Sanctuary in Pieces

McGill-Queen's Refugee and Forced Migration Studies

SERIES EDITORS: MEGAN BRADLEY AND JAMES MILNER

Forced migration is a local, national, regional, and global challenge with profound political and social implications. Understanding the causes and consequences of, and possible responses to, forced migration requires careful analysis from a range of disciplinary perspectives, as well as interdisciplinary dialogue.

The purpose of the McGill-Queen's Refugee and Forced Migration Studies series is to advance in-depth examination of diverse forms, dimensions, and experiences of displacement, including in the context of conflict and violence, repression and persecution, and disasters and environmental change. The series will explore responses to refugees, internal displacement, and other forms of forced migration to illuminate the dynamics surrounding forced migration in global, national, and local contexts, including Canada, the perspectives of displaced individuals and communities, and the connections to broader patterns of human mobility. Featuring research from fields including politics, international relations, law, anthropology, sociology, geography, and history, the series highlights new and critical areas of enquiry within the field, especially conversations across disciplines and from the perspective of researchers in the global South, where the majority of forced migration unfolds. The series benefits from an international advisory board made up of leading scholars in refugee and forced migration studies.

10 The Right to Research
Historical Narratives by Refugee and Global South Researchers
Edited by Kate Reed and Marcia C. Schenck

11 Kingdom of Barracks
Polish Displaced Persons in Allied-Occupied Germany and Austria
Katarzyna Nowak

12 Urban Refugees and Digital Technology
Reshaping Social, Political, and Economic Networks
Charles Martin-Shields

13 Migration Governance in North America
Policy, Politics, and Community
Edited by Kiran Banerjee and Craig Damian Smith

14 Write to Return
Huguenot Refugees on the Frontiers of the French Enlightenment
Bryan A. Banks

15 The Politics of Refugee Policy in the Global South
Ola G. El-Taliawi

16 Forced Migration in/to Canada
From Colonization to Refugee Resettlement
Edited by Christina R. Clark-Kazak

17 Sanctuary in Pieces
Two Centuries of Flight, Fugitivity, and Resistance in a North American City
Laura Madokoro

Sanctuary in Pieces

TWO CENTURIES *of* FLIGHT, FUGITIVITY, AND RESISTANCE *in a* NORTH AMERICAN CITY

LAURA MADOKORO

MCGILL-QUEEN'S UNIVERSITY PRESS
Montreal & Kingston | London | Chicago

ISBN 978-0-2280-2287-9 (paper)
ISBN 978-0-2280-2328-9 (ePDF)
ISBN 978-0-2280-2329-6 (ePUB)

Legal deposit fourth quarter 2024
Bibliothèque nationale du Québec

Printed in Canada on acid-free paper that is 100% ancient forest free (100% post-consumer recycled), processed chlorine free

This book has been published with the help of a grant from the Federation for the Humanities and Social Sciences, through the Awards to Scholarly Publications Program, using funds provided by the Social Sciences and Humanities Research Council of Canada.

Funded by the Government of Canada | Financé par le gouvernement du Canada | Canada
Canada Council for the Arts | Conseil des arts du Canada

We acknowledge the support of the Canada Council for the Arts.
Nous remercions le Conseil des arts du Canada de son soutien.

McGill-Queen's University Press in Montreal is on land which long served as a site of meeting and exchange amongst Indigenous Peoples, including the Haudenosaunee and Anishinabeg nations. In Kingston it is situated on the territory of the Haudenosaunee and Anishinaabek. We acknowledge and thank the diverse Indigenous Peoples whose footsteps have marked these territories on which peoples of the world now gather.

LIBRARY AND ARCHIVES CANADA CATALOGUING IN PUBLICATION

Title: Sanctuary in pieces : two centuries of flight, fugitivity, and resistance in a North American city / Laura Madokoro.
Names: Madokoro, Laura, author.
Series: McGill-Queen's refugee and forced migration studies ; 17.
Description: Series statement: McGill-Queen's refugee and forced migration studies ; 17 | Includes bibliographical references and index.
Identifiers: Canadiana (print) 20240393155 | Canadiana (ebook) 2024039318X | ISBN 9780228022879 (paper) | ISBN 9780228023289 (ePDF) | ISBN 9780228023296 (ePUB)
Subjects: LCSH: Noncitizens—Government policy—Québec (Province)—Montréal—History. | LCSH: Safe spaces—Québec (Province)—Montréal—History. | LCSH: Urban policy—Québec (Province)—Montréal—History. | LCSH: Montréal (Québec)—Emigration and immigration—Government policy—History. | LCSH: Montréal (Québec)—Emigration and immigration—Social aspects—History.
Classification: LCC JV7295.M66 M33 2024 | DDC 325.714/28—dc23

This book was designed and typeset by Lara Minja in 11 pt Adobe Jenson Pro.
Copyediting by Kaitlin Littlechild.

For Eli and Hanako (Koko), with all my heart.
And to Bruce Garside, in gratitude.

Contents

Figures

Acknowledgments

THERE ARE THE BOOKS you set out to write, and there are the ones you end up writing. *Sanctuary in Pieces* looks very different from what I initially planned to do and comes from the incredible assistance, insights, and inspiration offered by a number of people along the way.

I learned about each of the "cities" described in *Sanctuary in Pieces* thanks to the rich scholarship and generosity of opinion and insights from generations of scholars. I owe special thanks to many for their work and for taking the time to answer questions, provide resources, and shed light on topics that I was often only grasping in superficial ways.

As I worked through the "Prologue" and "The Underground City" chapters, Dan Rück helped me understand key aspects of the history of Kahnawà:ke and place naming in general. Similarly, Paul-Étienne Rainville provided me with important context for the different names for the city we now call Montreal. Kelann Currie-Williams helped me navigate the archives of the Negro Community Centre, as did Désirée Rochat, while Brian Young helped me with some key aspects of the legal history and family legacies I was exploring.

When it came to "The Fugitive City," I benefited from assistance from Jurretta Jordan Heckscher at the Library of Congress, who aided me with the nature of some of the sources I was working with. Don Nerbas helped me comprehend the city as a centre of merchant capitalism and clarified when and how certain rail lines started operating in the mid-nineteenth century, saving me from significant errors of interpretation.

Annick Desmarais was a cradle of information and assistance when it came to "The Hostile City" chapter. Sylvie Bourbonniere of Le Chaînon was equally supportive. They provided access to archival materials in a timely manner, as did historian Mikhail Bjorge, who shared digitized versions of Emma Goldman's correspondence with me during the early days of the COVID-19 pandemic. They all went above and beyond, and I am forever grateful. I am similarly appreciative of Franca Iacovetta and Cynthia Wright, who are embarked on their own research about Emma Goldman and the anarchist community in Toronto and took the time to engage with mine. I learned so much from the symposium they organized in the fall of 2022 and the feedback they later provided on an early version of this chapter. Moishe Volf-Dolman helped with translations. Kathy Ferguson also helped clarify some of the analysis. Much of "The Hostile City" chapter was inspired by Sonya Roy's brilliant and meticulous research and thinking on this topic, and she was also a tremendous help in identifying valuable sources. Merci Sonya!

Similarly, "The Wartime City" chapter results from passionate interlocutors who shared their time, insights, critiques, and archival materials with me. I am particularly indebted to the people I interviewed or corresponded with for this chapter: Bruce Garside, Jürgen Dankvort, David Rapaport, Mary Harman, Jackie Hyman, Ken Hyman, Dorothy Todd-Henault, Michael Klein, Bonnie Sherr Klein, Joanne Tompkins, and Marion Miller. Daniel Ross guided me in some early thinking around urban histories and politics of place, and I hope I have done justice to his suggestions here. Mary Harman's painting *The Epic and the Monumental* (2000) adorns the cover of this book and kept me company as I wrote. Part of the painting, of a young girl with big, fearful eyes, was cropped out in the design process and when I asked Mary if this was okay, she responded that it was "probably the best choice" to "stress the joyous figures and not the sad, lost one."

"The Occupied City" chapter was also the result of many people's efforts, most notably Laura Lopez and Flora Fernandez, who gave generously of their time and offered truly candid insights into their experiences of migration, settlement, and community solidarity. I also benefited from the views of retired civil servants, who were instrumental in setting the stage and allowing me to explore various questions about asylum and refuge in new ways. In this respect, I am deeply grateful to Raphael Girard, Ron Button, and Brian Lecomte. Lawyers William Sloan and Noël St-Pierre (who sadly passed away in January 2024) provided helpful context through phone and in-person interviews and several email exchanges. Similarly, Father Denis Prescott and Reverend Robert Warren helped me understand the occupations from the perspective of the church community, as did Janice Simpkins and Michel Gagnon. I spent an afternoon with Father Prescott at his home in the shadow of the Saint Joseph Oratory, and I appreciated the weaving together of place and life storytelling. Geneviève Dorais, and her elegant scholarship, helped me think through questions of solidarity, activism, and exile, more fully.

Finally, the making of "The Uneasy City" chapter came about because of the reflections shared by lawyer Stewart Istvanffy and Reverend Chris Barrigar. It was an absolute gift to be able to sit with these two individuals over the course of many years, including on Zoom during the pandemic, and I learned a great deal from them both. Reverend Barrigar also arranged for me to have a roundtable with members of the congregation who had been involved in providing sanctuary, which was a unique and helpful experience. I am also grateful to Rivka Augenenfeld and Rick Goldman, who provided critical context and insights, and to Nancy Oliver-Mackenzie, a community historian at the Union United Church, who helped me in numerous ways and also facilitated my site visit to the church (thanks in this respect also go to Svens Telemaque who showed me around).

Many people's contributions are woven throughout *Sanctuary in Pieces* and cannot be distilled into a single chapter. Megan Bradley and James Milner gave this work a home in the MQUP series on refugees and forced migration. Megan, along with Diana Allan generously organized a manuscript workshop for this project under the auspices of the McGill Refugee Research Group. Don Nerbas and Désirée Rochat (both mentioned previously) spent the day sweating it out – literally – with the manuscript, as did Sean Mills, Wendell Nii Laryea Adjetey, Elsbeth Heaman, Harald Bauder, Rachel Ida Buff, Shannon McSheffrey, Anna Sheftel, and Gada Mahrouse. I learned so much from each and every one of the participants whose own scholarship (and, in some cases, community-oriented work) has been so foundational to my own thinking. Jonathan Crago, who inherited this project at McGill-Queen's University Press, also attended the workshop (in addition to spending many other hours on this project), and I am grateful for the care and attention he brought to this work. Kaitlin Littlechild did some magical copyediting, Lara Minja did the design, Catherine Marjorbanks created the index and corrected mistakes as she went, and Lisa Aitken brought the whole thing home. My thanks to all.

A number of historians, librarians, and archivists also helped make *Sanctuary in Pieces* a reality, conjuring up the village that is required to raise a family. I owe them all tremendous thanks. These include staff at Bibliothèque et Archives Nationale du Québec, the Archives de Montréal, Library, and Archives Canada (thank you forever and ever, Alix McEwen!), the McCord Stewart Museum, the Library of Congress, the Ohio State Historical Society, the Montana State Historical Society, the Special Collections at Concordia University, Special Collections at the University of Arizona, Distinctive Collections at Arizona State University, the McGill University Archives, the Redpath Library at McGill University and MacOdrum Library at Carleton University.

Readers will likely notice that the theme of community is woven throughout *Sanctuary in Pieces*, and this is no doubt a reflection of the many communities and scholars who have supported and sustained this work. I learned a great deal from my exchanges on this subject from Patti Lenard, Mireille Paquet, Yael Schacher, Carl Lindskoog, Paul Kramer, Jessica Squires, and Steven High, and about refugee history more generally from Benjamin Thomas White, Evan Taparata, Sara Cosemans, Anna Macguire, and Anne Ifran. Anna Holian and Julian Lim supported me while I was on a Fulbright in Arizona, where I was also glad to connect with Johanna Skibsrud, John Melillo, Sarah Roberts, Blake Gentry, Miriam Davidson, John Fife, Pastor Alison Harrington, and the late Father Ricardo Elford.

I am incredibly grateful to the many scholarly friends who encouraged me as I plodded along. Some I have mentioned previously but I also want to make sure to thank CJ Alvarez, Erin Cressman, Amanda Ricci, Heidi Wendt, Leyla Vural, Lama Mourad, and Christina Clark-Kazak. Laura Ishiguro deserves special recognition for her solidarity and her wisdom through and through; so too do Shauna Labman and Jamie Liew who have proven endlessly patient with my random questions about the technical aspects of the law.

Thanks and appreciation go out to the long-suffering members of the Groupe d'Histoire de Montréal/Montreal History Group who have heard me work through this material for the past eight years and whose collective and individual works were foundational for the research I undertook here.

Un gros merci à vous tous! Similarly, much gratitude goes to the members of the Critical Refugee and Migration Studies Network in Canada, especially Thy Phu, Vinh Nguyen, Peter Nyers, Anh Ngo, Edward Ou Jin Lee, Gada Mahrouse, Fritz Pino, Maral Aguilera-Moradipour, and Udbi Ali. Thanks as well to Luna Vives and the other members of the Migration Research Collective.

Three anonymous peer reviewers provided me with substantive, thought-provoking feedback. I wish I knew who they were so I could give them more fulsome thanks, but at the very least, I want to recognize them here – especially the ways in which their questions and suggestions pushed me to stake out what I was doing.

The seed for *Sanctuary in Pieces* was planted during my time at McGill University, where I found a happy home in the Department of History and Classical Studies. I am grateful for the mentoring and encouragement I received in these critical early years when I was figuring out how to navigate teaching, research, and service demands in the academy. Thanks to Elizabeth Elbourne, Laila Parsons, Kate Desbarats, Jason Opal, David Wright, and Lorenz Lüthi for their guidance and for opening doors. Shanon Fitzpatrick taught me a great deal about courage and commitment. The late Jarrett Rudy welcomed me with open arms and is much missed. Sue Morton took me under her wings from day one and has been a constant friend from whom I have learned so much about work and life. This research came to fruition after a move to Carleton University and a global pandemic and took quite a different shape as a result. I am thankful for the encouragement I received throughout, and especially for the solid cheerleading as the end neared. I am also grateful for the financial support I received from the Social Sciences and Humanities Research Council, Fulbright Canada, the Fonds de recherche du Québec Societé et Culture, the Faculty of Arts (McGill University), and the Faculty of Arts and Social Sciences (Carleton University).

Throughout this research, undergraduate and graduate students asked transformative questions and inspired me with their work. For this, I am especially grateful to Rishma Johal, Chris Chanco, Sara-Marni Hubbard, Krenare Recaj, Amy Fung, and Steve Schwinghamer, as well as the MA and undergraduate students I have had the good fortune of working with over the years. Many students worked as research assistants on this project, including Sam Mickleson, Tyla Betke, Sybill Chen, Dexter Docherty, Shaden Hetu-Frankel, Amanda Hills, Macha Jauvert, Nicole Kim, Bernard Maftei, Laura Morlock, Aya Omar, Kahtryn Schmidt, Sara Wilson, Eleanor Wong, Michele Zampa, and Ed Dunsworth (who is now a colleague!). Jesse Moss, Tess Elsworthy, and Nicole Yakashiro, all brilliant scholars in their own right, went above and beyond, and I am truly indebted to them.

I owe a final round of thanks and acknowledgment to friends and family, near and far, and to those who have gone before (my dad and other loved ones are with me always). My sense of community has grown in leaps and bounds as a result of becoming a parent and our family has been sustained by many friends and neighbours who have been a source of levity, insights, and perspectives. My gratitude knows no bounds. Special thanks to Sarah Allen, who provided last-minute editing advice, and to Bruce Ainslie and Margaret Hicks (with Juan and Santi), who let me turn their annual holiday hockey camp into a personal writing retreat in the desperate, waning hours of this project.

Additional thanks to Dave, Mike, Ian, Melissa (and baby Felix), and all the other family members who got swept up in the ride. Fortunately, Tom is an ocean of calm and a true original. I am glad to be his complement and grateful for all he undertook to make this book possible. Koko and Eli have been curious and excited companions all along this journey. Their questions, ranging from "Are we safe in this world?" to "Do you love your book more than us?" to "What is the title?????" have kept me humble and attuned to the flurry of activity beyond these pages even if I was sometimes a little lost and distant along the way.

Finally, a word of thanks to my mom, Ann Rothfels, who inspires and encourages me in all that I do. She reminds me on a regular basis of all that is good in the world, and many of her life lessons are woven into the pages here.

On Naming and Language

THERE ARE BOTH more names in this work, and fewer.

I have attempted, wherever possible, to provide the Indigenous names of places alongside the English or French names. In the case of the city of Montreal, I have used the Haudenosaunee name Tiohtià:ke as well as the name Mooniyaang from the Anishnabemowin language. In other instances, I have named the traditional territories where cities in the United States and Canada now sit.

Using Indigenous place names is a way of underscoring that all the transformations described in this work unfolded in places with long histories of mobility, and settlement, prior to the sanctuary stories described here. It is also a way of ensuring that this history is not confined to the past but that the enduring connections might be considered in some way. Instead of a compass point, or longitudinal or latitudinal coordinates, I wanted to provide a different kind of mapping, and I sought to mention Indigenous names for places, in a variety of languages, for the sites I was discussing.

This proved to be an imperfect exercise largely because it was impossible to capture all the names for all the places. For instance, as the permanent exhibit at the Centre des mémoires montréalaises makes clear, there are many different names for the place we now call Montreal. It is called variously "molian" (N'diaki), ᒨᓇᔮᐤ (among some James Bay Cree), "Mounian" and "Moulial" (Innu), Moriak (Atikamekw) et ᒪᓐᑐᕆᐊᓪ (Inuit). I couldn't include all these names, but I chose two common names to help us think differently about the city and the other places people were living in and traveling to and from. In other instances, there was no Indigenous name for a place that settlers later established and so I referred to traditional territories in general terms. The results are uneven, and I see this as evidence of the need to do more work in this regard.

In contrast to the dense naming convention for places that I have adopted here, I have tried to avoid naming or offering any detailed descriptions of people still living without their sanction (a process that I describe in detail throughout this work). This means that in the later chapters, there are fewer personal names than might be expected given the subject of this study.

I am hoping that the layered place naming, combined with efforts to describe individuals in an ethical manner, will contribute to emerging conversations about how to do history differently, especially as we think about our accountability as scholars to multiple audiences and communities.

Sanctuary in Pieces

Introduction

> What is a sanctuary? The sanctuary often is something very small. Not a grandiose gesture, but a small gesture toward alleviating human suffering and preventing humiliation. The sanctuary is a human being. Sanctuary is a dream. And that is why you are here, and that is why I am here. We are here because of one another.
>
> — ELIE WIESEL[1]

IN THE WINTER OF 2017, as migrants began moving in increasing numbers across the Canada–US border to evade the Trump administration's various anti-immigrant efforts, city councillors in Montreal (known as Mooniyaang in Anishinaabemowin and Tiohtià:ke in Mohawk for "where the currents meet") made a unanimous sanctuary city declaration. This initiative was based in part on a sense that since the city's founding, it had offered refuge to "diverses vagues de réfugiés" in des "périodes sombres de l'histoire de l'humanité."[2] On 17 February 2017, council declared that people without legal status would be able to access municipal services and vowed to work with the Montreal Police Service to ensure that people in vulnerable situations often compounded by complex immigration statuses, could obtain services and protection without fear.

Formal federal immigration minister and then mayor Denis Coderre celebrated the move and asserted, "C'est un moment historique. J'ai vécu beaucoup de choses en politique, mais voir un conseil, à l'unanimité, faire de Montréal une ville sanctuaire compte tenu du contexte tant à l'échelle mondiale et même sur notre continent, je pense que ça envoie un message très très fort."[3]

In this case, being a sanctuary city entailed the development of an Access to Municipal Services Without Fear policy, which was created in February 2017.

The goal was to allow all inhabitants of the city "to benefit from municipal services, regardless of their immigration status." [4] The policy also aimed to address "the marginalization and abuse of non-status migrants and alleviate their fear of arrest and deportation."[5] This initiative was similar to other jurisdictions where there was a mix of "bottom-up and top-down approaches" to "protect illegalized and other vulnerable migrants."[6] Such policies have included access to education and health care for people without legal status, as well as the provision of legal aid to help address their precarious situations.

Just under two short years later, the city walked back the access policy, with the new mayor explaining that it had ultimately proven impossible to live up to the hopes and expectations of the sanctuary declaration. As Valérie Plante outlined at a press conference: "Il y a eu beaucoup de mots qui ont été dits, surtout dans des tweets, mais au bout du compte, nous ne sommes pas en soi une 'ville sanctuaire.'" She insisted instead that Montreal/Mooniyaang/Tiohtià:ke was a "ville responsable," a responsible city.[7] Activists were disappointed, holding that council had to do more to protect everyone in the city, regardless of their immigration status.

Proponents were correct to dispute the city's claims of being a sanctuary city, though not necessarily for the principles they cited. The idea of a city being a sanctuary is an anomaly largely divorced from the impulses that have animated much of the history around hospitality, protection, and refuge. Highly idealistic and aspirational, sanctuary cities are also contemporary instruments designed to gain jurisdictional influence, retain control over the discourse around justice and responsibility, and posture for political gain. In the series of case studies that follow, I trace the outlines of six different kinds of sanctuary experiences in Montreal/Mooniyaang/Tiohtià:ke over the course of two hundred years and show how, in most cases, the city was inaccessible, hostile, or closed to appeals for hospitality and protection. When sanctuary was received, it was often a contested and tumultuous experience, taking a toll on many of those involved.

In this analysis, "the city" is an organic entity made up of residents and non-residents. It is shaped by a physical landscape carved into the earth by surrounding waters and centuries of human activity, and imprinted with the political, social, cultural, and economic influences that cross visible and invisible borders. The exploration here could easily be undertaken in many other cities, all with histories of complicated refuge that predate any formal declarations of sanctuary.[8] In attending to the history of sanctuary in Montreal/Mooniyaang/Tiohtià:ke, we can see both the ways in which this phenomenon has been specific to place as well as the larger themes and undercurrents that have shaped practices around hospitality, protection, and refuge historically and into the present.

On Sanctuary

In making sanctuary city declarations or working towards this possibility, supporters of the concept regularly reference ancient and medieval traditions. Yet these historical connections are largely symbolic and are regularly presented in "radically idealized and fantastic" forms that are quite different from their original scope and purpose.[9] The idea of sanctuary for non-criminals and the public nature of many migrant justice efforts in the present are marked departures from the historical practices that inspire many contemporary initiatives.

In ancient times, sanctuary was closely tied to notions of criminal justice. In ancient Greece, dedicated sanctuaries where accused criminals could seek refuge were often located "on isolated outcroppings or mountainsides."[10] A similar philosophy was also at play in early Christendom where "religious asylum in Christian temples was an important defense for criminals," most notably operating with the approval of Emperors Constantine (ca. AD 274–337) and Theodosius (AD 346–95) and other fourth-century emperors.[11] In the Old Testament, Jews freed from slavery in Egypt and who moved to Canaan's Land were instructed to set up three cities of refuge to provide asylum to people who accidentally killed someone as a way of making sure that bloodshed did not beget further bloodshed.[12] Eventually, six cities were established along the Jordan River in Golan, Ramoth, Bosor, Kedesh, Shechem, and Hebron. There were rules around seeking refuge in these places, which included a confession and permission to stay until the death of the high priest.[13] In medieval England, beginning with the reign of William the Conqueror (1066–87), the practice of sanctuary in designated churches evolved so that people could seek sanctuary without fear of "arrest by royal, civic, or ecclesiastical officials."[14] The requirements for admission varied for each chartered sanctuary but generally included promises of good behaviour and the payment of entry fees.[15] Akin to England, France had a long history of formal sanctuary practices for people accused of a variety of crimes. Beginning in the fifth century, church sanctuary was guaranteed in France to ensure sufficient time for sentencing and punishment to be considered. However, King Francis I (a nephew to King Louis XII who ruled from 1515–47) ended sanctuary as a formal practice in France in 1539 as part of the evolving contest between church and state.[16]

Given the history of both French and British colonialism in North America, and its influence on shaping the history of Montreal/Mooniyaang/Tiohtià:ke, it bears asking whether sanctuary practices were part of the imperial outlook in either instance. This does not appear to have been the case. Discussions of safety or protection in New France occurred in the context of the physical landscape and religious outposts but not in terms of any formal religious designations.[17] In the British imperial context, it appears that beyond discussions of religious freedom in the Thirteen Colonies there was no direct translation of sanctuary practices to North America.[18]

When chartered sanctuary practices were curtailed in England beginning in 1540 (a process that would take almost one hundred years), the Crown decreed the creation of eight sanctuary towns: Wells, Westminster, Manchester, Northampton, Norwich, York, Derby, and Launceston.[19] A maximum of "twenty privileged persons" were allowed to dwell within these city spaces in that capacity.[20] Those who were already in sanctuary at the time of the legal change retained "their privilege and could continue to live there for the terms of their lives if they wished."[21] As historian Shannon McSheffrey suggests, it appears that only Westminster, with its famed Abbey, welcomed the designation. Other towns, such as Manchester, objected based on the potential economic impact of such an imposition.[22] Sanctuary as a formal practice between church and state was eventually abolished in England in 1634.

Still, the end of formal church sanctuary or medieval sanctuary cities in France and England did not mean the idea of sanctuary disappeared entirely.[23] One of the earliest references to a "city of refuge" in North America dates to a German settler named Christian Priber who arrived on the continent in 1735. He envisioned a city of refuge, which he called a "Kingdom of Paradise," among the Cherokees.[24] Priber had found "sure refuge" and hoped to create a utopian society in Tellico (located on Tellico Plains in present-day Tennessee where the Tellico River emerges from the Appalachian Mountains) that would operate as a "color-blind haven for debtors, runaway slaves, religious dissidents, and other oppressed people."[25] The idea was that such a city would be a place of just laws in the face of unjust laws that led people to commit crimes in the first instance.

The spirit of Priber's vision, the idea of creating cities of justice in the face of unfair laws, has been repurposed and reimagined in the present. Since the turn of the twenty-first century, the term *Sanctuary City* has referred to both a physical site and a political movement, particularly in the United States where such efforts are most numerous and where they are understood as part of the New Sanctuary Movement. This is a broad-based coalition involving a number of congregations and social justice groups who seek a multifaceted approach to effecting structural change to laws, regulations, and policies governing migration.[26]

The meaning and character of sanctuary have changed dramatically over the centuries, moving across the ages from the purview of religious authorities to community-based efforts and, most recently, to public declarations and policy frameworks that are meant to make cities safer for people without legal status or the requisite documentation. In the process, sanctuary has shifted from being "place-based," to extend beyond the geographic and geopolitical parameters of any urban space.[27] As historian Rachel Ida Buff outlines, sanctuary as it operates in the present involves not "only a specific place in a church or other building but a set of practices by which people come into relations of accompaniment and solidarity."[28] I see sanctuary in similar terms, defining it as an act or practice of hospitality and protection connected to a particular site, whether it be a church or a city. As I detail below, I also understand it as a western concept that operates in particular ways across various settler societies. Refuge, by contrast, is broader and captures the varied conceptual, epistemological, and philosophical approaches to seeking security, safety, or protection. Protection is common to both concepts, but it differs in scope and scale. I, therefore, use the terms *sanctuary* and *refuge* carefully and deliberately here.

Sanctuary (in the) City

Using the city as an analytical framework, *Sanctuary in Pieces* traces how sanctuary has been imagined and enacted in western contexts since the end of most formal religious sanctuary practices in the early seventeenth century. Crucially, since that time, sanctuary has moved from an informal form of protection to one that is increasingly informed by, and in conversation with, evolving legal frameworks that govern the conditions of asylum and refuge.

Studying sanctuary in an urban context, as is the case here, means we can trace the contours of refuge in line with, but also beyond, what state authorities had in mind. Even with sanctuary city declarations, protection and refuge are still being forged by various actors at the community level – usually beyond what local, provincial, and federal authorities are doing. As a result, historically and into the present, cities have both invited and refused the possibility of refuge. This paradoxical dynamic is central to any understanding of how it is that people continue to move to cities in the hopes of refuge and how, in some cases, they are bitterly disappointed.

On the surface, Montreal/Mooniyaang/Tiohtià:ke might appear as a natural site of sanctuary. It has been home to thousands of people seeking refuge in explicit or implicit ways over the years. Some were invited or accepted formally by authorities; others moved clandestinely, as was the case of Huguenot refugees in the 1600s. Unlike in the Thirteen Colonies, French authorities excluded people from settlement in New France based on religion, with the result that any Protestant refugee in the colony was there by stealth.[29] By the nineteenth century, people we might now describe as refugees had also moved to Montreal/Mooniyaang/Tiohtià:ke in significant numbers, including many migrants escaping economic and political turmoil in famine-ravaged Ireland. In the twentieth and twenty-first centuries, large-scale movements including from Europe and later Algeria, Vietnam, Cambodia, Laos, Rwanda, and Syria transformed the city.

Yet, beneath this general overview lies a much more complicated history, an underground marked by refusal and denial, selective compassion and solidarity, and outright animosity. There was never any guarantee of sanctuary, and it was often highly contingent. Nevertheless, as people made their way through the web of social connections, political pursuits, and economic realities at the core of any urban city, they tested the notion of the city and who it was for. They also imagined, and often enacted, a variety of possible futures. Crucially, the disappointments of the city didn't inhibit hopes and dreams and recognizing what a challenging place a city such as Montreal/Mooniyaang/Tiohtià:ke could be in the pursuit of sanctuary makes the lives that people were able to build all the more remarkable.

When I first began researching the history of sanctuary, I was interested in understanding the ways in which refuge, protection, and hospitality had evolved over time. I was especially curious about the relationship between community activism (broadly defined) in relation to state initiatives, especially as it involved legal regimes around asylum and citizenship. My starting assumption was that not only did sanctuary exist in various shapes, but that it was also always possible. Over the course of researching, writing, and thinking through *Sanctuary in Pieces*, however, it became clear that the history I was tracing was one where sanctuary had not transpired in the city very often, and if it had, it was the result of concerted efforts and, on occasion, state protection. It was rarely easy or obvious.

Contrary to my initial premise about the existence of a long history of sanctuary, I found a history of struggle for security and protection, where there was often an absence, or even hostility to the idea of offering refuge. The implications of this lack of generosity are profound and challenge the symbolic and substantive value of sanctuary city efforts and any activism around migrant rights in the present. In exploring sanctuary in six different keys over the past two hundred years I ultimately became concerned with the substance and character of sanctuary city policies, including the very public declarations that accompany such efforts and the ways in which they mark a radical departure from historical practices, including earlier ideas about "cities of refuge."[30]

The more I considered the experiences of sanctuary and refuge historically, most notably along the themes of flight, fugitivity, and resistance, the more I understood contemporary sanctuary city declarations and other public sanctuary work as a vocal response to unequal power structures. Drawing attention to inequities is meant to lead to broader social transformations. People are up against a great deal in their search for refuge and any help, however troubled, is therefore to be welcomed on some level.

As historian A. Naomi Paik observes, sanctuary practices have long been "pulled between their contestation of, and yet embedded place within, government structures."[31] This observation is particularly true for sanctuary cities, which operate as part of a larger state apparatus. The Black Lives Matter movement has drawn attention to police brutality at the municipal level and the complicity of local authorities in the context of state violence more broadly. Given the structures of settler states, cities cannot escape a "persistent complicity with, and consolidation of, state violence."[32] Yet for supporters, the idea of sanctuary cities speaks to social justice issues and aspirations for a more fair and equitable world.[33] They are a way of challenging the multiple injustices inherent in contemporary immigration laws, and it is not surprising that the movement grew significantly with the election of Donald Trump to office in 2016.[34]

Broadly speaking, sanctuary cities are meant to serve as a corrective and to facilitate further integration. Supporters do not see the people being assisted as being guilty of a crime; rather, they see laws around immigration documentation and detention as profoundly unjust. As political scientist Mireille Paquet has argued, "sanctuary policies are based on the promise of increased participation, interaction, and collaboration with the state for populations without status."[35] Sanctuary city declarations, therefore, emphasize the possibilities offered by the language of sanctuary and associated acts of hospitality and protection and, increasingly, solidarity. These acts are not always forthcoming, nor do they always live up to their promise, leading to frustration about the gulf between the language of sanctuary and the lived experience of those for whom such efforts are intended. In Europe, where thousands of migrants have perished in their attempts to cross the Mediterranean Sea in the first decades of the twenty-first century, the sanctuary city movement has been less about protecting individual migrants and more about ensuring that states uphold or expand their existing legal commitments for the provision of asylum.[36] For instance, City of Sanctuary UK "holds the vision that the United Kingdom will be a welcoming place of safety for all and proud to offer sanctuary to people fleeing violence and persecution."[37]

Such approaches point to the aspirational politics behind many sanctuary city efforts, where the goal is to create a different kind of society and a different kind of urban experience. Part of the problem is that even with sanctuary city policies in place, there is no guarantee of protection and, in some cases, the perception that there is increased security actually leads to greater vulnerability.[38] In Montreal/Mooniyaang/Tiohtià:ke, police officers continued to share information with the Canadian Border Services Agency (CBSA) even after the city's formal declaration and policy development around being a sanctuary city.[39] This was not an exceptional situation. Rather, it was reflective of the urban dynamics that shape refuge in many given contexts.[40]

The expectations and disappointments that become visible from thinking about cities as possible sites of refuge invite a return to the question of to whom cities belong – a visitor, a casual observer, a citizen, an asylum-seeker, an undocumented migrant? It also invites questions about who has a right to the city and who can remake the city, as suggested by French philosopher Henri Lefebvre in 1968 and later elaborated by Marxist geographer David Harvey.[41] Lefebvre understood implicitly the dispossession and alienation at the heart of many western cities, noting that the very phenomenon of the industrial city resulted in, and from, the dissolution of "old agrarian structures" where "dispossessed or ruined peasants" crowded into "cities to find work and subsistence."[42] As political theorist Dimitrios Roussopoulos elaborates, there are two key ideas contained within the idea of the "right to the city." The first is that cities are works in progress, always evolving. The other is that "all urban people" should participate in "the City's construction, directly and indirectly" so that the "space of everyday life" becomes a "site of resistance."[43] The need for resistance is obviously unevenly ascribed as people's experiences and lives in the city vary wildly. This unevenness stems from socioeconomic conditions and, increasingly, from legal status.

In moving to and within cities, people carried ideas about what sanctuary (and the city) should look and feel like. These expectations were not always met. In the cases I explore here, people such as Shadrach Minkins, who fled enslavement, may have expected more than legal security, but he was guaranteed little else. John Harrison Surratt, a Confederate messenger, expected to be able to hide, and he was able to do so for a time because of the political and religious actors in the city who supported him. By contrast,

Emma Goldman expected a city of revolutionary anarchist possibilities. She did not find this. War resisters arriving during the United States' war in Vietnam expected an easy transition, and the anti-colonial and anti-imperial politics in the city in the 1960s heartened some, even as they disconcerted others. Meanwhile, refugees and migrants seeking asylum and legal protection in Canada in the late twentieth and early twenty-first centuries expected much in the way of opportunity. When the city was not forthcoming in this regard, they alternatively challenged the city to do better, calling upon the humanitarianism and goodwill of residents, or sought refuge on their own terms. In thinking through the history of sanctuary, therefore, the city offers an important site in which to consider the seeking, making, denial, and forging of refuge on multiple planes.

On Public Sanctuary

In making sanctuary public and advancing declarations and policy initiatives that are intended to make cities safe, activists and policymakers are evolving an idea that is very different from its historical antecedents. The public dimension of sanctuary, as conceived by people offering religious sanctuary beginning in the 1970s and throughout the 1980s, as well as activists in the New Sanctuary Movement of the twenty-first century, is radically different from what was undertaken in ancient and medieval times when people used sanctuary as part of criminal justice frameworks. It is also different from refuge in the broader context of fleeing from slavery or law enforcement, when the goal was to hide, whether by adopting a different name or physical appearance, or by disappearing from sight.

The emergence of public declarations of sanctuary in the 1970s was bound up with the ways in which the practice of sanctuary was reclaimed and repurposed in the late twentieth and early twenty-first centuries. Insisting on the sacred and inviolable nature of western churches, religious leaders in the United States and Canada sheltered asylum seekers and migrants, and drew on customary law to assert that law enforcement could not disdain the holy ground of their institutions. This practice was largely respected, although the US federal government had FBI agents and informants infiltrate congregations and the meetings of sanctuary workers.[44] There have also been instances of law enforcement in Canada and the United States violating customary law to apprehend people in churches. By and large, however, since the 1970s, the idea of churches as sites of protected, if not guaranteed, religious sanctuary and physical security has been accepted in North America.

The first public declaration of sanctuary occurred in Berkeley, California in 1971 when the University Lutheran Chapel (located on xučyun, the traditional territory of the Ohlone people), along with seventeen other congregations, announced that it would shield US military personnel (including from the recently arrived USS *Coral Sea*) who did not want to fight in Vietnam.[45] This led the Berkeley city council to make a declaration of sanctuary. A decade later, Southside Presbyterian Church (built on the site of an ancient Tohono O'odham village) in Tucson, Arizona and a coalition of other churches made a public declaration of sanctuary for Central American refugees on 24 March 1982. At Southside Presbyterian, the congregation hung two banners on the outside walls of the church. One read, "This is a sanctuary of God for the oppressed from Central America." The other read, "La Migra [immigration enforcement] don't profane the sanctuary." Although people had previously been quietly helping refugees enter the United States and make asylum claims, this declaration officially launched the Sanctuary Movement of the 1980s. In a letter sent to the Attorney General of the United States, Southside Presbyterian explained: "We have declared our church as a 'sanctuary' for undocumented refugees from Central America ... We believe that justice and mercy require that people of conscience actively assert our God-given right to aid anyone fleeing persecution and murder. The current administration of US law prohibits us from sheltering these refugees from Central America. Therefore, we believe the administration of the law to be immoral as well as illegal."[46]

The sanctuary declaration was intended as a test to state authorities and represented a reassertion of church influence and an invitation to the public to become engaged in the issue of US foreign policy in Central America. It also sought to question the operation of asylum-determination procedures in the United States and the injustice of deportations, in particular.

There was a lot resting on public declarations of sanctuary in the 1980s, which supported thousands of Central American refugees and sought to fundamentally alter the way asylum cases were being heard and treated in the United States. The many public declarations that followed the first opening in 1982 galvanized activists, congregations, and, to some extent, interested observers. Public declarations were not without controversy, however, and congregations weighed the merits and drawbacks of making individual cases public. The question of publicity ultimately divided the 1980s Sanctuary Movement with the "Chicago branch" favouring the prominent use of migrant testimonies to contest US foreign policy in contrast to the "Arizona branch," which preferred to focus instead on reforming the asylum-determination processes and was much more physically involved with the provision of sanctuary on the United States-Mexico border.[47] Testimonies were crucial in many cases, but when the willingness to speak publicly began to determine which refugees organizers were willing to support, it created real strains within the Sanctuary Movement.[48]

Despite concerns about exploiting migrant experiences and the carceral dimensions of being confined to a physical site for extended periods of time, church congregations, lawyers, and activists have continued to use public platforms to draw attention to particular cases in the hopes of influencing elected officials, policymakers, and adjudicators.[49] The public dimension of sanctuary is now an integral part of how fights over deportation and immigration reform are being undertaken.[50] And yet, it comes at a cost. Sanctuary City declarations provoked the ire of the Trump administration, resulting in cuts to funding and menacing public rhetoric.[51]

As my research progressed, I came to see the public dimensions of sanctuary city policies and sanctuary acts as deeply problematic because of the gulf between providers' rhetorical aspirations and the experiences of people who sought sanctuary. With regard to sanctuary activities in the United States and Canada in the present, I found myself worrying about the public nature of this work and the ways in which sanctuary declarations play into a reinscription or reassertion of settler claims, even as they operate in the realm of solidarity and justice for all.

I came to this conclusion reluctantly believing very strongly in the good work and intentions behind any effort at protection and help. We live in a world where the need for refuge is all around us – visible in the growing populations of unhoused people across North America and environmental catastrophes and warfare across the globe. Too often, sanctuary is refused, denied, and even derided. The efforts to provide sanctuary and refuge remain, therefore, critically important and have palpable impacts on those who receive refuge or asylum with the state, as well as those who seek sanctuary beyond the state. They are not, however, unproblematic.

With public declarations of sanctuary, stories are instrumentalized for broader political objectives, meaning that individuals and families carry the burden of representation in addition to all their other hopes and fears. This is both an immediate reality and one that persists beyond the media spotlight (as several cases in this book show). The invisible costs and burdens of public sanctuary practices, therefore, raise questions at multiple scales about who and what sanctuary in the present is ultimately serving. This applies to state declarations about the purported humanitarian imperatives behind various laws and policies, city declarations, and individual pronouncements of sanctuary for people who take refuge in religious spaces.

My appreciation and admiration for the work that people do in offering protection and hospitality runs deep, especially given the contested aims and priorities that are often at the heart of these efforts and which must be overcome.[52] At the same time, the case studies in *Sanctuary in Pieces* reveal the troubling veins of power and authority that mark any question of shelter, hospitality, and protection. In case after case, we see the ways in which sanctuary has been deeply problematic historically in terms of dashed expectations, questionable motives, the fickle subjectivity of deservedness, the obfuscation of structural precarity, and exposure to public scrutiny and added state controls.

The title of this work, *Sanctuary in Pieces: Two Hundred Years of Flight, Fugitivity, and Resistance in a North American City,* speaks to some of these core concerns and evolving dynamics. In fact, the title can be read in two principal ways. In the first instance, it reflects the approach to this study, which is based on a series of six case studies throughout which the themes of flight, fugitivity, and resistance are interwoven. It also gestures to the overall conclusion of the work, which is that sanctuary as it has come to operate in the present – in the form of public declarations and high-profile media stories – is broken. It is shattered, and it is in pieces. As I noted previously, I came to this conclusion reluctantly, and it wasn't at all my intention in starting out. Yet, seeing how case after case, and person after person, negotiated disappointments and difficulties in the city as they sought to find some measure of economic, political, or social security led me to this conclusion. There were some exceptions, most notably the case of John Harrison Surratt, a Confederate messenger, as well as the war resisters I interviewed for the chapter "The Wartime City" – but by and large, what came through in this work was the gulf between the ideals and aspirations in seeking and offering sanctuary, and the reality of people's experiences of refuge. It's not that sanctuary as an ideal is in tatters entirely. Rather, in its present incarnation, it is being repurposed for political gain as part of larger state agendas. Only some of that gain is directed at the subjects of sanctuary themselves.

The themes of flight, fugitivity, and resistance recurred throughout the research and drew my attention to the idea of sanctuary in pieces. These three themes all speak to the possibility of refuge and the ways in which it has manifested differently over time.

Flight involves some kind of escape, either from captivity or justice. Although such an activity does not require crossing an international border, in the cases involving flight here, people did cross the US-Canada border to seek refuge; for instance, Shadrach Minkins (a fugitive slave) and John Harrison Surratt (a suspected accomplice in the assassination of US President Abraham Lincoln) and war resisters protesting the United States' war in Vietnam. In other instances, such as the women who took shelter with Notre-Dame-de-la-Protection in the 1930s or in the case of Laura Lopez, a Chilean migrant who was part of a series of church occupations in 1998–99, people did not flee far but rather sought protection and hospitality within the city. In doing so, they remade the city on their own terms. The notion of flight, therefore, operates at multiple levels, demonstrating the contrasting yet connected experiences of seeking refuge by crossing an international border or staying closer to home. Flight is neither unbounded nor bounded by geopolitical boundaries in the cases explored here.

The second theme, fugitivity, is closely related to the idea of flight. Historically, the term *fugitivity* referred to someone being made a fugitive or an exile. The significance of the term has changed over time, and many Black scholars now use it to convey the possibility of liberation and freedom through a refusal of existing power structures, including white supremacy, and a remaking or reclaiming of place.[53] Yet, in the context of seeking sanctuary, fugitivity was simultaneously both more literal and subjective. The term itself says nothing about the motives behind flight, which can range from the need to flee brutal oppression to the desire to escape criminal punishment. The one commonality historically was that to be a fugitive meant to hide. This is a stark contrast to the politics of display and the claiming of space that take places around sanctuary and notions of fugitivity in the present.

The final theme, resistance, is also closely related to the first two concepts and carries multiple connotations. Resistance played out among those who sought refuge, those who offered it, and state authorities who attempted to curtail or crush sanctuary practices entirely. In using this term, I asked about who was resisting, and what? The answers to these questions changed over time and depending on context. Fugitive slaves resisted their continued bondage and oppression by seeking refuge. People also resisted arrest, as was the case of John Harrison Surratt. They also resisted norms around propriety as was the case of Emma Goldman and, to some extent, Yvonne Maisonneuve, the founder and driving force behind one of the oldest women's shelters in Montreal/Mooniyaang/Tiohtià:ke.

War resisters (the name says as much) who left the United States during the country's wars in Vietnam, Cambodia, and Laos resisted military conscription but they also resisted US imperialism more broadly. In instances where people sought church sanctuary to delay or avoid deportation orders, they resisted state efforts to expel them from the country and the laws and policies that sought to cast them out. The offer of religious sanctuary itself was a form of resistance as customary law, in theory, inhibits the secular presence of law enforcement in sacred spaces.[54] However, there are no guarantees and, as noted previously, there are historical instances of police entering churches to apprehend individuals wanted for deportation. When this resistance has occurred in gurdwaras or mosques, law enforcement has proven much more willing to occupy sacred grounds.[55] And even more so in the case of secular spaces such as schools and hospitals.[56]

Considering flight, fugitivity, and resistance as part of the same landscape, or a refracting prism (to borrow historian Benjamin Hoy's way of explaining the impact of international borders) ultimately became a way of detailing the multiple perspectives that exist about or in any given city.[57] Too often people's views are dismissed if they are not long-term residents, or don't have an obvious stake in or claim on the city. Yet, there is no reason that outsiders or transitory perspectives should not be incorporated into our understanding of a city and the ways in which it operates, including around the making of sanctuary. These views might be misguided or superficial, as was the case for anarchist Emma Goldman's take on Montreal/Mooniyaang/Tiohtià:ke (discussed in the chapter "The Hostile City"), but they are no less significant or revealing as evidenced by the insights gleaned in asking war resisters about their impressions of the city during the turbulence of the 1970 October Crisis ("The Wartime City" chapter). This is especially important when considering the multiplicity of Indigenous perspectives and experiences within the city. The establishment and development of cities in settler-colonial contexts have largely erased Indigenous perspectives and marginalized urban Indigenous experiences. In thinking through the evolution of modern sanctuary practices in North America, part of the work entails considering the relationship to colonialism and settler colonialism, in particular.

Beyond Settler Sanctuary

Sanctuary was not easy for any of the people involved in the cases explored here, with the possible exception of John Harrison Surratt and the war resisters who moved to Montreal/Mooniyaang/Tiohtià:ke throughout the 1960s. In the case of the former, political and religious affinities and an existing network of Confederate supporters facilitated Surratt's time in sanctuary. In the latter, a combination of youth, intellect, resources, and activist connections – and ultimately, a sympathetic federal government – made seeking and fashioning sanctuary far easier than in other instances when the political climate was less inviting. The issue for many war resisters was that the city itself changed quite dramatically during the October Crisis of 1970, becoming a place of heightened violence and peaked tensions that contrasted wildly with the heady days of Expo '67, an extravagant event just three years prior that captured the imaginations of many people who later moved to the city. Most of the case studies explored here foreground the ways in which the city was a hostile or uneasy place to be and the ways in which people navigated the climate of the city and their own circumstances.

Significantly, none of the cases feature Indigenous experiences of refuge in the city. Although there are historical accounts of Kanien'kehá:ka seeking refuge in Ville Marie (as Montreal/Mooniyaang/Tiohtià:ke was known until the eighteenth century) and other instances of Indigenous Peoples seeking refuge during times of war, the settlement was not a natural site of refuge. In 1650, Wendat refugees, fleeing wars with the Rotinonhsión:ni, considered Ville Marie but settled instead on present-day Île d'Orléans, outside of Quebec City/Kebec.[58] In other instances, people were forcibly removed from their homes and installed within the fortified walls of the settlement in order for French authorities to offer some kind of protection. In 1689, many Kahnawákeró:non were relocated to Ville Marie, ostensibly for their own safety, in the context of King William's War (1688–97). Two hundred people were killed in Lachine when the village was attacked, and those in Ville Marie spent a year in the settlement before returning home.[59]

Rather than a site of refuge for Indigenous Peoples, Ville Marie (and later Montreal/Mooniyaang/Tiohtià:ke) was a site of colonial encroachment and a site of alienation. It continues to operate in this way even though people have forged community in the face of social structures that make it difficult to do so. As discussed in particular in the chapter "The Lonely City," part of what made and continues to make a city a site of sanctuary is the presence of some kind of community that can support and nourish individuals in need of assistance, protection, or hospitality. Colonialism and settler colonialism eroded the capacity for Indigenous Peoples to do so in the city, even as these same processes simultaneously amplified the need for sanctuary and community even more.[60]

The lack of inviting refuge for Indigenous Peoples in the city became abundantly obvious when I started to draft a chapter on Métis leader Louis Riel's experience of refuge in Montreal/Mooniyaang/Tiohtià:ke. Riel was instrumental in leading the province of Manitoba into confederation, but the decision to execute Thomas Scott in 1870 (following an insurrection against the provisional government) led to Riel's forced exile from Canada. The federal government later accused Riel of high treason for his involvement in the 1885 Northwest Resistance, which involved a number of Cree and Métis leaders who sought to repel colonial encroachment and who fought the coerced negotiations of the numbered treaties in the west. Riel was tried and convicted for this crime and executed on 16 November 1885.

As a young man, Riel spent seven formative years at the Petit Séminaire du Collège de Montréal from 1858 to 1865. Historian Max Hamon has shown how these years were critical in shaping Riel's lifelong negotiation of western and Indigenous political thought. They also created a range of associations from which he would later draw support during his time in exile.[61] When I first started working on this topic, I sensed that Riel's time in Montreal/Mooniyaang/Tiohtià:ke, as well as his time in exile in the United States (in 1870 and again after 1875), offered an opportunity to consider an experience of refuge involving a number of different Indigenous communities and political networks.

Yet, the more I read about and researched Riel's time in Montreal/Mooniyaang/Tiohtià:ke, the more I realized that this was not a story of sanctuary in the city. Rather, it was one where refuge and exile were facilitated by connections forged in the city. Classmates such as Persillier Lachapelle (who supported Riel during his by-election campaigns) and Joseph Dubuc (a lawyer who arranged for Riel's amnesty after 1870) supported the Métis leader during his time in exile.[62] Honoré Mercier, a nationalist French Canadian politician also encouraged Riel from his riding in Rouville (just south of Montreal/Mooniyaang /Tiohtià:ke) and later Saint-Hyacinthe (where John Harrison Surratt, discussed in the chapter "The Fugitive City," would hide for a time), but the city itself was never a site of refuge for Riel. Rather than a case study of refuge, Riel's story became a cautionary tale about the settler city as an unwelcome place for Indigenous Peoples. This does not mean that the possibility of refuge or sanctuary for Indigenous Peoples in Montreal/Mooniyaang/Tiohtià:ke did not exist. On the contrary. However, drawing on long-standing practices of support through kinship networks, refuge and protection generally came from other people and from elsewhere, not from the settler city proper.[63]

Sanctuary city declarations disguise this lack of refuge on the ground and in some ways reinforce the settler colonial practices within the city with little regard for Indigenous experiences.[64] The kinds of Indigenous resurgence described by Leanne Betasamosake Simpson and others who argue that "Indigenous peoples are enacting their own claims to urban places and spaces through (re)mapping and (re)storying their numerous and diverse presences and relations within urban spaces" is ignored in sanctuary city frameworks, as is the presence of people who can trace their familial and kinship connections to the land before there was any urban context to speak of.[65] The displacement and dispossession that might lead Indigenous Peoples to move to a city such as Montreal/Mooniyaang/Tiohtià:ke, and to require refuge, is similarly disregarded.

Early in my research on sanctuary, I had a conversation with an Indigenous woman that fundamentally transformed my approach to researching sanctuary in a settler context. In our very first call, I outlined my research project and observed that people had historically sought refuge in Christian churches because they were safe places. I had in mind the contest between sovereign and church authorities in medieval England. My interlocutor stopped me short. "The church has never been a safe place for Indigenous peoples," she said.[66]

Of course.

It was so obvious.

What was I thinking?

The answer is that I was thinking about many things, but I wasn't considering how different the history of sanctuary looks if we think about it in a settler-colonial context. Although the focus of this exchange was on the history of church sanctuary, I carried this intervention with me as I explored the nature of sanctuary in an urban context as well.

Indeed, that conversation utterly transformed how I have approached my research into the history of sanctuary. Although the focus here is not on Indigenous practices of sanctuary, *Sanctuary in Pieces* has been conceptualized, researched, and written with the understanding that western forms of sanctuary, whether in the form of church protection, state protection, or sanctuary cities, represent only one of the many affective, religious, political, kinship, and intellectual traditions that have shaped the landscape of sanctuary historically.[67] Tracing the evolution of sanctuary in a settler-colonial context means asking about the extent that western notions of justice and protection were imposed and, alternatively, the ways that

Indigenous practices were incorporated, refused, or ignored as practices around hospitality, protection, and asylum evolved.

Certainly, in the United States and Canada, the question of what land is being used in offers or claims of refuge is central. Indigenous activists made this point clearly in response to the Trump administration's efforts to exclude Arab and Muslim migrants in particular, advancing the "No Ban on Stolen Land" campaign in response to a series of Executive-Orders that denied admission to the United States from several Muslim-majority countries. In explaining the protest, Lakota scholar and activist Nick Estes stated, "the United States, as a settler nation, does not have the final say on who or what comes into the country because it's not theirs to own."[68] These efforts paralleled historian Elizabeth Ellis's argument that immigration issues cannot "exclude Native peoples and histories from the conversation," challenging the inherent rights of settler governments "to welcome some migrants while restricting and placing quotas on others."[69]

Settler states struggle with any defiance of what they understand as their authority over the land and their power to regulate the movement of people. The control of borders is intimately connected with notions of sovereign power. Yet this assumed and imposed authority has been regularly challenged by Indigenous Peoples who insist on their historic rights of mobility (including the 1794 Jay Treaty in the context of mobility across the US-Canada border) and whose kinship and adoption practices have sometimes been interpreted as a threat to the authority of the settler state.[70] Indeed, adoption practices and notions of kinship have long operated in tension with the legal frameworks around migration and citizenship managed by state authorities. When adoption practices among different Indigenous communities have been used to offer protection or to shelter people wanted for deportation, states have been relentless in undermining these practices. Such was the case for a member of the American Indian Movement who was adopted in Canada in the 1970s but eventually deported by the Canadian government to the United States.[71] So, too, for Sami activists adopted by a First Nations community in the 1980s only to be deported by the federal government to Norway. In 2012, the federal government similarly deported a Nigerian nun who had been adopted in Canada. Importantly, contrary to the kinds of church and city declarations we have seen in recent years, these efforts at protection were not publicized at the time. We know about them because of tribunal and court appearances, but at no point were the details of the adoptions made public to contemporaries. The adoptions were about community and protection and were not deliberately intended to counter the authority of the settler state in the realm of immigration and asylum, although they did.

Many traditional kinship and adoption practices continue into the present, though they are complicated by the long reach of colonial legislation, such as blood quantum laws in the United States and the Indian Act in Canada.[72] These practices have also been disrupted with the continued urbanization and city building among many settler societies. These processes have created a twinned effect where Indigenous Peoples move to cities, which are sometimes located on their traditional homelands, only to find that their needs are often exacerbated rather than assisted. In Montreal/Mooniyaang/Tiohtià:ke, there are now important community efforts to aid Indigenous Peoples in the city as evidenced by the work of the Montreal Indigenous Network and organizations such as the Native Women's Shelter.[73] Yet, the forces of colonization and gentrification regularly disrupt these efforts. The Open Door, a "culturally adapted" shelter moved away from the community it served after the building where it was located was sold for condominium development in 2008. Such decisions create additional strains and vulnerabilities for people in the city.

There are, as such, many stories to be told about the fostering and forging of refuge for and amongst Indigenous Peoples in the city. They take place at a different scale from the one revealed by the methodological and conceptual approaches I employed here but the knowledge of alternative ways of offering hospitality and protection informs this analysis nonetheless.

On Texture, Tone, and Method

The difference between sanctuary that was historically quiet and hidden and the public nature of discrete sanctuary cases since the 1970s shaped the structure of this work and the methods I used to explore the evolving nature of sanctuary experiences over two hundred years. The first half of the book reads differently from the second half because of this shift from hidden to public refuge, as well as the move to increasingly formal and legalized processes of asylum at the state level.

The origins of this book began with a project funded by the Social Sciences and Humanities Research Council of Canada called Sites of Sanctuary. The goal of this project was to document national and transnational instances of sanctuary in Canada historically, going beyond the 1980s and their aftermath, which had been the focus of previous research on this topic by political scientist Randy Lippert and legal scholar Sean Rehaag.[74] The research that I undertook along with an inspiring team of undergraduate and graduate students was much harder than I had initially anticipated. Working with digitized historical newspapers, we soon discovered how rarely sanctuary practices had manifested publicly in the past. The most frequent hit for keyword searches using "sanctuary" was for bird and wildlife sanctuaries. This was especially true in the late nineteenth century, though it remained the case for the entirety of the period we studied.

Given the lack of information available in digitized historical newspapers, we pursued other avenues, reaching out to community historians, local archivists, librarians, and heritage professionals to identify stories of community refuge that hadn't relied on the media but had, instead, embraced the idea of hiding as protection. These were less obvious histories, and they were informal in nature, which meant that we did not benefit from the sort of legal documents associated with formalized sanctuary in medieval England (something historian Shannon McSheffrey has been able to mine in detail to provide a vivid description of what sanctuary consisted of in this period).[75] In the case of the history we were investigating, the whole point of sanctuary was to be hidden. As a result, the historical record was often scarce (when it was not replete with exaggerated tales of sensational adventure, rescue, and escape, as was the case for many accounts of fugitives from the law).

In this respect, I was very much guided by my own childhood memories of growing up in the Eastern Townships (Wabanaki and N'dakina territory) and hearing stories of Donald Morrison, the famed "Outlaw of Megantic." According to local lore, Morrison had been sheltered for ten months by the local Scottish community over the course of 1888 and 1889 – hiding in the woods and among friends and kin – as police sought his arrest and capture for the murder of Earl Warren during a duel on the streets of Megantic. This tale has all the makings of a sensational movie, but beyond the dramatic plot line, it is a powerful story of community refuge and sanctuary, even as the significance of these efforts has changed over time.

As I pursued my research on sanctuary, the story of the "Outlaw of Megantic" served as an early conceptual reminder that refuge and protection were not always public. As a result, the first four case studies reflect a different methodological choice in terms of selecting stories to explore. Rather than the product of publicly identified newspaper accounts, they come from the question of what sanctuary and protection might have looked like at different moments in time. Here, I was guided by my sense of big temporal swaths: did sanctuary exist, and what did it look like, during legalized slavery, during times of war, and during economic turmoil? The first four chapters reflect an effort to answer these questions.

In attempting to do so, I wanted to provide more than an empirical narrative about the shape of sanctuary at a particular moment. I also saw an opportunity to connect all the case studies to broader themes in studies of the history of migration. As a result, each of the case studies has a specific thematic focus in addition to an empirical one. I was inspired in this vein by Italo Calvino's *Invisible Cities*, in which the author imagines Marco Polo recounting the personality and magical qualities of ten different cities to the aging emperor Kublai Khan. Each story, each city, has something to offer. Such is the case here. Each of the cities described in this book (The Lonely City, The Fugitive City, The Hostile City, The Wartime City, The Occupied City, and The Uneasy City) tells us something about the shape and character of refuge in the past and the present as it connects with cross-cutting themes in histories of migration. As a kind of prologue, I provide context to these cities with a discussion of "Before the City."

The first chapter, "The Lonely City," considers the history of the "Underground Railroad"[76] and the ways in which the city of Montreal/Mooniyaang/Tiohtià:ke failed to operate as a site of refuge in this period despite public depictions to the contrary. Exploring the lack of safety for fugitive slaves, across various legal jurisdictions, the chapter draws attention to what Saidiya Hartman describes as the "undeniably truncated opportunities available to the freed."[77] This is an important consideration because, as I discuss in the second chapter, notions of fugitivity are currently being revisited in terms of their liberatory potential. In interrogating the idea of formal sites of sanctuary and jurisdictional freedom through an exploration of Montreal/Mooniyaang/Tiohtià:ke and the surrounding settlements of Kahnawà:ke, Ahkwesáhsne, and Kanehsatà:ke, I attend to the role of community in shaping the substantive possibility and experience of refuge, drawing attention to the limits of legal protections to do so in both the past and present.

With "The Fugitive City" chapter, I turned my attention to the nature of sanctuary during the US Civil War and the role that Montreal/Mooniyaang/Tiohtià:ke played in sheltering fugitive John Harrison Surratt, suspected in the assassination of US President Abraham Lincoln in 1865. Here, I deliberately chose to explore recent work around Black fugitivity and refusal in conjunction with older definitions of fugitivity that underscore the idea of being "made a fugitive" or "exiled." Recent scholarship sees fugitivity as "the disavowal of and disengagement from state-governed projects that attempt to adjudicate normative constructions of difference through liberal tropes of freedom and democratic belonging."[78] Cultural studies scholar Tina Campt calls fugitivity "a refusal of the very premises that have historically negated the lived experience of blackness as either pathological or exceptional to the logic of white supremacy."[79] Inspired by these powerful evocations, I was interested in what fugitivity looked like beyond the suggestions of its liberatory potential, and so I made a deliberate decision to highlight how fugitivity operated historically for a white, Confederate, messenger (a figure almost completely contrary to the subjects evoked in studies of Black fugitivity in the present). In doing so, I emphasized the importance of race, class, and gender, as well as the religious and political networks that facilitated Surratt's flight into Canada and later to Europe and the ways in which these stood in stark contrast to the lack of refuge or sanctuary for fugitive slaves in Montreal/Mooniyaang/Tiohtià:ke in this same period.

The next chapter, "The Hostile City," is perhaps the most central to the arguments I make in *Sanctuary in Pieces* about the limitations, or what scholar Ananaya Roy calls "the horizons" of sanctuary historically and in the present.[80] It is, admittedly, a chapter that sits at the margins of conventional histories of sanctuary, in part because it explores the structures of global capitalism in fostering the need for economic refuge as well as the impact of political oppression in the 1930s (most work on histories of refuge and sanctuary continue to focus uniquely on the idea of political persecution, which has been central to understandings of refuge since the creation of the 1951 Convention Relating to the Status of Refugees). In doing so, I focus on anarchist Emma Goldman's time in exile in Montreal/Mooniyaang/Tiohtià:ke against the backdrop of charitable work in the city that provided housing and shelter to young women and girls. While Goldman focused on the problems of global capitalism and state authoritarianism, by the 1930s, she shared many of the cares and concerns of her immediate neighbours in the city who also struggled materially. The focus on economic considerations in the making of refuge led me to intertwine Yvonne Maisonneuve's work as founder of Le Chaînon, one of the oldest women's shelters in the city, with Emma Goldman's perspectives on the city during the fraught decade of the 1930s.

With this approach, "The Hostile City" ended up serving as a hinge chapter, moving from an interest in understanding the role of community, or the lack thereof, in the shaping of sanctuary to the relationship between community and legal frameworks of protection in the latter half of the twentieth and early part of the twenty-first centuries. The chapter that follows, "The Wartime City," reflects this gradual shift, exploring the experience of war resisters who moved to Canada as immigrants, not legal refugees, but who were nevertheless seeking refuge from forced conscription and US imperialism. Much has been written on this topic, most recently by geographer Allison Mountz, but I was interested in a very particular conceptual piece.[81] I wanted to know what happened, and happens, when the expected site of refuge itself changes. I was inspired to ask this question knowing that the October Crisis of 1970 and the federal government's use of the War Measures Act, which expanded the military presence in the streets of the city and suspended civil liberties, changed perceptions of the country for many residents. I wondered if the same was true for new arrivals and what these shifts signified in terms of a sense of refuge more broadly.

The last two chapters, which focus on the interplay between individual sanctuary cases, legal frameworks of protection, and acts of community solidarity and support are more aligned with conventional accounts of modern sanctuary practices. The "Occupied City" explores the history of sanctuary involving members of the Chilean community in Montreal/Mooniyaang/Tiohtià:ke in three acts in the 1990s. It explores the ways in which people seeking refuge or the normalization of their immigration statuses used the claimed religious authority and perceived security of church sanctuary to draw attention to their causes. In addition to tracing the relationship between diplomatic asylum, activism, and church sanctuary in the late twentieth century, the conceptual focus here is on the ways in which Chilean refugees and migrants fought for their right to the city, so to speak, and the way their activism and resistance were broadly seen as problematic.

The final chapter, "The Uneasy City," turns to church sanctuary cases in the early twenty-first century and troubles the public dimensions of sanctuary, most notably church and *Sanctuary City* declarations, in this period. Over the course of researching and writing this chapter, one of the families involved made it explicitly clear that they did not want their story included in the analysis I was offering; this refusal prompted me to consider the question of naming and what historian Anna Sheftel has called the "telling silence of untold stories."[82] I, therefore, opted to describe sanctuary seekers in this period in the vaguest of terms, focusing instead on what motivated sanctuary providers in the immediate years preceding the declaration of sanctuary by the city council of Montreal/Mooniyaang/Tiohtià:ke. For many modern sanctuary seekers, the choice to "go public" was coerced by circumstances and bound up with their hopes and aspirations for their futures. They were not necessarily willing public subjects, as discussed in "The Occupied City" chapter as well, and I was reluctant to foist them into the public gaze once more, even as I recognized that their stories remained accessible, and relentlessly present, online. This chapter ultimately explores the ways some church congregations came to offer sanctuary in this period and the troubling ways in which it was lived by those seeking to alter the outcomes of administrative decisions about their claims to refuge.

Sanctuary in Pieces concludes with a short reflection on the sanctuary city declaration in Montreal/Mooniyaang/Tiohtià:ke in 2017 and city council's decision to step back from this decision just under two years later. In tracing the lead up to the declaration, the response, and the eventual retreat, the epilogue considers the politics of public sanctuary declarations and their relationship to historic and ongoing acts of sanctuary. The conclusion considers possibilities for the future and the potential for conceptualizing fear, refuge, and need across broad categories of experience. It ends with a final reflection on the craft of history and the possibility and ethics of leaving history behind as a form of sanctuary or refuge in and of itself.

There is a sketch-like quality to many of the analyses and conclusions in *Sanctuary in Pieces*. This is deliberate and part of my methodological approach, which was to be as unfettered as possible when it came to interpreting the historical past and its connections to the present. I was guided in this work by the conversations I had with many people over the course of this project, including fellow researchers, but more importantly, with the people I interviewed about their own experiences with sanctuary or with the city of Montreal/Mooniyaang/Tiohtià:ke. I conducted formal interviews with eleven people for "The Wartime City" and eight people for "The Occupied City." I also interviewed three individuals and conducted one group interview for "The Uneasy City." The interviews and conversations varied in length, depth, and breadth. Some people I knew beforehand, including Ken and Jackie Hyman whom I consider close family friends but whose stories of sanctuary I had never asked about previously. Others I recruited through public sources, their own writings, or through word of mouth. Some of these interviews blossomed into friendships that I hold dear. None of the interviews were full life histories but many took place on repeated occasions, and all sought to convey their engagements beyond the immediacy of sanctuary, which was what drew me to them in the first instance. David Rapaport and Jürgen Dankvort talked about lifelong political commitments. Michael Klein and Bonnie Sherr Klein discussed their respective contributions to the fields of medicine and filmmaking, for which they have both been recognized with the Order of Canada. Yet, despite these accomplishments, it was Michael Klein's passing mention of supporting later generations of war resisters from the United State's war in Iraq that held my attention in terms of this project, reflecting a gap in what people wanted to emphasize and what I wanted to better understand.

As a result, I followed the crumbs; interviewing those who accepted my invitation to do so and respecting the wishes of those who indicated that they wanted to leave this history behind. This led me to omit any obviously identifying information from the text and to avoid citing any newspaper and other audio-visual evidence that might have easily led to their identification. I could do nothing about the continued digital record, but I knew that I didn't have to point to it directly.[83] I am hoping that my own attempt to reconcile the historical craft with issues around privacy and distance will provide some useful insights for others in navigating these complex ethical issues.

This process and other methodological concerns are detailed in the Notes from the Field that accompany each case study. These notes are an effort to capture the substantive deliberations that went into every aspect of this work and to be as transparent as possible about the making of this project. I don't think we talk enough about history as craft and all the iterations any given project involves. The Notes from the Field are repurposed from a research journal I kept throughout this project. Some of my journaling involved detailing the nature of my relationships with the people I interviewed, with the subject matter I was studying, with the archives I used, and with the city of Montreal/Mooniyaang/Tiohtià:ke itself. This is a place that I both know well having grown up in Quebec, as well as through work, friend, and family connections. In other ways, I don't know it all, never having immersed myself in its quotidian rhythms or participated in activist work in the city.

As the foregoing no doubt suggests, my interest in sanctuary is long standing, dating back to my earlier work around the history of Chinese migrants in the Cold War. At the time, I noticed the importance of activism in the face of states that continued to cling to race-based exclusion criteria and refused to assist refugees in Asia in any significant way unless there were political benefits to doing so. This determined activism drew me to questions of sanctuary in the first instance. In wanting to understand how sanctuary evolved, I opted to focus on a single city, Montreal/Mooniyaang/Tiohtià:ke, to better trace in a probing and burrowing manner the ways people sought, offered, and hoped for refuge. The numerous public sanctuary cases in the city beginning in 1983 were inviting, and I had assumed that there would be similar histories of sanctuary moving back in time, especially because of the way the city figures so prominently in the concluding chapters of

Harriet Beecher Stowe's antislavery novel *Uncle Tom's Cabin* and in the public imaginary more generally. Sanctuary was less forthcoming than I had anticipated, and I was surprised when my initial enthusiasm for the idea of sanctuary cities as promising sites of refuge began to abate. With case after case, and with only two exceptions, I began to see the ways in which the city had been a difficult and uneasy place for newcomers and outsiders.

I was surprised that I ended up feeling so down about cities as sanctuaries. I still admire and appreciate the efforts people make in getting municipal governments to engage, but overall, I was disappointed by what the substance and character of a formal declaration of sanctuary meant. Instead, I came to understand the significance of community connections and networks in creating the possibility of genuine and welcoming forms of hospitality and protection. I also came to see how isolating and vulnerable people were without substantial communities of support. These communities can take many shapes and forms. As the epigraph from writer and philosopher Elie Wiesel reminds us, "The sanctuary is a human being. Sanctuary is a dream. And that is why you are here, and that is why I am here. We are here because of one another."[84]

The emphasis on human connections is key. As the cases in this book show, sanctuary, in its various informal and formal expressions, has long been a part of the historical landscape. Crucially, ideas about sanctuary and for whom practices of hospitality and protection are intended continue to evolve. Increasingly, discussions are rooted in notions of solidarity with ideas focused on an open-ended practice of "coming together," instead of sanctuary proper.[85] As ideas around refuge and responsibility continue to evolve, we may see the shattered pieces of sanctuary as they exist in the present, collected up and reimagined.

Before the City

IN RECENT YEARS, thousands of people have sought refuge in cities. They have done so in places that often have long histories of mobility and contestation that have imprinted subsequent efforts to secure or provide sanctuary. Such is the case of Montreal/Mooniyang/Tiohtià:ke. Long before it was incorporated as a city in 1840, the settlement was a disputed and often uncertain site of refuge for Indigenous Peoples, colonists, and settlers alike. As a reminder, and to set the tone of the work that follows, this brief section emphasizes the character of this insecurity and flags transformative moments of conflict and vulnerability in the two centuries that followed the city's founding as a religious outpost. Unlike the rest of this book, this section is written in broad strokes to set the stage for the deep exploration of sanctuary that follows.

Established by French colonists in 1642 as Ville Marie, the settlement was an experiment initiated in the hope against hope (and with many prayers) that it would survive. The founders – members of the Société Notre-Dame de Montréal pour la conversion des Sauvages de la Nouvelle-France, including Paul de Chomedey; Sieur de Maisonneuve; and Jeanne Mance, an Ursuline nun – wanted a permanent settlement on the island of Montreal/Kawenote Teiontiakon for the purposes of religious conversion. They envisioned a religious community that would bring together Indigenous Peoples and French colonists. However, from its earliest history, Ville Marie was characterized by fear and insecurity; it was a "dangerous but divine post."[1] The geography of the land and the surrounding water made the location both attractive for settlement but also vulnerable to attacks.[2] François Dollier de Casson, a Sulpician priest and author of *Histoire de Montréal,* wrote about his fear that at any moment "Tous les arbres de cet Isle se devraient changer en autant d'Iroquois" (all the trees on this island might at any moment transform into as many Rotinonhsión:ni).[3] Dollier de Casson took it as an ominous sign that the Société had received the land for free from the Company of New France, whose associates "thought no French settlement there could survive its perceived dangers."[4]

The settlement's geographic exposure led the Société Notre-Dame de Montréal to encourage a "critical mass of settlers" to ensure the missionaries' security.[5] The site also became a key military outpost, first for the French Empire and then the British one. Still, Jesuit missionaries encouraged the idea of Ville Marie as a potential refuge, both as a physical site and a community. In 1642, one Jesuit missionary noted the need for "more security" to draw people in. If this could be done, he believed Indigenous Peoples would "form a village at Mont-Royal, and gather there those of the Island, and the other scattered nations, who see themselves to be the prey of the enemy here, and on the river where they have their haunts."[6] Still, the French at Ville Marie "could only offer security of a relative sort" given the site's geography and their own situation.[7] In the early 1650s, there were a number of documented attacks on the settlement as Ville Marie and the region generally became an "exposed frontier" in conflicts between the Algonquin and Rotinonhsión:ni.[8]

Ville Marie's vulnerability to enemy attacks led to the construction of increased fortifications in subsequent years, particularly following the transfer of power to the Sulpician Order in 1633. In this period, Ville Marie became increasingly garrisoned and visible as a physical site of refuge with the presence of reinforced fortifications, for which construction began in 1687.[9] A similar dynamic occurred outside the settlement as well. As one historian observed, "all observation posts, outposts, stores, and chapels had multiple uses," becoming places where people "would turn at the faintest whisper of an invasion."[10]

By 1681, there were fourteen hundred French settlers on the island of Montreal/Kawenote Teiontiakon and approximately three thousand two

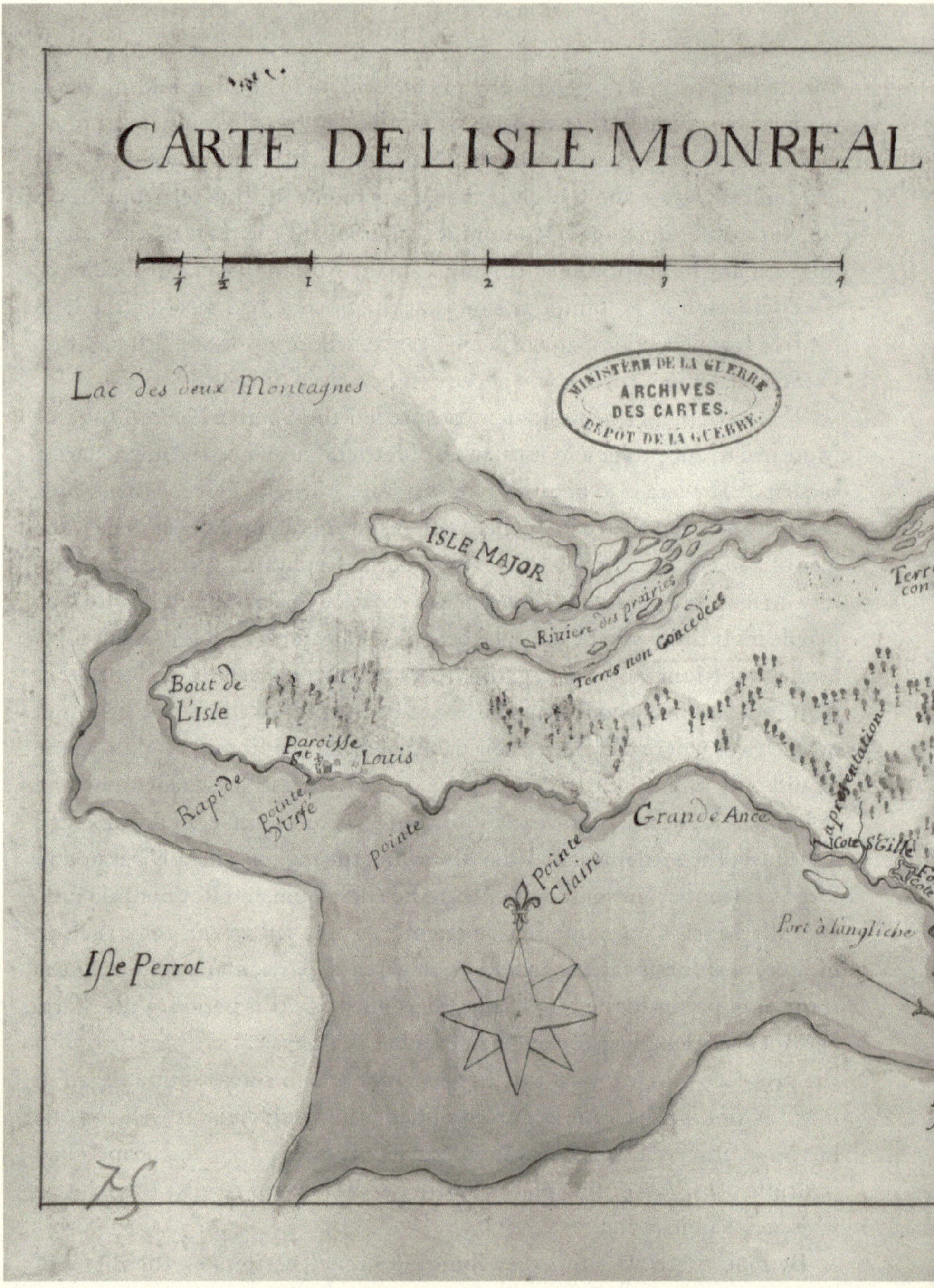

0.1 A 1730 map showing the geography of both land and water. *Carte de lisle Monreal.*

La Chanaye
Riviere des Prairies
petit Fort
Iesus
Boucherville
Nouvelle paroisse
aux Recollets
Redoute
Costes St Laurent
Fort de la Longuepoint
Le Tremblay
Cote St Caterine
Fort de longueuil
Ville Marie
Isle Ste Helene
Lac St pierre
La Congregation
cote St paul
Verdun
St Lambert
Saut St Louis
prairie de la Madelaine

decades later. Ville Marie was the largest town on the island but, in this period, it was still "outnumbered by the combined population of Native towns surrounding it."[11] In addition to the settlement of Ville Marie, the island of Montreal/Kawenote Teiontiakon was dotted with farms and Indigenous villages, such as La Montagne (populated by Wendat, Algonquin, and Haudenosaunee Peoples in the 1670s) and Sault au Récollet (originally intended as a refuge for Indigenous Christians), with whom merchants in Ville Marie traded.[12] As historian Brett Rushforth underscores, "this was just how colonial officials wanted it. Not only did a close body of Native allies provide military security, but they also drew pelts and goods to the French that otherwise would go to their English rivals."[13] Rushforth further notes that Indigenous Peoples within Ville Marie were also key to the settlement's evolution, "as consumers of French goods and traders who reexported French goods to other Native villages."[14] With these early developments, Ville Marie evolved to eventually become known as Montreal (after the mountain Mont-Royal so named by French explorer Jacques Cartier) and a major industrial centre and the "workshop of British North America" by the 1840s.[15]

Before these major transformations took place, however, the settlement was buffeted by major events that changed its very nature. Key among these was the defeat of French forces by the British in 1760, which led to a transfer of power – formalized in the Treaty of Paris three years later. This marked a critical juncture in the history of Montreal/Mooniyaang/Tiohtià:ke as the articles of capitulation preserved certain dimensions of the social, political, economic, and cultural life of the settlement but also introduced new ones, most notably a civil law regime that was layered upon the existing common law framework, new governance structures, protections for English-speaking and Protestant settlers, alongside a recognition of the existing French Catholic culture. The transfer of power created a new, contested dynamic, one which still plays out today in terms of language rights in the province of Quebec and an enduring sense of dual threat and survivance in terms of French Canadian culture.

This dynamic infused subsequent events, most notably during the War of 1812 when doubtful French Canadian and Indigenous loyalties were the source of considerable concern among British authorities.[16] In the District of Montreal, twenty-five hundred British soldiers and militia converged in an effort to secure the exposed settlement.[17] Yet the war never reached the city. The closest it came was in the fall of October 1813 when American forces attacked at Chateauguay and were defeated with the support of both French Canadian and Kanien'kehá:ka forces.[18] As such, perhaps the most fearful time for British authorities in this period came in 1837 with the emergence of armed rebellions in Lower and Upper Canada.

In Lower Canada, rebellion emerged when British authorities refused what became known as the "92 Resolutions" passed by the elected, majority French Canadian Legislative Assembly. These resolutions contained a list of grievances about the distribution of funds and political offices in Lower Canada. The refusal to consider the petition exacerbated the social strains already in place because of cholera epidemics, changing demographics and, more immediately, a struggling economy. The protests, initially both political and agrarian in nature, culminated in armed insurrection in November and December 1837.[19]

Much of the mobilization occurred in the countryside of the District of Montreal rather than the city proper. It was inspired in part by the American Revolution and events in France, but it was locally situated, growing "out of the campaign for colonial autonomy and democratic reform led by the middle-class radicals of the 'Patriot party.'"[20] Thousands became involved in the rebellion in a variety of ways. One account suggested that "in many parts of the District of Montreal almost every man had been implicated to some degree in the patriote movement."[21] Some of these entanglements led to conflict with Kahnawákeró:non when the Patriotes marched on Kahnawá:ke, while other conflicts took place across international borders.[22]

Hundreds of Patriotes and their supporters fled to Vermont and other parts of the United States after the first wave of violence in the fall of 1837, where they were "acclaimed" and celebrated as revolutionary heroes.[23] The residents of St Albans were particularly enthused, organizing a town meeting of two thousand people in December 1837, in which they "affirmed the inalienable rights as set forth by Thomas Jefferson in the Declaration of Independence."[24] Louis-Joseph Papineau, one of the leaders of the rebellion in Lower Canada, sought refuge in the United States and France from 1838 to 1845.

Crucially, when the rebels were defeated, the punishment was swift, and the humiliation and despondency that followed were palpable. As historian Allan Greer observed in his classic work, *The Patriots and the People: The Rebellion of 1837 in Lower Canada*, "from the moment the smoke cleared, it was open season on 'rebels': any could be arrested or imprisoned, their property seized or destroyed, with no trace of formalities, due process, or appeal."[25] More than one thousand people were jailed on charges of high treason in the wake of the 1837 rebellions. Twelve Patriotes were hanged, and fifty-eight were transported to Australia to serve time in a penal colony far away from the land, family, and friends they loved and had fought for.

The official investigation into the causes of the rebellions led to the recommendation to unite the two colonies, creating the Province of Canada in 1840. It was a union born of dissatisfaction with the imperial Crown, a desire for greater autonomy, and contests over the most appropriate form of governance for the colony. Crucially, it failed to resolve many questions around power and authority and the great sense of loss and injustice felt by many citizens of Montreal/Mooniyaang/Tiohtià:ke in the face of suspended civil liberties and punitive retributions. Those who arrived in Montreal/Mooniyaang/Tiohtià:ke after it was incorporated in 1840 encountered the "City of Wealth and Death."[26] It was a place of ongoing contestation over rights, responsibilities, community, and culture.

And it was here that many people sought, forged, and sometimes succeeded in finding sanctuary across the years.

The vexing issue as I prepared to write this chapter was how to tell the history of something that apparently didn't happen.

I first started to work on this section in October 2020. At the time, it focused on the history of the "Underground Railroad," sanctuary at the Union United Church (the first historically Black church in Montreal/Mooniyaang/Tiohtià:ke) in the 2000s, and the politics of writing during the early heady days of the Black Lives Matter movement. I wrote a first draft in a month and left it to ferment, knowing that I still wanted to do more in the way of primary source research.

When I returned to the chapter in October 2022, I was deeply uncomfortable with the direction I had taken. In trying to cover a vast historical period, I had framed the first chapter as a story of Black sanctuary from the nineteenth to the early twenty-first century. The problem, which should have been obvious at the time, was that this is way too much for one chapter. Worst, the way the original draft had been written inadvertently essentialized the idea of Black sanctuary as unchanging and Black people as always and forever reduced to marginalization and precarity. Read from a different vantage point, and with the benefit of two years of intermittent thinking and research, I knew that the chapter wasn't what I wanted it to be.

0.2 Early brainstorming sketches, spelling mistakes and all.

I got stuck and spent weeks gently poking at the chapter but couldn't move forward until I sat down and literally sketched out the historical past.

The resulting sketches were messy.

In both drawings, I traced out movements, and what I saw was an island surrounded by water. I realized that if fugitive slaves leaving the United States made their way to or through Montreal/Mooniyaang/Tiohtià:ke, they might have journeyed through Kahnawà:ke, Ahkwesáhsne, or Kanehsatà:ke before ever reaching the city, if they continued that far.

Sketching and seeing the geography helped me realize this chapter was actually about the ways Montreal/Mooniyaang/Tiohtià:ke was not a site of sanctuary for fugitive slaves in the mid-nineteenth century. It was about people moving in many directions, and often going elsewhere. Looking at my sketches, I wondered if people had found refuge among the Haudenosaunee. My idea was to make this history the focus of the chapter and to decentre the city in the process.

The historical record had other ideas.

Instead of documented adoptions or even records of a temporary presence in Kahnawà:ke, Ahkwesáhsne, or Kanehsatà:ke, I found only hints of encounters. There was no evidence of fugitive slaves in these settlements and only a few mentions of Black people more generally, such as Louis Cook's adoption into the community at Ahkwesáhsne where he received the name Akiatonharónkwen, "he unhangs himself from the group." Glasgow Crawford and Joseph Thompson, two Black men, lived in Kahnawà:ke for a time. These cases were documented by historian Frank Mackey in Done With Slavery, *who also identified an 1818 watercolour by Dudley Baxter, a rather elusive British artist who died in Mancetter, England in 1837, that shows a couple with "darkish" skin tones. Mackey suspected the subjects might have been fugitives from slavery, but there is no way of knowing for sure.*

The lack of information in the documentary record and in existing oral histories, combined with unpromising feedback in conversations with community members, forced me to wrestle with historical contradictions; with a geography of the land and water that would have made migration to Kahnawà:ke, Ahkwesáhsne, or Kanehsatà:ke possible but where there was only very sparse evidence that this had occurred for any length of the time.

It was precisely because of the space that opened from not knowing, from only having hints, that I was able to think through the relatively limited nature of sanctuary in Montreal/Mooniyaang/Tiohtià:ke during the era of the "Underground Railroad." This, in turn, led me to a broader negotiation with the ways in which the mythology around "following the North Star" has proven so powerful at the national level. In seeking to understand community perspectives on this history, I found a remarkable gap thanks to the insights of interdisciplinary scholars Désirée Rochat and Kelann Currie-Williams. Their familiarity with the Negro Community Centre collection, now preserved in Special Collections at Concordia University, was essential for understanding the almost complete disregard of this topic at the community level.

This gap provided an opportunity to consider the notion of absence more fully. Ultimately, I looked at it in the context of the original era of the "Underground Railroad" and attended to the fact that it has not been a prominent feature of community memory-making in the city.

Despite suggestions that I should pursue some form of creative fabulation to make the lived experience of slavery and freedom from slavery in the city more dynamic, I chose to emphasize instead lack and absence. In this way, I adopted Saidiya Hartman's earlier model, when "fabulation" was "latent, not yet emergent" in her work, choosing to "use the archive to create another order of statements, to produce a different account of what had happened and what might be possible."[1] *In this case, I used archival materials such as the registers from the Hôpital Général, the only established refuge in the city, to show how Montreal/Mooniyaang/Tiohtià:ke, with its own history of slavery and its relatively small community of Black residents until the twentieth century, was generally not seen or experienced as a site of refuge for fugitives from slavery.*

June 2023, January 2024

The Lonely City

1.1 John Henry Walker, *Skating on the harbour ice, Montreal, QC*, 1850–60.

THE WINTER OF 1851 was a typically cold one in the city of Montreal/ Mooniyaang/Tiohtià:ke. The average temperatures in February hovered at -10°C (13°F). Blizzards raged, and winds howled, with gusts sometimes reaching thirty kilometres (eighteen miles an hour), dusting the landscape with a "loose finally crystallized snow" that residents of the city described as a "poudrerie."[1] The frozen harbour was pure pleasure for some but the barren, snowy, frozen plains could be hostile elements.

For Shadrach Minkins, a fugitive slave from the United States, the icy landscape was a gift. After being sprung from a Boston/Shawmut jail in February 1851, Minkins made his way north to escape the reach of the 1850 Fugitive Slave Act, eventually becoming one of a small number of people who fled to the city of Montreal/Mooniyaang/Tiohtià:ke along the "Underground Railroad" (roughly 1790–1865). Recalling his escape, Minkins explained that "the weather was severe during the time, and we had to cross the ice twice; once the distance was nine miles (14.5 kilometres)."[2] The ice provided solid ground for his crossings and made the difference between safety and slavery.

Minkins' would not have been able to see the details of the settlement from his vantage point on the southern shore, and so if people had been frolicking in the frozen harbour, he would not have perceived this. Instead, his first impression as he gazed at the city was likely of a stilled settlement, quieted from the busy port activity of the summer months because of the frozen waters of the St Lawrence/Kaniatarowanenneh to the east.[3] The ferries that connected the railways of the mainland to the island would largely have stopped during the winter months. Had he arrived by a more westerly route, he might have been astonished to see the waters of the Lachine Rapids moving swiftly even as islands of massed snow and ice appeared among the currents. No bridge yet connected the island to the land masses in the south, or the north for that matter, and Minkins would likely have made his way across the ice near La Prairie, an early Jesuit mission for Christian converts including many Haudenosaunee.[4] If Minkins, aged thirty-seven, "was not too preoccupied with his own private uncertainties and fears" he may have marveled at the crisp air and the landscape around him, and wondered about his next steps.[5]

This opening teases out some of the obstacles and opportunities that Minkins navigated in his escape from slavery, including a settlement that wasn't designed or intended with him in mind. The city that Minkins encountered in 1851 was still negotiating the political and social aftermath of the 1837–8 rebellions. More immediately, the political and economic turmoil fuelled by outrage over the Rebellion Losses Bill (intended to compensate property owners for financial losses), which led to the burning of Parliament and its relocation to Toronto/Tkaronto in 1849, was still being felt. In 1851, Montreal/Mooniyaang/Tiohtià:ke was a small city of 57,000 people where class differences played out in taverns and other meeting places, at work sites, and in the streets. The affluent were protected by walls of stone, but two-thirds of the housing in the city was made of wood. In 1850, and again in 1852, major fires ripped through the city, destroying an estimated 15 per cent of the housing stock.[6] Charity in this period was piecemeal, formally limited to the work of the Hôtel-Dieu, which served as the medical hospital, and the Hôpital Général, which operated as a kind of refuge for those who were terminally ill or impoverished. As this chapter will explore, the Hôpital Général was simultaneously a place of refuge for some and unfreedom for others.

Nineteenth-century Montreal/Mooniyaang/Tiohtià:ke was, therefore, not a particularly welcoming place for impoverished, working class, or labouring people, nor for those fleeing slavery in the United States. Crucially, for the latter, the city never claimed to be. Still, a few people escaping slavery made their way there (some permanently, some temporarily), and the idea of the city as a site of refuge was subsequently mythologized, most famously as a result of the family reunion scene in Harriet Beecher Stowe's widely read antislavery novel, *Uncle Tom's Cabin*. We are, therefore, left with the complicated task of understanding refuge in a city that was never intended as such and was never a key part of the "Underground Railroad," even though it has been mythologized as such.

Rather than a place of refuge, the settlement and its surroundings were likely lonely and isolating for newly arrived fugitives from slavery. The history of slavery in the settlement and the ways people fled their situations when they could meant there were few Black residents in the city by the 1830s.[7] Census figures and narrative accounts outline how Black people left the city in greater numbers than they arrived during the era of the "Underground Railroad."[8] Within the settlement, Black fugitives would have been highly visible, making the kind of anonymity and freedom that is now synonymous with urban spaces illusory. Having to trust in the strange and unfamiliar, people largely did not shelter for long. Shadrack Minkins likely did not know this as he crossed the frozen expanses that lay before him. Perhaps in time, he came to think of that cold greeting as a metaphor for life in the city, even as he built a family and a series of businesses that would make him one of the only known fugitives from slavery to stay in Montreal/ Mooniyaang/ Tiohtià:ke during the era of the "Underground Railroad."

Slavery, Safety, and Freedom

Although scholars such as Saidiya Hartman have pointed to the "temporal entanglement" between slavery and freedom and the lack of an "absolute divide" between the two, the question of refuge in the context of legalized slavery has generally been structured around the question of freedom: freedom from bondage; freedom from exploitation; and freedom from sexual violence, physical punishment, and dehumanization.[9] Freedom is now deeply bound up with notions of liberty and civilization.[10] Yet freedom is not an unproblematic concept.

In colonial North America, freedom was understood to be the purview of a select few – most generally white, propertied men. Not surprisingly, therefore, the notion of freedom has, in many instances in the past and present, served as "a racist ideology" in which only certain people have been deemed worthy, or sufficiently trustworthy, to be free.[11] The language of freedom, however, disguises this underpinning racism as well as the persistence of class differences and economic exploitation. Liberal democracies now emphasize the allure of freedom in a way that erases the mixed motives that encourage migration, for instance, while also suppressing criticism of state and society. In terms of migration, some of the symbolic residue around freedom stems from the heady days of the Cold War when the idea of being a beacon of freedom and liberty for victims of communist oppression was a critical construction in US foreign policy in particular.[12] In other words, as with many examples when it comes to discourses around freedom, there is often a gap between what was claimed and what was experienced.

In conflating refuge with freedom, we lose sight of the important ways in which refuge was historically constructed in terms of safety. Safety is often defined as being protected or "guarded against hurt or injury." It can also mean "freedom from danger," showing how in some ways the concept of freedom and the notion of safety are deeply entangled.[13] The challenge is that because of the powerful discourse around freedom, we lose sight of how important it was to be physically safe, and the ways in which that safety could take many forms, ranging from moves across legal and international borders to changes in clothing and other physical transformations.[14]

In *The Refugee: Narratives of Fugitive Slaves in Canada (A North-Side View of Slavery)*, compiled by abolitionist Benjamin Drew in the 1850s, several interviewees highlighted safety as part of their efforts to leave slavery and find legal freedom, sometimes framed simultaneously along the lines of being on "free soil" and "perfectly safe."[15] A man known only as "James Adams" recounted: "We soon reached an old stable in the edge of a little town; we entered it and slept alternately one keeping watch, as we always managed while in the neighbourhood of settlements. We did not do this in the wilderness, – there we slept safely, and were quite reconciled. At cock-crowing in the morning we set out and went into the woods, which were very near; there we stayed through the day."[16]

Others dreamed about eluding "pursuit and reaching Canada in safety" or of being able to "safely return" to their old homes.[17] Although the emphasis here was on physical spaces, there were also temporal dimensions to safety. For example, for those who were enslaved, nighttime often provided some sense of safety. As historian Tiya Miles suggests, "Darkness carried with it a special kind of buffer that might at times have felt like a source of power to the enslaved."[18] Nighttime was, therefore, "a time of sanctuary to the enslaved when textiles were fashioned, rude quarters were made habitable, extra vittles were stewed in the pots and escape plots were planned and executed."[19]

Crucially, the laws around slavery could only demarcate the difference between free and unfree. When British authorities began to limit slavery in the 1790s, they only created the possibility of legal freedom. They did not govern safe or unsafe communities and places – these evolved entirely relationally. Mobility became key and people identified fellow human beings, places, and situations as potentially safe or unsafe. For many, safety continued to be difficult even after they were nominally free, seemingly forever marked by the colour of their skin and the resulting "travestied liberation, thwarted agency, coerced labor, interminable servility and blameworthiness of the free individual."[20] There was much at play and never any guarantees. Safety was, and remains, contingent on a host of factors that exist outside of legal frameworks. It depends on relationships, on the environment, on chance, on circumstance, and, in the case of migrants, what some scholars have described as the "furies" and "fortunes" of mobility.[21] And it could dissolve in an instant.

Montreal/Mooniyaang/Tiohtià:ke was not an especially promising city of refuge in the era of the "Underground Railroad." This was partly because of its own history of legalized slavery. Historians estimate that there were approximately 1,132 Black and Indigenous Peoples enslaved in New France by 1759.[22] Over half lived in Montreal/Mooniyaang/Tiohtià:ke.[23] Slavery was not only preserved in the articles of capitulation of 1760, which set out the conditions by which New France was to be surrendered to the British, but it actually grew in subsequent years.[24] In the aftermath of the American Revolution in 1791, the numbers of enslaved people in Lower Canada and Upper Canada increased significantly. Although an estimated four thousand Blacks also moved freely to British North America, hundreds of others were "kept as personal servants by soldiers, officers, or in common ownership by army units."[25] United Empire Loyalists, seeking refuge in British North America, brought an estimated three hundred enslaved people into Lower Canada alone.[26] For example, Sir John Johnson (a military officer, magistrate, and the son of the first British Superintendent of Indian Affairs) fled from Albany to Montreal/Mooniyaang/Tiohtià:ke and brought several enslaved people with him, some of whom were sold upon arrival.[27] Free and unfree lived side by side.

In Montreal/Mooniyaang/Tiohtià:ke, many powerful merchants owned slaves and derived huge profits from shipping and the sugar trade – enterprises that were also seeped in slave labour.[28] Advertisements of people for sale were commonplace, as were ads seeking information for the return of a fugitive slave. As art historian Charmaine Nelson has noted, the *Montreal Gazette*, which began to publish in August 1785, included its first fugitive slave ad a month later.[29] Some accounts suggest that the number of people fleeing slavery in Lower Canada was significant enough to constitute a "southbound Underground Railroad," especially after Vermont abolished new adult slavery in 1777.[30] For those trying to flee, the question of where to go loomed large and often did not have an obvious answer. Historian Afua Cooper explains the sparse options as follows: "Slave runaways could take refuge with sympathetic Natives in the Upper Country or disappear into some frontiers. Escaping to land held by a foreign power was another possibility."[31] Indigenous communities represented a potential refuge for some fleeing slavery, as did different jurisdictions depending on their evolving legal and political climates.

A series of court decisions rather than legislative action meant that the end of legalized slavery in Lower Canada was much messier than in Upper Canada where the slave trade, though not existing enslavement, was curtailed beginning in 1793. In Lower Canada, slave owners led by Joseph Papineau (the father of Louis-Joseph Papineau, one of the leaders of the 1837 rebellion) fought for the preservation of slavery, and the Legislative Assembly was loath to act as a result.[32] The move towards ending legal slavery in Lower Canada, therefore, rested on a series of court decisions at the Court of King's Bench, which occurred more or less by 1800.[33]

Still, even though new enslavement was not legally sanctioned after the court rulings, there were still 142 known enslaved people in Montreal/Mooniyaang/Tiohtià:ke in 1804.[34] In 1806, the state of Vermont introduced a Prevention of Kidnapping Act to prevent the removal of slaves to Canada "where slavery is established by law," suggesting that slavery endured in a substantial way with people being kidnapped from the relatively free state of Vermont and brought to bondage in Lower Canada and perhaps Upper Canada as well.[35]

In other words, a tenuous legal situation persisted in Lower Canada in the early nineteenth century. Only in 1829 did the Executive Council of Lower Canada formally endorse court decisions on slavery following a debate over the extradition of Paul Vallard (who had helped an enslaved person escape their owner) to the United States.[36] The end to legal slavery in Lower Canada was, therefore, the result of a collage of court decisions and an eventual willingness or desire to interpret the law in favour of enslaved people. For those involved, it must have been reassuring to see the courts and executive council moving in this direction, but it was also worrying to have to put so much faith in governing and judicial institutions. It was hard to trust the law. In the United States, the legal landscape flipped back and forth from the late 1700s to the mid-1800s, making the issue of where to find refuge and safety all the more challenging.

The Underground Railroad, Such as It Was

The term *Underground Railroad* generally describes a network of fugitives from slavery, free Blacks, Indigenous Peoples, and white abolitionists who facilitated the flight of an estimated 70,000 enslaved people between 1790 and 1865 to jurisdictions where they could be legally free.[37] People moved north, east, west, and south in what has been described as a "truly continental phenomenon" in an effort to escape slavery, which remained legal in parts of the United States until 1865.[38] People sought refuge with Indigenous communities where some were enslaved again or brought into community and adopted.[39] Several cities also became popular sites of refuge because of the employment, community, and sense of invisibility they offered. For instance, relative anonymity meant that even southern cities in the United States offered "greater safety from racist attacks prevalent in the relatively isolated woods and plantation lands."[40]

Contrary to popular impressions inspired by the name, the "Underground Railroad" was not a highly formalized or structured network. Rather, this evocative language came into use in the popular press in the 1840s. It was only later adopted by some of those involved or affected who employed terms such as "stations," "agents," and "routes" to describe how fugitives from slavery made their way to legal freedom.[41] An 1872 account by William Still (an African American abolitionist) was entitled *The Underground Railroad: A Record of Facts, Authentic Narratives, Letters, & c., Narrating the Hardships, Hair-Breadth Escapes, and Death Struggles of the Slaves in their Efforts for Freedom, as Related By Themselves or Witnessed by the Author, Together With Sketches of Some of the Largest Stockholders, and Most Liberal Aiders and Advisors, of the Road*. The title and the contents of the volume captured the essence of this change. Throughout his account, Still referenced the idea of "the mysterious road" with branches and "stockholders" who "did not expect any dividends" nor "require any special reports to be published."[42] Fellow abolitionist Frederick Douglass evoked the presence of an "upperground railroad," suggesting a similar if more public structure buttressed by "open declarations" of activity.[43] In reality, the networks of support were far more fluid than any system conjured by railway images of iron and ore, though some trajectories certainly became more established with time.

The exaggerated materiality and physical nature of the "Underground Railroad" has become a powerful symbol of freedom, liberty, and righteousness in the public imagination. Yet, it is not one that has been reclaimed by Black residents in Montreal/Mooniyaang/Tiohtià:ke. Community narratives and newspapers such as *Afro-Can* (published throughout the 1970s and 1980s) emphasize histories of liberation, mostly notably Garveyism and the efforts of the Universal Negro Improvement Association (formed in 1914). Articles penned by *Afro-Can* editor Leo Bertley in the mid-1980s focused on "The Establishment of the Negro Community Centre," "Matthew Alexander Henson and the Discovery of the North Pole," "James Somerset and the Abolition of Slavery in Britain," "First Canadian Emancipation (James Simcoe)," and "John Brown and Harper's Ferry."[44] There was no mention of any kind of Underground Railroad in Montreal/Mooniyaang/Tiohtià:ke. This is mirrored in community histories that largely disregard this earlier period beyond discussions of slavery in the city. As such, many see the roots of the present-day community in Montreal/Mooniyaang/Tiohtià:ke as a late nineteenth- and early twentieth-century phenomena bound up with the significant migration and settlement associated with railway workers (some of whom may have been fugitives from slavery) and, later, sleeping car porters.[45]

By contrast, much of the commemoration of the "Underground Railroad" emerges from redemptive national and local efforts to preserve and promote the history of former mansions, farms, and churches where people were known to have hidden. This has occurred in both the United States and Canada. The city of Philadelphia/Lenapehoking, which was a major centre for antislavery work, has a Harriet Tubman walking tour and numerous historic sites dedicated to promoting the history of the "Underground Railroad." In Canada, stories on this subject have spun a powerful thread of nationalism in which humanitarianism is foregrounded. The country's own history of slavery, of both Black and Indigenous Peoples, is often overlooked or denied as a result. For these and other reasons, scholars such as geographer Katherine McKittrick caution against conflating the "Underground Railroad" with "sites of liberation."[46] McKittrick insists on the need to attend "a radically different sense of place" in people's search for refuge, one that, as noted previously, should include attending to the very subjective and evolving nature of safety.[47]

Crucially, the emphasis on "sites of liberation," and on rescuers rather than fugitives, mirrors the bias in conventional histories where the humanitarian assistance provided to refugees often overshadows the intense decision-making and great challenges shouldered by refugees themselves.[48] Rescue narratives can be feel-good stories, but they are often perpetuated at the expense of more complicated and challenging dynamics.[49] Still, they remain doggedly alluring. As a result, the idea of certain places as "sites of liberation" and the "Underground Railroad" as a political antecedent have proven irresistible as reference points for generations of activists and humanitarians seeking to effect change. As historian Wendell Adjetey has documented, white war resisters from the United States' war in Vietnam used the term "Underground Railroad" to describe their efforts in "seeking broad legitimacy in their anti-war struggle" in a manner that would have "sounded contrived" to some.[50] In the 1980s, when the idea of sanctuary was reintroduced as a form of "civil initiative" to ensure Central American refugees had access to the US legal system, members of the Sanctuary Movement regularly referenced the historical precedent of the "Underground Railroad" in their efforts.[51] In the early 2000s, activists once again turned to the "Underground Railroad" as a powerful symbol, an "ethos" even, for their contemporary efforts around the protection of refugees and undocumented migrants, particularly after the introduction of the Safe Third Country Agreement between Canada and the United States in 2004.[52]

Beyond the evocation of a genealogical inheritance, however, there is little in the way of tangible connections between modern sanctuary practices and how fugitives from slavery sought sanctuary, safety, and freedom in the late eighteenth and early nineteenth centuries. While there were some main sites of refuge or "stations" and some popular routes along the Underground Railroad, none of these benefited from the claims to customary law and church protection, as was the case in the 1980s or the early 2000s. As historian Kristina Shull has detailed, the US government stepped back from apprehending people on church property in the 1970s after there was public outcry about people being arrested on sacred grounds. This led to an "unwritten rule" that churches were to be "hands-off."[53] By contrast, in the context of the "Underground Railroad," no place was inviolable, and violence was woven throughout efforts to escape slavery.[54] Abolitionist and minister William M. Mitchell described fugitives "being dragged out of their own churches and congregations."[55] People had to stay hidden. And in seeking refuge, they sought to hide until they could be nominally safe.

A great deal of discretion and secrecy were required about where, when, and how people moved in the era of the "Underground Railroad," especially following the passage of the 1850 Fugitive Slave Act. This act reduced fugitives' already limited rights by not allowing habeas corpus or providing the possibility for people to testify in their own defence. The act created the new office of the US Commissioner who heard the cases and could issue a certificate of removal, which was beyond the reach of any court. The 1850 Fugitive Slave Act marched over local and state laws and, perhaps most damaging, it was "retroactive, applying to all slaves who had run away in the past, including those who had been law-abiding residents of the free states for many years." As historian Eric Foner made clear, "It did nothing to protect free blacks from kidnapping."[56]

In a gesture that in some ways foreshadowed the Sanctuary City movement of the early twenty-first century, the mayor of New York City/ Manaháhtaan vowed to protect Black residents by "promis[ing] that the police would no longer participate in the apprehension of fugitive slaves."[57] The reality, however, was that the 1850 Fugitive Slave Act "posed a threat to every black family."[58] Thousands began to migrate in search of safety, looking to Indigenous communities and places in Mexico, Upper Canada, Lower Canada, and the Maritimes, to do so.[59] In the process of seeking refuge, the goal was to hide, and the larger the existing Black population or the further removed a community was from potential bounty hunters, the easier it was to do so. Even though some abolitionists made "open declarations" about their work and objectives, they provided little in the way of public detail about how they operated.[60] To speak publicly or to appear publicly when in flight were dangerous. Abolitionist Frederick Douglass recognized as much once he escaped from slavery. He declared, "open declarations are a positive evil to the slaves remaining, who are seeking to escape. They do nothing towards enlightening the slave, whilst they do much towards enlightening the master. They stimulate him to greater watchfulness, and enhance his power to capture his slave."[61]

Perhaps heeding Douglass's caution, abolitionists such as Sidney Howard Gay simply referred to people being "forwarded" without any further details.[62] In a similar vein, fugitive slave narratives often omitted any identifying information about the people and places involved, even as they elaborated the scale and scope of people's determined efforts to find safety and freedom in an effort to raise awareness and garner funds for the abolitionist cause. Frederick Douglass, for instance, declared, "It would afford me great pleasure indeed, as well as materially add to the interest of my narrative, were I at liberty to gratify a curiosity, which I know exists in the minds of many, by an accurate statement of all the facts pertaining to my most fortunate escape. But I must deprive myself of this pleasure, and the curious of the gratification which such a statement would afford."[63]

As a result, we know the details of abolitionist activities largely from the people who promoted their work as such. Abolitionist accounts, and even fugitive slave narratives, tell us very little about the important assistance fugitives from slavery received among the Seminoles, Cherokees, "Petites Nations," and other Indigenous Peoples in seeking refuge from slavery in this period.[64]

Land, Water, and Rail

The city that people such as Shadrach Minkins encountered as they fled from slavery and the reach of the 1850 Fugitive Slave Act was a foment of merchant capitalism and an outpost of empire.[65] Montreal/Mooniyaang/Tiohtià:ke had benefited from and exploited the fur trade from the seventeenth century on, serving as the easterly base for the Hudson's Bay Trading Company and the Northwest Company. As previously noted, merchants had also profited from the shipping trade and other industries that relied on enslaved labour, including sugar plantations in the South. By the nineteenth century, river and rail barons were financing and profiting from steamship operations and an expanding rail network that brought goods to and from markets. The Canadian Pacific Railway, the Canadian National Railway, and the Grand Trunk Railroad were all headquartered in Montreal/Mooniyaang/Tiohtià:ke. Banks such as the Bank of Montreal, the Montreal City and District Savings Bank, and the Banque du Peuple, in addition to money exchanges, populated the city's landscape with the result that Montreal/Mooniyaang/Tiohtià:ke was a bustling centre of finance and commercial activity.

The money and capital in the city resulted in a determined push to further expand markets and profit. The dredging of the Lachine Canal, beginning in 1843, further transformed the St Lawrence River/Kaniatarowanenneh from a source of food and transportation to a laneway for capitalism. Many of the limestone buildings, including bank headquarters, McGill University, churches, and mansions built in this golden age of merchant capital still stand – a testament to the wealth and exploitation that characterized the colonial city by the 1840s. The influential merchant class, the business elites, and the imperial powerbrokers did not have refuge or sanctuary in mind as they went about the work of building railways, pursuing markets, and accumulating capital. Those who made their way to Montreal/Mooniyaang/Tiohtià:ke did so with little encouragement from the established residents of the city.

The possibility of refuge in Montreal/Mooniyaang/Tiohtià:ke rested in large part on the sheer willpower and creativity of those fleeing slavery. Some people, such as Harriet Jacobs in North Carolina, stayed close to their families, wrenched by the idea of leaving. Writing in 1845, abolitionist Frederick Douglass suspected "thousands would escape from slavery, who now remain, but for the strong cords of affection that bind them to their friends."[66] In his own experience, "the thought of leaving my friends was decidedly the most painful thought with which I had to contend. The love of them was my tender point, and shook my decision (to flee) more than all things else."[67] In Jacobs' case, she hid "in the attic crawl space of her free grandmother's attached shed," which apparently was "barely larger than a coffin."[68] She lived in that space for almost seven years, in what Saidiya Hartman describes as a "loophole of retreat" that was simultaneously a "space of freedom" and a "space of captivity" (a paradoxical situation that would come to be used to describe extended stays in religious sanctuary in the early twenty-first century).[69]

For those who sought refuge through mobility, strategies about how to do so changed over time. Some simply disguised themselves, wearing "cross-gender dressing" or "someone else's clothes."[70] Others fled across juridical and international borders. As abolitionists and supporters became more involved, people could seek out help and safe places to hide, especially in borderland areas.[71] Such activities certainly became more formalized over time, beginning with Vigilante Committees in New York/Manahâhtaan and Boston/Shawmut after 1850.[72] Records from New York City/Manahâhtaan show the involvement of lawyer John Helder Isaacson in Montreal/Mooniyaang/Tiohtià:ke, who received US$100 in 1856 in what is thought to be a payment for his general antislavery work.[73]

Isaacson was an industrious lawyer who was involved in a number of organizations, including the Montreal Branch of the British American League (established in the wake of the 1837 Rebellions to consider constitutional issues and insist upon loyalty to the British Crown) and the Mechanics Institute (dedicated to the educational needs of workers in the city), acting as secretary for both organizations. Additionally, Isaacson was also a member of the Sixth Battalion, Hochelaga Light Infantry and served during the 1837 Rebellion as part of British efforts to supress rebel forces. Records show that he married Eliza McIver in an Anglican wedding in 1849. They do not appear to have had any children. We also know that he was the son of Robert Philips Isaacson, owner of Dolly's Chop House, a famed establishment frequented by "officers of the garrison and the merchants of the city." Perhaps given the reputation of Dolly's Chop House as a rather rowdy establishment, John Helder Isaacson was described as a "great improvement" on his father "in manner and sense."[74]

For fugitives from slavery, connections to people such as John Helder Isaacson were important, but their capacity to move was arguably shaped even more by geography and changing technologies that facilitated movement across sometimes difficult terrain and through different jurisdictions, including across the border that separated the United States from British North America. Some people may have traveled through the wilderness, though this would have been a hard slog. Vast sections of the border between Lower Canada and the states of Vermont and New York (traditional territories of the Lenape, Haudenosaunee, Oneida, and N'dakina), for instance, were densely forested and as in other parts of the expanding nineteenth-century border, the elements could be unforgiving.[75]

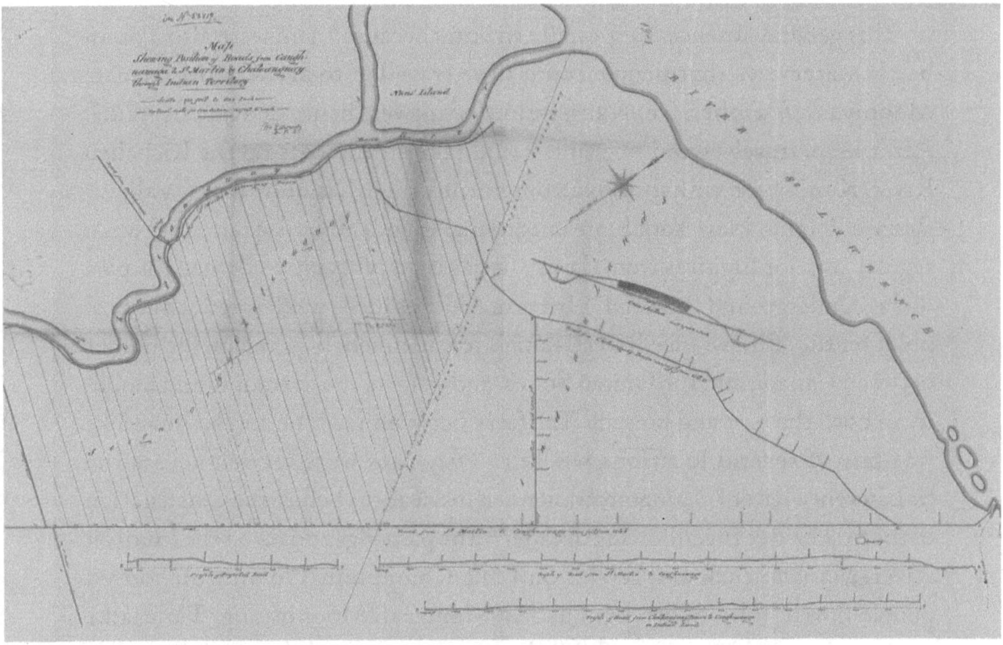

1.2 A map of the roads in and around Kahnawà:ke: Wm. Edwards, *Map showing position of roads from Caughnawaga to St Martin and Chateauguay through Indian territory.*

Still, as infrastructure expanded, movement became easier. Roads appear to have led some people to present-day Farnham, Quebec, about thirty-four kilometres (twenty-one miles) from the present-day Canada-US border.[76]

By 1743, a single dirt road ran along the south shore eastward from where Châteauguay and Chambly (traditional Haudenosaunee and N'dakina territory) now sit. Four years later, new roads linked Montreal/Mooniyaang/Tiohtià:ke to Saint-Jean-sur-Richelieu (traditional Kanien'kehá:ka and N'dakina territory) and New York City/Manahátaan.[77] Maps from the 1840s show a north-south road crossing the border between what was then Canada East and New York State, running just west of Kahnawà:ke, and providing a rapid connection between present-day Plattsburgh, New York /Tsi ietsenhtha and the lands to the north.[78] There were many roads, and many possibilities. It is significant, therefore, that few took the opportunity to flee to Montreal/Mooniyaang/Tiohtià:ke.

This general absence is especially striking because there were also a number of waterways that people could have travelled to arrive at Montreal/Mooniyaang/Tiohtià:ke, Kahnawà:ke, Ahkwesáhsne, or Kanehsatà:ke. After 1809, travelers and migrants could take steamboats up the Richelieu River/Kaniá:tare tsi kahnhokà:ronte or up the Missiquoi River Valley.[79] Rouse's Point in New York State (traditional Haudenosaunee territory) was a regular stop for fugitives from slavery (it has been officially recognized as part of the "Underground Railroad"). In turn, Ahkwesáhsne was located at a critical point on the St Lawrence River/Kaniatarowanenneh, bisected by the border between Canada and the United States, and a site of much trading and mobility in both the past and present. The ferry between Lachine and Kahnawà:ke was one of several locations where railway cars were ferried across the St Lawrence River / Kaniatarowanenneh in the 1850s before the construction of the first bridge the following decade.[80] The passenger boats on the Hudson River/Mahicantuck and ferries on Lake Champlain/Oniá:tarote moved people north. John Scott, who fled to Montreal/Mooniyaang/Tiohtià:ke in 1859, expected his wife to follow by boat but worried that with "so many boats coming here all times a day I may not know what time she will."[81]

In Wilbur Siebert's 1898 account of the Underground Railroad, there is a map that highlights a single line north to Montreal/Mooniyaang/Tiohtià:ke.[82] This lone route appears to cross both land and water. The reality, however, is that by the 1850s, people could also travel by rail. Indeed, one historian described railroads as "the principal means of flight" for fugitives from slavery as they drew places closer together and expanded the capacity for people to move.[83] Rail connections such as the Boston-Concord-Montreal Railroad were intended to facilitate access to markets and advance commercial trade, but they also made it easier for fugitives from slavery to move greater distances. Some of the new rail lines made settlements such as Kahnawà:ke more accessible, leading to further colonial encroachment while also elevating the possibility that fugitives from slavery may have journeyed there or passed through on their way elsewhere.[84]

Just as Montreal/Mooniyaang/Tiohtià:ke was connected to places near and far as a result of evolving transportation and community technologies, so too were Kahnawà:ke, Ahkwesáhsne, and, to some extent, Kanehsatà:ke. In 1852, the Lake St Louis and Province Line (LSL&PL) railroad opened,

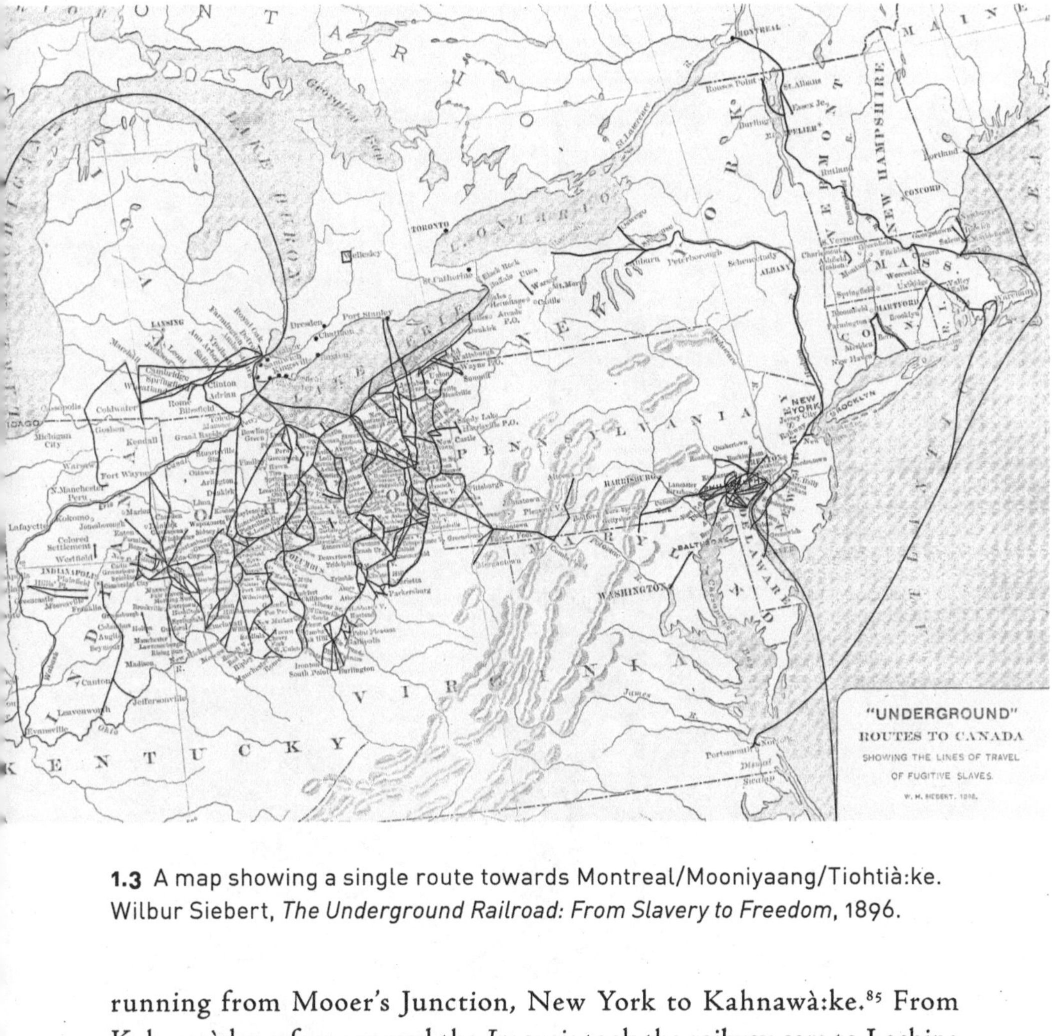

1.3 A map showing a single route towards Montreal/Mooniyaang/Tiohtià:ke. Wilbur Siebert, *The Underground Railroad: From Slavery to Freedom*, 1896.

running from Mooer's Junction, New York to Kahnawà:ke.[85] From Kahnawà:ke, a ferry named the *Iroquois* took the railway cars to Lachine where "they were pulled to Montreal along an eight-mile rail line running a route parallel to the Lachine Canal."[86] This line was eventually taken over by the Grand Trunk Railway in 1863, further connecting Kahnawà:ke with the northeastern United States.[87] Brown Thurston, a "veteran abolitionist,'" described some of the Underground Railroad as extending "from Portland (Vermont) to the provinces, by water to St John, New Brunswick and by rail to Montreal" as a result of the Grand Trunk Railway.[88] By 1860, when the Victoria Bridge was constructed across the St Lawrence River/

1.4 A Kanien'kehá:ka woman returning home from Montreal/Mooniyaang/Tiohtià:ke, watercolour by Francis George Coleridge, 1866.

Kaniatarowanenneh, people could also take the train directly to the island of Montreal/Kawenote Teiontiakon, bypassing conventional land and water routes. All of these developments amounted to increasing colonial encroachment as well as significant mobility between Montreal/Mooniyaang/Tiohtià:ke and the surrounding settlements.

In the case of Kahnawà:ke, people crossed the waters in both directions to work, and Kanien'kehá:ka went to the city regularly to trade and sell agricultural goods. An 1866 watercolour by Captain Francis George Coleridge depicts a Kanien'kehá:ka woman with the Montreal /Mooniyaang/Tiohtià:ke skyline visible behind her. The towers of the Notre-Dame Cathedral are there, as is the outline of the Victoria Bridge. Kanien'kehá:ka archivist Elizabeth Montour notes that the woman carries no bags, suggesting she has sold her wares and has crossed the bridge on snowshoes as she makes her way back to Kahnawà:ke.[89] She is looking away from the city, focused instead on home. The watercolour and Montour's study of this painting evoke the considerable movement between Montreal/Mooniyaang/Tiohtià:ke on foot, by rail, and by water in this period (even before the construction of the Honoré Mercier bridge that would link the city and Kahnawà:ke even more directly in the 1930s). There are no other people visible in this painting, but inspired by Montour's observations, we might ask if fugitives from slavery also travelled this route, walking the same path as the vendors, traders, and workers who connected Montreal/Mooniyaang/Tiohtià:ke and Kahnawà:ke through their movements and activities.

In the City

The absence of any other figures in the painting might also serve as a caution about reading too much movement into the history of this period. Indeed, the lack of evidence of any significant flight to Montreal/Mooniyaang/Tiohtià:ke and communities such as Kahnawà:ke, Ahkwesáhsne, or Kanehsatà:ke is arguably just as important in terms of how the possibility of refuge was perceived at the time. The lack of any tangible connections invites questions about the social climate of Montreal/Mooniyaang/Tiohtià:ke and perhaps the gulf that existed between how fugitives from slavery experienced the city and how it was presented to the world.

Author Harriet Beecher Stowe spent time in Montreal/Mooniyaang/Tiohtià:ke and may have found it quite agreeable. Perhaps it was her own personal experience that provided the setting for the concluding and joyous family reunion scene in *Uncle Tom's Cabin*. Crucially, it was not a typical experience for many. The abolitionist Samuel Ward (who had been formerly enslaved) stayed only briefly, writing to his counterpart Henry Bibb in October 1851, "I am, like yourself, a refugee … I have come to Canada, and I am now on my way from Montreal to your part of the province, making, or intending to make, Toronto my head-quarters for the winter. In full spring I may be a candidate for a job of hoeing in your garden."[90]

As suggested by the foregoing, any reference to Montreal/Mooniyaang/Tiohtià:ke as a site of refuge betrays the overarching character of the city in this period, which was dominated by an English-speaking commercial class interested in expanding profits and markets, not in providing for workers or offering sanctuary to people outside their social circles.[91] Despite the lack of significant refuge, author Harriet Beecher Stowe used the city to conclude *Uncle Tom's Cabin*, and its story of family dispersal, loss, and flight. Ending on a hopeful note, the surviving members of a once enslaved and separated family are reunited in the city. The Harris home is in a "small, neat tenement, in the outskirts of Montreal." In the evening:

> A cheerful fire blazes on the hearth; a tea-table, covered with a snowy cloth, stands prepared for the evening meal. In one corner of the room was a table covered with a green cloth, where was an open writing-desk, pens, paper, and over it a shelf of well-selected books. This was George's study. The same zeal for self-improvement, which led him to steal the much coveted arts of reading and writing, amid all the toils and discouragements of his early life, still led him to devote all his leisure time to self-cultivation.[92]

The reunion scene became an opportunity for Stowe to reflect on refuge more broadly and to highlight both the presence of the divine and the courage of those who fled slavery: "These shores of refuge, like the eternal shore, often unite again, in glad communion, hearts that for long years have mourned each other as lost … Deeds of heroism are wrought here more than those of romance, when, defying torture, and braving death itself, the fugitive voluntarily threads his way back to the terrors and perils of that dark land, that he may bring out his sister, or mother, or wife."[93]

The far reach and popularity of *Uncle Tom's Cabin* (it received mention from President Abraham Lincoln himself) is one of the reasons that Montreal/Mooniyaang/Tiohtià:ke became part of the conceptual geography of the "Underground Railroad."[94] The book was first published as a serial, chapter by chapter, in the *National Era*, edited by abolitionist Gamaliel Bailey. A year later, in 1852, it was published in London in twenty-three different editions. An estimated 1.5 million copies sold in Britain and its colonies in that year alone.[95] Historian Wilbur Siebert's early insistence on a railroad with Montreal/Mooniyaang/Tiohtià:ke as a terminus is another reason the city has been able to claim a long history of refuge.[96] Yet more than an endpoint, the city was often only ever a stopover for the few fugitives who did make their way there. This was due to the social and political climate in the city and the fact that there was only ever a very small community of Blacks in Montreal/Mooniyaang/Tiohtià:ke until the late nineteenth century.[97] As scholars have emphasized, the presence of growing Black populations in the free states of the American union, Mexico, Upper Canada, and the Maritimes was instrumental in thickening the assistance that could be provided to fugitives from slavery.[98] The relatively small Black population in Montreal/Mooniyaang/Tiohtià:ke undermined the possibility of refuge through community that was so critical.[99]

Given the small Black population in Montreal/Mooniyaang/Tiohtià:ke, newcomers might have found the city rather lonely, even frightening, if they did not have a sense of whom they might be able to trust. Census counts show eighty Black residents in 1852, though the number was likely slightly larger as people moved through and from the city.[100] In 1861, there were 160 Blacks in all of Canada East out of a total population of 1,110,664.[101] Historians estimate that "only a handful of fugitive slaves and free blacks" arrived in Montreal/Mooniyaang/Tiohtià:ke between 1852 and 1859."[102] For instance, Charles Williams fled north from Boston/Shawmut in 1850 and again in 1851 (after having returned to the United States to be with his wife for a brief period). On the second occasion, he stayed in Montreal/Mooniyaang/Tiohtià:ke, fathering a child with Margaret Maguire, a young Irish woman.[103] Williams apparently remained in the city from this point on and built a family with Maguire, abandoning his first wife entirely. One John Scott announced his safe arrival in the city in September 1859 and sent for his wife, indicating that she should "get a cab and go to the Donegana Hotel" (at the corner of Notre-Dame and Bonsecours). Scott continued, if "Edmund Turner is there he will take you where I live and if he is not there cabman take you to Mr Taylors on Durham St. nearly opposite to the Methodist Church."[104] One can't help but wonder what Mrs Scott made of the city upon her arrival. Did she find Edmund Turner, and was he agreeable? What did she think of the French she heard in the streets? Was she fluent in the language? What did she make of the city's glorious fall colours? Or of the streets "constantly sullied with vomit and other forms of bodily fluid"?[105]

Shadrach Minkins, whose story anchors this analysis, is probably the best-known fugitive slave to have arrived and stayed in Montreal/Mooniyaang/Tiohtià:ke. As noted previously, Minkins fled from Boston/Shawmut in 1851 and made his way north to escape the reach of the 1850 Fugitive Slave Act. Upon his arrival in Montreal/Mooniyaang/Tiohtià:ke around 20 February 1851, Minkins found himself in the largest city in Canada East but one that was far smaller than Boston/Shawmut, where there was a Black population of about 2,500 people (out of a total 136,000). Minkins appears to have had traveling companions, and they may have helped him get settled. Nevertheless, it would have been a disorienting time. The large fire that occurred in the city in the summer of 1852, which destroyed over a thousand homes and left ten thousand people homeless, would likely have been unnerving for someone who was still getting acclimatized to the city.

Nevertheless, Minkins seems to have found his way. He married an Irish woman by the name of Marylast around 1853, and together they had four children. Minkins moved through a number of occupations before opening a restaurant named Uncle Tom's Cabin at 12 Saint John Street.[106] This naming might have been ironic or opportunistic given the book's wide reception in 1852. In any event, Minkins prospered (despite a fire to his establishment in 1858). He appears to have been somewhat involved with the abolitionist movement, referenced in correspondence between Samuel Ward and Henry Bibb, though he did not publish any narratives about his experiences, unlike many of his contemporaries who recounted dramatic experiences in their search for refuge.[107] Minkins died in 1875 and was buried in a grave in the Mont-Royal Cemetery that was unmarked until it was adorned with a commemorative plaque in the fall of 2023.[108]

For Minkins and the handful of other fugitives from slavery who made their way to Montreal/Mooniyaang/Tiohtià:ke and stayed, the city was likely a mix of experiences. For one thing, it was questionably secure for fugitives from slavery even after the legal situation was seemingly resolved in 1834 with the abolition of slavery across the British Empire. Residents of the city appear to have been firmly opposed to slavery in the United States by the 1850s, as evidenced by articles in leading publications including the *Montreal Witness*, *Montreal Courier*, and *Le Canadien* and the positive response to lectures by leading antislavery advocates.[109] Yet there was also a significant exiled Confederate presence in Montreal/Mooniyaang/Tiohtià:ke after 1861, and agents received considerable encouragement from the city's residents (discussed in greater detail in the chapter "The Fugitive City").

There was also some suggestion of racial animosity, especially as the number of Blacks grew in the city after the introduction of the Fugitive Slave Act in the United States in 1850. Some, such as Israel Lewis who had failed in his efforts with the Wilberforce colony (which had been intended for black refugees) in present-day Manitoba, arrived in the city destitute. Lewis had passed through the city on previous occasions in his efforts to fundraise for the colony, and in 1852, he returned, this time in disgrace, accused of having used the funds for his own benefit.[110] Given the hostility to "pauperism" and any kind of dependency on charity in this period, Lewis' presence, and that of any other impoverished fugitive slave, would have likely been met with fear or hostility. In fact, in the same year that Lewis returned to the city, a writer for the *Montreal Courier* bemoaned the fact that Canada was becoming "a *cul de sac* for undesirable races."[111]

The other reality, in addition to the palpable presence of what abolitionist Samuel Ward called "negrophobia," was that the city's geographic location remained a blessing in terms of access but also amounted to a significant risk in terms of its proximity to the United States.[112] Bounty hunters sometimes disregarded the presence of the border to pursue fugitives from slavery. For example, in 1854, a "Kentucky bounty hunter was tried and convicted in Montreal" of "enticement" as a result of his efforts to lure a fugitive named Osbourne back to the United States.[113] In 1855, the *Montreal Gazette* published a letter from John R. Pape of Frederick, Maryland to the Sheriff of Montreal, John Boston. The letter proposed that the "latter should use his power to arrest Negroes who would then be turned over to Pape." The plan was to divide the proceeds from the sale of anyone arrested evenly between Pape and Boston.[114] This plan does not appear to have ever been carried out; however, any hints of such efforts would have been worrying. They may have planted a seed of doubt, if it did not exist already, about the extent to which the city was safe.

Beyond generalized insecurities about possible kidnappings and a return to slavery, people lived their lives as best they could, seeking employment in a number of different establishments, including the Donegana Hotel, St Lawrence Hall on James Street as well as the Ottawa Hotel, all of which would become Confederate haunts during the US Civil War.[115] Others worked in domestic service, carpentry, or brick making, or became barbers, what one author describes as "a privileged occupation among blacks."[116] Some of this work may have taken them to Kahnawà:ke, Ahkwesáhsne or Kanehsatà:ke given the close economic and trading relations between these sites and Montreal/Mooniyaang/Tiohtià:ke. These close ties brought many people to and from the city in their capacity as diplomats, crafts people, traders, performers, and labourers.[117] By the 1860s, many Black men in the city were in "skilled, semi-skilled, and small entrepreneurial occupations" making Harriet Beecher Stowe's representation of George Harris's employment in *Uncle Tom's Cabin* quite realistic.[118] Black residents could be found across the city by 1861 though most lived on St Urbain Street, below Place D'Armes and the Notre-Dame Cathedral.[119] It seems that those who did stay contributed to the small, but growing, community of Black citizens, one that would endure, expand, and diversify over subsequent generations with material evidence of "mutual assistance and shared responsibilities," especially among Blacks who had recently arrived from the United States.[120] Yet, such assistance would only begin to manifest with the growth of the community, most notably in the late nineteenth century.[121] Until then, the few Black residents in the city were often alone in their struggles. They could lean on one another at times, but they were generally at the mercy of the charity and goodwill of others. Such assistance appears to have been scarce and offered only on occasion. The records from the Hôpital Général, the closest entity to a formal charity in this period, show very few Black people in its care throughout its years of operation.[122]

The Hôpital Général was founded by François Charon and his brother in 1692. It was intended to serve as a refuge for "the aged, invalids, severely handicapped, paupers, orphaned children, and other needy males."[123] It was a vast building, surrounded by gardens, and built on the outskirts of the settlement's palisades.[124] It fell into disrepair after Charon's death in 1719 and Marguerite d'Youville and the Order of the Grey Nuns eventually assumed responsibility for the institution in 1747 (with financial support from the Sulpicians). The nuns provided care for the elderly and infirm and also for orphaned or lost children and women in need.[125]

Thousands of people stayed at the Hôpital Général over the years, but only a few Black people ever found their way there. Some were enslaved, apparently gifted to Marguerite d'Youville.[126] Of those who were cared for at the Hôpital Général, the first clear reference to a Black person in the registers involves "Coutin," aged fifteen, who died at the hospital on 23 September 1755. "François Dominique Mentor," infirm and "belonging" to M. Nafrechous entered on 8 April 1771 and died two years later. In 1772, "une petite négresse à M. Christie," aged ten, entered on 19 October and left sometime before the end of the year. In 1780, Jean Baptiste, "crippled" and aged twenty-four years, entered on 20 August and died eighteen days later. In October 1797, Marie Louise, "négresse esclave" (who had been owned by Mr le Chevalier de Lacome) was admitted to the Hôpital Général. She was eighty-seven at the time, and she lived there until her passing on 20 March 1802. The last reference to a Black resident was Marie, the widow of James Pharen. She arrived at the Hôpital Général on 13 July 1850 at the age of seventy-eight. She is notably absent from Marcel Trudel's *Dictionnaire des esclaves et de leurs propriétaires au Canada français,* no doubt because slavery had ended in Lower Canada two decades prior. The others listed in the registers may have been placed at the Hôpital Général by their owners in the hopes that they might recover and be returned to bondage.

Contrary to what might be expected, fewer Black and Indigenous Peoples appear in the Hôpital Général records after the abolition of slavery in the British Empire. This, despite the growing numbers of fugitives from slavery who made their way out of the United States. In the years after legal slavery was abolished in Lower Canada, we see only the names of three Black people in the registers. Marie, mentioned previously, as well as Paul McKay, who entered the hospital at the age of ninety-three on 19 November 1844 and died three years later. McKay was listed as a native of Philadelphia/Lenapehoking (but may, in fact, have traveled further afield given the history of mobility to and from this city in these years). On 20 May 1850, a Black man by the name of Robert arrived and lived at the Hôpital Général for eleven years until his passing on 11 April 1861. We don't know where Marie and Robert came from, but it is certainly possible that they were, at one time, fugitive slaves from the United States.

In almost all the cases noted in the registers, the identifiable relationships are between enslaved people and their owners. The only exception was the widow, Marie. The lack of known relationships and any broader sense of familial or kinship connections hint at the isolation of those who resided at the Hôpital Général. This is not to suggest that their lives were somehow empty, devoid of feeling and experience, or that they didn't have moments of laughter and joy, but rather to underscore the multiple scales at which isolation and alienation would have been experienced in a settlement that did not foster or encourage refuge for fugitives from slavery.

Community historian Dorothy Williams once described the apparent lack of a Black community in the city before 1897 as "odd" given the number of fugitives who were seeking refuge anywhere they could during the era of the "Underground Railroad."[127] Given the city's geographic location and its eventual legal liberalism, one might have expected Montreal/Mooniyaang/Tiohtià:ke to have been more of a site of refuge in this period. However, it appears that the social and demographic climate of the city continued to deter any kind of long-term or permanent settlement by fugitives from slavery in this period. The "Underground Railroad" rested on the volition of fugitive slaves themselves and on the capacity for community, and it is in this latter regard that Montreal/Mooniyaang/Tiohtià:ke was lacking in this period. It was a lonely city for newly arrived fugitives from slavery.

Conclusions

The history of slavery in Montreal/Mooniyaang/Tiohtià:ke, in addition to the economic and political climate of the city, meant that during the era of the "Underground Railroad," the focus of the city's most influential residents was on money and power, not on providing refuge. Religious leaders in the city were not invested in providing sanctuary to fugitives from slavery, though some church leaders would do so for Confederate fugitives, as discussed in "The Fugitive City" chapter. For those fleeing slavery who did make their way through the settlements and forests of what is now Vermont and New York, as well as those who traveled by water or rail, the city afforded legal protection and some defences against bounty hunters and kidnappers. It was not, however, able to provide a deep sense of community or the kinds of social capital required to survive the sometimes-turbulent forces, including the "great insecurity and loneliness" that came with arriving and settling in a new place.[128]

In the era of legalized slavery and sanctioned bounty hunting in the United States, escaping to freedom meant hiding or disguising oneself; it meant subterfuge; it meant finding somewhere safe/r. Some places have documented histories of being sites of refuge during the era of the "Underground Railroad" and have promoted themselves as such. In other cases, we have only hints of connections. In Ahkwesáhsne, there are stories about nearby structures and routes that people purportedly used in making their way north. One building, formerly the Tsiionkwanontiio Heritage Center, on Helena Road was rumoured to have been a hiding spot for fugitives from slavery and was later said to be haunted.[129] Fort Covington, just east of the reserve, has also been identified as a possible crossing site for fugitive slaves.[130] We also know that the Kanien'kehá:ka at Ahkwesáhsne supported Indigenous refugees fleeing Central America in the 1980s and that people continue to move to and through the territory in the present day.[131] In other instances, such as in Montreal/Mooniyaang/Tiohtià:ke, we have an exaggerated sense of refuge, one that is not borne up by the historical record. Harriet Beecher Stowe may have given the impression of possible refuge in the city, and historian Wilbur Siebert no doubt reaffirmed this impression with his insistence on a formal "Underground Railroad" with routes that could be mapped and substantiated.

In some ways, it doesn't matter at all where people went. The important thing was that they were safe. In other ways, the question of place matters a great deal, especially if the past is repurposed or used to make arguments about the shape and character of a particular site or city in the present. As noted in the introduction to *Sanctuary in Pieces*, contemporary activists draw on historical precedent to animate and substantiate their work around sanctuary and solidarity. The repurposing of the history of the "Underground Railroad" has been critical to activists' arguments around sanctuary on several occasions throughout the late twentieth and early twenty-first centuries. Yet, as this chapter has outlined, it is not an unproblematic referencing in large part because of the way the initiative of those who were in flight gets erased. It is further troubling for the ways in which the character of various sites of liberation becomes exaggerated, distorting what it meant to actually live in such places.

Even with laws in the United States that made the country unsafe and laws in British North America that, in theory, made the territory safe for Black people, Montreal/Mooniyaang/Tiohtià:ke was not a major source of refuge or protection for people fleeing slavery. Very few Black people stayed in the city after legalized slavery was abolished. Indeed, the scarce references to Black or Indigenous Peoples in the registers of the Hôpital Général after 1834 are another reminder (in addition to census records) that the few Black residents who had been in the city because of slavery likely left when they could. Tangled up in imperial politics and the pursuit of wealth and prosperity, Montreal/Mooniyaang/Tiohtià:ke was not a natural or obvious site of refuge for those who were poor, vulnerable, or enslaved.

In the opening passages of this chapter, I imagined what Shadrach Minkins might have thought about upon arriving in Montreal/Mooniyaang/Tiohtià:ke in the coldest month of the year and what he would have made of the ice, banks of snow, and blowing winds. The chilly landscape might have served as a metaphor for the cold reception of the city itself, one that was marked by a lack of community. In 1910, the federal state would use the phrase "unsuited to the climate or requirements of Canada" to exclude Black migrants from settlement, but in the period of the "Underground

Railroad," it was the social and political climate of a place that shaped where people went and for how long.

People were desperate to flee slavery, but this did not mean they were without choice about their destinations. This capacity is reflected in the limited settlement in Montreal/Mooniyaang/Tiohtià:ke in this period despite the perception of welcoming refuge generated by works such as Harriet Stowe's *Uncle Tom's Cabin* and the legal climate in British North America. In addition to exaggerating the character of refuge, *Uncle Tom's Cabin* also erased the shadows and spectres that danced around a city that had its own history of slavery. The last fugitive slave advertisement in the city "for an indented Black Girl, name of Eve" who "had a mark on her forehead occasioned by the Small-Pox" was placed in the *Canadian Courant* on 26 March 1810 by William Polley.[132] This was twenty-four years before the end of legal slavery across the British Empire. In some ways, this was a lifetime. Historian Frank Mackey suggests that by the 1830s, the memory of slavery in what had been New France and then part of the British Empire was already "lost."[133] But in other ways, this was a blip in time and people who moved to the city subsequently would have felt the strain of the hierarchical social structures, social views spoken and unspoken, and the uncertainty of an institution that was formally in its final thralls in the United States, but whose social and cultural implications would be long-lasting. The people who had the most at stake likely did not forget.[134] And they may have felt the legacy of slavery in the lack of community they encountered upon arrival. Indeed, while Black abolitionist Samuel Ward celebrated his freedom of movement while visiting Montreal/Mooniyaang/Tiohtià:ke in 1851, he also observed, "I do not, of course, find Canada free from Negrophobia."

Over time, a sense of community did evolve, as did a sense of place. In this early period, however, for fugitives from slavery, the experience of Montreal/Mooniyaang/Tiohtià:ke was most probably a lonely, isolating one if they were not able to forge bonds of friendship and affinity with others in the city. As mentioned previously, Israel Lewis, a co-founder of the failed Wilberforce colony for Black refugees passed away in 1852 "unattended and alone," having "found his way to a hospital in Montreal, where he soon after died, leaving not enough at all his gains to afford him a decent burial."[135] Lewis's lonely end was perhaps more common than the sweet and tender moments that Shadrach Minkins was able to forge in the city, with his family and various business undertakings. It wasn't just that people didn't seek out Montreal/Mooniyaang/Tiohtià:ke as a site of refuge, but that many of those who did were disappointed by what they encountered and continued on elsewhere.

The story of John Harrison Surratt was one of the very first ones I encountered as I began my research on the history of sanctuary. The members of the Société d'Histoire de Beloeil - Mont-Saint-Hilaire naïvely assumed that I knew this story and suggested it as a possible line of inquiry in an entirely modest way. As it turned out, I wasn't aware of Surratt's time in Canada, nor was I aware of the large Confederate presence in Montreal/Mooniyaang/Tiohtià:ke and surrounds, even though I grew up in the Eastern Townships (traditional N'dakina and Wabanaki territory) where Jefferson Davis (president of the Confederate States) and others sought refuge after the US Civil War. Over the course of my research, I learned that they had sent their children to be educated at Bishop's College School, which I had only ever thought of as a rival high school. As I learned, some stories of refuge from the past are seen as unsavoury now and aren't commemorated in any significant way.

I have spent a lot of time with John Harrison Surratt's story over the years. My first attempt at writing about this history appeared as "The Politics of Sanctuary: John Surratt, the Catholic Church and the US Civil War," in Undiplomatic History: The New Study of Canada and the World *edited by Phil Van Huizen and Asa McKercher (2019). In that chapter, I was specifically interested in the question of diplomacy and extradition and the state's take on Surratt's presence in Canada.*

This time around, I wanted to explore many of the threads that had escaped me initially. In particular, I was interested in the question of how Surratt moved and with whose help. In this vein, I was thinking about religious and political connections as well as the politics of mobility. Montreal/Mooniyaang/Tiohtià:ke was connected to the Civil War in the United States both in terms of people and capital. Exploring Montreal/Mooniyaang/Tiohtià:ke as a city where there was significant support for the Confederate cause helped me understand even more why it was such a limited site of refuge for fugitive slaves (as discussed in "The Lonely City" chapter).

It also made me see the limitations of the term fugitive and the ways in which it was simultaneously applied to people trying to escape from the injustice of slavery, as well as the people fleeing from justice – fleeing from accountability for violent crimes. Historically, the term has applied to people in wildly different circumstances, and I wanted to probe at this further. Surratt's movements as a fugitive were also vastly different from the ways in which fugitivity has been discussed in recent years, most notably by Black scholars who see great liberating potential in the concept of fugitive practices, refusal, and the remaking of place. I became interested in thinking through these extreme contrasts, even if reading the experiences of a Confederate messenger who went into hiding alongside this scholarship seemed egregious at first. With some hesitation, I proceeded, nonetheless.

The other thing that escaped my initial work on John Harrison Surratt's time in refuge in British North America and beyond was that one of the main sources I had used was not authentic. The Private Journal and Diary of John H. Surratt, the Conspirator *is available in print and digitally, courtesy of the US Library of Congress. It appears to be an account of Surratt's time in hiding and offers apparent details about the assistance he received, as well as explanations about why he remained in hiding while his mother was tried, convicted, and executed. It makes Surratt into a rather sympathetic figure, and at the time I was grateful for any evidence of his time in hiding.*

Only in hindsight, and thanks to a very helpful librarian, did I realize that the journal was a fake. Returning to the original catalogue entry at the US Library of Congress in the fall of 2023, I noticed that in very fine print, the entry for this publication read: "Probably fictitious." Shocked and intrigued, I emailed the Library of Congress to find out more about the reason for this label. They did months of sleuthing, and when they wrote back, they reported that the Library of Congress had, in fact, considered it a fake for more than forty-three years! This conclusion was based in part on assessments by scholars who deemed it a work of a "forgery and fabrication produced by a diabolical, money-mad, two-bit liar of the vilest hue."[1] *I noticed the lack of credibility more clearly going back though I admit I was still drawn to the flowery language in the "diary" about bidding "farewell to those kind friends who have so long given me a shelter" and wishes that "their safety never be endangered, or their peace and happiness disturbed."*[2]

I was aghast and mortified that early versions of this chapter had gone out to readers citing a fake source. I revised the chapter, yet again, over the course of a rainy December weekend and was pleased to discover that in the process, the idea of networked connections became all the more prominent as I turned instead to the testimony of Lewis J.A. McMillan, who was the surgeon aboard the SS Peruvian *and who befriended Surratt as he sailed to Liverpool in the fall of 1865. Questions persist about the reliability of this testimony, however, and I couldn't help but wonder if there wasn't some brilliant irony in the fact that Surratt's time in refuge is still so hard to detail despite all the available material (fake and otherwise).*

The whole point of hiding after Lincoln's assassination in 1865 was to be in the shadows, and with the help of a mixed network of political and religious contacts, Surratt did so rather effectively. His approach and his needs stand in stark contrast to the publicized sanctuary events that have shaped settler practices of hospitality and protection since the 1970s. Even in recent cases of fugitivity, involving people such as Julian Assange (founder of WikiLeaks), Edward Snowden (former CIA employee), and Chelsea Manning (former US military analyst), parts of their escapes were made public to garner protection from deportation and extradition through public opinion. This was not the case for John Harrison Surratt and those who aided him.

There is renewed interest in the story of John Harrison Surratt, evidenced by the publication of new popular non-fiction works, The North Star: Canada and the Civil War Plots Against Lincoln *by Julian Sher and the novel* L'Inconnu du Presbytère *by Josée Ouimet, both in 2022. Surratt's story is rife with possibilities for telling and re-telling, and there remains much to ask about. From my vantage point, one of the questions that sits with me still is how the fugitivity of an unsavoury character such as John Harrison Surratt is almost heroically celebrated in the present, as part of a great adventure, despite the terrible crime and repulsive politics at the core of his time in fugitivity. And I wonder about the connections between such celebrations and the societal backlash against those who advance a powerful vision of Black fugitivity, and liberatory politics, in the present.*

July 2023, revised December 2023

The Fugitive City

> Canada is a fine country for ice, snow, and cold weather, which I yet experience to a great extent. Montreal is really a beautiful city and what pleases me more there are a great many pretty girls here. It is more than probable that I shall lose my heart with some of them and then I ask myself have I one to give away? The answer comes back fully satisfactory. It is more than probable I shall give you a call as I return from Canada, but is very doubtful, as I am always in a hurry ...
>
> I am enjoying myself to my heart's content. Nothing in the wide world to do but visit the ladies and go to church.
>
> — JOHN HARRISON SURRATT TO BELL SEAMAN, 10 APRIL 1865, ST LAWRENCE HALL, MONTREAL/MOONIYAANG/TIOHTIÀ:KE[1]

AS WITH MANY expanding cities in North America in the mid to late nineteenth century, Montreal/Mooniyaang/Tiohtià:ke was a place where people were on the move. Crucially, much of this mobility was the product of criss-crossing networks – of merchant capitalism that concentrated money and labour in the city, of political networks that briefly saw Montreal/Mooniyaang/Tiohtià:ke as the capital city of the Province of Canada from 1844 to 1849, and of cultural networks that brought touring performers to various establishments such as the Theatre Royal, the first public theatre in

Canada. Social networks, including family ones, also transformed the demographics of the city through migration and the making of babies. Some networks were forged through movement; others enabled movement. As in the case of the "Underground Railroad," these networks were often loose and informal, yet they regularly overlapped and intersected, sometimes in surprising ways. Rarely did they remain constant or entirely distinct.

The relationship between migration and networks has become more pronounced in recent years as scholars, especially those interested in transnationalism across borders, emphasize the role of networks or relationships in the fostering and thickening of connections. In thinking through the impact of networks, historian Max Hamon emphasizes how people in exile build upon existing associations all the while deepening and expanding them. In considering the case of Louis Riel, exiled from Canada in 1870 and again in 1875 on a more permanent basis, Hamon argues that the Métis leader's "vast network" of correspondents while in exile "upset the restrictions of geography" and offered considerable opportunity to mobilize politically.[2] This was something that anarchist Emma Goldman also experienced after her exile from the United States in 1919, as she lived and worked within the context of transnational socialist and anarchist circles (discussed in the chapter "The Hostile City"). However, the idea of mobilizing and building a coalition in the pursuit of some kind of common objective is distinct to the experience of those who remain politically active in exile and contrasts starkly with other kinds of networked mobility, most notably that of fugitives.

As with the term *networks*, the idea of fugitivity has also taken on keen significance in recent times, especially among Black scholars who see in the concept "the disavowal of and disengagement from state-governed projects that attempt to adjudicate normative constructions of difference through liberal tropes of freedom and democratic belonging."[3] Given the close associations between fugitivity and freedom from slavery (discussed in "The Lonely City" chapter), this is an important reclaiming. The liberating potential inherent in the notion of fugitivity is now amplified as a pointed critique of the very structures that perpetuated and continue to propel the need for escape in the first place. As a result, the notion of fugitivity is now closely bound up with the idea of refusal, which anthropologist Damien Sojoyner describes as "the embodied knowledge at the core of social visions of being that are irreconcilable with liberal, difference-making state projects."[4] Cultural studies scholar Tina Campt calls fugitivity "a refusal of the very premises that have historically negated the lived experience of blackness as either pathological or exceptional to the logic of white supremacy."[5]

In these discussions of Black fugitivity and refusal, the very systems and societies in which people lived and struggled, and continue to do so in the present, are called into question. These critical interrogations draw attention to systemic and structural issues rather than faulting the motives or qualities of those refusing to perpetuate the current situation. This very much captures the spirit of what the New Sanctuary Movement has also espoused in recent years, which sees the structures of exclusion, racism, and labour exploitation as the root causes of any perceived problem with migration, not migrants themselves. Efforts around sanctuary city declarations and immigration reform are undertaken with a view that the current governance regimes are unjust.

In contrast to contemporary discussions of Black fugitivity, more traditional approaches to fugitivity, such as the definitions to be found in the Oxford English Dictionary, describe it as "the quality or state of being fugitive." Relatedly, the term *fugitive* as an adjective or noun is defined as "of immaterial things: evanescent, fleeting, of short duration." As a transitive verb, it means "to make fugitive, drive into exile." Crucially, the term is made to appear entirely neutral, with no distinctions drawn around the motives for becoming a fugitive. Yet there is a world of difference between those who flee unjust systems of oppression and those who flee because they have done harm and are wanted for their crimes. It is, therefore, revealing to see when and how assistance is rendered. As noted in "The Lonely City" chapter, there was very little in the way of assistance or community for fugitive slaves who made their way to Montreal/Mooniyaang/Tiohtià:ke and surrounds in the era of the Underground Railroad. By contrast, Confederate fugitives such as John Harrison Surratt were actively supported in the city as a result of religious and political affinities and despite accusations of violent crimes.

John Harrison Surratt was a suspected accomplice to John Wilkes Booth, who shot and killed US President Abraham Lincoln on 14 April 1865. In the aftermath of the assassination, four people were tried, convicted, and executed for their plot in the alleged conspiracy: Lewis Powell; George Atzerodt;

David Herold; and Mary Surratt, John Harrison's mother. Mary Surratt owned the boarding house where John Wilkes Booth hatched his plan and apparently supported him in his efforts. She was hung for her involvement, becoming the first woman to be federally executed in the United States.

Her son, John Harrison Surratt, was also named in the conspiracy, but he fled north to the Province of Canada and later to Europe in a bid to evade arrest. A wanted man, mobility became a form of protection. In fleeing from the United States, Surratt built upon contacts he had made during his time as a messenger for the Confederate cause, as well as religious networks stemming from his seminary years, to evade law enforcement for over a year. Unlike her son, Mary Surratt was trapped, bound by her ownership of a boarding house that had ironically served as a "safe house" for others in the Confederate cause.[6] Viewing John Harrison Surratt's time as a fugitive alongside his mother's fate is a study in stark juxtaposition, of flight versus entrapment, of life over death. Even though his innocence was questionable, the entangled race, class, and gender dynamics of the period meant that John Harrison Surratt was protected by political and religious networks that overlapped and intertwined and became all the more fused for a period, precisely because of his time in fugitivity.

Catholicism in North America

Exploring the question of political and religious connections as they involved John Harrison Surratt and his time as a fugitive means focusing on the relationships that emerged from important Sulpician education institutions in the United States and pre-confederation Canada and the role of Catholicism in forging bonds among some very unlikely historical actors. Catholicism was a central and defining aspect of life in French Canada and in Montreal/Mooniyaang/Tiohtià:ke specifically. The skyline of the city of "a hundred spires" was notably dotted with powerful visual symbols such as the Notre-Dame Cathedral, constructed in 1829. The religious imprint on the city is still visible in the built environment, even as it is now physically and symbolically overshadowed by the tall towers of the downtown core. Mary, Queen of the World Cathedral, erected in 1894 and the current home of Catholic Archdiocese of Montreal, and the Oratoire of St Joseph, which opened in 1904, are still prominent features of the city. A large, illuminated cross sits atop Mont-Royal, as it has since 1924. The very first cross to be planted on top of the mountain appeared in 1643, installed by Paul Chomedey de Maisonneuve as an answer to prayers and in gratitude for the end of disastrous flooding that had saturated the French settlement on the island. As noted previously, Ville Marie was established as a religious and military outpost, making religion, and the Catholic faith in particular, an essential part of the city's fabric from its earliest days.

A religious spirit also animated the early foundations of US nationalism and expansionism, evidenced most prominently in discussions of "manifest destiny."[7] In contrast to life in French Canada, however, Catholicism occupied a more marginal place in the social and political fabric of the United States. This, despite its rapid growth following the arrival of large numbers of Catholics following the end of the Napoleonic Wars.[8] By 1860, there were 3,500,000 Catholics in the United States," approximately 10 per cent of the population.[9] Many were new arrivals from Ireland, who sought refuge in North America following devastating economic, agricultural, and political conditions in their homeland.

In addition to favourable demographic changes, one of the ways in which Catholic influence was fostered and expanded across North America, beyond regular church attendance and services, was through the introduction of a series of seminaries. Catholic education was undertaken by a wide variety of orders, though the Jesuits and Sulpicians were perhaps most notable in this regard, establishing several colleges and seminaries across North America in the late 1700s. The goal of the Sulpician seminaries was, fundamentally, to train people for the priesthood. As one historian explains, "the primary aim of the Sulpicians was to create reflective subjects, not disciplined automatons. Sulpician schooling was an apprenticeship of the self."[10] In the process, they offered a classical education heavily focused on morality, but one that was influenced by the arrival of personnel from France in the revolutionary era.[11]

Religion and politics were closely connected in this period and major political events had a marked impact on religious life and vice versa. When civil war "sparked" in the United States in 1861 and then "burned, and smoldered" for four years, it divided families and communities.[12] For many Catholics in the country, whose religious beliefs were vilified and whose loyalties had been questioned, the conflict became an opportunity to prove their loyalties to either the Union or Confederate cause. Approximately two hundred thousand Catholics served in the Union Army, and dozens of priests and nuns worked in wartime hospitals. Thousands of others served and fought on the Confederate side.[13] This service had both domestic and international implications. Many Irish Catholics enlisted in the Union army and were "socialized into Fenianism," becoming ardent nationalists and opponents of British rule in Ireland.[14] In Canada, the threat of Fenianism was compounded by worries about a possible alliance with Indigenous Peoples as authorities looked with concern to Métis leader Louis Riel's activities in Manitoba, all too aware of his Catholic faith and the potential solidarities that might result.[15]

As for members of the Catholic clergy, many simply supported "the side under whose control their place of ministry was situated."[16] There was a certain degree of pragmatism involved. As the war progressed and the terrible losses and violence mounted, many Catholics withdrew their support for either the Confederate or Union forces. A number demonstrated vocal support for the anti-war faction. This shift heightened suspicions about Catholic loyalties, especially following the violent draft riots in New York City/Manahåhtaan in July 1863, in which there was heavy Catholic participation.[17] Some historians have suggested that the war ultimately "alienated most northern Catholics and their leaders, causing them to seek refuge in a separate Catholic subculture after the war."[18]

At the same time, it is important to note that the Catholic experience was not contained within any single national border. Catholicism also fostered networks across borders, entangling the Province of Canada in the turmoil of the US Civil War and the drama of President Lincoln's assassination. This entanglement was social and political and went beyond the recognized diplomatic implications of the war. Many people in the Province of Canada were engrossed by the conflict in the United States. For recently arrived fugitive slaves (discussed in "The Lonely City" chapter), the war held considerable significance, portending as it did the possibility of a very different future for them and their kin. Others were engrossed because of religious and political affinities. The war, for instance, was regularly discussed at Sunday services.[19] Many people also had personal connections. Over the course of twenty years, from 1851 to 1871, 105,000 people migrated to the United States from what is now known as the province of Quebec. The vast majority were French-speaking Catholics.[20] With friends and family immediately involved in or affected by the conflict, people in the Province of Canada were keenly attuned to events in the United States.

Catholic clergy in French Canada generally viewed the conflict waging in the United States with disdain. Newspaper editorials expressed the view that the United States was a nation "without cohesion" and the "most immoral country in the world."[21] Crucially, many Catholics viewed monarchies as better than republics; and parliamentary democracy as "superior to what they perceived to be American democracy run amok."[22] They also believed that "working the land was superior to urban living."[23] All this meant that French Canadians were often sympathetic to the Confederate cause, given their general view of the civil war in which both the North and Union troops were sometimes viewed as "barbaric" and guilty of "all sorts of excesses."[24] Following Lincoln's assassination, French Canadian Catholics – like many others – expressed outrage and grief at the shocking crime.[25] Yet it was members of the Catholic clergy, along with Confederate exiles and supporters, who assisted one of the alleged conspirators, John Harrison Surratt, in his flight from US law enforcement.

John Harrison Surratt

John Harrison Surratt was one of three children born to Mary Elizabeth Jenkins and John Surratt. As was generally the case in the United States in the nineteenth century, John Harrison Surratt and his siblings grew up in a religious household. Surratt's mother was born in 1823 to an English Protestant family. Her father died when she was only two years old. At that point, Mary's mother took over the management of the land and property, which included a number of enslaved people, and expanded the family's material wealth.[26] Mary converted to Catholicism at the age of twelve after being enrolled in the Academy for Young Ladies, which was attached to St Mary's Catholic Church in Alexandria, Virginia. She assumed the name Eugenia, although this does not appear to have stuck. Her new religious faith did, however.

The Academy for Young Ladies was run by the Sisters of Charity of Emmitsburg, a religious community established in 1809 by Elizabeth Ann Seton, following the Rules of the Daughters of Charity founded by St Vincent de Paul in 1633.[27] This long-standing community became active in the fields of education, social welfare, and health and expanded across North America. They opened a new Mother House in New York/Manahāhtaan (1849) and another one in Halifax/Kjipuktuk in present-day Nova Scotia, with the creation of Mount St Vincent (1856). During the US Civil War, they tended to the wounded and dying on both sides of the conflict.

Mary Surratt remained a devout Catholic throughout her life and raised her children in the faith, including John Harrison (her youngest) who attended St Thomas, a Jesuit establishment, and then St Charles College, a Sulpician minor seminary, near Ellicott's Mills in present-day Howard County, Maryland (traditional territory of the Susquehannock and Piscataway).[28] It was at St Charles College that John Harrison Surratt encountered some of the people who would become instrumental in his flight from law enforcement. It was also where Surratt met Louis Weichmann who remembered him as a "moral and exemplary young man" and yet became a witness for the prosecution in Surratt's trial, as well as in the case against Mary Surratt.[29]

St Charles College was incorporated in 1830 and named after its benefactor, Charles Carroll. Originally from Ireland, Carroll gained his wealth as a plantation owner and is distinguished in the historical record as the only Roman Catholic to sign the US Declaration of Independence. The history of Maryland also holds significance in terms of the history of sanctuary: the state was originally founded in part with the goal of providing refuge to Catholics fleeing the Glorious Revolution in England (1688–9). Indeed, many new colonists were drawn to the United States after the American Revolution by the principle of freedom of religion.[30]

At St Charles College, Surratt was exposed to a curriculum designed to "rear up a national clergy, accustomed from infancy to the manners and the country, and withal pious, learned, and sufficiently numerous."[31] The curriculum at the seminary focused on "moral training," and included courses in Latin, Greek, French, English, mathematics, history, and geography as well as bookkeeping, physiology, and religious doctrine.[32] The college drew students from across the United States and the Province of Canada.[33] St Charles College was located a short distance from Doughoregan manor, Charles Carroll's grand estate, which was described as an "elevated spot, with fertile, undulating lands in the front and rear, and bordered east and west by woods of chestnut and oak trees."[34]

Surratt spent only a short time at St Charles College as his studies were cut short by the start of the Civil War in 1861 and the death of his father a year later. Departing from the seminary, Surratt returned to Surrattville (renamed Clinton after the US Civil War), where he took up his father's position as postmaster and helped his mother run the family's tavern. As the business doubled as the local post office, it became a "natural stopping point" for travelers and soon became a "center of secessionist activity" as a result of the family's Confederate sympathies and the ease with which correspondence could be distributed.[35] When Mary Surratt moved to Washington/Nakotchank in the District of Columbia in the fall of 1864 and opened a boarding house at 541 H, a property previously purchased by her husband, she continued to be a source of safety for the Confederate cause.

According to the way John Harrison Surratt later presented his life story to the public, he became involved with Confederate forces upon leaving the seminary. He describes "sending information regarding the movements of the United States army stationed in Washington and elsewhere and carrying dispatches to confederate boats on the Potomac."[36] The Surratt family was certainly sympathetic to the Confederate cause from the outset. As a state where slavery was legal but one that bordered the North and South, Maryland was divided politically. People enlisted to fight on both sides of the Civil War, although numerically, more fought for the North. The Surratt family placed their fates with the Confederate government of Jefferson Davis, a "tall and gaunt" man whose wealth came from a thousand-acre cotton plantation and who led secessionist forces before ultimately fleeing to Canada at the end of the Civil War.[37] Indeed, both during and after the war, Confederate officials, volunteers, and soldiers made their way across international borders to organize, strategize, and, on occasion, to find some measure of safety. The war transformed Montreal/Mooniyaang/Tiohtià:ke, which was a site of convenience and heightened mobility in this period.

Confederates in the City

During the "vast" US Civil War, described as "four brutal, wretched years of misery on a scale never seen before," the Province of Canada was the site of considerable Confederate organizing.[38] Part of this had to do with financial considerations. By the mid-nineteenth century, even with the political turmoil around the burning of parliament and the Rebellion Losses Bill in 1849, Montreal/Mooniyaang/Tiohtià:ke was an industrial and economic powerhouse, described as the "workshop of British North America."[39] Industry and the indispensable role of labour drove this process, which benefited from the city's busy and established port and innovations in transport infrastructure (evident in enterprises such as the building of the Lachine Canal).[40] Approximately sixty new manufacturing establishments appeared along the canal from 1847 to 1867, feeding the growing trade in imports and exports. This trade swelled during the war, contributing to the enhanced material prosperity of the city.[41] Sympathetic merchants, who benefited in part from the conditions of war, also helped Confederate efforts on the ground.[42] For example, Augustin Cantin, one of the city's most important shipbuilders supplied the *Sumter* to the Confederate government to run the Union blockade (in addition to producing several lucrative vessels for the governments of Cuba and France).[43]

Confederate agents used Montreal/Mooniyaang/Tiohtià:ke as a site to organize and garner support for their cause. The city's proximity to the United States, as well as the significant number of residents who supported the Confederate cause, made it an ideal site in which to organize and potentially wage war against the Union. By 1863, the American consul was cautioning his government that steps should be taken to protect the border states "to prevent the consummation of contemplated deeds of wickedness."[44] Though the number of Confederates in the Province of Canada appeared to be relatively small, their presence was keenly felt, especially in Montreal/Mooniyaang/Tiohtià:ke and Toronto/Tkaronto.[45] There were, for instance, more Confederates than free Black people, including former fugitive slaves, in Montreal/Mooniyaang/Tiohtià:ke in this period. The Confederate presence included officials from the Confederate States of America and later prisoners of war who escaped and made their way north.[46]

2.1 St Lawrence Hall, a popular gathering place for Confederates in the city and their supporters. Photograph by James George Parks, 1865–70.

In fact, there were so many Confederates in Montreal/Mooniyaang/Tiohtià:ke that Dooley's Bar in St Lawrence Hall – a well-known Confederate haunt – served mint juleps, a classic bourbon cocktail and the official drink of the Kentucky Derby, year round. The Ottawa Hotel, located at 50 St Jacques Street, steps away from the Notre-Dame Basilica, was another establishment frequented by what was known as the Confederate Secret Service – a term that describes both the formal and more informal operations that supported the Confederate States of America during the war. The Bank of Ontario on Place d'Armes held more than US$400,000 (an estimated U$39 million in 2023) in Confederate funds for safekeeping.[47] Jacob Thompson was the Confederate commissioner in Canada and he officially established his headquarters at St Lawrence Hall on June 30, 1864. From his perch in Montreal/Mooniyaang/Tiohtià:ke, Thompson was responsible for the distribution of funds and for planning covert operations. This included a plan to free Confederate prisoners held at Johnson's Island, a Union prisoner camp located on the shores of Erielhonan (Lake Erie).[48]

These various schemes and incidents, such as the 1861 Trent Affair (when a US Navy official apprehended two Confederates aboard the British ship the *Trent*, creating a major diplomatic incident), worried the imperial government in London about the Province of Canada as a potential battleground. The result was a renewed military presence in Montreal/Mooniyaang/Tiohtià:ke and Toronto/Tkaronto, while officials and politicians kept a keen eye on the political landscape.[49] Indeed, the very real danger of being drawn into the conflict fueled some of the push towards confederation in 1867. Locally, the war had an important economic impact. In 1864, for instance, American influences sought to negotiate "an enormous cotton-for-contraband deal," which would have seen the purchase of cotton from the Confederate side in exchange for much-needed goods.[50] This was a major enterprise and as one account notes, "From the summer of 1864 until the assassination of Lincoln in April 1865, everyone interested in cotton trading was at … Saint Lawrence Hall, a mecca for investment bankers, cotton speculators, blockade runners, and US Treasury agents."[51]

The heightened activity in Montreal/Mooniyaang/Tiohtià:ke in 1864 coincided with a brazen attack by Confederate raiders on St Albans, Vermont, situated about 110 kilometres (sixty-eight miles south of the city) across the international border on traditional N'dakina and Wabanaki territory. Incorporated in 1859, St Albans was a bustling commercial and manufacturing centre with a population of approximately 2,000 by 1864. As with many other places, including nineteenth-century Montreal/Mooniyaang/Tiohtià:ke, rail lines were a crucial artery for the community.

Rail lines meant that fugitive slaves passed through or spent some time in St Albans.[52] It was also how the raiders arrived in the village in October 1864.

The raid on St Albans took place on 19 October 1964, when Confederates who had been quietly amassing in the village, posing as Canadian visitors, launched an attack. They began by robbing three banks to obtain funds to support the Confederate cause and proceeded to hold several people hostage in the village green before ultimately trying to burn St Albans to the ground. One person died in the violence. Fleeing to Canada, the raiders sought physical refuge and legal protection. They were welcomed by their southern counterparts in the city as well as by many sympathetic citizens. As one participant account detailed, "The prisoners were confined in the jail, but received the kindest attention possible from the jailer and his family. Indeed, the jailer set aside his parlo(u)rs for the accommodation of the prisoners." They noted further, "The large number of Southern people who were sojourning in (the city) vied with each other in kindness to the prisoners. The citizens of the city were equally conspicuous in their manifestations of friendship, sympathy, and courteous attentions."[53]

In a critical ruling, the justices determined that because the raiders or "soldiers" were under Confederate orders and because the Province of Canada was officially neutral, they could not be extradited to face criminal proceedings in the United States.[54] Tried in Montreal/Mooniyaang/Tiohtià:ke, the raiders were quickly set free, much to the outrage of US consular representatives. Historians note that the raiders celebrated their release "in a number of safe houses" outside Montreal/Mooniyaang/Tiohtià:ke, hinting at the network of supporters in the city and surrounds.[55]

Writing from Montreal/Mooniyaang/Tiohtià:ke, American consul John Potter was dismayed at the court's decision, describing the entire proceedings as "a mere farce."[56] News clippings reported how the crowd in the courtroom cheered upon the dismissal of the charges against the raiders. These stories were summarily dispatched to US officials, as was correspondence about how the city had become a hub for "refugees from the South, too cowardly to stay at home and fight."[57] Nevertheless, despite the celebrations surrounding the raiders' return and release in some quarters, the climate cooled in Montreal/Mooniyaang/Tiohtià:ke after the 1864 raid. The city was still appealing as a site of refuge; however, it became more difficult

2.2 Portrait of John Potter, American consul to the Province of Canada, 1863–65.

to use it as a Confederate operating base in the months that followed the raid, a time when John Harrison Surratt would have been making his way to and from the city with correspondence from Richmond, Virginia (traditional Powhatan territory).[58]

Part of this cooling in enthusiasm had to do with a sense that the border and the sanctity of the city of Montreal/Mooniyaang/Tiohtià:ke had been violated. Editors at the *Montreal Gazette*, who had previously expressed sympathy for the Confederate cause, as had those at the *Montreal Telegraph*, insisted: "It is the first duty of the Government and the people of Canada to see that the right of asylum which their soil affords is thus not betrayed and violated. The Government must spare no pains to prevent it; and it is the first duty of the inhabitants of this country, especially those who live on the borders, to give instant information of any attempt they may see to the nearest magistrate, and the duty of the magistrate immediately to inform the Government."[59] The raid affected the sense of who the city was for and how it should be used. Issues around authority, the rule of law, justice, and the right of asylum all came to the fore. The editors at the *Montreal Gazette* were particularly concerned about how an abuse of the right to asylum might affect the Province of Canada's claims to neutrality. Titled, "Outrage of St. Albans," they declared, "We must, we repeat, preserve our neutrality, and the right of asylum which British soil affords inviolate, and punish with the sternest severity any breach which can be discerned. If we do not, we shall find ourselves dragged into the war for needless cause; our eastern frontier lit up with the fires of now peaceful hoes, and the country on both sides of the line made red with murders."[60] From the vantage point of this editorial, to offer refuge was to risk political instability and this was undesirable. The spectre of being drawn into the raging conflict in the United States loomed large.

As a result, discussions about a possible federation between the Province of Canada and the Maritime Provinces became more urgent. The Canadian government also introduced the Frontier Outrages Bill, which officially became known as The Alien Act. This law allowed "for the expulsion from the Canadas of any foreign person suspected of engaging in hostile acts against a friendly nation."[61] Crucially, in introducing the bill, then Attorney General John A. Macdonald indicated that it was necessary because those seeking asylum "in consequence of war, may have in their own land by their conduct, proved themselves unworthy of that asylum."[62]

According to newspaper accounts, Macdonald insisted that when war first broke out in the United States, "a number of refugees" had moved north. They were largely, he believed, from "the class whose sympathies were with the Southern Confederacy." He noted "these unfortunate people" who had "been driven from their homes, many of them ruined in their circumstances" were "received" with "kindness and consideration."[63] The raid, however, had altered the empathy that characterized the initial response to "refugees" arriving from the United States. The result, as noted previously, was the introduction of more robust mechanisms for deportation. The Lincoln administration, meanwhile, introduced passport controls, for the first time requiring people in the Province of Canada to carry documentation if they wished to enter the United States. In this way, the border between the Province of Canada and the United States hardened, or at least became more demarcated, as a result of Confederate activities. It certainly led to increased patrolling and enforcement, for a time.[64] Despite these controls, John Harrison Surratt fled across the US-Canada border after Lincoln's assassination. However, the trajectory of his subsequent movements had as much to do with the idea of the border as a divide between safe and unsafe spaces as it did with the reality of who was willing to assist him.

Religious Contacts, Political Networks

In April 1865, John Harrison Surratt was twenty-one years old. He had recently been engaged to work as a messenger in the Province of Canada for General Robert Edward Lee, a Confederate general, and was busily crisscrossing the US-Canada border on a regular basis. As detailed previously, a number of Confederate supporters and sympathizers had taken refuge in the Province of Canada during the war, and keeping communications open and swift was considered a key element in the fight against Union forces. In his work as a messenger, Surratt came into contact with a number of Confederates and their supporters in Montreal/Mooniyaang/Tiohtià:ke. He also became familiar with the landscape around the border as well as various train schedules and access points. On 14 April 1865, President Lincoln attended a performance of *Our American Cousin* at the Ford Theatre in Washington/Nakotchank. Approaching Lincoln from behind, Booth shot and fatally wounded the US president. Booth's accomplice, Lewis Powell, assaulted Secretary of State William Seward, causing critical but not fatal injuries.

Within days of the assassination, notices appeared indicating that John Harrison Surratt was a suspected accomplice and that there was a bounty of $25,000 on his head. Surratt, who had just returned from Montreal/Mooniyaang/Tiohtià:ke, was in upper New York State at the time of Lincoln's assassination.[65] He heard news of the events in Washington/Nakotchank and later saw a notice for his arrest. He immediately sought refuge. His initial plan was to go to Baltimore (traditional territory of the Susquehannock and Piscataway), and he boarded a train from Elmira to Canandaigua,

2.3 A portrait of John Harrison Surratt in his "Canada Jacket," ca. 1866.

originally a Seneca village, in order to do so.[66] However, once in Canandaigua, he changed course and went to Montreal/Mooniyaang/Tiohtià:ke via St Albans, the site of the Confederate raid just a few months prior.[67] According to author Julian Sher, Surratt was wearing a "distinctive 'Canuck-style' jacket he had made sure to buy ... to escape any undue attention."[68]

The city of Montreal/Mooniyaang/Tiohtià:ke, which Surratt had frequented regularly over the previous months, had changed following Lincoln's assassination. There was significantly less public support for the Confederate cause, though some people still celebrated Lincoln's passing. The US consul was dismayed at the gleeful behaviour on display on the day of Lincoln's assassination, recording "I am sorry to say there were some so devoid of all feeling, so wicked and depraved, as to exult over this great crime."[69] However, as people (including Andrew Johnson who became president of the United States after Lincoln's death) began to overtly suggest that the assassination plot had been facilitated in Montreal/Mooniyaang/Tiohtià:ke and that Confederate agents were "being harboured" in Canada, the mood cooled even further.[70] People did not like the idea of being drawn to, or involved with, something they considered nefarious.[71] The *Courier de Ste-Hyacinthe*, which served the community of St Liboire where Surratt would eventually go into hiding, declared that the assassination "would wither the Confederate cause."[72] This, from editors who had previously been supportive of the idea of secession.[73]

In response to the assassination, there was a groundswell of support in the Province of Canada for Union forces. When Governor General Charles Monck received news that "persons who had planned the assassination of Lincoln were on their way to Quebec," he promised his full assistance.[74] Spontaneous groups of vigilante citizens also organized themselves to patrol the border with the intention of apprehending any suspected assassins. Despite their efforts, John Harrison Surratt arrived in the city on 16 April 1865. He likely traveled by train, though some accounts reported that he walked across the border.[75] Upon his arrival, John Harrison Surratt checked into St Lawrence Hall Hotel on St James Street using the alias Charley Armstrong. The clerk at the desk described him as "being a tall man, 24 or 25 yrs. old, no beard or whiskers, light brown hair, not very gentlemanly in appearance."[76]

From there, he sheltered with John Porterfield, a Confederate agent originally from Nashville, Tennessee (traditional Cherokee, Yuchi, and Shawnee territory), whom Surratt described as a "poor man, with a large family." The key was that "money could not buy him."[77] Porterfield appears in the contemporary city directories as a partner in Porterfield & Lyon, at 3 Merchants Exchange (St Sacrament) and as residing at 1 Prince of Wales Terrace at 887 Sherbrooke Street.[78] The enterprise was too small to be listed in the business directory, but given the location of the office, it might have well been involved in some kind of trading activity or simply been a front for Confederate activity as Porterfield's political leanings were well known.[79]

From Montreal/Mooniyaang/Tiohtià:ke, which was soon crawling with detectives from the United States, Surratt was taken to St Liboire, located about 100 kilometres (sixty miles) east of the city on the traditional territory of the Wabanaki and N'dakina. Apparently, Surratt evaded law enforcement in Montreal/Mooniyaang/Tiohtià:ke by leaving Porterfield's residence with an accomplice at the same time. Each went in a separate taxi, and the detectives did not know whom to follow. A man "previously engaged" to take him across the river did so and "a young lady guided him across the country to a village on the Grand Trunk Railroad called San Leben (St Liboire)."[80]

This escape was likely orchestrated by Father Pierre-Larcille Lapierre, whom many see as "instrumental in marshalling the network of the French Catholic Church in aid of John Surratt."[81] Father Lapierre had served as Canon to the Catholic Bishop Ignace Bourget, with whom General Robert Lee and Jefferson Davis both had associations.[82] Although Catholic clergy would later be criticized for harbouring a known and wanted fugitive, supporters, including the editors of the *Courier du Canada*, defended them vigorously. They claimed that the priests, at least, had acted only upon a letter of introduction penned by General Lee:

> Surratt est arrivé au Canada porteur d'une lettre d'introduction donnée par le général Lee pour un prêtre catholique qui l'a accueilli uniquement par des motifs de charité, dans un esprit absolument indépendant de toute préoccupation politique, comme il aurait donné asyle à un esclave fugitif venant réclamer l'hospitalité que ne refuse jamais un prêtre chrétien aux affligés et aux proscrits.[83]

The emphasis was on charity and hospitality, not political favoritism. The editors insisted that Father Lapierre had acted in the same way that he would have if a fugitive slave claimed this hospitality. This may have been true, but it is striking that there is no record of Catholic clergy in Montreal/Mooniyaang/Tiohtià:ke doing so in the context of the "Underground Railroad."

Contemporaries described the settlement as "an out-of-the-way place, and so a good place in which to hide."[84] An agricultural area, the terrain was and remains quite flat. The region is much less wooded now than it would have been when Surratt sought refuge there but as a fugitive, Surratt may, nevertheless, have felt quite exposed given the lay of the land. He certainly would have been noticed as being from away, and he spent much of his time in hiding.

In this rural village, Surratt was sheltered by Father Charles Boucher, the local Catholic priest. Boucher was born in Trois-Rivières (traditional territory of the Nitaskinan and N'dakina) on the north shore of the St Lawrence River/Kaniatarowanenneh. His father was a master carpenter. Little else is known about his early life, but it appears that he was in his second year of service when Surratt arrived in the small village. According to all available accounts, including his later testimony during Surratt's trial, Father Boucher did not know that Surratt was a wanted accomplice in Lincoln's murder. Apparently, he knew only that a Catholic American in ill health needed to recover from his bouts of "chills." Boucher testified that Surratt's "health was very poor." According to Boucher, Surratt "remained in bed whole days at a time. At such times he could hardly move. He was very pale and weak."[85]

The Catholic connection is interesting as there were immediate allegations that Surratt was hiding with Roman Catholic faithful after Lincoln's assassination, hinting at some of the misgivings about Catholicism in the United States discussed previously. C.H.A Buckley, a former chaplain to the first Regt. Excelsior Brigade immediately targeted Surratt's faith. In correspondence with the Secretary of War, Buckley observed that Surratt had once been "patronized and petted by the priests of Georgetown" and insisted that since Surratt had yet to be found, he must "have taken refuge in one of their monastic or conventional establishments." To make his case, Buckley further charged, "As the Papal government only has shown favor to the Southern Rebellion and as the loyalty of a large proportion of the Catholic clergy is, to say the least, questionable, is not the presumption fair that Surratt is harbored in some of their secret sanctuaries, more likely in Georgetown?"[86] Buckley was correct to suspect a Catholic refuge, but mistaken in assuming that Surratt was still in the United States.

As it was, Surratt spent most of his four months in St Liboire, located on the traditional territory of the Wabanaki and N'dakina, in hiding, "secreted in a dark room, from which he never came out except a few times, when he would go out late at night and take a walk."[87] Newspaper accounts continued to speculate that Surratt was in Canada and so he remained discreet.[88] Surratt reportedly received regular correspondence from friends and acquaintances who assured him that all was going well with his mother's trial.[89] Yet a quick scan of any newspaper in English or French in Quebec would have suggested otherwise as *Le Courier du Canada, Le Canadien, Journal du Québec, Montreal Herald,* and smaller local newspapers all carried details of the trial. Nevertheless, Surratt later claimed to have been oblivious to the fate awaiting his mother. He would, on occasion, go hunting with Joseph Du Tilley (Father Boucher's brother-in-law) and Father Lapierre from Montreal/Mooniyaang/Tiohtià:ke, but it seems that he spent most of his time in the rectory.[90]

Midway through the summer, a young servant apparently discovered Surratt hidden away in the back room of Father Boucher's residence when she peeked under a crack in the door. Dr Lewis J.A. McMillan, who encountered Surratt on his later voyage to Europe, recounted that "the story was immediately circulated around the village that the priest had a woman in his bed-room hiding. Then the priest told him that he could keep him no longer; that he must find other quarters."[91] Surratt was quickly removed from the priest's house and returned to Montreal/Mooniyaang/Tiohtià:ke. Father Lapierre appears to have once again assisted with Surratt's furtive movements and his need for shelter. On this second occasion in the city, Surratt took refuge at 116 Cemetery Street, "a quiet place just behind the Catholic Bishop's Place."[92] This was the home of Father Lapierre's parents where Surratt was apparently "secreted in a dark room, from which he never came out except a few times, when he would go out late at night and take a walk."[93] Despite Surratt's efforts at subterfuge, the US consul was able to report to the State Department at the end of May that Surratt was in Canada.[94]

Consul Potter suspected early on that the Catholic Church in Canada was involved in sheltering Surratt. In making this suggestion to US Secretary of State Seward, Potter made mention of Dr Luke Blackburn, a Confederate runner and one of the St Albans' raiders. Blackburn had been arrested earlier in May 1865 for his plot to murder people in the United

States by mailing clothing infected with yellow fever. Potter made pointed reference to the fact that Catholic institutions had sheltered Blackburn and implied they were doing the same with Surratt.[95] Still, despite Potter's alerts, no immediate action was taken. Nevertheless, Surratt and his supporters must have felt that he was in danger of arrest in Montreal/Mooniyaang/Tiohtià:ke. Its geographic proximity to the United States was both a blessing and a potential problem. Arrangements were, therefore, made for Surratt to board a sailing vessel bound for the port of Liverpool. He left Canada on 5 September 1865.

The SS *Peruvian*, a steam and wind-powered ship that had taken her maiden voyage across the Atlantic the previous year from Liverpool, sailed first to the port of Moville, just outside of Londonderry, Ireland, before continuing to her city of origin.[96] The ship's physician, Dr Lewis J.A. McMillan, described John Surratt as having dyed hair, a narrow moustache, and using eyeglasses as a disguise.[97] Surratt was apparently "very thin, and nervous and careworn" though McMillan added that "his general conduct (on the boat) was gentle." The main thing that McMillan observed was that Surratt would "show signs of nervousness whenever any one came suddenly behind him. He would turn around and look about as if he expected some one to come upon him at any moment."[98] The inference was that Surratt was suspicious in appearance and, therefore, likely guilty. At the same time, the mention of his gentleness undermines any impression of him as a bloodthirsty accomplice, perhaps providing some insight into how his personal character, along with his various networked connections, helped him move through difficult circumstances.

McMillan befriended Surratt aboard the ship, perhaps at the behest of Father Pierre Lapierre, who seems to have asked for assistance in this regard (though without revealing Surratt's identity, introducing him only as "McCarty"). Surratt apparently became more open with McMillan over the course of the voyage at sea, and the latter's testimony against Surratt during his criminal trial would prove deeply incriminating, though not fatal. Surratt apparently first hinted at his fugitive status by asking McMillan if he thought there was an American detective onboard. When McMillan asked him, "What you have done that you should be afraid of an American detective?" Surratt ostensibly said, "that he had done more things than I was aware of, and that very likely, if I knew, it would make me stare, or something to that effect."[99] Surratt then pulled out a "a small four-barrelled revolver" as a way of emphasizing the seriousness of the situation.[100]

In recounting their various conversations, McMillan claimed during Surratt's trial that "one day, in talking of the mere possibility of his being arrested in England, he said he would shoot the first officer who would lay his hand on him." McMillan suggested he "would be shown very little leniency," to which Surratt replied, "I know it, and for that very reason I would do it, because I would rather be hung by an English hangman than by a Yankee one, for I know very well if I go back to the United States I shall swing."[101] Such testimony was critical for the prosecution as it sought to establish Surratt's guilt, though the reliability of McMillan's words is somewhat dubious in places.

Although McMillan made it appear as though Surratt stayed on the ship all the way to Liverpool only after having too much drink, other sources suggest that this was his intended destination all along.[102] Liverpool in 1865 was a city with many Confederate sympathizers as it had important economic ties with the American South. The trade in tobacco and enslaved people had been key to Liverpool's prosperity. It dominated the transatlantic slave trade after the 1740s when it surpassed the competing ports in London and Bristol, making it tops in the grotesque exploitation and violence wielded in the context of this trade.[103] According to one account, once in the port city of Liverpool, Surratt when directly to the Oratory of the Holy Cross "where, if he was not expected, (he) was indeed welcome."[104] The church, located in a "crowded and impoverished" ward, had been built only five years prior and served a largely Irish Catholic congregation. It was still a rather novel presence when Surratt arrived.[105] The church survived considerable damage as a result of air raids during the Second World War, but it closed in September 2001 and was torn down several years later.

At the Oratory of the Holy Cross, Surratt was sheltered by Father Charles Constant Jolivet. The priest was born in Pont-l'Abbé, France in 1826 and took his vows in 1848. Of his early studies, one teacher wrote bluntly that he "has finished his theology course and seems to have sufficient intellectual ability. He would have gained more from his studies if he had been more studious; he is naturally lazy and frivolous. He has lost a lot of time.

Nevertheless he is quite devout and is endowed with much docility, simplicity and gentleness."[106]

In the end, Jolivet was successful in his studies and was ordained in 1849. He went first to Everingham in England and then became the supervisor in Liverpool in 1857. He would have been seven years into his position when Surratt presented himself, fully capable of determining the desirability and merits of assisting the fugitive Catholic Confederate messenger. It seems that Surratt was "secreted" at the church though accounts of hiding in an obscure room or closet that once again were made to characterize his time in Liverpool appear somewhat exaggerated.[107] Stephen J. Cameron, who was engaged by the Confederate service and was in Liverpool at the time, told the judge in Surratt's criminal trial that "he was sensible in concealing himself, though he did not take any particular pains to conceal himself. He went round to public places seeing curiosities with Dr. McMillan."[108]

US consular officials in Liverpool were also aware of Surratt's presence in the city but were slow to seek him out.[109] By this time, there was a great deal less urgency around his arrest as the original trials of the conspirators were completed and the executions of four people, including Surratt's mother Mary, had taken place on 7 July 1865. Even though the US federal government knew of Surratt's movements to England, officials did not pursue him in part because his return might have renewed the controversy around his mother's execution and that of other accomplices. The reward for John Harrison Surratt's arrest was revoked on 24 November 1865, further discouraging any urgency around his apprehension.[110]

Despite these evolving and less pressing circumstances, it appears that Father Jolivet only ever intended to shelter Surratt for a brief time. The latter eventually made his way to Rome with some financial support and perhaps letters of introduction from Jolivet or Father Pierre Lapierre.[111] It seems that Surratt was first assisted in Rome by Frederick Neve, rector of the English College (1863–7), who hosted students for the priesthood. Surratt initially stayed at the college before enrolling in the Papal Zouaves forces. According to author Julian Sher, Surratt "was a Zouave Third Class in Company C of the 3rd Regiment, stationed outside Rome."[112] The largest contingent of Papal Zouaves came from the Low Countries, but there were also a significant number of volunteers from France, Italy, and Canada.[113] Joseph Royal, who had attended the Sulpician Collège de Montréal alongside Louis Riel, was a founding member of the Zouave committee in Canada, which was quite active on a number of fronts.[114]

Surratt seems to have joined the Papal Zouaves largely out of a desire for anonymity and financial necessity, though his Catholic faith may have also inspired some interest in their cause. Although Surratt appeared safe under the pseudonym "John Watson," he had, in fact, been identified by a former schoolmate from his time at St Charles College. Henri Beaumont de Sainte Marie conveyed his suspicions, and Surratt was arrested and jailed on 7 November 1866. Surratt nevertheless managed to escape. He then proceeded to convince the English consul in Rome that he was a Canadian, perhaps using his Charley Armstrong alias again, and sailed shortly for the port of Alexandria.[115] He arrived, still wearing his Pontifical Zouave uniform (and not his famous "Canuck" coat), on 23 November 1866.

By then, Surratt had been fleeing justice for almost a year and a half. Crucially, while there had been all kinds of protection for Surratt as he moved along and through Confederate and Catholic networks, there was little in the way of such contacts or support in Alexandria. Moreover, as historian Andrew Jampoler makes clear, "extraterritoriality empowered ambassadors, ministers, and consuls general in the empire with almost complete legal authority over their resident citizens. By landing in Alexandria, Surratt had unwittingly made himself subject to US law as exercised there by American government officials."[116] Surratt was arrested and returned to the United States aboard the "man-of-war ship *Swatara*," to face a civilian trial.[117] A mistrial was eventually declared, and because the statute of limitations had run its course, Surratt was free to go. He chose to head south to Mexico, rather than his previous haunts in Montreal/Mooniyaang/Tiohtià:ke and spent his later years teaching school and lecturing about his life across the United States, starting in Montgomery County, Maryland (traditional territory of the Piscataway) in 1870.

Conclusions

John Harrison Surratt's story is a reminder of the very real implications of being able to move physically and what this meant in terms of the potential for escape beyond the conceptual emphasis on fugitivity advanced by scholars in the present. Flight and expansive mobility were not possible for everyone. Unlike her son, for instance, Mary Surratt was not mobile. She was trapped. The boarding house she operated in Washington, DC/Nacotchtank lands was known to be a meeting place and a safe house for the Confederate cause. Her son John Harrison told everyone as much. People, therefore, came to rely on her, and her fixity, to advance their own plans. In addition to providing shelter, prosecutors alleged that Mary Surratt helped John Wilkes Booth procure and store weapons. She was arrested before she could flee, and ultimately tried, convicted, and executed.

Still in hiding in St Liboire, John Harrison Surratt apparently had no idea about the gravity of his mother's situation. It remains a matter of debate as to whether he was sheltered from news about her circumstances by people who did not wish him to risk his life in going back to the United States, though it certainly soured public opinion against him.[118] Instead of returning to be at his mother's side during her trial and in the days before she was hung, Surratt inadvertently wove together a network of Catholic and Confederate supporters as he made his way geographically further and further afield. At each step of his journey as a fugitive, connections born of his time at St Charles College and his work as a Confederate messenger facilitated his movements. Surratt was supported because people alternatively thought him innocent, were misled about who he was, or continued to believe in the Confederate cause.

Many present-day audiences consider the story of Surratt's time as a fugitive in an unsavoury light, seeing the wild differences around sanctuary today (even if the language of "illegal" or "undocumented" is often applied to those seeking refuge in an effort to sully any impression of virtue) versus the resolute protection offered to Surratt, a wanted suspect after the assassination of President Lincoln and somebody who knowingly or unknowingly abandoned his mother to the gallows. Nor was Surratt's case an example of the transformative fugitivity imagined in the present.

Indeed, the objectionable nature of John Harrison Surratt and his cause makes it difficult to square the protection he received with the dynamic and empowering contemporary politics around Black fugitivity and refusal in particular. Yet it is precisely because his case is so contrary to these ideas that it bears considering the vast gulf revealed by this variation and the implications of this gap for how we understand arguments about oppression, responsibility, and possibility in the present.

The Black fugitivity that scholars have detailed in recent years is an empowering fugitivity that is ultimately, as cultural studies scholar Tina Campt says, about the possibility of living "unbounded" lives.[119] Freedom is part of this story, but even more central to this concept is the notion that people need to find escape and alternative ways of being within societies where many of the fundamental structures of power and authority operate against them. The pressing issue woven through ideas about Black fugitivity is not physical mobility, rather it is about the possibility of social transformation *in situ* and within. In teasing out the ways in which John Harrison Surratt was able to evade law enforcement for over a year and a half and the contrasts between his experience and those of fugitive slaves seeking refuge in Montreal/Mooniyaang/Tiohtià:ke or the Black fugitivity espoused by scholars in the present, we can see much of what was subjective about the making of sanctuary and fugitivity in the past. The entangled dynamics around race, gender, and class, in addition to the presence of networks and connections, endure into the present, albeit in varied forms.

The story of John Harrison Surratt's time in fugitivity stands in stark contrast to the experience of fugitives from slavery described in "The Lonely City" chapter, and it also diverges from many of the other cases explored in *Sanctuary in Pieces* where people were seen as worthy of assistance precisely because they weren't guilty of any criminal offence. In a number of cases analyzed here, people were assisted because supporters saw them as blameless victims. They found flaws with the social and economic circumstances that contributed to the need for refuge or identified failings in the adjudication of asylum.

Innocence is essential to how sanctuary operates in the present and in state-led efforts around asylum. This expectation is reflected in societal norms and international laws such as the 1951 Convention Relating to the

Status of Refugees, which denies the possibility of asylum to war criminals. John Harrison Surratt was suspected of a grave crime and yet he was aided nonetheless by people who had sufficient power and connections to do so. His innocence was highly suspect, even among some of his supporters, and yet he was helped. This stands in stark contrast to the ways in which discussions about sanctuary for migrants across North America in the present take place in the present, characterized by a political environment where people are seen as guilty of something, anything, simply for moving. It draws further attention to the power structures that make it simultaneously difficult and necessary to offer refuge in the present. It also explains, in part, why people are willing to make public declarations about sanctuary to obtain support and assistance. I still see this as deeply problematic but exploring the ways in which networked support played a crucial role in facilitating sanctuary helps explain the sense of urgency and the desire for broad-based support that animates many of these contemporary practices. There is a great deal that people must overcome in the search for refuge in the present.

Given that this book is organized chronologically, I always suspected that the 1930s would have something interesting to say about sanctuary because of the Great Depression and the ways in which economic precarity became so pronounced in the early part of the decade. There was no obvious entry point, however. None of the newspaper research students and I had undertaken indicated any instances of church sanctuary, partly because mediatized and public-facing sanctuary didn't begin to appear until the 1970s and only became a significant phenomenon in the 1980s. And yet, I couldn't help but sense that in an epoch when many people were mobile as they searched for economic security, there must be something particular to the idea of sanctuary in the city in this period.

In the end, I chose to focus on anarchist Emma Goldman's time in Montreal/Mooniyaang/Tiohtià:ke during the 1930s. I am not sure when I first realized that she had spent a significant period of her time in exile there, but the more I read about and by her, the more I wanted to understand the significance of her time in the city as part of a larger history of sanctuary.

Exiled from the United States in 1919, Goldman's situation was far from what people think of when they think of sanctuary, and she would have chafed at the idea of sanctuary as it manifests today, with its dependence on charity (often religious charity) and with the ultimate goal of having approbation from the state. This was something two of the peer reviewers observed, wondering if her story even had a place in this book. I spent weeks thinking about this, but I couldn't let her story go. I was hooked, and I doubled down. As a result, Goldman's exiled time in Montreal/Mooniyaang/Tiohtià:ke became all the more important as I picked, probed, and prodded, trying to figure out what Sanctuary in Pieces *was really all about. My struggle with this chapter was reflected in the many names I came up with for it: The Exiled City, then The Sheltering City, and finally, The Hostile City. In the end, the name was as straightforward as I could make it: the city was basically a hostile place for Goldman and thousands of others during the Great Depression.*

Despite the hostility she experienced, Goldman used and sometimes favoured Montreal/Mooniyaang/Tiohtià:ke as a site of exile in the 1930s in large part because of its proximity to friends, family, and lovers in the United States. This meant that Goldman never really understood the city and never engaged with the immediate plight of those around her. This would have been interesting in and of itself, but the problem with Goldman's remove is that writing only about her distance, and, in some ways, her antipathy keeps the city itself at a remove. Preserved. Under glass. And the city of Montreal/Mooniyaang/Tiohtià:ke was not still or frozen during the 1930s, far from it (even if Goldman saw things very differently).

I wrestled with how to capture this twin dynamic: the foment of Montreal/Mooniyaang/Tiohtià:ke, where thousands were unemployed, in contrast to the perceptions of a fierce, struggling, anarchist woman who disdained much of her time in the city. Goldman struggled economically throughout the 1930s, as did many people, including single and married women who shared in the economic burden of the period and sometimes carried an additional weight because of the gendered relief policies advanced by charities and various levels of government. This shared economic struggle and its gendered nature encouraged me to pair locally based efforts with Goldman's anarchist worldviews. I wanted to capture how women in the city thought about relief in this period, and I ultimately turned to Yvonne Maisonneuve's efforts with what is now known as Le Chaînon to do so.

Originally known as the Foyer Saint-Viateur and then L'Institut Notre-Dame-de-la-Protection, Le Chaînon is one of the oldest women's shelters in the city, dating its establishment to 1932. It struggled to gain a foothold in the city throughout the 1930s, even as its very raîson d'être was largely a product of this period. In exploring the organization's early history, I couldn't help but see parallels between Goldman's struggles in the city and Maisonneuve's, as the latter laboured to find funds to support the young women and girls who sought assistance in the shelter that she oversaw.

A deeply devout Catholic, Maisonneuve could not have been intellectually and spiritually more unlike Goldman. She had an entirely different sense of the city in this period and of what was possible in terms of solutions. And while Goldman's massive correspondence gives some insights into her time in Montreal/Mooniyaang/Tiohtià:ke (correspondence I was able to access digitally during months of pandemic lockdowns thanks only to the generosity and assistance of historian Mikhail Bjorge), Maisonneuve's written record is sparser. Fortunately, historian Annick Desmarais offered last-minute assistance in the early part of winter 2023 to help me better understand Maisonneuve and her work. Kevin Ledo's image of the mural he painted of Yvonne Maisonneuve further helped amplify the documentary record.

Still, the archival record, as such, is a study in contrasts, as was the women's time in Montreal/Mooniyaang/Tiohtià:ke. I am not sure if Maisonneuve and Goldman ever met. I like to think they might have at least passed on the streets of the city, although Goldman gives no sense of walking the city in any of her correspondence. She wrote and lectured, but the spaces of movement and mobility in between aren't mentioned. Maisonneuve, by contrast, roamed the streets in search of funds, furniture, and food. Perhaps somewhat ironically, I first encountered Yvonne Maisonneuve's name as I passed a park named after her on my way to and from work in the early 2000s (a reminder of the importance of public history for making stories known).

"The Hostile City" is about the ways in which people of diverse backgrounds, including local and foreign-born, found a hostile city in the age of economic and political turmoil. It also highlights a key commonality, namely the gendered ways in which precarity and solutions have been understood historically. "The Hostile City" also serves as a hinge chapter, swinging between the major themes of this book, namely community and legal protection and the way they began to intersect in more immediate ways over the course of the twentieth century. It moves from the focus on community and networked protections, or the lack thereof (highlighted in previous chapters), to the beginning of legal protections that were organized through various forms of immigration status and refugee determination processes that are detailed in the later chapters. In the process, it offers a glimpse into the making and receiving of sanctuary for women in Montreal/Mooniyaang/Tiohtià:ke throughout the challenging years of the Great Depression.

December 2023

The Hostile City

IN THE SPRING OF 1932, young women began to pass through the doors of the third floor at 366 Fairmount Street, the location of a rather inconspicuous building in the shadow of Mont-Royal, an urban mountain that dominates the geography of Montreal/Mooniyaang/Tiohtià:ke. They were seeking refuge offered by a group of society women under the umbrella of the Comité Secours aux Chômeuses à Collet Blanc (The Rescue Committee for Unemployed White-Collar Women Workers).[1] The ravages of the Great Depression were being felt throughout the city and the needs of girls and young women were of particular concern. The worry was that if they were not protected, some might turn to prostitution to provide for themselves and their families.[2] Yvonne Maisonneuve, a French Canadian woman and a "spinster" at the age of twenty-nine, was tapped by committee members to manage this makeshift shelter.[3] She worked desperately hard to make the committee's vision, and her own, a reality, sharing in the poverty of the many women the organization sought to assist.

These modest origins of what was known as "Foyer Saint-Viateur" led Yvonne Maisonneuve to establish L'Institut Notre-Dame-de-la-Protection in 1933, which would eventually be renamed Le Chaînon in 1978. Le Chaînon means "link" in French, suggesting a kind of bridge or connection. The organization is still active today, making it one of the oldest women's shelters in the city. From its origins as a refuge for the unemployed and unhoused, its efforts expanded over the years to include unwed mothers and their babies, as well as new arrivals to the city. Girls as young as seven stayed at the shelter on some occasions.[4] Throughout the 1930s and beyond, the organization expanded its cadre of volunteers and workers, with new "associates" coming on board to assist. These women took secular vows of service instead of religious ones, but their work was very much undertaken in the same vein.

Protection and charity were woven throughout the organization's early work. This was also the case for many of the activities undertaken by religious entities and community organizations in this same period. These efforts were intended to make up for the inadequate responses by municipal, provincial, and federal authorities who largely relied on existing infrastructure to offer support to people during the straining, anxious years of the Great Depression.[5] The city lived and breathed the economic turmoil of the 1930s, expanding and collapsing like a pair of lungs.

Into this urban mix moved the famed anarchist Emma Goldman, who had been exiled from the United States since 1919. A dedicated activist and public intellectual, Goldman was destabilized by the experience of exile. Describing herself as a "woman without a country," Goldman recognized that "to have a country implies ... the possession of a certain guarantee of security, the assurance of having some spot you can call your own and that no one can alienate that from you."[6] She found no such place in exile. As a result, Goldman spent decades abroad in search of security, community, and refuge until her death in Toronto/Tkaronto in 1940. It was often a discouraging existence, leading friends such as publisher Joseph Ishill to wish for Goldman "a place of sanctuary, the inviolate home where you could rest and be at ease."[7]

In exile, Emma Goldman spent a considerable amount of time in Montreal/Mooniyaang/Tiohtià:ke in 1926 and 1928, and again for intermittent but extended periods from 1933 to 1935, and once more in 1939. These later years were particularly difficult. Increasingly out of step with her anarchist colleagues, Goldman found herself buffeted by the same economic circumstances and political oppression that confronted her neighbours in Montreal/Mooniyaang/Tiohtià:ke and elsewhere. Yet her experience was also distinct as a result of her transnational anarchist connections, and because of the nature of her relationship, or the lack thereof, with Montreal/Mooniyaang/Tiohtià:ke. The city had no claim on her, and she had no claim on it. Rather, throughout the 1930s, Goldman lived and worked in the city but proved uninterested in engaging with the fate of the majority working-class French Canadians, or the anti-Semitism and fascism in her immediate surroundings. She kept her attention perpetually on events elsewhere.[8] She was also more concerned with advocating for radical change to disrupt the "intricate machinery of the industrial system," rather than the question of immediate relief for the unemployed.[9] This stood in stark contrast to the efforts of Yvonne Maisonneuve, who was deeply invested in the city and the many neighbourhoods where L'Institut Notre-Dame-de-la-Protection established itself over the years.

In bringing the early history of L'Institut Notre-Dame-de-la-Protection, the work of Yvonne Maisonneuve, and Emma Goldman's time in exile into a single narrative frame, we can better understand the diverse, gendered experience of women involved in the provision and seeking of refuge in this period. Yvonne Maisonneuve's efforts reveal the hopes and ambitions of a devout French Canadian Catholic who understood an urgent need among young women and girls for shelter and support in the early years of the Great Depression. She immersed herself in relief work and the welfare of women and girls, regardless of whether they were newly arrived or long-term residents of the city. By contrast, Emma Goldman's time in the city reveals the perspectives of a brilliant, radical intellectual who was perpetually preoccupied with events and people elsewhere and who only ever experienced Montreal/Mooniyaang/Tiohtià:ke superficially as a site where resources could be gathered and connections could be nurtured or renewed, but rarely made.

Together, Yvonne Maisonneuve and Emma Goldman offer a surprising portrait of the diverse ways that women experienced need and created refuge in the economically and politically turbulent years of the 1930s. It is a study in contrasts, but also connections, especially in terms of the gendered experience of precarity at a time when the need for sanctuary was structurally driven, born of both economic and political oppression. Underscoring the nature of Maisonneuve's efforts alongside Goldman's makes it possible to see how their energies and experiences were bound up and shaped by a larger landscape of precarity. Too often, migrants and refugees and their search for economic or political security are positioned as distinct – or entirely removed – from the communities from which they seek shelter when, in fact, there are many points of intersection.

Generally, the young women and girls at L'Institut Notre-Dame-de-la-Protection found the city hostile and were grateful for the community and guidance they found with "Mère Yvonne" (Mother Yvonne). Emma Goldman would also come to find the city a rather hostile place to be. The global rise of fascism and political repression throughout the 1930s exacerbated the tenuous position that Goldman had long occupied as a leading critic of state oppression and advocate for freedom of thought and expression. The 1937 Act to Protect the Province Against Communistic Propaganda inhibited her capacity to speak and disseminate anarchist literature in Quebec, further troubling Montreal/Mooniyaang/Tiohtià:ke as a site of exile. Yet, Goldman continued to labour regardless, just as Yvonne Maisonneuve sought to advance her efforts to provide refuge and protect young women and girls in the city.

The mix of needs, along with the charged tensions of this period, provides an opportunity to connect the experiences of citizens and non-citizens within a single urban context and explore the hostile nature of 1930s Montreal/Mooniyaang/Tiohtià:ke. The ways in which Yvonne Maisonneuve and Emma Goldman moved through the world and imagined their lives and commitments is also an invitation to rethink the substance of sanctuary in this period. Maisonneuve and Goldman forged refuge on their own terms, complicating conventional notions of sanctuary and blurring the citizen/non-citizen divide that animates many contemporary discussions of these practices. The work to which Maisonneuve and Goldman dedicated themselves was simultaneously a product of their immediate circumstances and a response to it. Refuge shaped their efforts, just as they shaped the character of refuge for themselves and others.

L'Institut Notre-Dame-de-la-Protection

In 1929, the population of Montreal/Mooniyaang/Tiohtià:ke was approximately 850,000 people. Within three years, there were an estimated 906,000 people in the city, a shift that was largely the result of migration from the surrounding agricultural areas as well as an influx of migrants from across the country who hopped on the trains and made their way to "Canada's Metropolis" in the hopes of finding employment.[10] Instead of employment, however, they encountered barriers that prevented them from accessing work and relief because of their lack of residency status in the city.

Just as nation-states have done historically, municipalities have used differences in status, such as residency, to limit responsibility for care and protection, especially during periods of economic duress.[11] Most recently, new arrivals were blamed for straining the shelter system in New York/Manaháhtaan as well as Toronto/Tkaronto over the course of 2022 and 2023. In the case of New York/Manaháhtaan, the edges of the "right to shelter" that had governed the city's approach to the unhoused since 1987 began to erode in the face of thousands of new arrivals, some of whom were deliberately bused to the area by Republican governors in the states of Florida and Texas who were determined to move the issue of border control into other parts of the country. Overwhelmed, city staff in New York/Manaháhtaan responded by introducing a thirty-day limit on beds for single men, requiring them to reapply for shelter upon the expiry of this timeframe. This approach was reminiscent of efforts during the 1930s when many urban centres in the United States and Canada dissuaded potential applicants for relief by creating barriers to shelter and actively encouraging their participation in "back to the land" colonization schemes, which would have removed people from any urban considerations.[12]

In the 1930s, Montreal/Mooniyaang/Tiohtià:ke became a destination for many unemployed workers in Canada because of the numerous corporate headquarters in the city and the major train lines that could shuttle people there.[13] Residents from local communities and rural areas also sought what economic gains they could in the city. Angela Morris, of Kahnawà:ke, recalled of these years: "During the depression people used to help each other ... People also traded what they had a lot of for something else. I used to sew for people and sometimes they would pay me in beans. No one had money then to pay with cash so we settled for food and other things that we needed. A lot of women did beadwork and went to Atwater Market to sell. These are some of the ways that we kept ourselves from starving."[14]

At the height of the economic crisis in Montreal/Mooniyaang/Tiohtià:ke, there was a 27 per cent unemployment rate in the city, and about

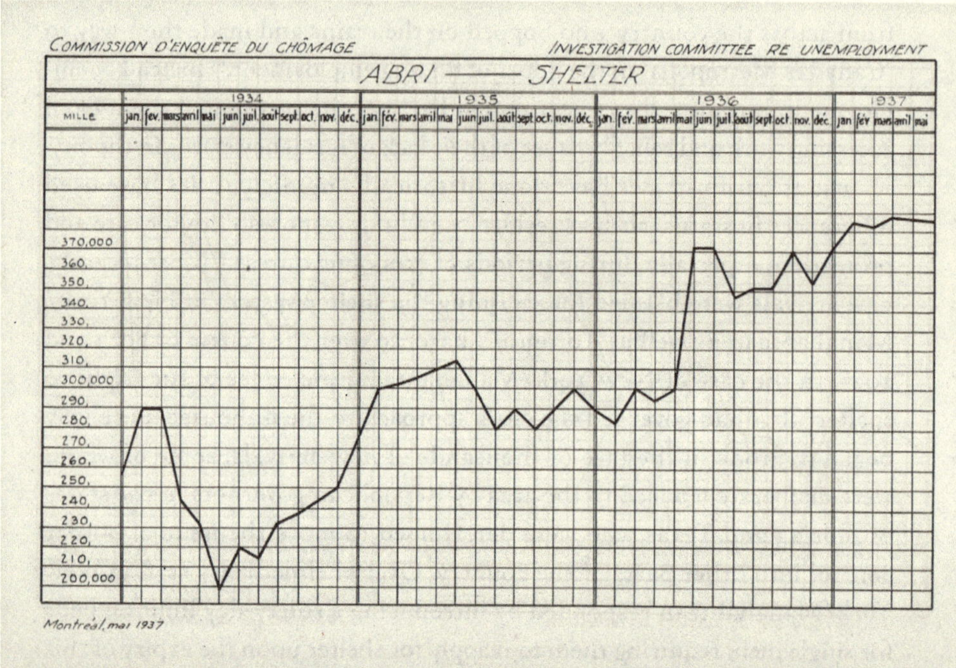

3.1 A 1937 graph showing the housing situation in Montreal/Mooniyaang/Tiohtià:ke.

33 per cent of the population was relying on some kind of relief.[15] Efforts to mitigate the brutal effects of the swirling economy were rather piecemeal, embodied in Mayor Camillien Houde's penchant for personalized largesse.[16] Accepting relief also carried considerable stigma and exposed people to additional control and regulation by state authorities – including obligations to produce identity cards, to report, and to account for their efforts in finding employment or undertaking relief projects.[17] Statistics from the city's Unemployment Relief Commission in 1937 show a stark rise in the housing challenges that many urban residents faced. These difficulties persisted even as the economic and employment situation in the city improved.

Those who were already in economically precarious situations were especially hard hit by the financial downturn. Novelist Gabrielle Roy captures some of this tumult in her famous novel *The Tin Flute,* about life in the working-class neighbourhood of St-Henri in these years. Giving soul to statistics, *The Tin Flute* conveys the story of one family's declining welfare, exemplified by the deterioration in their living conditions over the course of the decade to the point that they ended up at the very bottom of the city (socially and geographically), in a shack by the railroad tracks, where the windows of their home, like their spirits, were darkened by the coal exhaust of the passing trains. The protagonist, Rose Anna, whose family is forced from one poor living condition to another, sees a newspaper headline about the situation in Europe that reads "Refugees on the March" and thinks "just like us ... Always on the march."[18]

Municipal, provincial, and federal efforts were largely inadequate, relying heavily on existing infrastructure to provide relief. Moreover, they carried the ancillary objective of discouraging demands and responsibilities for assistance. For instance, throughout the 1930s, the Unemployment Relief Commission in Montreal/Mooniyaang/Tiohtià:ke instituted rolling cut-off dates to ensure that new arrivals would not have access to municipal relief efforts.[19] The last thing the city wanted was to encourage migration through seemingly generous welfare support.

Relief programs in the city privileged male workers, meaning that women – even longtime residents of the city – were regularly disadvantaged. This was most noticeable for single women and those who were divorced, though it was also evident in discussions of "women's work" and the question of whether such employment took opportunities away from their male counterparts. Expert reports eventually concluded that the "material requirements of modern living" were burdensome on family budgets and that a father "with an average salary is necessarily obligated to obtain the help of his daughters."[20] The "work of women," including single, young women, was, therefore, to be tolerated if it supported family life.

The search for relief took place at multiple scales in this period. For those who were economically marginalized, including people who already operated with a sense of "secondary status," the need for self-reliance became paramount.[21] Community organizations, such as Chinese clan associations and the Coloured Women's Club of Montreal, attempted to alleviate some of the most severe effects of the Great Depression. The Coloured Women's Club organized a soup kitchen and continued to maintain beds at the Grace Dart Hospital (something members had undertaken since the influenza outbreak following the First World War).[22] Charles Este, minister at the Union United Church, gave out food vouchers and regularly signed paperwork to assist members of the congregation in obtaining municipal relief.[23] In the Jewish community, people were helped by the Baron de Hirsch Institute's Employment Department. This communal support was much needed as they also confronted the challenge of anti-Semitic economic campaigns such as the "Achetez chez nous! Buy from us!" slogan introduced by French Canadian and English Canadian merchants.[24] As noted previously, Yvonne Maisonneuve and L'Institut Notre-Dame-de-la-Protection provided free shelter to unemployed and homeless women regardless of religious faith, though they tended to serve mostly French Catholic women.

The creation of L'Institut Notre-Dame-de-la-Protection marked a rare instance of dedicated refuge for a diversity of women in the city of Montreal/Mooniyaang/Tiohtià:ke.[25] Prior to this period, there had only ever been sporadic efforts for designated groups such as women workers moving to the city from agricultural areas or for victims of prostitution. The Refuge de la Passion, which was opened by the Sulpicians in 1861, is an early example of this approach. In 1874, the Young Women's Christian Association also began to provide support to working-class women in the city, especially those who moved from nearby farming communities to find employment. Beginning in 1864, with the establishment of the Magdalen Asylum and the Female Home four years later, there were dedicated spaces in the city for former prostitutes. Ten years later, the Protestant Home for Friendless Women was created to provide for those suffering from alcohol abuse, and for former prostitutes and prisoners. The Society for the Protection of Women and Children was established in 1883 to aid victims of domestic violence, and in 1886, the Women's Christian Temperance Union opened the Female Home for homeless women. Five years later, the Salvation Army introduced an Industrial Home for both men and women.[26] As such, charitable relief efforts in Montreal/Mooniyaang/ Tiohtià:ke grew over the years, largely bound up with the perceived ills of a rapidly urbanizing and industrializing city and always with the needs of particular groups in mind. The Great Depression exacerbated these dynamics while also inspiring broader gender-based organizing in the city.[27]

Historians of L'Institut Notre-Dame-de-la-Protection, and especially of its founder Yvonne Maisonneuve, who headed the organization for thirty-three years, celebrate the dedication with which she undertook this work, noting that in the early years, "son seul salaire sera celui de la joie de server."[28] Born in 1903, Maisonneuve grew up in an established household with a devoted, educated mother and a blacksmith father "with true Christian convictions."[29] Throughout her life, she evinced a strong sense of responsibility and service, perhaps due to the family responsibilities she undertook at the age of eleven after her mother died. As Maisonneuve wrote, her mother's passing left "an atmosphere of sadness that penetrated her very being and which she never fully got rid of."[30] She found considerable relief when she went to board with the Sisters of the Congregation just north of the city, as well as in her subsequent work with L'Institut Notre-Dame-de-la-Protection.

The initial goal of the Comité Secours aux Chômeuses à Collet Blanc, which first dreamed up the "Foyer Saint-Viateur," was to simply provide free shelter. Members had previously made direct donations to individual beneficiaries so that they could pay for housing, but when the economic crisis hit in the early 1930s, safe and affordable housing became more scarce. As a result, women could often only find rooms in worrying situations, including "houses of prostitution" where they were "exposed to the worst dangers!"[31] Some of the women ended up at the Miséricorde (a hospital for those who were pregnant and unwed) because they had only been able to find housing in "des maisons louches."[32] The solution the committee envisioned was a home for young women and girls, and through Helene Lemoyne (one of the committee's members), Maisonneuve was tapped for the task of supervising this work. She was intrigued by the invitation, though hesitant. Maisonneuve saw her calling more with the aged, the very young, or in the poorhouses.[33] Moreover, her father was vocally opposed. Revealing a rather conventional outlook where motherhood and marriage were normalized, he was angry that she was unwilling to get married and did not like the idea of her living in a home with other women, seeing it as contrary to societal expectations for a woman of Maisonneuve's standing.[34] Despite the lack of support from her family, Maisonneuve agreed to take on the work of managing the shelter.

In entrusting Yvonne Maisonneuve with their vision, the society women chose someone with a deep religious commitment and a seemingly unwavering faith in God's will.[35] Indeed, Maisonneuve appeared to have found her vocation with the Foyer St-Viateur and later Notre-Dame-de-la Protection, and invested a great deal of herself in making sure that the shelter in its various incarnations would survive. Maisonneuve was devoted in particular to the young women and girls for whom she considered herself responsible. Unfortunately, the available archival record reveals very little about who these women were, though Maisonneuve says that "Il y en avait de toutes sortes, ruinées, abandonnées, dégoutées de la vie."[36] Many were newly arrived from nearby farming areas and had moved to the city in search of employment in its many manufacturing industries.[37] In recalling how difficult the early years were, Maisonneuve insisted that all the hard work, including the humiliating scavenging, did not bother her. What she was interested in, were the young women and girls who came to the shelter: "je les aimais : je les voyais revenir au bon Dieu tranquillement; et quand je voyais un pauvre sourire sur leur visage, pensez-vous que les charges que je portais, et les bêtises que je recevais, me fatiguaient beaucoup?"[38]

Reflecting the strains of this period, the organization moved many times over the course of the 1930s, always searching for greater physical and economic security. The first edition of the shelter on Fairmount Avenue was small and modest. As Maisonneuve recalled, there were eight rooms, and a single mattress on the floor awaited her when she first arrived. A few committee members showed up with some modest furnishings a few days later and more beds, which were much needed. Adèle Roy was the first girl to appear at the Foyer St-Viateur. She had initially taken shelter with L'Aide à la Femme, which was also starting to organize help in this period. Roy was disdainful of her situation and the proffered charity, saying at once that she was tired of being eaten by bedbugs while simultaneously emphasizing that she didn't want to start over again.[39] Maisonneuve entreated her with food. She had scavenged a chicken and "différentes petites choses" (other little things) and promised her that with this, they would be able to celebrate a kind of Christmas.[40] Several young women and girls followed and soon Maisonneuve was living among five or six others in "la plus grande promiscuité" (the "most cramped conditions") where "je faisais pratiquement toute la besogne" (she did "practically all the work.")[41]

From its original location as the Foyer Saint-Viateur, the shelter moved a few doors down to 384 Fairmount Ouest in 1933. There, it became known as Notre-Dame-de-la-Protection after it was decided that Saint-Viateur was too lofty a figure for their enterprise.[42] The shelter moved several times over the next few years, relocating from 384 Fairmount Avenue in 1934 to the second floor of a small building on Visitation Street (near the intersection with Dorchester Boulevard, what is now known as René Lévesque Boulevard) where rent was a mere $90.00 for the year. It was a building that required considerable repair, and Maisonneuve and the women and girls in the shelter at the time washed cracked walls, painted, replaced carpets, and did all kinds of handiwork. About fifteen girls lived among the eight rooms at any given time.[43] They then relocated to a site within the St-Louis-de-France Parish before moving to the plateau neighbourhood in 1935 (where the shelter remained for five years).[44]

This movement reflected the same kind of instability that prompted considerable mobility in this period, including Emma Goldman's shifting sites of exile. However, whereas Goldman felt buffeted by the fickle operation of state power, Maisonneuve believed that everything was the result of Providence.[45] In her unpublished autobiography, she wrote, "Nous cherchions quand même dans différents quartiers de la ville : nous n'étions pas stables; nous étions des pauvres; nous nous fiions à la Providence, ballottées ici et là sur ses ailes; pouvions-nous craindre quoi que ce soit, ainsi dirigées par le bon Dieu? Alors, c'est de cette façon de tout marchait!"[46] Maisonneuve understood the organization's impoverished conditions as a form of solidarity with those it was trying to help, especially in terms of the immediate neighbourhoods where the shelter was variously based. About the original location, she later said, "nous étions dépaysées avec une oeuvre de pauvre que l'on prisait plus au moins."[47] When they moved downtown, she found that the neighbourhood "cadrait plus avec notre oeuvre; la classe ouvrière, du bon monde pieux, puis les Pères Oblats qui cultivaient la dévotion dans leur paroisse."[48]

In her own way, Maisonneuve, like Goldman, worked against or at least outside many of the existing social structures and norms, refusing to seek financial support from municipal or provincial authorities, chafing against the perceived bureaucracy and control that would result. As much as Maisonneuve would have liked the additional funding, she remained principled about the need for freedom of action in her work.[49] She sought, instead, to manage L'Institut Notre-Dame-de-la-Protection on the basis of private gifts and fundraising efforts alone.[50] Advertisements regularly appeared in *Le Devoir* and other newspapers for card games to raise funds to "protect young girls at the very moment when danger menaced after they found themselves without work and without money."[51] It was largely inadequate in terms of fundraising but it afforded Maisonneuve the freedom she sought to pursue relief work on her own terms. Only in later years would the organization receive more institutionalized support.

L'Institut Notre-Dame-de-la-Protection was nominally secular, but it was nevertheless informed by Catholic teachings and moral coding, and by a strong sense of rescue. Its efforts were, therefore, appreciated and supported by local parish priests who regularly referred young women to its care. It was also encouraged by the St-Jean-Baptiste Society and lawyers such as Arthur Laramée who were involved with the criminal justice system and could see the impacts of the housing shortage on the people they worked with.[52] Yet, despite this support, as well as Maisonneuve's own's efforts, the early days of L'Institut Notre-Dame-de-la Protection's existence were "extremely difficult."[53] Maisonneuve worked and foraged for everything – food, furniture, and money to pay bills. Faced with unending challenges, Maisonneuve innovated. Desperate for soap, she made her own. At the market, where requests for donations were rebuffed (often with the rejoinder that the shopkeeper was already donating food to the religious orders), Maisonneuve begged for bits of carrots and cabbage that had fallen to the ground. She was able to fill bags and bags this way, making sure that the people residing at the shelter at any given time were fed, if not nourished.[54]

Within its first eight years of operation, L'Institut Notre-Dame-de-la-Protection hosted 3,007 women, a period that was arguably the most difficult in terms of the economic crisis that was ravaging Montreal/Mooniyaang/Tiohtià:ke.[55] By 1940, the city's finances were in such disarray that it was put into receivership for four years. The society women who had first imagined a shelter for young girls and women had clearly identified a need, and Maisonneuve worked hard to fulfill it, seeing the shelter's work expand in size and scope over the years. A great deal of effort took place on the ground in these years in the face of an inadequate public response by various levels of government. These efforts were recognized by those who benefited directly from charitable support even as they struggled to establish or re-establish themselves in the city. Others, such as the famous anarchist Emma Goldman, who lived in Montreal/Mooniyaang/Tiohtià:ke for extended periods during this difficult time, struggled on their own terms. In Goldman's case, she fought for financial survival all the while condemning what she perceived to be the total failure of imagination among those around her. She was oblivious to all that Yvonne Maisonneuve and the associates at L'Institut Notre-Dame-de-la-Protection were undertaking, and she likely would have been critical of their willingness to accept the parameters of the societal structures in which they lived, working to improve them rather than call for their destruction.

Emma Goldman in Montreal/Mooniyaang/Tiohtià:ke

Emma Goldman was one of the leading anarchists of her generation. Born in Kovno (present-day Kaunas, Lithuania) in 1869, Goldman migrated to the United States at the age of sixteen. The labour organizing of the 1880s and the execution of the Haymarket martyrs in 1886 (all events that occurred before Yvonne Maisonneuve was even born) aroused Goldman's interest in politics as well as her passion for justice. She became a leading public intellectual and a deeply polarizing figure, both within the anarchist movement and beyond.[56]

Deported from the United States to Russia in 1919, Goldman was "unmoored" by her experience of exile, something scholar Kathy Ferguson describes as an "enduring loss."[57] The great cultural critic Edward Said, born in British mandate Palestine, conjured the "utter loneliness of exile" as a deeply pervasive condition. Reflecting on his own trajectory, Said concluded there was "nothing more painful and paradoxically sought after" than "the many displacements from countries, cities, abodes, languages, (and) environments" that kept him "in motion."[58] This was Goldman's experience as well, especially in her later years where the toll of being away from family, friends, and lovers in the United States was profound. Goldman foreshadowed Said's later sense of exile being "a condition of terminal loss" with "something left behind forever."[59] Much of Goldman's time in exile was spent hungering for the United States, even as she worked for an anarchist future, evoking historian Walter Benjamin's "angel of history" who looks back on the wreckage of the past as a "storm irresistibly propels him into the future."[60]

Emma Goldman spent twenty-one of her seventy years and most of her mature anarchist career in exile. Much of this time was spent in Saint-Tropez, France (where Peggy Guggenheim had gifted her a small cottage in 1936), England, and Canada, with several months in Spain in 1937. To some contemporaries and scholars, Goldman "seemed to personify the uprootedness of an entire generation of political refugees."[61] Goldman came closest to channeling this in her own work with her 1934 essay "The Tragedy of Political Exiles," which distilled the particular experience of political persecution amidst the economic turmoil of the interwar period.[62] While she insisted that her own "struggle to survive was hardly worth mentioning," she foreshadowed political philosopher Hannah Arendt's compelling analysis of refugees as people who had lost the right to have rights, describing the world as a "huge penitentiary" for political refugees.[63]

Goldman further emphasized the general precarity of political exiles even after settlement, noting that they were "sometimes lucky enough to find an abode, but that by no means includes the right to work. Anything they do to eke out a wretched existence, such as lessons, translations, or any kind of physical labor, must be done furtively. Should they be caught, it would again mean the wearisome round of seeking another country."[64] Although Goldman attempted to distinguish her situation from that of the political exiles she was discussing, some of her lived experiences were, nevertheless, reflected in her writing. She observed that before exile, radicals "lived, dreamed, and labored incessantly for the liberation of their native lands." In exile, however, work was no longer "a salvation."[65] In some ways, it was just work, and in Goldman's case, it was coated with layers of anxiety about material circumstances throughout the 1920s and 1930s, worries that were further exacerbated with the onset of the Great Depression.

In exile, Emma Goldman relied on the generosity of supporters (which she refused to call charity, emphasizing all her labour instead) and income from her lectures and publications to survive. All her work, therefore, including the two-part publication *My Disillusionment in Russia* (1923) and *My Further Disillusionment in Russia* (1925); her two-volume memoir, *Living My Life* (1931 and 1934); and hundreds of articles had the dual purpose of advancing anarchist efforts and ensuring her material survival. Comrades later criticized her for selling articles to the *Nation* and other liberal magazines. Goldman herself struggled with the ethics of writing commercially; however, the funds were much needed.[66] As she would later insist, "In my long public life I have raised tens and thousands of dollars for all kinds of causes and for all kinds of people. But for myself, personally, it has always been desperately hard."[67]

Goldman lived in Montreal/Mooniyaang/Tiohtià:ke for extended periods in 1926, 1928, from 1933 to 1935, and again in 1939, splitting her time in Canada between Montreal/Mooniyaang/Tiohtià:ke and Toronto/Tkaronto. During the 1930s, Goldman shared the need for shelter and financial security with many of those around her although she never thought of herself as personally needing refuge. She had obtained legal protection in the form of British subjecthood by marrying James Colton (a Welsh coalminer) in 1925. Her concerns were, therefore, both more material and abstract than people who did not have legal protections, such as her longtime comrade Alexander Berkman (who relied on the Nansen Passport for stateless people to remain a resident of France). The only time Goldman used the term *sanctuary* was in discussions of the needs of refugees from the Spanish Civil War in 1938 and 1939.[68] Rather than as sites of sanctuary, Goldman was drawn to Montreal/Mooniyaang/Tiohtià:ke and Toronto/Tkaronto largely because they had the benefit of being close to the United States where she desperately wanted to be. The idea was that if she couldn't get to the United States, then at least friends, family members, and lovers could come to her. Once in Montreal/Mooniyaang/Tiohtià:ke and Toronto/Tkaronto, however, Goldman needed to live, and it is here that the connections between material security and refuge, beyond legal protections and social connections, became more pronounced.

In Montreal/Mooniyaang/Tiohtià:ke, Goldman was supported by the small Jewish anarchist community, one that was at once rooted in the politics of place while also maintaining a broadly transnational outlook. As a port city, Montreal/Mooniyaang/Tiohtià:ke had been an important site of refuge for Jewish migrants arriving in the wake of political and economic persecution in Russia in the late 1800s.[69] It was such a magnet that when the numbers of people arriving threatened to disrupt the workings of the local Jewish community, serious efforts were made to send people further afield, most notably to New York City/Manahátaan. Others were directed to settlements in the Canadian west after 1887, including one near Assiniboine, Manitoba, Treaty 1 Territory (traditional territory of the Métis nation) and another at Hirsch, Saskatchewan, on Treaty 4 Territory (situated on the traditional homelands of the Cree, and Saulteaux people).[70]

This community gatekeeping generally did not extend to the numerous Jewish anarchists who also settled in the city in this early period. Some came directly from Eastern Europe, while others moved from the United States. Montreal/Mooniyaang/Tiohtià:ke was soon described as a "hub of radicalism" and as a "satellite" of the activities in nearby New York City/Manahátaan.[71] In addition to a popular bookstore opened by Hirsch Hershman in 1903, there were other anarchist gathering places as well as regular lectures to attend, many of which were held at Coronation Hall, which stood at the corner of Ste-Catherine and Bishop Streets in the downtown core.[72] By 1920, however, immigration had slowed considerably, and the period of "rapid growth and colossal change" that had characterized the evolution of the Jewish community in Montreal/Mooniyaang/Tiohtià:ke in the first two decades of the twentieth century was over.[73] Subsequent decades compounded the community's vulnerability, amplifying a sense of not being quite "rooted" in the city, the province, or the country.[74]

Goldman had distanced herself from the Jewish faith early in her career, maintaining a cultural rather than a religious interest, but the small size of the anarchist community in Montreal/Mooniyaang/Tiohtià:ke meant that Jewish comrades were key to her material survival in the city. Max Zahler, Louis and Lena Shlakman, Rose Bernstein, Minna Baron, and Anna Aron all provided different forms of assistance over the years.[75] Beyond this small circle of anarchist comrades, Goldman developed a dear friendship with Rabbi Harry Stern, a pillar of the Jewish community, with whom she was very "impressed."[76] Hannaniah Meir (H.M.) Caiserman-Wital, one of the co-founders of the Canadian Jewish Congress, also became a close friend. He and his wife hosted Goldman while she was in the city, and she later referred to them as "enthusiastic Judaists" who "were proud that I was as one of their race."[77] In Montreal/Mooniyaang/Tiohtià:ke, Goldman regularly offered Yiddish lectures (with some in English and none in French), and her activities were well documented in the local Yiddish newspaper, the *Keneder Odler*.[78]

The bonds of affinity that Goldman nurtured with the Jewish community, and anarchists in particular, stood in stark contrast to her marked lack of interest and even antipathy towards the majority French Canadian population in the city.[79] Her first recorded impressions of Montreal/Mooniyaang/Tiohtià:ke during a lecture tour in 1908 was of a "city of the dark ages, priestcraft and churches."[80] It was indeed, as noted in "The Fugitive City" chapter, a city imprinted with religion. Goldman nourished her antagonistic view of the city during her time in exile, seeing Montreal/Mooniyaang/Tiohtià:ke as "essentially a French city" where "75 per cent of the million population are French body and soul, under the dominion of the Catholic Church, and as far removed from the cultural efforts and life of the English-speaking part of the city as if they lived thousands of miles away."[81] Goldman recognized the linguistic – and to some extent the class —divide in the city, noting French-speakers "never attend English lectures, in fact live separate and distinct as if they were not in the same city."[82] However, instead of empathizing with the situation of French Canadians who made up the majority of the working class or engaging with French Canadian anarchists, Goldman dismissed French Canadians outright for their perceived subservience to the Catholic Church. She accused them of being "under the thumb of the priests" just as she railed against the church itself.[83]

Goldman's approach to the circumstances of French Canadians reveals her more general removal from the immediacy of the city, most notably the anti-Semitism that was palpable from the early 1900s onward.[84] In the mid-1930s, there were attacks on Jewish businesses and anti-Jewish riots and accusations that Jewish people were making "important preparations ... for future disturbed occasions."[85] Flags with the swastika symbol "surrounded by maple leaves, with a curious beaver as its crown" were displayed in parts of the province.[86] This flag represented the Parti national social chrétien (Socialist Christian National Party). Its co-founder,

Adrien Arcand, was a "vicious anti-Semite" who once suggested that Jewish people should be deported to Hudson Bay.[87] He was not alone in his racism. Until the onset of the Second World War, "Arcand and his followers were legally tolerated and sympathetically supported" by a range of elites including the editors of *Le Devoir*, nationalist organizations such as Les Jeunes Canadiens, and Maurice Duplessis (who would be elected premier in 1936) and Abbé Lionel Groulx.[88] There was a pronounced anti-Semitic dimension to Canadian and Quebec politics in this period, which in the case of the latter had been inflamed during debates over religious education.[89] At the federal level, senior government officials sought to curb Jewish migration, and would later refuse to admit refugees fleeing Nazi Germany during the Second World War.[90] The federal government was also willing to tolerate the presence of Vichy War criminals in the country until public allegations about Count Jacques de Bernonville, assistant to the "butcher of Lyon," Klaus Barbie, and others began to appear in 1948.[91]

Yet, what is striking about Goldman's activities and correspondence in this period is how little she cared about the particular dynamics of Montreal/Mooniyaang/Tiohtià:ke, Quebec or Canada beyond the impact they had on her material existence and capacity to survive financially in exile. Goldman tended to see anti-Semitism as a fact of life, the product of a "tradition of centuries, ingrained antipathies, and what not."[92] Goldman was of the view that with most "Gentiles, when you scratch deep down to their inner being you will find an anti-Semitic streak lurking somewhere in their make-up."[93] And although the French Canadian working class might have been a useful source of insights and organizing, it is clear from Goldman's public lectures, published works, and private correspondence that she was not attentive to their situation. Rather than taking on currents of anti-Semitic thought and other local battles, Goldman used Montreal/Mooniyaang/Tiohtià:ke simply as a base where she could meet family members and friends as well as her lovers from the United States, such as Leon Malmed and Frank Heiner, with relative ease. She also used it as a site of anarchist organizing and fundraising, a place from which a legal return to the United States might be realized. Goldman's efforts were rarely directed at conditions in the city. She took shelter and material refuge in Montreal/Mooniyaang/Tiohtià:ke, but unlike Yvonne Maisonneuve, her energies were directed elsewhere.

The Precarity of Capitalism

Goldman's main goal in moving to Montreal/Mooniyaang/Tiohtià:ke from Europe in 1933 was to see if she could regain entry to the United States, something she had yearned for since her forced deportation from the country fourteen years prior. She was also financially strained, and her dire economic situation mirrored the reality of many people during the global economic downturn of the early 1930s. While she wrote, traveled, and lectured to raise funds to support herself and various anarchist causes, many others also migrated in search of economic opportunities. In North America, where farmers experienced the environmental devastation of drought and winds, which led to repeated crop failures, single men and families hopped on trains moving east and west. Large urban centres experienced an increase in poverty and strained housing conditions, compounded by the arrival of significant numbers of transient people. In California, police introduced a "bum blockade" and attempted to prevent people from entering the state.[94] As noted previously, the city council in Montreal/Mooniyaang/Tiohtià:ke also sought to deter movement by distinguishing between long-term and newly arrived residents of the city, making relief inaccessible to those who had only recently migrated. Moreover, the federal government deported those who sought relief without citizenship, meaning that the impact of being out of work could be especially profound for those without status.[95]

Emma Goldman had no idea how bad the situation was in the city before she returned after having last been there in 1928, and though she was appalled at the visible distress, she was rather muted about it publicly in contrast to previous economic downturns when she had spoken passionately to audiences about their rights as workers. In 1893, when there was considerable anarchist activity in New York City/Manahâhtaan in the face of serious economic difficulties, she caused a near-riot when she railed against the state and the church, which had "been on the side of the rich against the poor." Goldman told a large crowd in Union Square: "You, too, will have to learn that you have a right to share your neighbour's bread. Your neighbours – they have not only stolen your bread, but they are sapping your blood. They will go on robbing you, your children, and your children's children, unless you wake up, unless you become daring enough to demand your rights. Well, then, demonstrate before the palaces of the rich; demand work. If they do not give you work, demand bread. If they deny you both, take bread. It is your sacred right!"[96] Almost twenty years later, Goldman was still vocal about the plight of workers "in the throes of unemployment." The winter of 1914 marked a sharp downturn in the US economy. According to Goldman, "over a quarter of a million persons were out of work in New York/Manahåhtaan, and other cities were stricken in no lesser degree," a situation compounded by the "extraordinarily severe weather."[97] Calling up the events of 1893, Goldman charged that "nothing had changed since then. Now as then capitalism was relentless, the State crushing every individual and social right, and the Church in league with them. Now as then those daring to give voice to the suffering of the dumb multitude were persecuted and jailed, and the masses too seemed to have remained as ever in their submissive helplessness."[98]

By contrast, in the early 1930s, Goldman's personal circumstances seem to have inhibited such provocative discourses. Her own financial situation was strained as people had less money for lecture subscriptions, publications, and donations. When Goldman voyaged to Canada in the late fall of 1933, she did so out of despair rather than with a powerful, radical voice. She was still committed to the anarchist cause, but her personal preoccupations in terms of finances and the possibility of returning to the United States were more pressing.

Friends and supporters, including Roger Baldwin of the American Civil Liberties Union and Mable Carver Crouch, a political activist, had been lobbying the US government for months on Goldman's behalf, and she was finally permitted entry for a few short weeks in the spring of 1934.[99] Emma Goldman returned from the United States three months later, claiming an "excruciating pain" at having to leave the country again just when, as she said, there was "an awakening among native born men and women."[100] She described it as being a thousand times more bitter than her departure fifteen years prior. Goldman had been reminded of what it felt like and what it meant to be surrounded by family, friends, and lovers, and too soon, she was wrenched away again. She returned to Montreal/Mooniyaang/Tiohtià:ke for a short time and immediately organized English and Yiddish meetings in addition to holding many newspaper interviews, including on this rare occasion with the French press.[101] It is possible that Yvonne Maisonneuve would have read about Goldman's recent trip to the United States, though she was probably preoccupied with one of the many relocations of Notre-Dame-de-la-Protection in this period and it is very likely that she did not.

Goldman's lectures on Hitler and Nazism, "The Collapse of German Culture," and her autobiography were well received by audiences, though there was little in the way of substantive action or financial uptake in response.[102] Part of this muted response may have stemmed from Goldman's own conflicting views about key issues in this period, most notably the rise of fascism in Germany. She abhorred what was happening under Hitler but also vehemently opposed "national wars", which she disparaged as "capitalist rivalries between essentially similar states."[103] At the same time, she was concerned about the bourgeois inclinations of her Jewish audiences and comrades in Montreal/Mooniyaang/Tiohtià:ke and the general lack of engagement with the situation in Europe.[104] Goldman also differed in opinion from those who sought a Jewish homeland in Palestine. She was fundamentally opposed to the idea of a Jewish state, insisting in 1934 that "the final emancipation of the Jew lies only in an international movement such as anarchism ... Nationalism of any kind is not the answer to the Jewish question."[105] Her disdain for the nation-state as a political solution endured throughout her anarchist career.

Goldman left Montreal/Mooniyaang/Tiohtià:ke for Toronto/Tkaronto in relatively high spirits, though her mood clouded in November 1934 when she returned to much smaller audiences, pointing to the overarching importance of material considerations for Goldman in this period. By this time, she was financially strained to the point where almost all the proceeds from fundraising lectures were going to support her living costs as opposed to anarchist causes. The cost of living in the city was expensive as she opted to stay in a hotel. She claimed there was no one in the city she "would care to stay with except the Bernsteins" and they did not have "enough rooms" and "lived too far."[106] Goldman seems to have cooled on her relations with Max Zahler and Shlakmans, with whom she had resided previously. For instance, she accused Max Zahler of being too absorbed in his grocery store chain and complained of his poor efforts in organizing lectures.[107] Goldman

3.2 1935 Tupper Street where Emma Goldman lived over the course of 1934–45.

had long felt there was insufficient depth to the anarchist movement in the city, and she became even more ruthless in her assessments in this period. She declared that "we have no comrades in Montreal. There are a few stodgy couples who for some unknown reason call themselves anarchists. They are really nothing but trades people absorbed in their business, leading a comparable existence."[108]

Despite her disappointment with her immediate surroundings, Goldman decided to extend her stay in the city to see about another return to the United States. Reflecting at least some modest means, she proceeded to rent a small apartment at 1935 Tupper Street, just west of where Concordia University's downtown campus now sits. It was physically distant from

Yvonne Maisonneuve's work, which was based out of 5168 Papineau Avenue by this time, but Goldman's experience of economic need paralleled that of many women who stayed at the Notre-Dame-de-la-Protection shelter in this period.

Goldman was horrified at the cost of her apartment, describing it as "the cheapest I could get and the nastiest which is always the case when anything is cheap."[109] Nevertheless, Goldman had observed the considerable poverty in the city, especially relative to Toronto/Tkaronto, and she tried to be grateful for her modest accommodations.[110] In correspondence with Jeanne Levey (who founded the National Parkinson Foundation in the United States in 1957), Goldman explained that the apartment had been equipped by "the wives of the few comrades" in the city who had "made a 'shower' and brought a few dishes, pots, pans and linen." Despite this generosity, Goldman derided the results, "It looks like a rummage sale only I have no customers either for the rummage or anything else."[111] She also objected to the noise and the "thin walls" that separated her from her neighbours. As she told Levey, "I cannot only hear them talk, but also breathe. As to the radio, it goes from morning until night. Well, that will have to be endured. For I certainly don't intend to move again. Besides there is no place to move within my reach."[112]

Alone in her noise-drenched apartment, Goldman complained of having "no intellectual companionship," the prohibitive cost of "anything artistic," and how there was "no one here among the comrades to do anything."[113] There was far less press attention than there had been on previous occasions, and little had been done to organize for her visit.[114] Now aged sixty-five, Goldman complained, "I have to be jack of all trades. I am worn out before I have to face the audience. But this is nothing new."[115] More worrying were the growing restrictions that foreshadowed the political oppression that mushroomed with the election of Premier Maurice Duplessis in 1936. When prevented from distributing anarchist publications by Canadian Customs officials and a 1934 provincial law in Quebec that required the approval of the police for such undertakings, Goldman decried, "It is to laugh when Canadians boast of their liberty. Every line that comes into the country goes through rigid censorship. Imagine such an old pamphlet as the 'Place of Anarchism in the Socialistic Evolution' [Peter Kropotkin, 1884] to be held up."[116]

In waiting on a decision about readmission to the United States, Goldman operated in a difficult environment and attempted to make the best of the situation.[117] In her last letter of 1934 to her dear friend Alexander Berkman she observed, "What a year it has been. The struggle in Canada is often beyond me and you know what a hide I have. The experience in America was hectic enough to break a bull. I went through it like a house on fire without being scorched. Some hide eh? Jesus I worked hard and at the end I am as poor as I began."[118] The new year marked little improvement in Goldman's mood as she continued to wait on news about whether she would be readmitted to the United States. Goldman had been warned that it would be difficult to "break grounds" in the darkening political climate in Montreal/Mooniyaang/Tiohtià:ke, but she was determined to try for both political and increasingly pressing financial reasons. When these initial efforts failed, however, she commented that "more and more it seems to me that the workers don't want to be roused from their leaden sleep, or have their chains broken. There is damned little unrest in their ranks. Whatever there is of awareness is in the young generation, student and middle-class and they are entirely in the meshes of the Bolshevik humbug." [119]

Goldman's failure to secure audiences led her to alter the subject of her lectures in the hopes of drawing more people to her talks and raising more money. She noted that subjects such as youth and women's emancipation and birth control "have a wider appeal than the political issues."[120] She, therefore, presented popular material, such as "the element of sex in unmarried people" to ensure sufficient attendance.[121] Material concerns are, therefore, a caution against the idea of exile as a liberating creative force as has been suggested of the works produced by Theodor Adorno and Edward Said in exile.[122] It is clear from Goldman's time in Montreal/Mooniyaang/Tiohtià:ke that her intellectual efforts were stymied by the political climate in the city (and the province and country more generally) as well as her daily concerns about how to raise funds to support herself.

Even with her efforts to develop more popular lectures, Goldman's English-language series at the Windsor Hotel and the YMCA on topics such as the work of George Bernard Shaw, the individual in society, and a comparison of Bolshevik and anarchist communism were all poorly attended. The expenses for her Windsor Hotel lecture were $45, and yet she only made $12. Goldman began to describe the city as her "Waterloo." She invited Alexander Berkman to commiserate with her, explaining "you can imagine what it meant speaking before an empty hall with the thought pressing on my mind that I will have to cover a huge deficit. I have no one else to blame but my own stupidity of trying to chase wind mills."[123]

In the winter of 1935, Goldman was immensely worried about her grim financial situation, probably the worst of her career, noting how close she was to being in a "pickle."[124] She confessed, "It is, indeed, the first time in my life that I feel the ground slipping a bit from under my feet."[125] Goldman's material circumstances contributed to a sense of being trapped, as did her ongoing and seemingly never-ending wait for news about potential readmission to the United States. Suspecting she would not be allowed to return, Goldman indicated that if she could, she would "sail back to France" in March. "Unfortunately," she noted, "the ship companies still want to be paid for transportation. My work of a year in Canada hasn't left me even that … I am caught in a vice."[126] Goldman was trapped even as she felt unmoored. She despaired, observing that "the anti-alien spirit is spreading all over the world like wildfire." She suggested that "the deepest modern tragedy is the homelessness and hearthlessness of all political refugees. Well, one cannot make plans now. One just drifts from day to day."[127]

Although Goldman used the language of drifting, her correspondence from this period reveals that her time was actually quite structured and grounded, though perhaps not in a conventional sense. In 1934 and 1935, arguably Goldman's most difficult moments in exile, the rhythm of her days was marked in large part by the coming and going of ships carrying correspondence from comrades overseas and trains bringing mail from America. Goldman was buoyed by correspondence and bereft when hoped-for letters did not appear. When she didn't hear from Alexander Berkman for an extended stretch in late 1934, she declared, "I can't understand why it should have taken so long. No wonder I was so anxious having to wait so long to hear from you. I hope it will not happen again. The god damned post office always does such tricks."[128] But when two letters arrived, she was delighted, exclaiming "I have not had so many letters from you in one week for a long time. You bet it helps to stand so much of the misery this town has given me."[129]

Goldman was such a prolific correspondent during her time in Montreal/Mooniyaang/Tiohtià:ke that she had ships' schedules memorized. Writing to Alexander Berkman in early February 1935, she observed, "This is the second letter this week one sailed away in the Olympic to day. This will sail on the Ile de France Saturday. So you have no cause for complaint."[130] Goldman also knew the speed of the boats, writing to Berkman on another occasion and explaining, "This will not sail until Saturday and even then I will have to make an exception and send it by the Rex. There is no fast steamer on any other line until the 7th of Feb (1935). And this is too important to wait so long."[131] The subject of that letter was the serious issue of censorship by Canadian Customs, but on other occasions, Goldman felt compelled to "scribble a few words" to catch the Cunard Line's "RMS Berengaria" even though she confessed that she did not "have anything important to write."[132] The arrival of mail ships, in this case in New York/Manaháhtaan from where the mail would travel north, was met with anticipation. "Perhaps there will be a letter from you," Goldman would write.[133]

Not surprisingly, Goldman's politics were woven through all aspects of her correspondence, including her choice of mail ships. With the rise of fascism in Europe, Goldman opted to boycott ships sailing under German or Italian flags. In the summer of 1934, Goldman was hard at work on an article on communism, so much so that her regular correspondence was interrupted. She felt badly, especially as far as Alexander Berkman was concerned, writing,

> My dearest, I wanted so much to get out a letter to you yesterday in time to catch the "Empress Britain" that left today from Montreal, a five-day boat. But it was impossible. I was still in labor pains with the Communist article. Now this won't go until Wednesday. Of course it will leave Toronto Monday. But it will not sail until Wednesday. There is a German boat on the 19th. But of course I never use the damned nazi ships.[134]

Goldman recognized that her boycott of the "damned German or Italian lines" probably didn't matter since, as she said, "nearly every other country is fascist." It was just her "own feeling about the matter."[135] She continued to express strong opinions, even as she struggled to make her way in Montreal/Mooniyaang/Tiohtià:ke.

Goldman remained primarily preoccupied with her own circumstances, even as the political climate in her immediate surroundings and in Europe deteriorated. When her entry to the United States was denied in 1935, Goldman was devastated. By this time, Goldman had been exiled for sixteen years from the country she held most dear. She glumly concluded: "I know now that I will remain an alien abroad for the rest of my life. Not a happy feeling. But it will have to be endured."[136] At the same time, Goldman determined that she could not stay in Canada where she felt she had been a "complete failure."[137] Boycotted "by the Communists, pseudo-Communists and all the others who see in Russia the crutches of life," Goldman concluded there "is nothing to be done but to sail back."[138] The situation in Europe, "where Communism and Fascism" were the "order of the day" worried her, as did her own future circumstances.[139] As she said, "I am going into a very unsafe and disturbed Europe. I don't know what might happen to me."[140]

Continued Precarity

In Europe, the situation was even more dire than when Goldman had departed two years prior. Fascist leaders in Germany and Italy had consolidated their hold on power, and their influence was spreading. In Goldman's personal world, tragedy struck when Alexander Berkman killed himself in the spring of 1936 after a persistent illness. Lost, Goldman seemed to regain some strength of purpose after being invited to Spain to work for the anarchist cause. Goldman would later admit that the situation in Spain initially engaged her more than the plight of Jewish people in Nazi Germany. As she told one correspondent, she felt "deeply the plight of the Jews," but she was "not a good enough Jew to feel their suffering more than I do that of the struggle of the Spanish people." She suspected that these sentiments were because the "epic greatness of the Spanish struggle" appealed more to her "imagination." As Goldman explained, "It is terrible to see people outraged and degraded without anyone fighting against it, and it is wonderful to see people fight so heroically for their freedom."[141]

Goldman soon became very active on behalf of refugees from the Spanish Civil War, which pitted conservative Catholic Nationalist forces against Republicans and their anarchist and communist comrades. It was a cause that engaged people globally. Cardinal Villeneuve in Quebec, for instance, roundly condemned the "Godless army" of people who supported the Republican side.[142] Goldman had long been interested in events in Spain, dating back to the United States' war with the country in 1899. At the time, she was "profoundly in sympathy with the Cuban and Philippine rebels who were striving to throw off the Spanish yoke."[143] Over the years, Goldman had followed political developments in Spain closely, including the growth of the anarchist movement and setbacks such as the arrest and execution of anarchist Francisco Ferrer in 1909.[144] She was, therefore, receptive when the call came to assist. People who encountered her in Spain, including Samuel Abramson, a Montrealer who had joined the International Brigades, described her as in "the best of health, looking younger than ever and full of energy."[145] Goldman had found a cause, in the same way that Yvonne Maisonneuve had a few years prior.

From Spain, Goldman traveled through France to England in 1937 to raise funds and work with International Antifacist Solidarity (SIA). In London, Goldman helped organize the committee to aid Homeless Spanish Women and Children. Despite her efforts, few donations were received, and Goldman found it difficult to engage audiences in a country that she found perpetually frigid.[146] Goldman's own circumstances were dire as she could only afford "squalid" accommodations in London.[147] As a result, she gave thought once more to traveling to Canada to fundraise and to see, yet again, about a return to the United States. The pull of her adopted homeland remained strong and became even more intense as Goldman neared her seventieth birthday. Suggesting an even deeper commitment to returning to the United States (and an even greater financial need) than had previously been the case, Goldman sold the Bon Esprit cottage. She also sold her papers and those belonging to Alexander Berkman to the International Institute for Social History.[148]

As Goldman began to organize for a return, her correspondents in Montreal/Mooniyaang/Tiohtià:ke warned her about the political climate in the city. The environment had become very oppressive following the election of Maurice Duplessis in 1936. Duplessis was a devout Catholic and a fierce French Canadian nationalist. He considered radical ideas, especially communism, dangerous, declaring in 1937 that "tant que j'aurai un souffle de vie, je n'épargnerai rien, je ferai tout en mon pouvoir pour faire disparaître le communisme de la province de Québec."[149] These efforts included bans on freedom of expression for communists and anarchists, which by the late 1930s, greatly curtailed Emma Goldman's capacity to organize, distribute reading materials, and influence the anarchist movement.[150] As Goldman prepared to return to Montreal/ Mooniyaang/Tiohtià:ke, Rose Pesotta, an anarchist with the International Ladies' Garment Workers' Union who was in Quebec to organize workers, cautioned that "we can not even mention a word about Spain – there is a ban on everything."[151]

The Act to Protect the Province Against Communistic Propaganda, a project driven by Duplessis, came into effect on 24 March 1937. It gave provincial authorities and law enforcement the power to "padlock" any premise suspected of hosting communist or Bolshevik activities. These terms were not defined, and the impact of the law was far-reaching, affecting any group considered anathema to Duplessis' nationalist and Catholic sympathies. The law dampened political organizing in Quebec, inhibiting the number of people that could gather, even privately.[152] Potential targets were fearful and restrained as a result. The Canadian Jewish Congress, for instance, did not challenge the religious suppression that resulted under the law, particularly vis-à-vis Jehovah's Witnesses or address the oppression of left-leaning radicals in the Jewish community.[153]

Writing in the anarchist publication *The Vanguard,* socialist Jack Fitzgerald blamed the Catholic Church in Quebec for this situation, amplifying a sentiment that Goldman had been expressing for years. He wrote, "It is the Church that educates and tells the people who they may vote. It is the Church which sanctions the open, French Nationalist, anti-English, anti-Jewish, propaganda of Adrian Arcand, leader of the Quebec Fascists." It was, according to Fitzgerald, "the Church that says to Duplessis, "Pass a Padlock Law."[154] Goldman herself was wary of the situation in Quebec, but conditions in Europe were so grim by the spring of 1939 that Goldman felt it was worthwhile to attempt a return to the United States. Once again, Montreal/Mooniyaang/Tiohtià:ke was to be a site of transit.[155] Goldman declared she was not "deceived" about her "chances" in Canada but concluded, "I have to be near America so that our friends in New York can begin once more some kind of campaign for my re-entry. Small as their chances are, they would be still smaller if I remained in England. Coming near there is a possibility."[156]

Goldman set sail from Liverpool (where John Harrison Surratt had stayed for a time in 1865) and arrived in Montreal/Mooniyaang/Tiohtià:ke on 17 April 1939, months before the outbreak of the Second World War. There was little fanfare upon her arrival in the city, and Goldman found it difficult to reach any potential audiences.[157] The restrictions imposed by the Padlock Law on gatherings and free speech meant that the city was, indeed, "forbidden for anything about Spain."[158] Moreover, there was considerable support for the Nationalist side and several publications, including *Le Droit* and *Action Catholique*, voiced their enthusiasm for General Franco and his defence of Catholicism.[159] Pierre Trudeau, who would become prime minister in 1968, was part of a group that protested the writer André Malraux when he came to Canada to encourage support for the Republicans.[160] Others, including many first-generation migrants, supported the left-leaning National Front and volunteered in the ranks of the Mackenzie-Papineau Battalion. This battalion included a significant number of French Canadians.[161] Still, Goldman found the situation in Montreal/Mooniyaang/Tiohtià:ke desperate, describing anarchists in Canada as "living corpses."[162] Her frustrations with the city had only mushroomed over the years and she was perhaps more alienated during her time there in 1939 than at any other moment.

Conclusions

Emma Goldman's perspective on the city of Montreal/Mooniyaang/Tiohtià:ke was always and forever that of an outsider. She never understood the city and never found what she was looking for there, even if she shared much in common with the small Jewish anarchist community and, more generally, with the thousands of men, women, and children who lived economically precarious lives in this period. By and large, Goldman found the city oppressive and was despondent about its politics and

3.3 Mural of Yvonne Maisonneuve by Kevin Ledo.

culture. She ignored the experiences of French Canadians and railed against the Catholic Church. This contrasted starkly with the experience of Yvonne Maisonneuve whose work with L'Institut Notre-Dame-de-la-Protection bound her to Montreal/Mooniyaang/Tiohtià:ke. With every relocation within the city, the shelter grew in size, scope, and influence. This enabled Maisonneuve to make a noticeable contribution to life in Montreal/Mooniyaang/Tiohtià:ke, particularly for women and girls who were unemployed or in need of some kind of shelter. Although some of her approaches invited criticism, Maisonneuve and her efforts are now appreciated more fully. As historian Annick Desmarais writes, "Yvonne Maisonneuve dedicated her entire life to the cause of marginalized women and the improvement of their living conditions. As society changes, as charities and social works adapt and modernize, the essence of her unique, family-like welcome endures. Her work remains, to this day, incomparable and invaluable."[163] Indeed, Maisonneuve's contributions are now a permanent feature of the city's landscape (or as permanent as anything can be in the age of perpetual urban change). In addition to the continued existence of Le Chaînon itself, as well as a not-for-profit retail store on St-Laurent Boulevard that supports the organization's operations, there is now a park named after Yvonne Maisonneuve on Pine Avenue near McGill University. Since 2022, a large mural with her portrait (painted by acclaimed muralist Kevin Ledo) adorns the side of 4382 Saint-Urbain, close to Mont-Royal.

There are, by contrast, no obvious traces of Goldman's time in the city, though members of the Jewish community continue to recount stories about her time there.[164] Still, there is no plaque to commemorate her stay at 1935 Tupper Street, nor are there any other kind of public memorials. Goldman's presence in the city was ultimately fleeting, reflecting, in part, her failure to inspire any radical change during her time there. It also reflects the way the city largely refused her, just as she refused it. In exile in Montreal/Mooniyaang/Tiohtià:ke, Goldman was often out of sync with those around her. She lived her days perpetually connected to places and rhythms beyond the city proper, reflected in her attention to ship schedules, correspondents, and events elsewhere. Her refuge and community connections were small and narrow as a result of her unwillingness to engage with the experiences of the majority of the population in the city. Seeing the dominant influence of the church, Goldman summarily dismissed French Canadians and the city as a result.

In many ways, Emma Goldman and Yvonne Maisonneuve could not have been more different in outlook and vocation. Maisonneuve was involved in the kind of patchwork relief efforts that Goldman would have disdained, seeing the "impenetrable dullness of official government marionettes, of religion, patriotism, marriage, parliament of the press and the critics" and the "charity of the uplift movements" as a combined problem.[165] Goldman opposed the idea of the state and its "trimmings," and believed in getting along "without the state or dictatorship," not trying to help governments function through good works.[166] At a fundamental level, Goldman also resented the idea of needing refuge, relief, or protection, especially from the state. In Goldman's view, the "formidable State machine" had to be corrected so that refuge wouldn't be required in the first place.[167]

The relief efforts provided by Yvonne Maisonneuve through L'Institut Notre-Dame-de-la-Protection did little to alter the structural causes of unemployment and homelessness in the city, just as Goldman's refuge in Montreal/Mooniyaang/Tiohtià:ke did little to solve the political and social structures that had led to her exile in the first instance. These problems continue to plague sanctuary efforts in the present, where the protection of individuals and families often achieves some personal benefits or gains with very little impact on existing social and political orders as a whole. Nevertheless, we can take inspiration from Yvonne Maisonneuve and Emma Goldman – two very different women who encountered a world of hurt, turmoil, and upheaval and who, in their own very different ways, sought to make it better. Yvonne Maisonneuve and Emma Goldman both lived materially impoverished lives as they dedicated themselves to their work. They had limited personal economic security, dedicating much of their material resources and energies to their respective causes. This connection binds them together, even if they were vastly different in outlook and disposition. Their efforts mattered in the lives of those who followed them, and their ideas continue to reverberate in various ways across the decades, even if they are remembered unevenly. In negotiating the workings of political power and economic precarity in the critical interwar period, Maisonneuve and Goldman blurred the conventional lines around relief, action, and the kind of social transformation that was deemed possible in part by being physically, intellectually, and, in the case of Maisonneuve, spiritually present and active in the city.

What is it like to move to a place that you think is safe and then discover differently? This is the question that inspired my interest in the history of US war resisters who found themselves in Montreal/Mooniyaang/Tiohtià:ke during the 1970 October Crisis when fears of an armed insurrection led the federal government to suspend civil liberties and expand the military presence on the streets of the city. In fleeing one war, the United States' war in Vietnam, resisters found themselves in another (hence the title of this chapter).

In researching this project, I was fortunate to interview or exchange correspondence with several war resisters, including Bruce Garside, Michael Hendricks, Mary Harman, Jackie Hyman, Ken Hyman, David Rapaport, Jürgen Dankwort, Bonnie Sherr Klein, and Michael Klein. Sherr Klein introduced me to Dorothy Todd-Hénaut, who gave generously of her time to help me better understand 1960s Montreal/Mooniyaang/Tiohtià:ke. Although Todd-Hénaut was not a resister, she moved in both resister and French Canadian intellectual circles and was able to provide invaluable perspectives on the political and social dynamics of the city in this period. Todd-Hénaut became a kind of bridge, playing the same kind of role in my research that she did in connecting war resisters and French Canadian intellectuals in the 1960s.

In asking the question about "after," I discovered I needed to think about "before" in terms of the kinds of politics and ideas people had about Montreal/

Mooniyaang/Tiohtià:ke and Quebec, more generally, before moving. I was curious about the extent to which the anti-colonial and anti-imperial politics in Montreal/Mooniyaang/Tiohtià:ke and Quebec translated to people who were themselves fleeing because of opposition to an imperial war. As critical refugee studies and refugee studies scholars have long emphasized, what happens before matters to what happens after. The past isn't just left behind at a border. People's experiences with politics, the US state, and the language of decolonization shaped their perceptions of the city, their experience of refuge, and, in some cases, how they lived the 1970 October Crisis.

This focus on the "before" means that the end of this chapter is quite abrupt. It concludes with the October Crisis, but this was not the end point for many of the individuals who contributed their stories to my efforts. Their lives continued to unfold after the political events I described. As Bonnie Sherr Klein observed of an early draft,

> *We disappear from your manuscript but that's not the end of our immigration story … (Michael and I) both got landed immigrant status and became citizens when we were eligible. After my stroke in 1976, Montreal became inaccessible to me because of the weather and the general lack of accessibility. We looked at the US again because Michael still had a California Medical license, but again chose to return to Canada, this time to the milder and more accessible climate of Vancouver … I was proud and honoured to be named an Officer of the Order of Canada. Our children, Seth Klein and Naomi Klein, are proud Canadians.*[1]

Sherr Klein's intervention is a reminder that the stories captured in these pages are not necessarily the stories that people lived. Rather, they are an amalgam of insights, evidence, and perspectives. They are both larger and smaller than any one individual's experiences. And they have been assembled as part of a focused inquiry on the meaning and significance of refuge in a place that appeared safe to outsiders. Just as David Rapaport observed in one of our conversations that "the memory of an event is forged by where you stood at the time," this chapter is soldered out a very particular desire to understand the impact of tumultuous events on the expectations and conditions of refuge.[2]

By asking people about how they experienced a specific event, I was at once approaching them as resisters but also seeking to understand their experience in the city more fully, as more than resisters. This speaks to my approach to histories of migration, displacement, and refuge more generally, where I understand that this is only ever one aspect of someone's life experience (or that of their family or their communities). It might be a large and consuming facet, or it might be seemingly insignificant, and it might stay with people forever after, but regardless, people are always more than their experiences of displacement. The result means thinking about how people are involved with other events beyond their own decisions around moving. Somewhat ironically, as I discovered with this chapter, telling a full history of refuge sometimes means decentring the very question of refuge.

As with the previous three studies, there is no instance of church sanctuary or church/state contestation around refuge of the sort that has come to characterize contemporary sanctuary practices. That analysis can be found in the last two cases. Here, sanctuary is once again constructed in loose and informal ways, though it is interesting to see the many ways in which it is threaded through the life of the city, even when there was no sanctuary declaration as such. Federal politicians such as Prime Minister Pierre Trudeau stated publicly that Canada would be a place of refuge for war resisters only after 1969, and even then, they did so by interpreting the existing regulations around admissions rather than creating something new. The refuge that war resisters sought and received was much less confrontational than in the cases that unfolded in subsequent decades. It was a rare instance where refuge was relatively easy to obtain on a structural level. It was the evolving character of the city, the deepening understanding of anti-colonial activity, and the nature of the Canadian federal government itself that gave some people pause, especially during the October Crisis of 1970.

June 2023

The Wartime City

THE UNITED STATES' WAR in Vietnam sparked resistance across the country and beyond. The protracted conflict, along with images and news stories of US atrocities, such as the 1968 massacre at Mỹ Lai, raised questions about the nature and morality of the conflict. Inspired in part by the civil rights movement, many US citizens questioned the role their country was playing in the suppression of national liberation movements, even as successive leaders talked about freedom in the face of communist aggression at home and abroad. As the war progressed and intensified, it became increasingly difficult to recruit soldiers and the military-age draft was repeatedly expanded. By the time the US military withdrew from Vietnam in 1975, over three million people had been deployed to Southeast Asia.

Resistance to the war and the draft took many different forms. There were efforts to sever the relationship between academic research and companies such as the Dow Chemical Company (the producer of Napalm). Students held sit-ins and protests and, along with other activists, helped organize various marches and boycotts across the country. Twenty-five thousand people attended the March Against the Vietnam War in Washington, DC/Nacotchtank lands, on 17 April 1965. There were also public displays of people burning their draft cards. In 1971, following the lead of churches that offered sanctuary to deploying servicemen aboard the USS *Coral Sea*, city council declared Berkeley, California xučyun to be a sanctuary for the soldiers.[1] The men who refused to serve were understood to be part of a larger movement to resist the war, one which included military deserters and draft dodgers. The term *deserter* referred to someone who had left active military service, while *dodger* implied that someone had evaded the draft. Both groups were captured in the more general term *resisters*. For those crossing international borders, this term also referred to supporters, including many women who moved as girlfriends, wives, and activists in their own right.

Thousands of resisters left the United States during the war, especially after 1965, when the military draft became more expansive. Some moved to Mexico while others went to Europe or Canada. Estimates suggest that as few as thirty thousand and as many as sixty thousand people made their way to Canada from 1965 to 1974, where there was also a significant anti-war movement as a result of the federal government's complicity in supplying military material and providing chemical testing grounds for US efforts.[2] This mobile resister population was the result of a relatively open and unassuming border, as well as a vague immigration policy around the treatment of war resisters, which only became clearer in 1969.[3] Many people moved to Toronto/Tkaronto and Vancouver, which sits on the unceded territories of the xʷməθkʷəy̓əm (Musqueam), Sḵwx̱wú7mesh (Squamish), and səlilwətaɬ (Tsleil-Waututh) Nations. These cities became the hubs of resister activity in Canada.

Notably, for our purposes, a significant number of people also moved to Montreal/Mooniyaang/Tiohtià:ke. There, resisters with radical politics had the distinct experience of reconciling their perspectives with the storm of intellectual and political activity underway in Quebec during this period. These politics were born of a distinct history of nationalist, anti-imperialist thought, which was invigorated in the 1960s by anti-colonial and national liberation movements abroad (the influence of the domestic Red Power movement would only be felt later). They were imbued with various strands of class ideologies, feminist discourses, and, to a certain extent, the politics of race. Newly arrived war resisters, therefore, discovered a city "filled with revolutionary possibilities" even though it appeared "sedate" and "relatively calm" to some.[4]

Most radical groups in Canada sought transformation through existing political channels; however, the Front de Libération du Québec (FLQ) was committed to the use of violence to alter the status quo. Over a seven-year period, beginning with its founding in 1963, the FLQ planted or mailed almost two hundred bombs, often directed at highly symbolic targets. In the fall of 1970, members escalated their activities, kidnapping British Trade

Commissioner James Cross and the Deputy Premier of Quebec, Pierre Laporte. The members of two FLQ cells held them hostage and made a series of demands involving the publication of the organization's manifesto and the release of political prisoners, including many FLQ members jailed for earlier bombing activities.[5] The use of the War Measures Act by Prime Minister Pierre Trudeau (himself a child of Montreal/Mooniyaang/Tiohtià:ke) and the death of Pierre Laporte in captivity shocked many.

The invocation of the War Measures Act on 16 October 1970 outlawed membership in the FLQ, suspended *habeas corpus,* and gave law enforcement widespread authority. It was a decision that was welcomed in some quarters but incited anger and alarm in others. On the streets of Montreal/Mooniyaang/Tiohtià:ke and in homes across the city, people were confronted with the possibility of detention and arrest. For some, this possibility quickly became a reality. For others, the crisis unfolded at a distance. Newly arrived war resisters from the United States, some of whom had been in the city less than a year, observed and experienced the crisis in various ways. Many moved in activist circles and were sympathetic to the views of French Canadian intellectuals, including to some extent the FLQ. As former war resister David Rapaport explained, "the resistance in Quebec was viewed as part of (an) international uprising against colonialism."[6]

As the national liberation movement in Quebec evolved, resisters sometimes found themselves torn between supporting the federal government (the legal source of their refuge) and radicals in Quebec, with whom they were sympathetic and often allied politically. This was certainly the case in October 1970. Yet, as relatively new arrivals, resisters had the luxury of deciding if, when, and how to engage with the events around them. The fact that they did so in various and uneven ways is revealing, pointing to how the situation they encountered was simultaneously familiar and strange, connected to national liberation movements elsewhere, but also born of decades of contestation within Canada. In many cases, people absorbed and magnified the existing and highly complex politics in the city rather than transforming them. Crucially, this generalized remove (something we also observed of Emma Goldman's time in the city) meant that the October Crisis did not necessarily alter people's sense of security, although it did raise troubling questions about the kind of society in which they were now living.

Montreal/Mooniyaang/Tiohtià:ke in the 1960s

As in many other places, Montreal/Mooniyaang/Tiohtià:ke was part of a generalized post-Second World War affluence with high employment figures and a wide array of manufacturing, industrial, and transportation jobs. But like many other cities in North America, this affluence wasn't evenly shared. Visitors to the city throughout the 1950s and 1960s commented on the poverty visible in certain quarters, and documentaries from the period captured some of these inequities.[7]

Black Montrealers continued to live and work in informally though markedly segregated conditions, experiencing what historian Steven High has described as the "territorial stigmatization of racialized urban poverty."[8] Indigenous Peoples in the city, and in nearby Kahnawà:ke, Ahkwesáhsne, and Kanehsatà:ke faced similar challenges, compounded by continued contests over treaty rights and state paternalism, displacement, and territorial

4.1 An image of graffiti in St-Jacques, from *VTR St-Jacques*.

encroachment, particularly during the construction of the St Lawrence Seaway, completed in 1959.[9] The seaway, which was meant to connect Montreal/Mooniyaang/Tiohtià:ke with the rest of the world in a more immediate way, came at the expense of the residents of Kahnawà:ke, who lost large amounts of territory and traditional waterfront access. In Ahkwesáhsne and Kanehsatà:ke, the construction disrupted traditional fishing practices and the surrounding ecosystems. It was a devastating moment of colonial intrusion and one that damaged the health and welfare of shoreline communities.[10]

Distinctive decolonization efforts, vis-à-vis the Canadian state and to some extent the United States, flavoured the political discourse in the city, as did other broad-based social movements, including civil rights, New Left ideologies, labour activism, feminist, and, later, anti-war efforts.[11] Much of the discourse was led by French Canadian youth who chafed at their economic and political circumstances in the face of continued domination by English-speaking elites. There were frequent protests and demonstrations.[12] Workers at the newly revived Port of Montreal, for instance, staged regular strikes throughout the 1960s; workers at *La Presse* went on strike in 1964, and two years later, nurses across the province did the same. Independence groups such as the Rassemblement pour l'Indépendence Nationale (RIN) organized sit-ins and protests when companies such as Canadian National Railway (CN) failed to observe Saint-Jean Baptiste Day in 1964.[13] In 1965, there were demonstrations on 24 May (Victoria Day) and 1 July (then known as Dominion Day), two symbolically important days where tensions were rife. Participants described them as "very violent" to the point where they "almost turned into riots."[14] There were also street protests with thousands of participants in support of Opération McGill Français and a wildcat police and firefighter strike in October 1969, during which time conflict over taxi monopolies in the city also came to a head. As historian Will Langford has observed, throughout the 1960s, "independence and social transformation were entangled goals" for many.[15] Protests were also the result of a variety of ideological outlooks and political agendas, making it sometimes difficult for new arrivals in Montreal/Mooniyaang/Tiohtià:ke to grasp the extent of the ambitions and divisions at play.

Some of this activism was a direct result of the Quiet Revolution, described as a "form of collective dissent against an established order which oppressed French Canadians economically and socially."[16] Although there had been some change over the course of the post-Second World War period, the death of longtime premier Maurice Duplessis in 1959 (whose oppressive policies are explored to some extent in "The Hostile City" chapter) and the election of Jean Lesage and the Liberal Party provincially fuelled efforts on the ground and in the halls of power to collapse the "marked cleavage between what politics was and what politics ought to be."[17] Lesage's vision for Quebec's future was rooted in the idea of "economic liberation" and a form of nationalism where French Canadians could famously be "maîtres chez nous."[18]

The change in political leadership was electric, but it also operated within the realm of the legible and the familiar. The Liberal government focused on modernization and secularization, particularly in terms of the economy and education where there was a sense that French Canadians had fallen behind. Generalized sentiments about inequity and oppression were confirmed by figures from the 1961 census, which revealed a 35 per cent wage gap between anglophones and francophones provincially and a 50 per cent gap between unilingual anglophones and unilingual francophones in the city of Montreal/Mooniyaang/Tiohtià:ke.[19] English was the language of commerce and English-speaking elites dominated the business district in the city, where only 17 per cent of administrative jobs were held by French Canadians.[20] Despite the progress of the Quiet Revolution in addressing some of these issues, or perhaps precisely because the changes failed to be as radical as some would have liked, a sense of inequity and impatience continued to fester.

Jean Drapeau, elected mayor of Montreal/Mooniyaang/Tiohtià:ke in 1960, proved to be highly conservative, almost uniquely attuned to entrenched business interests that supported his party and his candidacy.[21] The upshot was a "city government hostile to social activism" and dedicated to urban development and a "modern internationalist vision."[22] As a result, the city pursued several high-rise and large-scale infrastructure projects, including eleven new bridges and massive expressways that continue to define first impressions of the city for people arriving by car or bus. The city expanded outward, becoming a "metropolis" as communities on the north and south shores grew, while the population on the island of

Montreal/Kawenote Teiontiakon declined and, in some neighbourhoods, became further impoverished.[23] These growing inequalities inspired the emergence of important citizen action committees in the 1960s, such as the Saint-Jacques citizens' committee, which would later involve newly arrived war resisters in their work.[24] In other instances, residents attempted to resist massive urbanization projects without success. To make way for the Ville-Marie Expressway, much of Little Burgundy (home to many Black residents of the city and an area once described as a "refuge for the poor") was razed, undermining the many crucial cultural, social, and economic dimensions of a vibrant community.[25]

Inequities in the city were felt perhaps most palpably in terms of living conditions. In 1962, a report indicated that 36 per cent of families in the largely French-speaking neighbourhood of St-Henri lived in uninhabitable buildings.[26] Poor living conditions meant that childhood in these quarters was "stalked by malnutrition and disease, too often accompanied by abuses in familial and institutional settings."[27] These differences cemented divides in class, culture, and experience.[28]

Pierre Vallières, a leading intellectual in Quebec and later a member of the FLQ, grew up in a working-class family. Vallières is most famous for his work, *White N** of America*, published in 1968, which was part memoir and part political tract. In this work, Vallières describes how "one of the most critical problems of the postwar period was housing." His father worked at Usines Angus, a railway car manufacturing and repair company that serviced the Canadian Pacific Railway, and according to Vallières "the workers talked all day long about their housing problems."[29] Vallières describes one of the houses he grew up in as follows: "The shack was made of wood covered with *"papier brique,"* a kind of tarpaper designed to look like brick … The (three) rooms were separated by walls of 'donnacona,' which could be bought quite cheaply from any dealer in building materials …. Many of the shacks that went up in Ville Jacques-Cartier in the years following our arrival were built entirely out of two-by-fours and broad panels of this economical cardboard, which was then covered with tarpaper. It was not exactly warm in winter, but it didn't cost much."[30]

Vallières' emphasis on housing insecurity and economic precarity is a visceral reminder of the vast gulf between Montreal/Mooniyaang/

Tiohtià:ke as a city of affluence and Montreal/Mooniyaang/Tiohtià:ke as a city of insecurity in the 1960s. It is also revealing of the various interconnected strands of activism and resistance in the city in this period as people sought better social and economic conditions, as well as different kinds of political formations and futures.

While Vallières' revolutionary ideals provided radical inspiration in some quarters, *White N*** of America* has since been criticized for effectively "de-racializing colonial history, of turning race into a politically insignificant (and acquirable) category within the settler colony."[31] And although Vallières casually insisted there was "no black problem" in Quebec, he was, nevertheless, influenced by the rhetoric of Black Liberation. As historian Wendell Nii Laryea Adjetey has observed, there was a marked tendency on the part of French Canadian intellectuals to appropriate the "African American narrative to illustrate their historical subordination and suffering."[32] In addition to borrowing a discourse of oppression, French Canadian intellectuals also sought to affirm the virtue of their cause by emphasizing their alliance with Black radicals. Despite his ignorance of Black experiences in Montreal/Mooniyaang/Tiohtià:ke, Vallières made a point of emphasizing the support he and Charles Gagnon received from "many partisans of the Black Power movement."[33] Other French Canadian intellectuals sought similar affirmation by advancing a sense of shared oppression.

In 1968, students at Sir George Williams and McGill University organized the Congress of Black Writers. Held in the memory of Martin Luther King and Malcolm X, the goal of the gathering was to move towards a "second liberation." It was attended by activists and intellectuals from across North America, and the anger and impatience among attendees was palpable in what was described as the "militant atmosphere of the conference."[34] One of the featured speakers was Stokely Carmichael, author of *Black Power: The Politics of Liberation*, head of the Student Nonviolent Coordinating Committee, and one of the people who had written to Vallières and Gagnon while they were in jail in New York City/Manaháhtaan to lend his support. In his speech, Carmichael suggested an affinity with the French Canadian experience while also making all white people complicit in "the rape of Africa."[35] Speaking to an impassioned crowd, Carmichael charged "Portugal, Spain, the Netherlands, Belgium, France, England, the US,

Canada, an extension of the US [applause and laughter]." He then quipped, "except for the French Canadians."[36]

Indeed, question of where French Canadians sat in this landscape of imperialism, colonialism, and violence, changed radically depending on one's perspective. For his part, Vallières maintained that race "was not present" when it came to issues of economic exploitation. Rather, "one just talks about a group of people who are taking advantage economically of another group. But when one talks about colonisation, the question of race comes into play because in colonisation it is one race that seeks to entirely dominate another race."[37]

Gérald Godin, the publisher of *White N** of America*, attended the Congress and may have been in the audience for Carmichael's talk. He certainly listened to activist Rocky Jones document his sense of the Black experience in Canada as one defined by inequality. Absorbing Jones's words, Godin noted, "that's how French Canadians feel!"[38] It seems that it was easier to express shared sympathies than to wrestle with the fundamental question of French Canadians as colonial oppressors, something that certain Indigenous leaders had been insisting upon in this period. At the 1965 hearings of the Commission on Bilingualism and Biculturalism, for instance, Mohawk activist Kahn-Tineta Horn suggested that the French be considered "the first invading race" in Canada.[39] This was something that Vallières and other French Canadian intellectuals would only begin to do in later years, in the context of massive hydroelectric developments in the north. In 1980, Vallières shifted his gaze to consider the experience of Indigenous Peoples such as the Cree and Inuit in Northern Quebec. He described them as "indigenous survivors of genocide" who had met "with philanthropy and contempt from those White power groups who stole everything they had."[40] Such observations would only come later, however. In the 1960s, French Canadian nationalists and intellectuals were not engaged with questions of their own community's history of colonialism.[41] Instead, they were intent on (re)claiming space and place.

René Lévesque, one of the founders of the Sovereignty-Association Movement and later premier of Quebec from 1976 to 1985, published *Option Québec* in 1968. He wrote: "We are Québécois. What that means first and foremost … is that we are attached to this one corner of the earth where we can be completely ourselves: this Quebec, the only place where we have the unmistakable feeling that 'here we can be really at home.' Being ourselves is essentially a matter of keeping and developing a personality that has survived for three and a half centuries."[42]

The idea of a French Canadian homeland and distinct nationhood has been central to separatist politics in Quebec since the 1960s, and yet, this idea has regularly been challenged by Indigenous Peoples who point to historical relationships with the land and to laws and relationships that have not been honoured.[43] Neverthless, Nationalist claims to place and land, including affirmations of sovereignty continue to manifest in contemporary Quebec society.[44] As such, even though people arriving in the city might feel as though they are starting afresh, they aren't encountering a blank slate. Rather, they are moving to a place shaped by multidirectional histories of oppression and resistance. Very few war resisters had a sense of the depth and breadth of these currents before arriving in Montreal/Mooniyaang/Tiohtià:ke. David Rapaport, who moved from New York City/Manaháhtaan in 1968, recalled reading Harold Cardinal's *The Unjust Society* (1969) and Dee Brown's *Bury My Heart at Wounded Knee* (1970) but confessed to knowing little beyond the fact that Indigenous Peoples in Canada "were colonized" with some sense that "sovereignty" was an issue.[45]

Making the Move

Many war resisters who moved to Montreal/Mooniyaang/Tiohtià:ke from the United States in the 1960s never had any plans to do so. Rather, it was US imperialism overseas, the expanding military draft, the end of the marriage deferment option in 1965, and the introduction of a lottery system in 1969, as well as increasingly oppressive measures on freedoms of association, protest, and expression that prompted people to depart the United States. Others moved to Montreal/Mooniyaang/Tiohtià:ke after serving in Vietnam and determining they could not and would not go back. Within the broad category of war resister, there existed a range of experiences and motives among people seeking refuge.

Generally speaking, draft dodgers were most often young, well-educated, and politically engaged, a profile that largely distinguished them from deserters who had less education and often enlisted for economic reasons before leaving the military after one or two tours of duty. While some of the people I interviewed, such as Jürgen Dankwort, gave voice to feelings of rootlessness, few people spoke of classic conditions such as poverty or economic strain as part of their reasons for migrating.[46] Uniquely, Mary Harman, who grew up in Putnam County, Ohio (long traveled by the Peoria, Myaamia, Shawnee, Kaskaskia and Kickapoo peoples) and moved to Montreal/Mooniyaang/Tiohtià:ke in 1967, says that she "always felt insecure," a feeling that was compounded by her experience with childhood poverty, her mother's deep unhappiness, and her father's own sense of alienation as a first-generation migrant from Europe.[47]

"John" (last name now unknown) was one of the estimated one thousand Black war resisters who moved to Canada in the late 1960s. He was interviewed about his experiences in 1971 and emphasized the economic circumstances that encouraged the poor and disenfranchised to enlist: "I haven't seen many blacks from the States this is true, but from where I was the tendency for the blacks was to go into the army because that was a way out. Well you know that the situation is pretty bad – monetarily and sociologically, and from any other viewpoint that you want to attack the situation. So the military represented a way out for blacks. It represents a way out for any poor person."[48] For those with means and educational or professional opportunities, leaving the United States was another "way out." Ken and Jackie Hyman (née Korschun) were students, happily pursuing options from their base in Philadelphia/Lenapehoking when the possibility of graduate studies at McGill University encouraged a move to Montreal/Mooniyaang/Tiohtià:ke. David Rapaport was living in New York City/Manaháhtaan when he received his draft notice and decided to move as a result of his mother's tearful urging. Michael Klein, a doctor, and his wife Bonnie Sherr Klein, who had graduated from film studies at Stanford University, decided that moving to Canada was the best option if Michael was going to avoid going to jail after being drafted as a medical officer. Klein was resolutely opposed to using his medical skills to support the United States' war in Vietnam.[49]

As a result, people moved to Montreal/Mooniyaang/Tiohtià:ke and Canada with varying degrees of familiarity about what awaited them and different ideas about the nature of the country as a safe space. "John" couldn't really explain the draw to Canada, according to the surviving 1971 interview notes. He mused that it was perhaps something "subconscious," which suggested to him that "the North was a place of milk and honey, and that the North was the place to be if you are trying to make it." He also conceded, "I really couldn't see how the situation could be any worse than the situation I was in at the time," and since he was "sort of grasping at straws," he moved to Montreal/Mooniyaang/Tiohtià:ke. Bill Wittmeyer, who described himself as a one-time "right-wing" and "fascist" thinker was a tank crewman in Vietnam before eventually deserting.[50] When he was interviewed about his experiences in 1971, he admitted that he initially thought he would be extradited if he moved to Canada. As a result, on the advice of a staff member at the Russian embassy in Washington, DC (where he had first sought refuge), he moved to Mexico in the hopes of eventually getting asylum in Cuba. When that didn't work, he headed north. As he recalled, "I didn't even know I was safe in Canada."[51]

Others had a bit more of a sense of the country, however impressionistic. Mary Harman's father, originally from Belgium, had worked for years on tobacco farms in southern Ontario before settling in the United States. She recalls visiting "relatives in tobacco country" in the summer and going to dances at the Belgian Club, where the evening would end with everyone standing on the dance floor, listening to "God Save the Queen." Many of her dance companions were French Canadians who worked the local farms, and would "whisper sweet things" in their dance partner's ear.[52] Some of these early impressions shaped Mary's sense of what Montreal/Mooniyaang/Tiohtià:ke might portend, though she suggests that in hindsight she really "had no idea" about the city as she was "pretty sheltered" in her life and had limited exposure to the currents of French Canadian nationalist activity around her.[53]

Many people moved north because it was relatively easy to do so. Geographically proximate, Montreal/Mooniyaang/Tiohtià:ke was a four-to-five-hour drive from Boston/Shawmut, along I-89 or a six-to-seven-hour drive from New York City/Manaháhtaan, thanks to the I-87 (designated in 1957). It was also a very short flight from Logan International Airport or La Guardia to Dorval (which opened in 1941). People also crossed over Quebec's sparsely populated land borders from Vermont, Maine, and New Hampshire. Those who had been active in the anti-draft movement in the United States benefited from networks of assistance that led them to Montreal/Mooniyaang/Tiohtià:ke. As Mary Harman recalls, "We got information as to what was needed for entry at the border and names to contact in Montreal for support finding housing and other needs."[54]

Others chose the city as their destination because of their previous experiences. Jürgen Dankwort, for instance, was familiar with Montreal/Mooniyaang/Tiohtià:ke due to his father's posting as West German ambassador to Canada from 1951 to 1956.[55] He felt a sense of familiarity upon arriving in the city even though he hadn't lived there previously. More typically, others experienced a sense of discovery, especially following visits to Expo 67, which in some cases encouraged their move to the city or left lasting impressions of the place where they had arrived. Held from 27 April 1967 to 29 October 1967 and inspired by the theme "Man and his World," Expo 67 emphasized human progress and the capacity for innovation and change. Michael Klein, who arrived in the city in October 1967, declared that "Montreal was exuberant!" while Bonnie Sherr Klein described it as "exhilarating."[56]

Even within the "spectacular novelty" of Expo 67, there were critical contestations about modernity and liberation at play, and these marked people's sense of the period.[57] Some participants subverted the federal government's plans for the Indians of Canada Pavilion, using the space to suggest that amidst the presentation of harmonious relations, Indigenous Peoples "had suffered enormously from non-Native Canadians' insensitivity, intolerance, and selfishness."[58] Members of the Youth Pavilion lobbied Expo organizers to name 6 August Youth Day, and as one participant recounted, "Expo would learn later it was also Hiroshima Day!" A planned anti-nuclear protest for this day was disrupted when protesters were denied entry at the border, but activists still managed to bring their protests directly to Expo 67. The underground newspaper *Logos*, for instance, famously "presented a Vietnam Pavilion to Expo in the shape of a coffin, covered with pictures of napalmed Vietnamese."[59]

The international fair also became a focal point for other political actors. Cuban anti-revolutionaries attempted to sabotage their country's pavilion and carried out a series of intermittent bombing attacks in Ottawa (traditional territory of the Algonquin Anishnabek) and Montreal/ Mooniyaang/Tiohtià:ke beginning in 1964.[60] General Charles de Gaulle created a diplomatic incident and galvanized French Canadian nationalists when he shouted "Vive le Québec! Vive le Québec Libre! Vive le Québec en français … Vive la France!" from the heights of the city hall balcony on 24 July 1967, pausing between each phrase for dramatic effect and to let the applause and cries of the rapturous crowd roll over him. In doing so, de Gaulle captured some of the language of oppression and the spirit of anti-colonialism that animated French Canadian nationalists at the time, a deeply ironic move given France's violent response to independence movements in Vietnam and Algeria.[61]

Paradox was, therefore, woven throughout the Expo 67 experience. Ken Hyman, a war resister, remembers the excitement of the period, but the tensions and divisions that were apparent also stand out in his mind many years later. When asked, he quickly recalled the walls Mayor Drapeau had ordered to be painted white and blue along the route to the Expo 67 site in an effort to disguise some of the poorer quarters of the city.[62] The divisions and differences that were barely visible at the edges of Expo 67 were, in fact, profound fissures in a society where change was largely desired and deeply contested.

Refugees from Imperialism

Debates about the nature of oppression in Quebec during the 1960s hinged, in part, on ideas about who should be held accountable for the conditions in which French Canadians found themselves. Some intellectuals impugned English Canadians and the structure and outlook of the federal state, others blamed the autocratic and entrenched power of the Catholic Church, and still others held that US imperialism was at fault.[63] Pierre Vallières, for instance, charged "the adversary of the Quebec revolution is not Ottawa (which does not have the means to oppose it!) but Washington."[64] He believed that US imperialism, not just questions of nationalism, needed to be addressed by those seeking revolutionary social change. As he wrote, "Quebec, and especially the region of Montreal, is in a situation of *absolute financial dependence* with regard to the United States which, like France and England in the past, cannot but oppose the autonomous development of the

Quebec economy." Vallières insisted that "the United States derives enormous profits from its economic domination of Quebec" and maintained that "unless it is forced to do so by the violence of the Québecois, it will never consent to end its domination."[65]

The ambiguity of being a kind of refugee from the United States in Montreal/Mooniyaang/Tiohtià:ke and Quebec was reflected to some extent in the ways in which war resisters interacted with French Canadians and French Canadian society and culture upon their arrival. Many of these encounters were shaped by linguistic affinities or socioeconomic circumstances. When Jürgen Dankwort, a German national who had been active in radical circles in the United States, first got to the city, he stayed "with a very nice lady (who) had a room for rent." Noting that she was French Canadian, he added, "they had their experience with conscription and they remembered that and they didn't appreciate it."[66] Bruce Garside, a specialist in Greek and medieval philosophy who took a job in the Department of Philosophy at McGill University, recalled a sense of isolation because of his limited French, though he also explained that he "very much" believed in the idea of national liberation. He noted that "the role of the Church and Duplessis in terms of stifling Quebec" was a "clear example of a fascist state." Having only arrived in the city in 1965, Bruce hadn't lived through the Duplessis era, but he had absorbed enough of the social and political intelligence from this period to understand the significance and importance of what he was seeing around him.[67] He was sympathetic, as were many others, as evidenced in part by the numerous articles about the French Canadian experience in the underground press. Pierre Vallières, for his part, recalled receiving support from "certain 'draft dodgers'" while in jail in 1966.[68]

Some resisters remained quite isolated and developed very few connections with French Canadians, even though they constituted a majority of the city's population (64 per cent according to the 1971 Census and 67 per cent by 1978).[69] Mary Harman remembers "feeling isolated and quite detached from the external politics of the city." As she explains, "With no understanding of the French language and no close friends, I was lonely – I missed my home in Ohio, my parents and my seven brothers and sisters."[70] Others such as Bonnie Sherr Klein and Jürgen Dankwort spoke French and were able to move relatively easily across linguistic boundaries.

4.2 Bonnie Sherr Klein during filming of *VTR St-Jacques*.

After arriving in Montreal, Bonnie Sherr Klein found work with the National Film Board of Canada (NFB), where she became friends and colleagues with Dorothy Todd-Hénaut, developing extensive connections with French Canadian communities as a result of her films. For her part, Dorothy Todd-Hénaut, originally from Ontario, had moved to Montreal/Mooniyaang/Tiohtià:ke in 1954 after studying at the Sorbonne. Her perspective on relationships in the city was, therefore, somewhat more profound than those who were newly arrived. For instance, Todd-Hénaut herself had the experience of being told to "speak white" (a derogatory phrase used against French Canadians) in downtown restaurants.[71] In her view, this was "not something that was forgivable," and she felt the injustices experienced by French Canadians keenly.[72] Together Todd-Hénaut and Sherr Klein made the film VTR *Saint-Jacques* (1969). Sherr Klein would also make *Citizens' Medicine* in 1970 about the community health clinic in St-Jacques. These films provided important insights into French Canadian experiences in the city. Sherr Klein herself emphasized how meaningful it was for her and her husband, Michael Klein, to work with organizations such as the citizens' committee in Saint-Jacques.[73]

Even those war resisters who moved in largely English-speaking circles felt a sense of solidarity among their French Canadian neighbours. One interviewee suggested there wasn't any "prejudice against draft dodgers who didn't speak French" for "it was clear there was a solidarity to be had."[74] Indeed, Bonnie Sherr Klein emphasizes that it was the local French Canadian community that "had been so welcoming."[75] For his part, Bruce Garside believes "an exception was made" for those who moved to Montreal/Mooniyaang/Tiohtià:ke in the context of the United States' war in Vietnam. In his opinion, "as soon as you said you were American, doors opened so to speak in terms of people's willingness to speak English and people's willingness to humour you when you tried to speak French."[76] Indeed, an anonymous letter published in an info letter for arriving war resisters declared: "Many French Canadians are anti-American, for many reasons, among which economic domination. Therefore, an American who is critical of his own government's behaviour usually merits the esteem of someone who himself is struggling for a greater degree of 'real' liberty."[77] As further evidence of this solidarity, students in the city organized anti-war marches and urged "Canadian universities to open their doors to Americans, who because of their convictions, had deserted the forces or had refused induction."[78]

These sentiments shaped concrete strategies. For instance, people were counseled to arrive at Dorval Airport after midnight in order to be received by sympathetic French Canadian officers. Michael Klein and Bonnie Sherr Klein followed this advice and recalled that "in those days the French Canadians had the less desirable night shift. The day shift would be an English Canadian, many of whom had served in the Canadian military. They could be expected to be less sympathetic to an American deserter from the US military. In contrast, French Canadians were in general against conscription, especially 'fighting for the queen.' They were also likely to be against the Vietnam War."[79]

Michael Klein remembers being embraced by the visa officer at the airport while Bonnie Sherr Klein developed a great deal of sympathy for the position of Quebec nationalists, voting for René Levesque and the separatist Parti Québécois party in 1976. Yet, the structure of the Canadian federation meant that the possibility of legal refuge, in the form of landed immigrant status, came from the federal state. It was a local, French Canadian officer who had made Michael Klein and Bonnie Sherr Klein's admission to Canada possible and the citizens of Montreal/Mooniyaang/Tiohtià:ke who made them feel welcome, but until 1971, when the Lang-Cloutier Accord was negotiated, it was the federal government that ultimately decided immigration admissions while retaining unique authority over questions of citizenship.

Here was a situation where resisters benefited from the openness of a federal state they also understood as antagonistic to the aspirations of their French Canadian neighbours.[80] Few had a sense of this incongruity before arriving in Montreal/Mooniyaang/Tiohtià:ke, but many would become aware of it over the course of their time there. People in sanctuary in the United States in the 1980s and in recent years have had to wrestle with a parallel tension, holding a sense of obligation to the same federal state that caused them to seek refuge in the first place, as exemplified, for instance, by US political and economic interference in Haiti and Central America.[81] Seeking sanctuary does not necessarily mean condoning the state, though it is often taken as such.

Organizations that emerged to help war resisters move and settle in Montreal/Mooniyaang/Tiohtià:ke throughout the 1960s navigated these tensions, and there was considerable debate about the role of the exile community as a result. While some believed that it was important to find work and build new lives, others maintained that the priority for war resisters should be to support the ongoing fight against US imperialism.[82] This meant turning one's gaze south, which in turn invited criticism about the "uncritical importation of US ideas and tactics."[83] When Tom Hayden, of the Students for Democratic Society, spoke at an international conference of war resisters organized by the Montreal American Deserters Committee in May 1970, he declared: "There's nothing political you can do for Canada without getting Canadians very upset eventually. Canadians don't need American advisors in their struggle against U.S. imperialism. You must oppose the U.S. as American exiles, not as Canadians or expatriates."[84] Perhaps reflecting some of this sentiment, organizations such as the Montreal Council to Aid War Resisters (MCAWR) would prove particularly attuned to French Canadian concerns by the 1970s, and a number of war resisters would eventually evolve their activist efforts towards anti-poverty efforts in the city.

MCAWR was founded in 1966 by a group of Canadian citizens and US exiles, including Ed Miller who had worked in New York City/Manaháhtaan on behalf of David Mitchell, a conscientious objector who had attempted to use the Nuremberg Principles as he defended his refusal to serve in Vietnam.[85] Another founder was Nardo Castillo, identified in RCMP records as a Spanish Canadian anarchist. Castillo passed away in 2017, but it is possible to find traces of his time in Montreal/Mooniyaang/Tiohtià:ke in the archival record and through oral histories. He appears in the documentary *Sur Les Traces d'Arthur* and in the memories of Dorothy Todd-Hénaut, who lived with Castillo from 1966 to 1968. According to Todd-Hénaut, Castillo was born in Spain, where his father was "very involved in the anarchist syndicalist movement." When Franco took over, Castillo was five years old, and "he and his mother walked over the Pyrenees into France," becoming part of the refugee community that so inspired Emma Goldman in her later years (see discussion in "The Hostile City"). According to Todd-Hénaut, Castillo was eighteen years old when his father brought him to Canada to avoid the draft in France, and he remained very involved with the Spanish anarchists throughout his life, publishing a newsletter with his father for the community.[86]

MCAWR's early efforts focused on providing practical advice and support, taking on much of the work that critics thought the federal government should be assuming.[87] For those without connections, MCAWR ran a temporary shelter called Gandhi House for which they asked people to provide a $1 donation per night.[88] Paul Kirby, one of the founders of the independent, underground magazine *Logos*, was hired by MCAWR to run Gandhi House. He remembers, "It was big, and we could put up a lot of people, it had a huge kitchen. The draft dodgers and resisters didn't stay very long, a lot of them moved into I guess what is Mile-End now. It was cheap as hell."[89]

By 1970, Gandhi House was operating from May to August and had enough bunk beds to house a maximum of twenty-five people. Those who did "not have much financial support" were "lodged with Montreal families," and MCAWR staff and volunteers provided job and immigration counselling services.[90] One of the main challenges for new arrivals in the city was finding work. Jesse Winchester, who would later gain fame as an accomplished folk musician, joined a French-speaking band called *Les Astronauts*. They toured north of Quebec City/Kebec and Winchester recalls,

> We were up on the north side of the St. Lawrence where the road ends. I had never experienced that before. We were driving down the road. It was gravel all the way, very rough. There were no bookstores and no restaurants and no nothing. I did get really depressed just for someone to talk to. That was hard, yeah, but like I said, I learned French and it was one of the steadiest jobs in music I've ever had. I got hundred dollars a week rain or shine. In the music business that's rare.[91]

Ed Miller, Bruce Garside, and Vance Gardner registered MCAWR formally in 1971.[92] By this time, the goal of the organization was to serve as an information and counselling service, and its work was quite pragmatic as a result. Indeed, the organization prided itself on being non-political "as far as possible." As Bruce Garside explained in 1969, "we do not ask for any justification for a person's decision not to serve in the military and we make no attempt to 'politicize' a person once he is in Canada."[93] As a result, MCAWR's goal was to integrate war resisters "into Canadian life as quickly as possible," and while organizers hoped people would be "politically active in Canada" they did not see the purpose of the organization as providing the "base for such activities." Crucially, MCAWR organizers positioned their work in relation to the larger anti-war movement. In a fundraising letter, Bruce Garside explained:

> We do not contend that immigration to Canada is the best or the most effective method of opposing the draft or the war. However, we do feel that for those who oppose the draft, the war, and the US government, and feel either that they cannot comply with the dictates

> of Selective Service and file for a CO (Conscientious Objector) classification or that they would be wasting precious years in the federal prisons (and concentration camps) coming to Canada provides a very exciting alternative.[94]

At the height of its activities, in the spring of 1971 (following a successful fundraising "Together" concert at Place-des-Arts featuring Jesse Winchester and Bruce Cockburn), MCAWR was engaging with one hundred people a week (in-person and through correspondence). Bill Mullen was employed as a full-time staffer, and there were five part-time employees.[95] MCAWR publicized its work and the opportunity to migrate to Canada with a circular entitled "Immigration to Canada and its relation to the Draft." It is possible that this is the material Michael Hendricks received in 1968 when he visited "The Purple Onion, a head shop" where he was told he could "find American resisters who knew how to fix the immigration thing." As he explains: "I went. They were nice college boy draft dodgers, around 20 years old, and they had published a pamphlet explaining how to immigrate (to get through the immigration process with no hiccups or hassles). I went home to New York, packed my bags and came back."[96] Like the Toronto publication prepared by Mark Satin, *Manual for Draft-Age Immigrants*, thousands of copies of "Immigration to Canada and its relation to the Draft" were distributed through various anti-war networks. A copy survives in Bruce Garside's personal papers and is annotated with the following information:

> Money
> Job confirmation
> Documents – educational
> Letters of reference from parents, clergymen etc, birth marriage divorce child support
> Border points avoid: L. Champlain, Highway 87, Blackpool / Lacolle, Rouses Point
> Dorval best. Never immigrate by bus.
> Don't bring car in. esp. if loaded up.
> Below 22 – Air Canada Savings Club – ½ price stand by flights
> Form – letterhead – date of starting work stated

Job to last at least 4 months (do not say 'temporary')
Immigration checks with new employer 6 to 8 weeks later when applicant goes to receive L.I card
At land borders – no permission to work until after medical (2 wks), And this you get at Dorval at the same time.

Goodnight

As the additional handwritten notes suggest, the work of MCAWR was very practical, and in some ways, this underscores what was at stake for people seeking refuge in this context.[97] Broadly speaking, they needed places to live, a means of financial support, and to avoid deportation. These needs were more immediate for some depending on their social and economic backgrounds and their situations upon arrival. Michael Klein, for instance, came with an offer of employment, but many others did not. In such cases, MCAWR used Gandhi House and the homes of sympathetic supporters, many of whom were war resisters themselves, to house people and offer short-term support.[98]

At the same time, as MCAWR's work and relationship with the local community evolved, activists turned to the question of how to foster deeper relationships with their French Canadian neighbours. By the spring of 1970, MCAWR was offering a "budding programme of resister-Québecois cultural relations including regular classes in conversational French." Additionally, MCAWR attempted to provide some context about the English-French divide in the city to new or possible arrivals, highlighting the "increasing isolation of English and French speaking interests in this province," suggesting that it was best not to approach this complicated and delicate subject with any "prejudgements." Indeed, MCAWR recommended that people "live and work in Quebec" before attempting "any conclusive appraisal."[99]

Returning to the archival file he first gathered in the 1970s, Bruce Garside noted the work of other organizations in this period, most notably the American Refugee Service, where David Beauchesne played a key role. Beauchesne was part of the "Québecois diaspora in the United States," having been born in Hanover, New Hampshire (traditional N'dakina territory). He had joined MCAWR "wanting to work specifically with deserters."[100] Beauchesne's interests eventually led to the creation of the American Refugee Service.[101] Michael Hendricks (another war resister who moved to the city in 1968) was Beauchesne's friend and neighbour for a time. He recalled that Beauchesne wanted to make sure that "his gang, the deserters, got (the) same treatment and benefits as the dodgers." Hendricks observes that this was generally "impossible" because they "lacked the background, the maturity and the $ to get more education at McGill or Sir George. So, David used his charm, his incredible speaking ability, and his boyish good looks to get as much as he could for them."[102] Reflecting further, Hendricks recalls the "enormous gulf that existed between us (those who were 'prematurely moral' – draft dodgers) and those that got morality after a touch of US Army life."[103]

Hinting at some of the underlying tensions around community solidarity and activism in this period, Bruce Garside recalls of MCAWR's work that they "were concerned that working with deserters" would "endanger" the war resister movement. He noted there was less resistance in Quebec because of the history of anti-conscription sentiment, but they were still worried. As Garside explains, "we were afraid that if we became publicly associated with helping deserters disappear in Canada (which a lot of them did quite successfully) that would feed that whole opposition to accepting war resisters as refugees."[104]

Support for war resisters in Canada moved in line with the sentiment about the United States' war in Vietnam more generally, but it also rested in part on the good behaviour of the war resisters themselves.[105] Any evidence of too much radicalism was cause for concern among law enforcement and government officials who considered draft evaders and military deserters to be a highly politicized group and who paid considerable attention to their activities, particularly if there were any communist or anarchist overtones.[106] Federal civil servants frequently received letters accusing them of mismanaging the situation and permitting lawless, dangerous elements into the country.[107] Nevertheless, most of the war resisters I spoke with felt a general sense of acceptance in Montreal/Mooniyaang/Tiohtià:ke, though some did get caught up with the politics and suspicions that circulated in official circles, particularly in the lead, and in the aftermath of, of the October Crisis in 1970.

October 1970

The roots of the October Crisis were decades, if not centuries, in the making. In 1963, FLQ was announced in Quebec. A loose organization, the FLQ sought the liberation of French Canadians from economic and political control by English Canada. Its founding was highly symbolic, coinciding with the two hundredth anniversary of the transfer of New France to British control. Placards at protests during this anniversary year read "1763–1963 – 200 years of servitude."[108]

The FLQ made itself known initially through a series of bombs that it deployed against targeted and highly emblematic entities, including large corporate enterprises, Mayor Jean Drapeau's Rosemount home, McGill University – a perceived "symbol of imperial domination" – and, in 1969, the Montreal Stock Exchange (an attack in which twenty-seven people were injured). In pursuing a violent bombing campaign, the FLQ was taking up what it considered to be a historic fight, which we might understand in some ways as a war within a war. Although the language of decolonization in Quebec in the 1960s was in some ways new, reflecting shifting global currents, it was also very old, building on long-standing anti-imperial sentiments and including previous efforts at resistance, most notably during the 1837 rebellion.[109]

In the fall of 1970, two FLQ cells, operating distinctly from one another, decided to pursue their radical aims of national liberation by kidnapping first James Cross, British trade commissioner, on 5 October 1970 and then, five days later, Pierre Laporte, a senior member of the provincial Liberal government. Their goal was to use their hostages to negotiate a series of demands comprising the publication of the FLQ Manifesto and the liberation of political prisoners, including many FLQ members. It was a tense, uncertain, worrying time. Roger Goodleaf, who was involved with the fire brigade in Kahnawà:ke, recalls, "When someone needed an ambulance, we left whatever we were doing, sometimes in the middle of a meal and just did what we had to do. Even when the FLQ were in Montreal, it was scary but we had to go."[110] For his part, Jürgen Dankwort remembers, "one of the first things I realized was that there was a lot of sympathy for the FLQ because, I was in a tavern … on the 'Main,' Saint-Laurence Blvd." Dankwort said he "walked in there" because the "TV was on" and "people were sitting around and when they heard about Laporte being kidnapped," they clapped. He notes somberly, "that was before he was murdered…"[111]

The kidnappings and the declaration of an "apprehended insurrection" to justify the enactment of the War Measures Act triggered fiery discussions about the goals of the FLQ, national liberation, and the debatable necessity of suspending civil liberties. Within hours of the War Measures Act being introduced on 16 October 1970, the Canadian military (which had been in the city even prior to the legislation being invoked) and police forces across Quebec were raiding homes, workplaces, and businesses in their search for FLQ militants and sympathizers. This included the homes of anti-poverty activists in Saint Henri and members of the federally funded Compagnie de Jeunes Canadiens, some of whom (including Louis-Philippe Aubert and Bernard Mataigne) had previous ties to the FLQ.[112] A total of 1,600 raids took place over the following days and months. Some of these took place at hostels that served the war resister community. Almost five hundred arrests were made, some involving high-profile individuals such as Pierre Vallières and Pauline Julien. Michel Brault's 1974 film *Les Ordres,* based on the testimonials of people who were imprisoned, captures some of the random detentions and the abuses of power that took place in this period. A letter from the Canadian Council of Churches to MCAWR leaders also hints at generalized harassment, noting that members "very much regret" hearing "that the Aid groups have had so much difficulty since the implementation of the Military Measures Act."[113]

The discovery of Pierre Laporte's body in the trunk of a car belonging to one of the kidnappers the day after the War Measures Act was invoked, shocked people across the political spectrum and sowed additional fear about the size and scale of the FLQ's operations and possible future violence. David Rapaport describes being "horrified."[114] For some, the use of the War Measures Act appeared all the more justified in light of Laporte's death while others continued to believe the federal government was overstepping, exploiting the FLQ's actions as a means to suppress the Quebec nationalist movement as a whole.

As a young mother, Mary Harman lived the events of October 1970 at a distance, or as she put it, "only peripherally."[115] As she explained, "with a one year old child and 5 months pregnant with the second, I barely had time for my Women's Lib Conscious-Raising meetings."[116] She later elaborated on this sense of detachment by explaining, "We were white, English-speaking, living in the McGill Ghetto (the Milton-Parc area near McGill University)." The distance between English and French was sometimes vast. Mary recalls being told "by someone that if I did go out for a walk, it was not safe to go east of 'The Main' (Saint Laurent Blvd) because that was 'where the French lived.'"[117] Despite, or because of, such comments, there was considerable sympathy among US war resisters for French Canadians during the October Crisis. As Harman recalls: "Our left-leaning politics were those of two naive American twenty-year olds who lived through the 60s: we had no deep understanding of the French/English divide. We felt no threat from the FLQ, in fact we were always sympathetic to the separatist cause. However, when private citizens began getting arrested during the War Measures Act (including only one person we knew, a French doctor working at a clinic with my husband) did we feel some concern for our own situation as immigrants with a US Federal warrant outstanding."[118] As this explanation suggests, the actions of the Canadian federal state weren't shocking to people who "lived through the 60s" and already distrusted the actions of the US government though they created a certain amount of disillusionment with Prime Minister Trudeau and their chosen country of refuge.[119]

Writing in the *New Republic*, Roger Williams declared, "I [had] lived as a draft-refusing fugitive in the US before coming to Canada and I can honestly say that I was never as afraid of the authorities as I was in Quebec in October."[120] Yet, none of the people I interviewed expressed the same level of fear, even those who were interrogated directly by the police, in some cases months before the October kidnappings. David Rapaport was called in for questioning in the spring of 1970 because, as he says, he was "identified … incorrectly of course," as being an FLQ sympathizer by an undercover agent who had heard his name mentioned at a party.[121] The police were interested in verifying these claims. As Rapaport explained:

> I used to have deserters stay in the house … part of the Underground Railroad, that's what we called it … This one guy called me who was staying there, I was at work, and he says that some cops just came to

> the house and they were asking about you and they were looking over your books. My books were all revolutionary books, stuff on China, stuff we read … And they were asking about it and everything.[122]

Although all of this was rather standard fare, Rapaport was, nevertheless, called in for an hour of questioning. Rapaport's sense was that at that particular moment was that he was "pretty vulnerable," especially to deportation, though he had never previously worried about his safety in Canada.[123] However, Rapaport was fortunate that through his employment at Tundra Books, he had access to Philip Cutler, the owner's husband, a high-profile lawyer who was eventually appointed a Quebec Superior Court Judge in 1987. Cutler's impression was that, although the course of the interview and its outcome were predictable, "the police were also desperate because they didn't have anything."[124]

This perceived desperation is amplified in descriptions of other encounters between war resisters, the police, and the military. Jürgen Dankwort, who was writing for the underground *Montreal Free Press* at the time, came to the attention of police because of the Front d'Action Politique (FRAP) posters he had plastered in his basement apartment window. The FRAP was a left-leaning party made up of labour activists, students, and citizens' committees. It was accused of supporting the FLQ during the municipal election held on 25 October 1970, in which Jean Drapeau and the Civic Party were triumphant. The FRAP was soundly defeated.[125]

In Dankwort's case, he felt generally safe because he believed police were mostly interested in anyone who was French, "les sympathisants" as he calls them, rather than a German national. Still, it was unnerving for him to have the police in his small, "damp" basement apartment. As Dankwort recalls, one police officer stayed with him in the kitchen while the other looked around. He remembers thinking, "I am in trouble now because I have books on Marx, Engels, all that stuff in the bedroom where the guy was looking." In the end, they didn't seem to take notice or to care if they did. More critically, they also didn't pay attention to the stacks of copies of the *Montreal Free Press* in the small entranceway to the apartment. Dankwort now recognizes how fortunate this was for those issues carried copies of the FLQ Manifesto, which the paper had decided to publish in violation of the War Measures Act. Instead, what Dankwort experienced was a mild scare and the mocking attitude of one of the police officers who trilled "Love and Peace" as he departed.[126]

Yet, despite this close brush and a later encounter with a soldier on the street (who stopped him on his way back from getting groceries and commented on the amount of celery in his shopping bag), Dankwort never felt unsafe. I asked him about this, and he said, "never." Without prompting, he then explained his sense of things this way: "I was certainly ... well look ... JÜRGEN DANKWORT ... that's not a Tremblay, Pauline Julien or Paul Rose."[127] Dorothy Todd-Hénaut echoed this sentiment, responding that she never felt vulnerable during the crisis itself. For her, the scarier moments had come previously, when she had her phone tapped because of her involvement with the Voice of Women for Peace organization.[128] Similarly, as historian Wendell Nii Laryea Adjetey has shown, fear in the Black community manifested itself most powerfully in the wake of the violence at Sir George Williams in the winter of 1969, less so during the October Crisis. As with the idea of feeling safe, any sense of fear was also deeply contingent on and shaped, in part, by the politics of race, class, and gender.[129]

Akin to Jürgen Dankwort and David Rapaport, Ken and Jackie Hyman had direct encounters with law enforcement during the October Crisis even though they had moved outside the city and were living near Mansonville (traditional N'dakina territory) in a house on a "country road with no other houses near," when James Cross was kidnapped.[130] Their problems stemmed from the fact that they owned a green VW beetle and "some friends, fellow students" had come to visit. Their friends happened to own a red VW beetle; combined, these two vehicles matched the profile of cars suspected of belonging to one of the FLQ cells. The Hymans later learned there had been aerial surveillance of their property. The result, as Ken Hyman remembers, was an early morning raid by the Quebec Provincial Police (QPP). It is an event that still stands out in his mind five decades on. He recounted the experience this way: "I was of all things, sitting at the kitchen table, cleaning a rifle (for hunting) ... I look up, at the kitchen window, and there is a QPP officer with a gun, and at the same time there are two doors downstairs and other police burst in ... What was most frightening was that these guys were more terrified than me. This guy's hand was shaking.[131] The police spent a couple of hours combing the house, "searching around," and "asking a lot of questions," but found nothing to connect the Hymans to the FLQ (there was nothing to be found). Ken Hyman's lasting impression was that they "were so incompetent and so unprepared" that he ended up worrying most about the state of affairs among provincial law enforcement.[132]

Asked about his experiences, Bruce Garside was similarly nonchalant about the actions of the police and the military during the crisis.[133] In October 1970, Garside, his wife, and children were living with filmmaker Peter Katadotis and his family in a collective in a big old house in the neighbourhood of Westmount. Katadotis was viewed with generalized suspicion by authorities for his involvement in the Greater Montreal Anti-Poverty Coordinating Committee, which insisted "poverty is political!" and devoted considerable energy to housing issues and matters of health and welfare, including childhood malnutrition.[134] Their program was characterized by "open leftist," feminist and anti-racist agendas.[135] As a result, on the night the War Measures Act was introduced, Garside and Katadotis slept elsewhere and only an intervention by a wealthy donor who was sympathetic to the work of MCAWR and the anti-poverty movement kept the authorities at bay. Garside felt personally safe because he had been "vouched for."[136] As outlined previously, the overarching concern for many war resisters in the city seems to have been overreach by the Canadian state rather than the FLQ itself.

When I interviewed Dorothy Todd-Hénaut in 2021, she laughed about her experiences during the October Crisis and said: "Well, it was very funny because I had a couple of old lovers, former lovers, who showed up (fortunately not on the same night) to hide … both of whom were Anglophone." When I suggested that she offered sanctuary, she said "yes" and giggled some more.[137] Similarly, Michael Hendricks sheltered two friends after the War Measures Act was introduced "for a few days until the raids were over." As he explains, "both of their apartments had been raided by the police during the mailbox bombing days (1963 and 1966) and they did not want to be picked up in the sweep that was going on."[138] He, himself, felt quite removed from the events. He suggests that, for him, "the October Crisis had little effect" except "to make things more exotic and strange in Montreal."[139] He remembers that "on the evening following the kidnapping of the Minister of Labour (and Manpower), Pierre Laporte" he and his "friends were in a gay disco on Stanley Street in downtown Montreal and there was a raid; the cops cleared the place out but let us all go home." He found this to be "just weird."[140]

As the crisis wore on, quotidian concerns returned to the fore, though David Rapaport suggests that people never forgot that James Cross was in captivity.[141] The fluid shift from crisis to quotidian concerns was also reflected in the way that former war resisters remember the October Crisis decades later. There are certain early moments that stand out in their memories but much of the day-to-day is now a blur. Some of the strongest memories relate to how people were personally affected by the crisis and where they were when the crisis came to an end. In official terms, the October Crisis concluded on 3 December 1970 when James Cross was released following a series of negotiations that resulted in the exile to Cuba for his FLQ captors and their relatives, including Jacques Lanctôt, his wife, and child; Pierre Séguin; Marc Carbonneau; Jacques Cosette-Trudel, and Louise Lanctôt. Somewhat ironically, the exchange of prisoners took place at the former Expo 67 pavilion on Île Ste-Hélene, the very site that mesmerized many war resisters arriving in the city a few years prior. Bruce Garside remembers "being glued to the TV as the exchange took place." As he says, "I was both surprised and relieved when that exchange came off peacefully. Surprised, because I thought it likely that the police and military would make an attempt to capture the kidnappers. Relieved, because I didn't want another innocent person to lose their life through the actions of the FLQ. As with many progressive folks at the time, I was very impressed by the manifesto they insisted be broadcasted, but happy to have an end to the violence."[142]

Like Garside, David Rapaport recalls that "everything stopped" as he and his employer, May Cutler (later mayor of Westmount from 1987 to 1991), listened to the radio broadcast that detailed "play by play" the news of the release and transfer. Similar to Bruce Garside, David Rapaport recalls a kind of collective exhale, a "sigh of relief" when the exchange was successfully completed. Nevertheless, reflecting on the events of that season fifty-one years later, Rapaport also understands that although "the incident was over," nationalist politics were not, pointing to the election of the Parti Québécois in 1976. When I asked about whether there was a sense of finality to the crisis on that December day, Rapaport simply quipped, "does anything ever end?"[143]

Conclusions

Reflecting on the events of 1970, war resister Michael Hendricks suggests: "If anything about the October Crisis caused me to question my choice (by then irreversible) to immigrate and live the rest of my life in Canada, it was the strange contrast of the welcoming the Canadian government offered me and what they served up to their own citizens who supported the independence option. It seemed 'out of place' or in contradiction with the seemingly open English Canadian worldview and character."[144]

Yet, despite a sense of disappointment with the Canadian state and its actions in the fall of 1970, many people stayed, becoming more established and committed to their new homes. For some, such as Jürgen Dankwort, who eventually pursued doctoral studies in social work at the Université de Montréal, this meant a shift away from anti-war work to a more pronounced focus on anti-poverty issues, inspired by concerns about the "alienation and disempowerment of the poor."[145]

Deteriorating economic conditions in the city and the province certainly fuelled concerns about housing and welfare issues among anti-poverty advocates.[146] The changing economic conditions also affected the way resisters experienced the city and the kinds of politics they engaged with. By 1971, the economic high of the 1960s was clearly fading. As a result, some thought it was irresponsible for people to seek refuge in Montreal/Mooniyaang/Tiohtià:ke and Quebec given a situation where jobs were "next to non-existent."[147] As a circular from MCAWR explained in May 1971: "Unemployment in Quebec is normally twice as high as it is in Canada. In 1971 the unemployment figures 'seasonally adjusted' and compiled by the Department of Manpower and the Dominion Bureau of Statistics reached 12%. The true figure is probably closer to 17% or 18%."

For MCAWR, which was at its height in terms of the number of people it was assisting, the economic situation meant it was harder "to help people find jobs" and get "the job confirmation letters necessary to obtain Landed Immigrant Status." It was also difficult to obtain shelter for new arrivals as "the number of people willing or able to provide housing (had) dropped sharply." Most significantly, MCAWR underscored a sense of responsibility for the situation in Montreal/Mooniyaang/Tiohtià:ke and eventually announced that it was "unwilling to aid or encourage anyone, for whom it is not necessary in seeking employment in Québec when hundreds of thousands of Québecois are without jobs."[148]

This attention to the economic circumstances of friends and neighbours suggests a heightened sense of community feeling and a continued focus on the part of MCAWR on immediate and proximate circumstances in contrast to the work of other organizations, such as the American Deserters Committee, with were characterized by more of an exilic gaze. Yet, developments abroad also affected how organizations operated in these years. The withdrawal of US troops from Vietnam in 1975 and President Jimmy Carter's proclamation of a general amnesty on 22 January 1977 changed the need for refuge, and the number of United States' war resisters arriving in the city declined.[149]

Instead, new refugees from US imperialism began to arrive, namely thousands of refugees from Vietnam, Cambodia, and Laos who were resettled through private citizen and government efforts after 1978. Many would remain in Montreal/Mooniyaang/Tiohtià:ke and Quebec, drawn, in part, by linguistic affinities because of the long history of French imperialism in Southeast Asia. They, too, would live and experience the city in different ways, with varying degrees of interest and comfort in becoming engaged with issues of concern to their neighbours. In some cases, they would also absorb the paradoxical nature of refuge in the city in these years, and the implications of moving to a country that had played a part in their own displacement.[150] As refugees from communist oppression, however, their relationship with leftist, national liberation currents of thought in the city was even more complicated than it was for United States' war resisters opposed to the actions of their own government in Vietnam, Cambodia, and Laos.[151] Nevertheless, they, too, would negotiate the politics of refuge in a complex, dynamic city in the years to come.

When I first started working on this chapter in the fall of 2021, I was first and foremost concerned with physical sites of refuge. I was struck by the descriptions of Chilean refugees and migrants occupying churches over the course of 1998 and 1999 and by the ways in which they identified potential sites of refuge and acted upon them, changing the nature of those spaces, if only fleetingly. In undertaking research about these events, I was cognizant of the earlier parallels around discussions of people seeking refuge in the Canadian embassy in Santiago, Chile following the military coup in 1973. I have always had a sense that the federal government's response would have been much less significant than it was (and it was already quite minimal) were it not for the fact that people sought asylum in a diplomatic space.

There was something about the physicality involved in the act of taking sanctuary in the embassy and later in churches in downtown Montreal/Mooniyaang/Tiohtià:ke that drew my attention from the outset. However, as many religious leaders have noted, a church is more than a building, it is a community. As a result, I had to think through the relationship between different physical spaces and the kinds of communities attached to them. In the case of diplomatic asylum offered in 1973, this community essentially amounted to the long reach of the state. In the case of church sanctuary over the course of 1998 and 1999, people encountered communities of faith and were simultaneously exposed to, and shielded from, the power of the state in certain respects. The result was an emotional and tense series of events, and I decided to explore this history in a three-part drama, reinforcing the sense of theatre I encountered as I interviewed people involved and read through the news coverage from this period.

In the cases described in "The Occupied City," having a physical space in which to shelter was critical for the possibilities that ensued. On a certain level, they evoke C.S. Lewis' Narnia series about children evacuated to the English countryside during the Second World War who discover and enter a magical wardrobe, which opens to a wildly different land. By entering physical refuge, people changed the landscape of possibilities available to them, sometimes minutely and sometimes dramatically. One of the participants, Laura Lopez, reminded me of this point during our many wide-ranging conversations. She is a fearless interlocutor and I was inspired by her candour to think about what notions of community and being in physical sanctuary or occupying churches meant for those who were involved.

My conversations with Laura Lopez also led me to reflect on the significance of returning to these events over two decades later. Throughout our discussions, Lopez spoke freely about topics that I would have struggled to discuss publicly. As I have gotten to know her over the years, I have come to understand that she is a very forthcoming person. I don't think her openness in this case was out of the ordinary, but I do think there was something about being asked about previous events and about having personal experiences taken seriously and considered as part of a larger history that proved meaningful for both of us. "The Occupied City" is, therefore, about the physical occupation of space, the making of sanctuary, and people's relationships to particular sites and communities.

Laura Lopez wanted to see her name attached to this history, and so I have kept it here with her permission. As in "The Uneasy City" chapter,

I have anonymized the sources around other aspects of this history and omitted identifying information for anyone whose permission I did not have to name them in the print. Unlike in "The Uneasy City" chapter though, I have retained the names of the churches so that the sense of physicality that I was interested in foregrounding initially did not disappear as well.

July 2023, April 2024

The Occupied City

> At that time Chile was a haven of peace, isolated from the world. Santiago slept in the foothills of the Cordillera detached from the rest of the world ... Nothing ever happened. The presidents of the republic walked unescorted through the streets. Only the present moment existed. One day this peaceful life came to an end. A revolutionary tide swept us to the centre of the world.
>
> — *NOSTALGIA DE LA LUZ*, PATRICIO GUZMAN, 2010

IN FEBRUARY 1998, a group of approximately thirty Chilean refugees and migrants occupied the Church of St-Jean-de-la-Croix in Petite Patrie, Montreal/Mooniyaang/Tiohtià:ke. It was the first in a three-part drama that would see Chilean refugees and migrants challenge perceptions of post-dictatorship stability in their homeland in different ways. Politicians, religious leaders, labour organizers, activists, and fellow Chileans in the city, along with the general public were called upon to witness and act on their behalf. Some intervened as a result. The drama that subsequently unfolded over the course of a year involved two different congregations. Crucially, the sanctuary seekers were not invited in; they occupied the church premises and used the physical structures of the churches and, to some extent, the religious communities associated with them to stake their claims for the future.

The group involved in Act One, what we might call The Thrust, represented over a hundred people who were facing deportation. To create awareness about their circumstances, some participants went on a thirty-eight-day hunger strike as their lawyers and supporters, along with federal and provincial negotiators, worked to resolve the impasse. A temporary solution was eventually found, but when the federal government failed to review the many cases in question in an expedient manner, some members of the group returned to St-Jean-de-la-Croix in the fall of 1998 in what we might call Act Two, The Riposte. Refusing to accept the government's failure to meet the negotiated terms, they countered with a second occupation, entangling their initially reluctant hosts yet again. This time, tensions with the congregation and among the sanctuary seekers were more pronounced and harmful to the sanctuary cause. The group left St-Jean-de-la-Croix after two months.

Four months later, a different, smaller group of Chileans took sanctuary in another church, the Church of the Advent, in what I am calling Act Three, The Expulsion. This sanctuary incident was largely separate from the previous two in terms of participants. Nevertheless, it reflected a similar set of concerns about what would happen to those in sanctuary if they were sent back to Chile and a parallel refusal on the part of state authorities to countenance the sanctuary seekers' claims. It also involved a threatened hunger strike, which violated the group's conditional entry into sanctuary and led to their expulsion from the church. All the members of this group were eventually deported.

The actions of the sanctuary seekers and the nature of their reception were shaped by several concurrent factors: the immediacy of having people physically present in church sanctuaries; the complexity of late twentieth-century immigration regimes; the imminent threat of deportation; gender dynamics; and the politics of solidarity such as they were in the 1990s when the overarching focus of governments in North America was on freer and faster trade. They were also shaped by earlier histories involving refugees from Chile, especially those who sought to escape the 1973 coup that brought General Augusto Pinochet to power and other instances where people contested state efforts to curb migration from Chile to Canada and the United States during the transition years of the early post-dictatorship period.

The challenge of being legible as a refugee was critical in the aftermath of 1973, and it continued to be critical in the intervening period as the contours of the archetypal refugee figure of the Cold War, that of the persecuted political actor, began to dissipate. As the hard divisions that marked out the Cold War era blurred, receiving states often saw economic opportunism when people made claims about ongoing difficulties, rather than the need to provide protection from persecution. As a result, there was a lot of history to overcome in the final years of the twentieth century. There was also a lot of history to rely upon. People who had fled Chile after 1973 came to the assistance of those insisting on their need for protection in 1998 and 1999. There was also considerable solidarity between labour organizers, intellectuals, and politicians in Quebec and Chile over this same period. Sanctuary seekers themselves turned to some of this history as well in making their own claims to refuge in 1998 and 1999.

As such, the physicality of refuge is the main actor in the drama explored here, with the weight of history as a prominent plot line. The term "physicality of refuge" refers to the physical spaces of the church and the physical presence of people in sanctuary. It also points to the manner in which people used their bodies, and stories about their bodies, to insist on their need for protection in the face of marked ambivalence on the part of the Canadian state and, to some extent, among religious circles. They made their bodies count.

Writing about the militarized use of refugee bodies, critical refugee studies scholar Yến Lê Espiritu has reconceptualized the term "body counts." It was the lead title of her influential 2014 book and repurposes the conventional military term used to document fatalities to account for how refugee bodies have shaped a distinct politics of humanitarianism and memorialization among settler societies. Although Espiritu's focus was on troubling state practices in this regard, we can also see how migrants used their bodies to evoke "the lives that could or would have been."[1]

In occupying churches, sanctuary seekers challenged what sociologist David Fitzgerald describes as an "architecture of repulsion," one that has only grown more expansive over time and that contains both invisible and visible barriers.[2] By being physically present and sometimes pursuing or threatening hunger strikes, sanctuary seekers sought to disrupt ideological barriers such as the myth of post-dictatorship recovery in Chile. They wanted to force state actors to consider their immediate responsibilities to migrants in their midst. Sanctuary was seen as a vehicle by which to accomplish these crucial objectives. It was also an opportunity to galvanize supporters and sway public opinion. Church leaders and congregations became inadvertent participants in the sanctuary theatre that unfolded.

The twinned threads of exclusion and resistance came together over the course of three acts in a society that was, itself, wrestling with questions of power and self-determination as debates over sovereignty for Quebec peaked and then simmered after a major referendum on the issue in 1995. The sanctuary seekers' actions revealed the terrible need to be seen and to be heard in this period of political tumult. They also showed the lengths required for this to happen in an era when religious influence was flickering, and the federal government was focused on trade and economic relations, to the detriment of considered responses to ongoing human rights violations in a society scarred by decades of dictatorship.

On Chile

On 11 September 1973, a military coup d'état in Chile brought down the democratically elected Parti Unidad (UP) government and President Salvador Allende. Supporters had been euphoric at Allende's election in 1970, and many people around the globe took heart from his victory. Lawyer Noël Saint-Pierre, who was in Germany at the time and later became involved in the 1998 sanctuary case at St-Jean-de-la-Croix, called Allende's victory a "proposition d'espoir" (a hopeful project).[3] All this was dashed by the coup d'état, which was led by generals from all sections of the Chilean military and backed by the Nixon administration and the CIA in the United States. Allende was killed in the attack on the presidential palace. Reprisals against organized labour, sympathetic priests, nuns, educators, and students were swift, in what one historian has described as a "war of annihilation."[4] An estimated two thousand people perished in the weeks immediately following the coup.[5] Anywhere from twelve thousand to twenty thousand others were held in the Stade de Chile, a site that soon became synonymous with torture and executions.[6] In fact, scholars have described the entire country "as a huge concentration camp," noting that the regime blocked international air travel for almost two weeks after the coup, making it difficult for people to leave.[7]

Despite these initial restrictions, about twenty thousand people managed to flee the country in the months that followed, with an estimated thirty-five hundred people using embassy routes to do so.[8] Following in the tradition of political asylum in Latin America (guaranteed in the 1933 Montevideo Convention on the Rights and Duties of States and the 1954 Caracas Convention on Diplomatic Asylum), some Allende supporters and foreign nationals sought refuge in foreign embassies in the days and weeks following the coup.[9] The ambassadors of Sweden and France were very active in providing refuge. Those of other countries, less so. In the Canadian context, this reluctance stemmed in part from the fact that it was not a signatory to the conventions on diplomatic asylum in Latin America, as well as its relative disengagement with the region.[10]

Up until that point, successive Canadian governments' interest in Chile had largely consisted of providing food and material relief in the wake of "calamitous" flooding, avalanches, and earthquakes throughout the 1950s and 1960s. Along with other western governments, the Canadian government had also negotiated with the government of Chile over its repeated requests regarding foreign debt refinancing.[11] Generally speaking, however, Chile had been considered one of the more "stable" Latin American countries and had not garnered much attention from the Canadian state beyond these few occasions when the latter's relative economic fortunes were revealed.[12] This perceived stability was also reflected in Chile's own history as a site of refuge. In the 1930s, Spanish Republicans had crossed the ocean to relative safety during and after the civil war in that country (where anarchist Emma Goldman sought to lend a hand, as discussed in "The Hostile City). This history of migration and refuge was made richly complicated in Isabel Allende's 2019 novel *A Long Petal of the Sea*. Twenty-five thousand refugees from neighbouring countries also sought refuge in Allende's Chile in the early 1970s, including Brazilians and Uruguayans fleeing violence in their homelands.[13] The story of refuge after the 1973 coup, therefore, involved more than Chilean nationals, there were all kinds of people who suddenly found themselves in dangerous situations.

At the time of the military coup, Canada's ambassador to Chile, Andrew Ross, was away on a short sojourn to Argentina to buy a luxury car.[14] In Ross' absence, people desperate to avoid the violence of the military regime began to present themselves at the chancery, located on the tenth floor of 11 Ahumeda in Santiago. They also went to the ambassador's official residence at 33458 Avenida Presidente Kennedy (Las Saldes) and the residences of some of the junior embassy staff. In the case of the latter, staff drove people to the embassy to give them refuge. This particular action worried civil servants in Ottawa (traditional territory of the Algonquin Anishnabek), who suspected diplomatic overreach. In a flurry of telexes to embassy staff, they emphasized the lack of authority and the outright danger of civil servants undertaking such actions.[15] Nevertheless, within two weeks of the coup, there were eleven Chileans and two Brazilians (in addition to eight Canadians who were relying on the custom of national protection) sheltering in the Canadian embassy.[16]

Despite the generally favourable view of the refugees, described in one report as making a "good impression" with the appearance of being "fairly decent people," the Canadian government approached the practice of providing what it called "temporary protection" with considerable trepidation.[17] The government worried about the implications of giving shelter to people in the embassy, fearing that they might be "saddled with long term guests." Civil servants pointed to the case of Cardinal Mindszenty, who lived in the US Embassy in Budapest for fifteen years after the Hungarian Revolution in 1956, as a cautionary tale.[18] Nevertheless, over the course of the fall of 1973, public sentiment in Canada increasingly favoured doing more for people in Chile.

Much of this support came from intellectuals and students, as well as religious and labour leaders, in Quebec. There were distinct religious connections between Quebec and Chile, the result of a French Catholic missionary presence in Chile from 1853 on.[19] Clotilde Bertrand, a nun from Quebec and someone who was considered suspicious by the Pinochet regime, returned home to play an active role in the reception of refugees, as did missionary Jean Ménard.[20] French Canadian priests, including Jean Latulippe, Maurice Hébert, and Pat Donovan, did the same, providing reports on the conditions in Chile as they did so.[21] Early religious solidarity with Chilean refugees was, therefore, born of people's own experiences in the country and their testimonies gave additional weight to the situation being described by refugees themselves.

There were also important ideological connections. Many activists were inspired by Salvador Allende's socialist views. For instance, he was celebrated by supporters for his "violent diatribe against American imperialism" when he spoke at the Hemisphere Peace Conference to End the Vietnam War in Montreal/Mooniyaang/Tiohtià:ke in 1968.[22] The socialist politics and anti-imperial discourse in Chile resonated with the "movement for national liberation" in Quebec, although it alienated some of the province's financial and more conservative elite.[23] The 1973 military coup came only three years after the October Crisis in Canada and the persecution of Allende's supporters was felt forcefully among like-minded thinkers.[24] Articles in left-wing publications such as *Maintenant* and *Chili - Quebec Informations* (1973–9) spoke to a sense of shared destiny.[25] As a result, all the major unions in Quebec, including the Confédération des Syndicats Nationaux (CSN), the Fédération des Travailleurs et Travailleuses du Québec (FTQ), and the Centrale de l'Enseignement du Québec (CEQ), voiced their support for the victims of the coup.[26]

These interests coalesced in the establishment of the Comité de Solidarité Québec-Chili in 1973, which included a mix of intellectuals and labour activists (such as Michel Chartrand, president of the Montreal Central Council for the CSN, who had been arrested and imprisoned during the October Crisis).[27] Described as a "revolutionary group" by the federal government, the Comité de Solidarité organized fundraisers for opponents of the military junta, raising the ire of the Chilean ambassador in Canada.[28] Members also occupied federal immigration offices to protest the slow response to the situation in Chile.[29] Additionally, the Comité de Solidarité coordinated a tour of Canada in December 1973 by Hortensia Bussi de Allende (Salvador Allende's widow). Allende gave talks in Toronto/Tkaronto and Montreal/Mooniyaang/Tiohtià:ke, which were all well attended. In Montreal/Mooniyaang/Tiohtià:ke, on 1 December 1973, Allende spoke alongside Caesar Chavez of the United Farm Workers and Louis Laberge of the Quebec Federation of Labour at the Montreal Forum. The organizers' intention was to "show Quebec workers solidarity for their under-privileged brothers in other countries of the world."[30] Also on the stage, according to government reports, were "numerous spokesmen from various North American Indian Bands."

Unbeknownst to those advocating publicly for a more substantial response, the federal government had already developed a "Special Chilean Immigration Programme" in late November 1973.[31] However, few details of the program were announced publicly for fear of drawing attention to the embassy in Santiago as a potential site of refuge. The program facilitated departures from Chile by providing people with loans for their airfare and financial support to help with their settlement upon arrival in Canada. The initiative treated people as immigrants, not refugees. "Sympathetic consideration" meant that the usual selection criteria, in terms of skills and language qualifications, were suspended, but medical and security screenings remained in place. People were given three-month entry permits and told they could not engage "in any international subversive activity in Canada."[32] In addition to receiving applications initiated by Chileans seeking to leave the country, the government also worked with religious leaders and missionaries in Chile (including Quebec nuns Marie-Denise Dubois, Denise Caron, and François Lapierre) and others in Canada to identify people held in Chilean jails for "acceptable protests" who could then be selected for migration to Canada.[33] Religious actors, therefore, played a key role in shaping the possibility of refuge in the immediate post-1973 period.

Crucially, work on behalf of political prisoners continued beyond the scope of the Special Chilean Immigration Program, which ran from 1973 to 1978. Seven thousand people ultimately moved to Canada under the auspices of this program, even though it had initially been designed with only three hundred to one thousand people in mind.

Flora Fernandez was one of the people who moved to Canada as a result of the program. In 1975, Fernandez had been detained for four days by the military junta in Chile, which was interested in her political allegiances. It was also concerned about her father's sympathies as he had been active in socialist circles. When she could not or would not provide her interrogators with the information they were looking for, she was transferred to a women's prison for four months.[34] Upon her release, her family encouraged her to go into exile, and she was selected by the Canadian embassy as part of the original program for political prisoners.

Fernandez was first sent to Edmonton, Alberta (located on Treaty 6 territory and the traditional homelands of the Métis Nation), where she worked in chicken factories and cleaned hotel rooms. However, Fernandez explains she never felt quite at ease in Alberta. English, as she underscored, was the language used by the military in Chile. To her, it was the language of the coup. French felt more comfortable, and she happily moved to Montreal/Mooniyaang/Tiohtià:ke in 1979.[35] From the moment she arrived in the city, Fernandez became deeply involved in women's rights campaigns, eventually serving as a member at large for the National Action Committee on the Status of Women. When we first spoke in the winter of 2022, she had been working with the Assistance aux Femmes women's shelter for forty-one years. She became part of the support network for the people in sanctuary in the winter of 1998, drawn to their cause as a fellow Chilean but also out of concern for the safety of the women in the group.

The Transition Years

Even with the ongoing operation of programs to support political prisoners, the Canadian state and others were happy to forget the violence of 1973 as the Pinochet regime stifled dissent and presented a veneer of relative calm and normalcy.[36] Banks and businesses were also quick to forget, or at least to ignore the continued violence.[37] American economists aided in the development of a market economy during the Pinochet era and Canadian companies were eager to participate, especially in the mining sector. In 1975, Noranda (a major Quebec mining company) returned to invest and operate in the country through its subsidiary Chile Canadian Mines, even as news of Chileans who were disappeared by the state became more frequent.[38] Noranda's ambitions were vehemently opposed by the Comité de Solidarité Québec–Chili.[39] Two years later, a consortium of Canadian banks, including Toronto-Dominion, the Royal Bank of Canada, and the Bank of Nova Scotia, floated a considerable loan to the Pinochet regime, provoking an outcry among clients in Canada, one of whom described the funding as the equivalent of "bankrolling Hitler."[40] Nevertheless, the arguments in favour of closer and better economic relations with Chile held considerable traction in official circles.

The impression of an improved political situation at the macro level belied the lived experience of many Chileans who continued to endure physical and economic insecurity. The country felt the 1982 global recession keenly.[41] Women, in some cases deprived of their loved ones and in various states of grief and mourning, bore a considerable amount of the political and economic violence of this period.[42] Thousands of women were detained by the Pinochet regime and in some cases they suffered "sexual torture" at the hands of the regime.[43] The particular plight of women political prisoners attracted international attention as people campaigned to raise awareness and get women released from prison, and sometimes into exile.[44]

Yet, as the situation in Chile became less immediate, it also became more and more difficult to argue for the need for protection. Violence could be manipulated, erased, or dismissed, as evidenced by evolving immigration and refugee policies in Canada in this period. By 1987, there was a considerable backlog in the refugee determination processing system, which prompted the federal government to undertake major efforts to streamline and reduce the number of applicants. This included increasing the use of the "safe country" designations (which denied the right of certain nationals to make asylum claims based on the perceived stability in their homelands), visas, and other control mechanisms, as well as expanding the powers of interdiction at sea and developing an expedited refugee determination process.[45]

Even though Chilean nationals constituted a relatively small number of those filing claims for refuge in the late 1980s, officials began to consider migration from the country as generally suspect.[46] Their suspicions were seemingly affirmed after authorities identified thirteen people at Mirabel Airport in September 1987 as having been smuggled in from Chile.[47] Civil servants also heeded reports of fraudulent travel agents in the Valparaiso region (on the west coast of Chile), who were allegedly counselling clients on how to obtain tourist visas and then make refugee claims in Canada.[48]

As a result, officials started to take a sterner view of people's narratives of persecution, alleging that "the fact that someone has been detained in Chile does not in itself mean anything. Many people were detained in general round ups and were released after being checked out by Government."[49] This approach created a confrontational dynamic between a federal government interested in enforcement and reducing its obligation to asylum-seekers and refugees and activists who maintained that Chile was unsafe for many people, especially for women. The Canadian government's efforts to streamline the asylum-determination system and narrow its scope of responsibilities led to a series of protests throughout the late 1980s as migrants and their advocates sought to elucidate alternative and more expansive conceptions of what safety looked like.

In 1987, for instance, people undertook a hunger strike in opposition to the newly imposed federal requirements that necessitated a transit visa for anyone who also needed a visitor's visa to travel.[50] Protesters began by demonstrating on 25 February 1987 in front of the federal immigration offices in Montreal/Mooniyaang/Tiohtià:ke. The offices were then occupied by over two dozen people who went on a hunger strike to press provincial and federal authorities to act. Juan Iturriaga, a Chilean community leader and pastor at the unregistered Église Chrétienne Espagnole de Montréal, became a spokesperson for the group (he would later take on prominent roles during another hunger strike in 1989 and during the Church of the Advent sanctuary incident in 1999). The protesters also received support from the Table de Concertation des Organismes au Service des Personnes Réfugiées et Immigrantes, an important refugee rights organization in the city.[51]

The federal minister for employment and immigration at the time, Benoît Bouchard, sought to undermine the merits of the protest by questioning the integrity of those involved. Bouchard declared, "I find it absolutely staggering that, after two or three days in a country, one can find the time and the ability to contest its laws ... That bowls me over. You've hardly had time to arrive in the country, and you're already contesting its laws."[52] The minister's effort to equate a long-standing presence with the right to have rights was galling. Still, despite Bouchard's dripping condescension, the hunger strikers garnered a lot of support, especially after it became public knowledge that people as young as thirteen were involved. One woman eventually obtained a court order to stop her daughter from taking part. Her child had gone eleven days without eating and later explained to the media she felt it was important to join the strike because she didn't "want people to suffer."[53]

Two years later, people undertook another hunger strike to draw attention to the children who had become separated from their families as a result of visa restrictions imposed by the federal government.[54] After a year of campaigning on this issue, with delegations going to Ottawa (traditional territory of the Algonquin Anishnabek) to plead their cause with parliamentarians, organizers determined that further pressure was required. As a result, almost two dozen people embarked on another hunger strike. They used Juan Iturriaga's small church offices on Papineau Avenue as their base and decorated the outside with banners to draw attention to the events unfolding inside. It took weeks for the strike to have any real impact, prompting two of the participants to refuse water as well as food on 2 January 1990 in a bid to emphasize the seriousness of their concerns. Three Quebecers also joined the strike as a sign of support, and in early January, the media began to take notice of the protest.[55] Much of the coverage involved a hunger striker who lost twenty-one pounds over twenty-four days and twice had to be taken to hospital.[56]

Parti Quebecois MNAs (members of the Quebec National Assembly), including Michel Bourdon, Louise Harel, and Gérald Godin spoke out on behalf of the migrants and refugees, as did former MNA and minister Bernard Landry. Additionally, Nicole Boudreau, the former president of the Société Saint-Jean-Baptiste/St-Jean-Baptiste Society, Gérald Larose of the CSN, and singers Pauline Julien and Gilles Vigneault all lent their support. In supporting the strikers' cause, Boudreau emphasized the solidarity of Quebecers, explaining, "Everyone is asking you to give up your hunger strike. You are no longer alone." She added, "Many Quebecers find it altogether inacceptable that something so simple as the family – a father, a mother and children – should be turned into something so complicated." According to news reports, the strikers applauded at this point, and cries of "Vive Québec!" could be heard.[57] Throughout the 1980s, therefore, at every point that the federal government sought to suggest that Chile was safe, these claims were met with opposition not only from Chilean refugees, migrants, and their supporters, but also from certain political leaders in Quebec who understood that migration control was an essential way of claiming and exercising sovereign power.[58] They became important backers when people sought to contest federal interpretations and authority over their situations.

Debates about the nature of life in Chile evolved in the late 1980s and throughout the 1990s. In August 1988, Decrees 1197 and 1198 issued by the Pinochet regime permitted the return from exile for many.[59] In 1991, Patricio

Aylwin (Christian Democratic Party) was elected to power, and the rule of the military regime came to an end.[60] While the political transition was significant, the new coalition government (the Concertation) followed the economic approach previously adopted by the military regime, resolutely determined to become a "model" free market.[61] This aggravated existing inequalities. Moreover, in the rush to change and establish a difference between the military regime and the new one, the state's inclination was, paradoxically, to avoid public discussions of human rights violations. Scholars have described the result as a "seemingly endless transitional amnesia," emphasizing the inadequacies of the government's 1991 Truth and Reconciliation Commission.[62] Hurt and fear didn't just vanish with the formal change of a regime or the introduction of a commission of inquiry. Well into the early 2000s, the mothers and relatives of the disappeared were still combing the Atacama Desert in the hopes of recovering the remains of their loved ones. In the documentary *Nostalgia de la Luz*, a grieving sister tells of finding the skeletal remains of her brother's foot and communing with it in her family home. She grieved him so much that even being able to sit with his partial remains was better than nothing.

Flora Fernandez, who visited Chile three years after Pinochet's fall from power, recalls "a heaviness" to the general mood and a leanness to people's bodies. As she said: "on sentait qu'ils avaient vécu quelque chose de grave" (we sensed that they had lived through something serious).[63] Aylwin's rise to power did not stop violent retributions on the part of military, paramilitary, and police, and women continued to be discriminated against in Chilean society. Yet it proved difficult to prioritize women's issues amidst the larger, yet still largely private, reckoning with human rights violations in Chile. As psychologist Gonzalo Bacigalupe explained, "initially many activists rejected efforts to have women talk about domestic violence in women's groups because they felt that state violence had priority."[64]

Despite legal changes, such as amendments to the 1989 Civil Code so that women were no longer considered their husband's personal property, the problem of domestic violence persisted. In recognition of the ongoing challenges, the first public shelter in Santiago opened in 1996 for women fleeing troubled situations in their homes.[65] Yet despite the continued difficulties in Chile, the emphasis in Canada, as well as the United States, was increasingly on trade and on a return to "normalcy" in Chile. These efforts were capped by the 1997 Canada-Chile Free Trade Agreement, during which time the government suspended the use of visas for Chilean nationals in a show of goodwill. Even the political prisoners program (PPOP) was oriented elsewhere by this time, most notably in El Salvador and Nicaragua. As a result, by the late 1990s, Chileans had a very hard time making the case to the federal government that they were people in need of, and worthy of, the Canadian state's protection.

A Drama in Three Acts

As the foregoing shows, there had been considerable activism prior to the events of the late 1990s, and so the sanctuary theatre (what might almost be described as guerrilla theatre) that unfolded over the course of 1998 and 1999 was not without context. It was inspired by the history of post-1973 relationships and the experiences of Chileans in Canada, as well as broader shifts in activism in the early 1980s that used the physical presence of migrants on state soil to challenge the legitimacy of state actions in the realms of migration, asylum, and international affairs.

Historically and into the present, states have refused uninvited migrants in part because they understand from historical precedent and decades of vocal protests and community organizing that it is difficult to refute claims of belonging and effectively manage deportations once people are on national soil. The physical dimension of the 1980s Sanctuary Movement, in which people were sheltered within US and Canadian churches, is a critical example of this phenomenon. Beginning in the early 1980s, migrants from El Salvador and Nicaragua, and later Guatemala, encountered disproportionate levels of refusals when it came to their asylum claims precisely because of the Reagan administration's simultaneous involvement and denial of the "dirty wars" in their homelands.[66] Compounding this harm, the Reagan administration also restricted access to the asylum-determination systems by preventing entry or deporting people before they could even make their asylum claims. Refusal rates were, therefore, much higher than reported.[67]

The Sanctuary Movement that emerged in response involved the physical protection of people in churches and local communities across the United

States and, later, Canada. People's bodies were critical for drawing attention to the toxic foreign policy that the Reagan administration was pursuing in Central America and the injustices at play in the operation of the asylum-determination systems. As noted in the introduction to *Sanctuary in Pieces*, these campaigns were often based on the testimonies, storytelling, and public witnessing of those in sanctuary.[68] This marked a fundamental and not unproblematic shift in the way sanctuary had played out historically and the ways in which it would evolve into the twenty-first century.

Some of the people who were assisted by US sanctuary workers continued north to Canada. At the same time, these efforts also inspired independent sanctuary efforts in Canada. The first Central American refugee denied by the Canadian government took shelter in 1983 in a church in Beloeil, Quebec (traditional Wabanaki and N'dakina territory). Several other cases followed. By the time the first Chileans claimed sanctuary in February 1998, community activists and religious communities in Montreal/Mooniyaang/Tiohtià:ke had become much more familiar and comfortable with sanctuary as a practice. Nevertheless, the physical presence of people in sanctuary continued to generate layered and often divergent responses.

Act One: The Thrust

In February 1998, a group of thirty Chileans, representing a total of 160 families, sought sanctuary in the Church of St-Jean-de-la-Croix, then located at 6651 Boulevard St-Laurent in the city's Little Italy neighbourhood.[69] They believed that the church was a safe physical space, one that was removed from the reach of immigration authorities and law enforcement and one where they could make their case for admission to the federal and provincial authorities responsible for their fate, as well as to the general public. Some members of the group were facing deportation after over-staying recently imposed visa restrictions; others had been in Canada for years and were seeking to regularize their status. At the time, the church was led by Father Denis Prescott of the Congregation of the Holy Cross (connected with the Saint Joseph's Oratory of Mount Royal, with its imposing dome that is visible across the skyline of Montreal/Mooniyaang/Tiohtià:ke).

Born in Drummondville, Quebec (traditional Wabanaki and N'dakina territory), Prescott was ordained in 1964. Over the course of his career, particularly because of his leadership in the International Boy Scout movement, Prescott spent considerable time abroad. He studied Spanish in Mexico and spent time in Uruguay, Paraguay, Colombia, Brazil, and Chile. He was, therefore, seen as potentially sympathetic, and he himself admits that because of his order's connections to Chile, he was intrigued by the case being made by the sanctuary seekers.[70] St-Jean-de-la Croix, therefore, seemed like a welcoming place compared to some of the other churches the group had considered, and had actually approached previously. The fact that the church was in the riding of the Quebec immigration minister, André Boisclair, was key as participants hoped to leverage federal-provincial conflicts in the realm of immigration policies to their advantage.[71]

When several people arrived for a Sunday mass in late February and stayed, Father Prescott's initial reaction essentially amounted to "a desire to get them out." However, he was unsure about how to proceed.[72] He first contacted Brian McDonough, who was Director of Social Action in the office of the Catholic Archdiocese to determine next steps.[73] McDonough shared some of Prescott's concerns: the church was not built to house people, and so there were no showering or bathing facilities available.[74] The basement of the impoverished church was also regularly rented out to community groups for much-needed income, and this was a consideration in determining how to proceed as sanctuary might negatively impact the church's precious revenue.[75] Moreover, as with all sanctuary cases in this period, the church leadership was truly concerned about the possibility that law enforcement might enter the confines of the church to arrest and deport people (as had occurred at the St-Bernard Church in Paris, France the previous year when a number of "sans-papiers" had sought sanctuary).

The eviction of the "sans-papiers" from St-Bernard had garnered international media attention, and Father Prescott and other members of the Catholic Diocese did not want a repeat situation where they might be seen as casting people out of St-Jean-de-la-Croix.[76] Archbishop Jean-Claude Turcotte, appointed 17 March 1990, who saw the sanctuary seekers as "vulnerable" and who believed in social action by the church, especially in the realm of human rights, was likewise concerned about what it would look like if police entered St-Jean-de-la-Croix.[77] After on-site consultations, it was agreed the church would offer sanctuary for one week, after which time the group would then be transferred to a more appropriate church, if necessary.[78] In the end, the group stayed for about three months. Although members of the congregation and the diocese were concerned about the length of time that people were spending in sanctuary, church members voted on three different occasions to allow them to stay on.[79]

This first group of sanctuary seekers was quite diverse, and participants essentially came together to ask the federal government to review all their cases individually. Some were solo applicants, while others were married, and many others had children, often quite young – there were several infants among the group. Some were failed refugee claimants; others had overstayed their visas. Most were women, though this was not obvious at the time because the public-facing roles were largely taken up by male participants.[80] Together, the members of this varied group made an initial thrust, insisting that they had legitimate concerns that the federal government needed to address.

For one of the participants, Laura Lopez, the search for refuge resulted in part from her precarious immigration status in Canada. More pressingly, however, was her need to escape domestic violence. Lopez was twenty years old when she arrived at Mirabel Airport with her daughter and her boyfriend, the father of her child, in November 1995. She was leaving a precarious domestic and economic situation in Chile, which had involved her working from 8 a.m. to 3 p.m. at a bank and then from 4 p.m. to 9 p.m. at a computer distribution warehouse. Her daughter had been in daycare since she was three months old, and the long hours that Lopez worked were in large part for a child that she rarely got to see. When her boyfriend decided to move to Canada, she decided to go with him, wanting to improve her daughter's circumstances. Unfortunately, Lopez's time in Quebec was marked with difficulties similar to what she had endured in Chile. The domestic violence she had experienced repeated itself in her home in Montreal/Mooniyaang/Tiohtià:ke, and her precarious immigration status meant that she was vulnerable to economic exploitation. Like many migrants without legal status, she worked long hours as a farm hand harvesting vegetables and also in the underground economy, replacing labels on clothing merchandise from China with ones that read "Eaton's" or "Zellers."[81]

Lopez was denied asylum in 1996 and had determined to hide and essentially go underground rather than be returned to Chile. When she became pregnant a few months later, she decided to have an abortion, believing that she would be deported if she had the baby in a hospital.[82] She continued to feel insecure. When a massive ice storm hit the city in January 1998 (weeks before people sought sanctuary at St-Jean-de-la Croix), Lopez and her family lost power for ten days. She remembers being cold, hungry, and incredibly fearful. When a neighbour told them they might get food and support at a nearby church, Lopez refused to go. She worried that she might be asked for her documents and deported.[83]

As a result, when Lopez heard rumours that a group was organizing to go into sanctuary, she asked to be a part of the effort. Lopez was initially refused, and she suspects it is because some of the women in the group were jealous. Listening to Lopez recount the events from this period, often in tears, it becomes clear that there was a certain amount of friction within the relatively small Chilean community in the city, with a number of accumulated grudges and grievances.[84] Undeterred, as sanctuary got underway Lopez grabbed her daughter and her stroller and made her way to St-Jean-de-la-Croix. There, she tried to make herself indispensable by cleaning toilets and other spaces so that the group would consider her case alongside the others. Certainly, some of the organizers were aware of Lopez and her efforts and also what she was enduring. One day, Lopez came to the church with a swollen eye, and one of the leaders immediately surmised that she had been harmed at home.[85] Even then, Lopez didn't stay in the church as she needed to work to support her family. She was nevertheless very invested in having her case for asylum reviewed. Lopez knew that she was not a political refugee in the conventional sense of the term, though she might have been considered a refugee under the Immigration and Refugee Board's 1993 guidelines to address gender-based persecution.[86] Lopez was simply scared about what awaited her and her daughter if they returned to Chile.

Many of the people who occupied the church felt the same way. Yet they were also apprehensive about their fate in Canada. The possibility of being swept up, detained, and deported was ever-present, even for those inside. They knew the stakes were high. As a result, in response to considerable intransigence couched in sympathetic utterances from the federal government, the sanctuary seekers organized a committee called Non à l'Indifférence (No to Indifference). Eighteen members of the group then decided to undertake a hunger strike, which they initially described as a "fast" to draw further attention to their situation.[87] In the end, the hunger strike lasted thirty-eight days and was assessed at the time as the longest immigrant hunger strike ever undertaken in Quebec. Participation ebbed and flowed, though it appears that at least ten people participated from beginning to end, lying prone on cots provided by the Red Cross with signs reading "Future Canadiens."[88] One sanctuary seeker who began the hunger strike alongside the others, was quickly rushed to hospital when her condition deteriorated.

Hunger strikes were, and continue to be, a powerful way for people, especially migrants who do not necessarily have recourse to conventional political channels, to draw attention to issues of concern.[89] They are a powerful tool of resistance that historian Nayan Shah insists is "unlike any other."[90] Hunger strikes draw attention to injustice, often framed in anti-imperial or anti-capitalist terms. They regularly propel at least some sympathetic observers to action as people see someone causing themselves physical harm; they see the anguish and the obvious diminishing. However, as historian Kristina Shull has detailed, hunger strikes by migrants in detention in the United States in recent years have led to brutal reprisals, including rapid deportations, assaults, and a deterioration in living conditions.[91] In other words, they can sometimes invite harsh reprisals and lead to unintended consequences. As discussed previously, Chilean nationals in Canada had undertaken hunger strikes in 1987 and 1989 to protest immigration controls. They obtained considerable publicity for their cause but may also have contributed to the state's perception of certain migrants from Chile as a "problem."

Crucially, when people decided to go into sanctuary in 1998 and undertake a hunger strike to gain support for their situation, they weren't just building on previous hunger strikes in Quebec and Canada, they were following on a long-standing practice of full-bodied activism in Chile.[92] Inspired by the coordinated international strike in the summer of 1978, five hundred political prisoners went on a hunger strike in Chile in December 1986 to demand better conditions, and several were eventually hospitalized. There were other hunger strikes in Chile in 1991 and 1992, one of which coincidentally took place in front of the Canadian embassy in Santiago, though it was "not directed at Canada or the Embassy itself."[93] Nevertheless, the ambassador worried that if one of the strikers died, the situation might "deteriorate further."[94]

A similar, anxious, tone was apparent in the spring of 1998 as the hunger strike attracted media observers, as well as a range of interested parties to St-Jean-de-la-Croix. The hunger strikers had the support of many residents, including members of immigrant support groups and others whom journalists described as "Québecois de vielle souche" (old stock).[95] Flora Fernandez recalls that she went to the church after following reports about the hunger strike in the news. Fernandez was aware of previous protests in this vein in Quebec and Chile, and by day twenty, she said, "je ne pouvais plus" (she couldn't take it anymore), and she went to visit the group. She was alarmed about the potential long-term health issues for the hunger strikers. Additionally, and in part because of her work with Assistance aux Femmes, she was concerned about the fates of the women and children in the group.[96]

Despite the ongoing negotiations, finding a solution was difficult because the federal government did not want to be perceived as conceding. It was a challenging situation to overcome, and supporters from the church and leading unions in Quebec played a critical role. As Brian McDonough recalls, "The feds were perfectly happy to wait things out until the situation would become manifestly intolerable." Minister André Boisclair, the provincial member of parliament for the riding was also frustrated, describing the situation as "intolerable" and asking that the church "expel the Chileans."[97] The stumbling block for the protesters was the federal government's insistence on receiving a full list of names of all the cases to be considered and the group's concern about how this information might be used. An almost complete lack of trust or faith meant that members of the group worried that the federal government would employ any detailed biographical data to deport rather than admit.

The hunger strikers were finally convinced to stop on 27 March 1998 when a support committee made up of influential representatives, including Archbishop Jean-Claude Turcotte, Father Denis Prescott, Gérald Larose of the Confédération des Syndicats Nationaux, and the Table de Concertation des Organismes au Service des Personnes Réfugiées et Immigrantes intervened. According to Brian McDonough, who was similarly involved, Flora Fernandez also "had an important role of liaison with the Chileans themselves."[98] As McDonough later recalled, it was difficult work. The political situation between the federal and provincial governments was so charged that the committee members found themselves "communicating with officials from the two levels of government about what procedures to resolve the crisis might be seen as acceptable to each other."[99]

Although the federal government refused to make any special concessions, it did agree to a speedy review of individual applications. This was noteworthy because there was a considerable backlog of cases at the time. The Quebec immigration minister also expressed an inclination to accept applications made provincially, seeing an opportunity for his government to take a more active role on the question of immigration more broadly. There was a lot of jurisdictional manoeuvring. The role of the support committee, which worked closely with lawyers William Sloan (a former professor at UQAM) and Noël Saint-Pierre (who had worked on behalf of Chilean refugee claimants previously), was critical to ensuring that the merits of each case were clearly presented. With his union connections, Gerard Larose was often able to secure employment offers, which helped with specific situations.[100]

The trick with the government review was that people had to leave the country to file new claims. Many eligible families exited the country to Mexico (they were ineligible to enter the United States, which would have been an easier destination to access) and re-applied for a Certificat de Sélection du Québec (CSQ) to be admitted as immigrants. The Société Saint-Jean-Baptiste/St-Jean-Baptiste Society provided financial support when necessary.[101] For her part, Laura Lopez was too afraid to go to Mexico, not trusting what might happen to her or her daughter there. She eventually presented herself to be deported, having given up all hope of staying in Montreal/Mooniyaang/Tiohtià:ke. Yet, instead of being deported, she was given the opportunity to apply as an immigrant when a new visa officer heard her story. Her admission was, therefore, largely tangential to what happened at St-Jean-de-la-Croix, though her capacity to make her claim was propelled by the activity in sanctuary.[102]

Act Two: The Riposte

The seeming success of the initial compromise was betrayed when five families were deported, even though their cases were still under consideration as part of the general review. At the end of June, many of the protesters left for Mexico to resubmit their applications for admission, but the federal government failed to move quickly.[103] It may have been an instance of out of sight, out of mind. Without the physical presence of migrants in Quebec and Canada, the need to engage was less urgent. This absence seemingly confirmed the approach the sanctuary seekers had taken previously in occupying St-Jean-de-la-Croix and ensuring the various levels of government were aware of their physical presence so that their concerns could be fully addressed.

Whatever the circumstances, by August 1998, the situation was still not resolved. None of the 160 people involved in the cases being reviewed had been accepted as refugees by the federal government or immigrants by the Quebec government. Supporters continued to highlight the "cas de risque de retour, en particulier pour les grévistes de la faim, sur les cas de violence conjugale, sur les cas problèmes liés à l'orientation sexuelle et sur les cas où un enfant ne pouvant pas recevoir des soins appropriés au Chili."[104] They emphasized the material, emotional, and psychological difficulties of being without status: "(les familles) sont exclues du système d'assurance-sante, leurs enfants ne peuvent fréquenter l'école, ils n'ont pas de permis de travail, et s'exposent à travailler pour 3$ ou 4$ dollars l'heure sans avantages sociaux, sécurité au travail."[105] Activists soon decided on a second occupation of the Church of St-Jean-de-la-Croix. As one participant explained: "Il a fallu le faire, parce que le Canada avait commencé à déporter les gens : ils allaient chercher les personnes partout, entrant dans les écoles pour prendre les enfants, et les gens étaient obligés de se rendre … L'occupation a donc été un moyen d'achever ce que nous avions commencé avec la grève de la faim, afin d'arrêter les arrestations."[106] This second sanctuary incident lasted from 17 September to 23 October 1998. In conversation in 2023, Father Prescott drew a distinct line between the two experiences. The first one was good, the second one was not. The second occupation was angrier, more intense, and potential solutions seemed more elusive, though people were just as determined to have their cases considered favourably by the federal and provincial governments. The press coverage, especially in *Le Devoir* and *La Presse*, was highly favourable, if only initially and briefly. The end story does not appear in newspaper accounts of the period.

Nevertheless, for the brief moment during which the story held their gaze, journalists and op-ed contributors detailed unjust deportations and offered critiques about the insensitivity of the Quebec government in failing to process applications in a timely manner. They also attacked the federal government for pursuing detentions and deportations. One account detailed how a woman was held at the detention centre in Laval despite a difficult pregnancy. Another family had been separated upon deportation, leaving a child of fourteen behind in Montreal/Mooniyaang/Tiohtià:ke. There were also accounts of children being detained on their way to school, and parents were consequently apprehended when they went to find them.[107] The outrage was palpable.

Nevertheless, Father Prescott noted that, within the congregation and the community, the second occupation resulted in "tensions allant jusqu'à des menaces de violence de la part de certains individus du quartier."[108] On this second occasion, the sanctuary seekers were decidedly unwelcome in the church even as journalists and many members of the public continued to support them, perhaps even more so given the disappointing government responses. Despite the mood within the church, Father Prescott felt it would look bad to turn people away even as conservative parishioners complained of people being in sanctuary, taking issue in part with the fact the children were biking in the aisles of the church.[109] It was a difficult situation to resolve. Although General Pinochet had been made a senator for life in March 1998, he was arrested for crimes against humanity on 10 October 1998, and charged with the murder and disappearance of over three thousand people in what was considered a major achievement in international human rights law.[110] Still, Pinochet's arrest further complicated arguments about the extent to which Chile was safe. For people in the church, the news of Pinochet's arrest must have aroused mixed feelings. The brutal dictator was no longer free, but neither were they as they continued to contest their treatment at the hands of federal and provincial authorities in Canada. In the end, however, people simply left St-Jean-de-la-Croix and hoped for a promised resolution. There was little more to be done in the church, and the church itself had little left to offer beyond the building itself.

Act Three: The Expulsion

Critically, this was not the end of sanctuary for everyone.

The story continued in the spring of 1999 when a small group of Chileans sought sanctuary in the Church of the Advent in Westmount. This historic church was built in 1892. At the time of the sanctuary incident, it carried the address of 4119 De Maisonneuve Boulevard and was located near the Atwater metro station. The church was, therefore, frequented by many English-speaking parishioners from across the city, as well as a number of local residents. As such, it was perhaps more socioeconomically diverse than might be expected given the neighbourhood's long-standing association with the affluent and influential in Montreal/Mooniyaang/Tiohtià:ke. Moreover, the church had a history of engaged political action. This spirit was reflected in part in the character of Reverend Robert Warren, who led the church at the time of the sanctuary incident. Warren grew up in British Columbia and the Yukon Territory before moving to Quebec at the age of twenty. He was a beloved church leader, described by many people as "dynamic," and his departure from the church was keenly felt when he left in 1999 to become head of the Old Brewery Mission in the city.

From the outset of the sanctuary incident, Reverend Robert Warren and many parishioners recognized that their church was in a prime location for such action, situated as it was in the riding of the federal immigration minister, Lucienne Robillard. As with the Church of St-Jean-de-la-Croix, the Church of the Advent made for a strategic choice.[111] As a result, in April 1999, a family of five, along with another man who appears to have been a family friend, "arrived unannounced" for a Wednesday, noon-time service.[112] After the service, they declared they were staying. There were only a few people in attendance, likely five or six elderly members of the congregation who preferred this service and the Bible Study that came afterwards. Most members of the congregation only became aware of the presence of these "strange visitors" the following Sunday when the decision to offer sanctuary in response to the occupation was announced.[113]

According to Reverend Warren, the church leadership was familiar with people "who were working helpfully with refugee claimants" in Montreal/Mooniyaang/Tiohtià:ke.[114] However, Reverend Warren and congregation members were unfamiliar with those involved with the new group. As Revered Warren later explained, "We had no basis of trust upon which to agree to work with them."[115] Instead, given the way events unfolded, the reverend suspected they were "looking for a conflict, first with me as a 'representative of the church' and therefore evocative of authority, and then ultimately with the Minister of Employment and Immigration." As the reverend explained, "we happened to be in a building in exactly the right place."[116]

Like Reverend Warren, Janice Simpkins (who was the church warden at the time) recalls the sanctuary experience as somewhat forced, reflecting some of the anxieties that both parishioners and sanctuary seekers likely endured in this period.[117] As she recounted, the group literally walked into the church and started to camp out, "with all their stuff."[118] Church leaders then met to discuss what to do. They felt trapped because, in their view, the group did not have an especially strong case. Still, they did not want to expel them. At the same time, they also recognized that the church space was inadequate in terms of living conditions for people in refuge; it simply wasn't designed to house people. Much like the situation at St-Jean-de-la-Croix, meeting rooms were rented out in the summer and there were no showers or bathing facilities.[119] One parishioner described the basement of the building as "swampy" and recalled that the "sink in the kitchen (was) not in good shape."[120]

Church leaders were led to understand that the six people were part of the group that had sought sanctuary in St-Jean-de-la-Croix and made their way to Mexico in order to reapply for admission to Quebec and Canada; however, this was not the case.[121] The family friend had been in the United States for many years and had come north believing that the Queen would be visiting Canada and would provide some kind of amnesty for Chilean refugees, in contrast to the policies of the US Republic.[122] These ideas struck several parishioners as quite odd. Similarly, some people had misgivings about the father who seemed "paranoid," although they suspected from what they knew of conditions in Chile, that these might have taken quite a toll on him.[123] Still, even though they had reservations about the small group, in part because of the manner in which they had presented themselves for sanctuary, the church leadership resolved to let them stay.[124] Reflecting on the incident decades later, Janice Simpkins observed that refugees often have little in the way of "cushions" and hard times are, therefore, especially hard.[125] This sense of being able to provide some kind of padding encouraged the decision to offer sanctuary. As a result, the parish council agreed that the group could stay "on the condition that nothing take place which put the health and wellbeing of the families, especially the children, at risk."[126] Given the events of the preceding months, they were acutely worried about another hunger strike.

This hopeful goodwill did not persist for long, and things soon "deteriorated."[127] The congregation had little to do with the families (they only saw them at Sunday Service), although they seem to have been generally well-liked. One of the members, Michel Gagnon, remembered the children years later and recounted how his youngest daughter (who was a one-year-old at the time) was a source of interest for them. Janice Simpkins taught Sunday school to the "lovely" children.[128] However, the mood among the congregation soon soured. There was a certain amount of unease about the publicity that the Chileans' case generated, especially for those congregation members who were themselves also moving through the refugee determination and immigration selection processes.[129] Additionally, members of the congregation sensed that the group's supporters weren't always acting in their best interests. There was a feeling that some supporters "hated being in a church" (a theme discussed in "The Uneasy City" chapter as well) but nevertheless felt that it was politically necessary in order to challenge the authority of the federal state to deport.[130]

There was also considerable mistrust about the motives of Juan Iturriaga, a pastor and immigration consultant. As noted previously, Iturriaga had been involved in earlier protest cases involving Chilean migrants, including the 1989–90 hunger strikes. Significantly, although Iturriaga was the pastor at the Église Chrétienne Espagnole de Montréal, the church was unregistered for tax purposes. It had, therefore, been determined that it would be unsafe for people to take sanctuary there.[131] Instead, Iturriaga worked on behalf of the group while they sheltered at the Church of the Advent. These efforts became increasingly politicized, eventually prompting church leaders to ask the group to leave. The tipping point appears to have been the announcement of a planned hunger strike. As Reverend Robert Warren put it, "When they declared that they would go on a hunger strike and that this would include the children, we took this to mean that the sole condition of their remaining on the premises was being breached."[132]

During my research, I attempted but failed to contact any members of this last group. As such, I can only imagine what their time in sanctuary was like and how they might have received the order to leave the church. I assume the message was conveyed through Pastor Juan Iturriaga, who was involved with their initial entry into sanctuary. I wonder how he framed the issue to them. And I wonder how they responded. Were they saddened? Or did they feel some sense of relief in knowing that their future options, if constrained, were now more obvious? Perhaps they were tired of the uncertainty, or perhaps they were still hopeful. They may have felt angry and defeated, or maybe they were defiant. I would still very much like to know what all of this meant to them.

It certainly was a difficult decision for the congregation and the church leadership. Janice Simpkins recalls "feeling sorry" for the families.[133] Others worried about the backlash. Reflecting on the perceived hostility at the time, the church leadership went so far as to arrange for a police escort when the families departed to ensure that activists didn't enter the sanctuary for fear that they might damage some of the church's property as retribution.[134] Reverend Warren recalls that he "worked out a deal with the police that (the sanctuary seekers) would be removed from the premises but NOT handed over immediately to the Immigration folks – that they would have essentially a safe passage from the church premises."[135]

After the group was removed from the church, the father attempted to go into hiding again, leaving his wife and three daughters exposed. He apparently trusted that the federal government would not separate them through deportation (even though there was precedent for such action). While the father went underground, the rest of his family took shelter in Juan Iturriaga's Église Chrétienne Espagnole de Montréal. When authorities learned that at least some members of the group were at Iturriaga's church, they verified "with the city of Montreal and with the police, who confirmed that the site was not registered as a church."[136] Armed with the knowledge that they wouldn't be violating customary law, authorities proceeded to enter the site. When news of the arrests became public knowledge, protesters physically occupied the federal immigration offices on St-Antoine Street but to little avail. All the members of this last group were ultimately deported.

Conclusions

In tracing the ways in which the "architecture of expulsion" has been reinforced in recent years, David Fitzgerald ultimately insists on the role of civil society in "guard(ing) the paths to refuge from the duplicitous attempts to close them."[137] It is a tall order. As the description of the sanctuary theatre here makes clear, civil society has only ever been inclined or able to do so much. In 1998 and 1999, sanctuary was not willingly offered to Chileans contesting their treatment at the hands of federal and provincial authorities, it was taken. This created a ripple effect as those immediately involved were forced to consider the merits of the sanctuary seekers and their cases, as well as their own sense of responsibility. Protesters had previously occupied spaces, most notably embassies and federal immigration offices, but this was the first occasion where they used the sanctuary of the church to argue for asylum. Their choice of location gave additional substance to their undertaking for it invited the participation of a much wider range of actors, most notably church leaders and congregations, in addition to existing networks of support among activists, lawyers, and labour organizers.

All of this theatre took place in a heightened political climate of strained federal and provincial relations that were being actively renegotiated. For sanctuary seekers in 1998 and 1999, a key challenge involved finding ways to have concerns about their treatment attended to by authorities in multiple jurisdictions. This meant overcoming immediate dangers, such as the threat of deportation, as well as addressing decades of perceptions about the nature of life and politics in their homeland and their own desirability as citizens. The history of contestation and protest associated with the Chilean community in the city and abroad made the sanctuary seekers desirable to some and unattractive to others, even within the communities where they sheltered. Although people found physical refuge in church buildings, labour organizers, activists, lawyers, church leaders, and congregations, as well as the general public, all played a supporting role in extending refuge beyond the immediate confines of the church. Crucially, this support only extended so far and when the conditional terms of entry were violated in the spring of 1999, the last group of sanctuary seekers were expelled from the Church of the Advent and deported.

In a twist of fate, neither of the two church communities involved in the sanctuary events of 1998 and 1999 exist in the same way today. The Church of St-Jean-de-la-Croix was sold in 2000 for financial reasons and was de-sanctified and turned into condominiums three years later. The Church of the Advent was sold in 2004 and is now the House of Prayer for all Nations. In some respects, this is a fitting analogy for the way congregations became involved with seeking sanctuary in the late 1990s. Organized religion could play a role in offering space with a certain symbolic impact, but its own status in Quebec and Canadian society was increasingly constrained. Moreover, as Reverend Warren perceived, sanctuary seekers (or at least their advocates) could, on occasion, appear hostile to the very communities with whom they were seeking protection. As a result, religious congregations and leaders made a series of cautious decisions about what they were willing to do, and it was ultimately the decision of one church that put an end to the third occupation. Still, the fact that sanctuary seekers were able to achieve any compromise at all from the federal and provincial governments is a testament to their determination, evidenced most powerfully in the undertaking of an extended hunger strike and the ways in which the solidarity between Chilean nationals and certain socialist and labour circles in Quebec endured across the decades.

The sanctuary in three acts described here raises questions about the possibility and character of refuge and the duty of individuals and collectives to those in their midst. The theatre also invites questions of the sanctuary seekers themselves and how they perceived their roles and responsibilities in what was unfolding. For her part, Laura Lopez understood what was at stake in being part of a group of people laying claim to the state. She also recognized the limitations, pursuing her own path when the negotiated outcome proved contrary to her own interests. Lopez stayed in Montreal/Mooniyaang/Tiohtià:ke after participating in the first occupation, raising her children, and observing and participating in the changing city around her. When we spoke in the summer of 2023, she was employed at the local library and remained unwavering in her determination to make sure that people were well cared for. She was volunteering with the local food bank and talked about keeping an eye on young women in distress. She had also reconnected with Flora Fernandez and was serving on the board of Assistance aux Femmes. Lopez was proudest of her children, of her daughter Natalia, who was pursuing studies in the law, and her son. And she had no regrets about the first sanctuary occupation, even if the weight of what they were all up against is still with her.

I initially heard about some of the cases described in the study that follows from lawyer Stewart Istvanffy, who responded to a very early inquiry of mine through the Canadian Council for Refugees about people who might be able to offer insights into sanctuary cases in Canada. When I first met Istvanffy in 2016, he spoke passionately about the cases he was involved with from 2002 to 2014. I was immediately interested. Still, it was only when I dug into these cases more deeply that I came to appreciate that they occurred during a period of consolidated activism and organizing in the face of restrictive and punitive immigration measures introduced by many western states, including the Canadian one, in the wake of the attacks on 11 September 2001. All the people involved in these cases used formal church sanctuary to gain time for their appeal processes. Supporters and lawyers worked to garner public support and governmental approval for people's bids to stay in Canada permanently. Some of these cases followed very shortly on the heels of the Chilean refugees who occupied churches in the city in 1998 and 1999 and some of the same advocates were involved, including the Committee to Aid Refugees and lawyers such as Noël St-Pierre.

From the outset of the research, I wanted to speak to the activists concerned as well as the people who were in sanctuary. However, that proved more difficult than expected. Activists were reluctant to discuss their work, and I suspect, in many cases, the often transient and volunteer nature of their activities meant that they were largely unable to do so, caught up with other cases and preoccupations. Their lack of voice or perspective on the cases described here is unfortunate in part because there is so much to learn across generations of activists.

It was similarly difficult for me to find people who had been in sanctuary and were willing to speak about their experiences. Although people's time in sanctuary was very mediatized in this period, in contrast to the quieter and more quotidian forms of sanctuary that characterized fugitivity and refuge for much of the past two centuries, it was very hard to locate and communicate with the people implicated a decade after they had left the media spotlight.

Four years after I first started trying to reach the people involved, I reached out to an intermediary who graciously offered to help. It was at that point, admittedly after many versions of this chapter had been drafted, that I learned of a request to desist from one of the families. Not only did they not want to speak about their experiences, they also did not want their case to even be mentioned. They wanted to leave this story in the past and asked that I help them do so by not pursuing their story further. I respected their wishes and shifted the scope and focus of this chapter accordingly.

Not only did I not write about their case, but I also decided to write about the people and churches involved in as general terms as possible. As a result, I generally wrote about the people involved in broad terms without naming the churches. Only in the case of the Union United Church, a historically Black church in the city, was it important to provide the name because of the long and complicated history of refuge, or lack thereof, for many Black citizens and visitors in the city. In other cases, I identified neither those who sought sanctuary nor the name or location of church, though some of the people who provided sanctuary are named.

This approach stands in contrast with my strategy in "The Occupied City" chapter, where in exploring the physical dimensions of sanctuary, I named the churches and some of the participants. I proceeded this way because, in those cases, I had permission and even encouragement to do so. In all cases, however, I made sure that where I hadn't been given permission to write about a situation, any identifiable sources, such as newspapers, were only cited in broad terms. This was a compromise between the citational demands of the historical discipline and the expressed interests of the people involved. It was a messy and complicated way to proceed, and the results are no doubt uneven, but I am hoping that it opens up possibilities for historians to do things differently, especially because (as one of the peer reviewers for this work highlighted) the past is never very far from the present here.

The interesting thing about the methodological shift in "The Uneasy City" is that I realized I could write about what was at stake in this period without having to name names or provide revealing details. The decision to proceed in a more general fashion, working to sketch only the faintest outlines of sanctuary experience, had all kinds of implications in terms of how I thought, and now think, about the stories that historians can and should tell, about the relationship between the past and the present, and the idea that people have the right to leave history (something I explore in the conclusion – "Beyond the City").

Ultimately, the request not to write about some of this history came as a relief. After months of not knowing whether I should proceed or how, there was some clarity. And it was absolutely the right decision. One of the things I had been concerned with in earlier versions of this chapter was that I was replicating the very the critique I was making about the use of public sanctuary. I worried about the toll of the public gaze, and I worried about the instrumentalization that was evident in some of the cases. In initially proceeding without explicit sanction, I feared that I was perpetuating the very same harms.

In some ways, the request not to proceed confirmed what I had suspected in terms of the toll of certain forms of public sanctuary. Unlike the people seeking sanctuary, those who offered sanctuary were much more willing to talk about their experiences, and this difference is striking. It speaks to some of the power dynamics involved. And, in a somewhat removed but related vein, it also speaks to what my friend and legal scholar Shauna Labman once observed in conversation: the striking difference between people who have been hidden and want to tell their stories and those who have been in the public eye and choose not to.

The public nature of sanctuary has been of paramount importance since it was first adopted as a strategy in the 1970s and came to prominence during the 1980s Sanctuary Movement. It has been effective in terms of immediate relief and in terms of helping people overcome some rather significant obstacles. However, it has come at a cost. Unlike the early examples of refuge explored in this book, sanctuary in the late twentieth and early twenty-first centuries has been politicized and shaped in large part by evolving legal frameworks, including refugee determination processes that are increasingly complex and difficult to navigate, part of a paradox where, as sociologist Azar Masoumi has shown, access to protection has been "simultaneously, and systemically, expanded and restricted."[1]

As a result, people were not just involved in making their own sites of refuge; they were participants in a system where the historical practice of church sanctuary had become part of the state's legal apparatus around admissions and refugee determinations. This is a crucial shift and one that needs to be addressed and considered both now and in any future effort to shift the parameters of how we think about refuge, hospitality, protection, and solidarity. I ultimately wrote this chapter with this goal in mind.

April 2023, January 2024

The Uneasy City

SHORTLY AFTER the attacks on the United States in 2001, a Pakistani woman moved to the United States from Kuwait, where she had been working as a maid. Soon after, she filed an asylum claim. She was refused and ordered deported but continued to appeal her case through various legal channels. When Donald Trump was elected in 2016, on a platform that included several anti-immigrant initiatives, the woman's options seemed to foreclose, and she came closer to the reality that she might be deported to Pakistan, a country she had not seen in decades. Her family was desperate. When members of a church in Kalamazoo, Michigan (traditional territory of the Ojibwe, the Odawa, and the Potawatomi), heard about her case, they decided to offer sanctuary. In the wake of the Trump election, the church had opted to be an "immigrant-welcoming" space, and providing sanctuary to a woman facing deportation spoke to this goal.[1] The Pakistani national spent three years in the church and was finally permitted to stay in the United States in 2018. In describing their actions, church representatives spoke of justice and of a previous history of sanctuary at the church, which had "wilfully violated the 1850 Fugitive Slave Act" to provide protection to people fleeing slavery.[2]

The sanctuary offered by the church in Kalamazoo (traditional territory of the Ojibwe, the Odawa, and the Potawatomi) was part of what has been described as the New Sanctuary Movement that emerged in the first decades of the twenty-first century following the 9/11 attacks and which expanded after the election of Donald Trump in 2016. This movement was and remains transnational in shape and structure. It involves the protection of individuals and families in church sanctuaries as well as campaigns for broad-based immigration reforms, including moratoriums on deportations, regularization initiatives, and more transparent refugee determination processes. It has also led to the designation of entire cities, states, and campuses as sanctuary spaces.[3]

By 2017, there were more than six hundred declared sites of sanctuary, including cities, states, and campuses across the United States.[4] In Canada, there were an estimated thirty church sanctuary cases from 2000 to 2010.[5] The Southern Ontario Sanctuary Coalition, the Canadian Council of Churches, the Canadian Council for Refugees, and a variety of local support groups all worked on behalf of people in sanctuary.[6] In Montreal/Mooniyaang/Tiohtià:ke, the Comité d'Aide aux Réfugiés/Committee to Aid Refugees and the Table de Concertation des Organismes au Service des Personnes Réfugiées et Immigrantes provided crucial support to individual sanctuary seekers. Some of the cases became quite protracted and mediatized. For example, there were dozens of news stories about a blind refugee who took sanctuary in a church in the working-class neighbourhood of Pointe Ste-Charles in Montreal/Mooniyaang/Tiohtià:ke in 2005. The man spent almost four years in the church before being permitted to stay, becoming one of the longest and most thoroughly documented church sanctuary cases in North American history.[7]

The important media and academic attention that this case received was symbolic of a larger shift that began with the 1980s Sanctuary Movement and became much more pronounced in the 2000s, namely that of making sanctuary public. As I have suggested throughout this work, sanctuary took many different forms historically. It was part of criminal justice frameworks in ancient and medieval times. Across North America in the nineteenth century, it was usually covert and quiet. It was intended and designed to help people hide. The idea was not to be known or discoverable, so as not to be captured, arrested, extradited, or deported. Over time, however, sanctuary has become more public, an evolution that can be seen in the very cases explored in this book.

Shadrach Minkins and John Harrison Surratt hid when they arrived in Montreal/Mooniyaang/Tiohtià:ke in 1851 and 1865, respectively. By contrast,

American war resisters and their protests in Canada became more visible as their legal status became more secure. Church sanctuary also became more public as the activities described in "The Occupied City" chapter suggest. Crucially, by the 2000s, church sanctuary was conjoined with other forms of activism so that people often took inspiration from individual cases to organize and advocate for general amnesties, moratoriums on deportation, and sanctuary city declarations across North America and Europe.

The public dimension of many modern sanctuary cases provides an opening through which to understand the complex, layered, and multifaceted factors that characterized practices of refuge, protection, and hospitality in the early twenty-first century. It was an uneasy time. States were treating migration as a security issue, and activists were divided on how best to respond. The number of people attending established churches was also dwindling, binding any religious intervention on behalf of sanctuary seekers to questions about the health and survival of individual church congregations more generally.[8] As a result, there was considerable uneasiness in the alliances, ambitions, and strategies pursued in the making of sanctuary. This discomfort or "governmentality of unease," which international relations scholar Didier Bigo identifies in relation to state efforts to manage migration, was rooted in fear and insecurity. Geographer Jennifer Bagelman has also employed this concept to consider how acts of sanctuary contribute to governmental practices and has flagged the issue of when and how sanctuary practices "threaten to ease" problems associated with not knowing, and with unpredictable outcomes, in a manner that enables state authority, rather than challenging or reforming it.[9]

There was certainly a sense of uneasiness about sanctuary amongst the very people who were subject to its vagaries in the early twenty-first century. Members of activist organizations and church congregations were also nervous about sanctuary.[10] Some of this uneasiness came from the uncertainty about challenging the law in the twenty-first century as well as trepidations about the merits of specific sanctuary cases. On occasion, people's time in sanctuary became quite extended and was almost carceral in terms of the constraints on their freedom of mobility and their capacity to live with dignity.[11] On such occasions, the uneasiness at play evolved into concerns about what was being undertaken and to what ends. In some ways, the spirit of sanctuary remained the same as it had throughout the ages. It was, at its core, about providing some kind of shelter or protection. In other ways though, sanctuary in the early twenty-first century was more complex, bound up with larger concerns about the treatment of migrants, the politics of deportation, and an ethic of care that sometimes meant a migrant's case was instrumentalized in the pursuit of broader reforms. As we saw in "The Occupied City" chapter, sanctuary could sit uneasily in a landscape where there were multiple actors, not all of whom agreed about the best course of action.

Sanctuary in the early twenty-first century was characterized by its high visibility, as well as the active engagement of sanctuary providers and church congregations in adjudicating the merits of whether an individual or family deserved to be in sanctuary. Similarly to the events documented in "The Occupied City" chapter, in the first decades of the twenty-first century, churches needed to be convinced of the merits of a case before accepting someone into sanctuary. There were many concerns about the legality of sanctuary and the potential implications of what they were undertaking.[12] Journalists regularly described the offer of sanctuary as a kind of protest and one that challenged the authority of the federal state. Offering sanctuary was often undertaken with considerable apprehension as a result.

The fact that church leaders and congregations had to be convinced of the merits of a sanctuary case is a reminder that people were only asked to consider the most exceptional cases in this period, acting during what one participant described as a "peak crisis moment" in the life of someone seeking refuge.[13] The case had to be meritorious in terms of protection, as well as in its capacity to sway public opinion. Lawyer Rick Goldman, who was involved in a number of sanctuary cases in these years, affirmed that a sanctuary offer needed "to create enough public support for government to realize that it had made a mistake and to correct it."[14]

As a result, representations about individuals, families, and their sanctuary cases were carefully constructed to convince state and non-state actors of their worthiness. The voices of people seeking sanctuary are, therefore, almost entirely absent from accounts of this period, even as the surviving public record seems to offer some of the most visible and detailed claims to sanctuary historically.[15] Where their voices do appear in the public record, we have only short clips or the equivalent of a soundbite on the page. These snatches were generally chosen by sympathetic journalists to spotlight the humanitarian element, not to provide insights into the complex lived experience of sanctuary. As a result, the performative dimensions of sanctuary in this period reflect some of the core concerns voiced by scholars in the field of critical refugee studies about the nature of "liberal humanitarianism."[16] Given the emphasis on "rescue" in many humanitarian practices, the capacity of people seeking refuge to be understood in full and complex ways is constrained by the need to make their case convincing, to appeal for help, and to express gratitude for any assistance received.[17]

The uneasy dynamics that characterized sanctuary offers in the early twenty-first century are outlined in a case involving the Union United Church in Montreal/Mooniyaang/Tiohtià:ke in the early 2000s and a later case at an Anglican church from 2013–14. In exploring these histories, we can better understand how sanctuary seekers and refugee advocates convinced churches to serve as hosts. We can also see the ways in which this assistance was exceptional and how the need to convince multiple audiences (not just the legal system) of sanctuary seekers' deservedness and worthiness led to very circumscribed understandings of the people involved, and their experiences, despite the very public record that outlines their time in sanctuary. The uneasy relationship between the law, human agency, voice, and the politics of refuge is foregrounded here. So, too, is the uneasy relationship between the past and present and the capacity to be alternatively known or forgotten as a subject of sanctuary.

The New Sanctuary Movement

Many migrants and citizens were caught up in the anxious climate that emerged in the wake of the attacks on 11 September 2001 as governments, responding to the generalized fear and insecurity in the aftermath of the violence, closed borders, further scrutinized asylum claims, and operated in an environment that insisted on divisions between "us" and "them." In the United States, migrants encountered a "hostile immigration bureaucracy" and a range of reforms that led to the increased securitization of migration.[18]

These included coordinated domestic raids on workplaces thought to be susceptible to terrorist activity and the implementation of the National Security Entry-Exit Registration System (NSEERS), which required men over the age of sixteen from twenty-five countries to register and be screened by the federal government. It also included a reorganization of federal departments, with the result that the Immigration and Naturalization Service moved under the jurisdiction of the Department of Homeland Security.[19] Migrants and citizens of Arab and South Asian backgrounds bore the brunt of these changes (because ignorance caused conflation), which perpetuated a climate of fear and hostility as the United States and its allies led a broad-based "War on Terror." Anger, hostility, and fear perpetuated further alarm and unease.

These sentiments traversed borders. In Canada, the Immigration and Refugee Protection Act (IRPA), which had been introduced in February 2001, was withdrawn and revised with new, more stringent measures introduced. Early allegations that terrorists had used Canada's refugee determination system to gain access to North America led to restrictive reforms and a tightening of admission procedures.[20] In 2002, the United States and Canada negotiated the Safe Third Country Agreement (based on an idea that was first floated in 1996) that further constrained migrant mobility by forcing people to make refugee claims in their country of first asylum, regardless of the fairness or effectiveness of these respective systems. The agreement came into effect in December 2004, and within a year, the Canadian Council for Refugees was warning of its damaging impact in terms of gender-based claims, a decline in asylum cases, and an increase in human smuggling and irregular border crossings.[21] The federal government elected in 2006 under Prime Minister Stephen Harper also chilled refugee admissions in the country with new legislation in 2012 that curtailed both refugee resettlement and convention determination processes. And yet, people continued to move and to seek refuge. As such, the "War on Terror" combined with local conflicts, layered with histories of decolonization and oppression, meant that the early 2000s were a time of great violence and uncertainty where refugee determination processes became more contested, and safety seemed all the more tenuous.[22]

Although the "War on Terror" and the revenge attacks on Al-Qaeda in Afghanistan by an alliance of fifty nations occupied much of the world's attention, political tumult unfolded elsewhere. To cite two examples based on the sanctuary cases discussed here: Algeria was wracked by civil war from 1991 to 2002, in a conflict that pitted the government (National Liberation Front) against various Islamic rebel groups, including the Islamic Armed Movement and the Armed Islamic Group. It was a nasty war with many civilian casualties – estimates range from 100,000 to 200,000 deaths. There were also keen moments of violence, most notably during a series of massacres in 1996 and 1997. This included the Thalit massacre, in which almost all the villagers in an enclave south of Algiers were murdered. Western states issued travel warnings to their citizens, and the Canadian government put a halt on deportations to Algeria in 1997, given the conditions in the country.[23] In Pakistan, the Taliban and associated groups carried out widespread attacks in public spaces such as "marketplaces, hospitals and religious processions."[24] There were also targeted killings against many political opponents, especially in Karachi. To make matters worse, the precarity and vulnerability created by the violent situation was compounded by devastating flooding in 2010. An estimated one-fifth of the country was flooded and twenty million people were displaced as a result.

Migrants were caught up in this turmoil, and some of them made their way abroad in the hopes of finding refuge. What many encountered instead was a deep mistrust of migrants and immigration systems that had been hardened to exclude, as terms such as "Fortress Europe" suggest. Immigration lawyer Stewart Istvanffy described a similar situation in the Canadian context saying that "the way the system reacts to seeing a whole bunch of people arrive at the border (is) to think how can we keep them out."[25] One federal immigration official explained (in the context of migrants from Algeria), "les agents d'émigration sont plus attentifs quand le pays connaît comme actuellement un gros flux de réfugiés. On se méfie des visiteurs qui cacheraient de faux réfugiés."[26]

In the wake of 9/11, activism around migrant justice took many forms, including public protests, marches, petitions, and targeted media campaigns. Advocates recognized the impact that the generalized climate of fear and anxiety was having on the capacity of western states and their citizens to empathize with refugees and their interest in maintaining their legal commitments to protection. It became obvious that people needed to act. As a result, there was a noticeable rise in the tenor and tone of civil society activism in this period.[27] The American Civil Liberties Union worked tirelessly against racism and Islamophobia, as did local community organizations across the United States. There was visible transnational political organizing as a result. The No One Is Illegal movement, co-founded in 2001 by Harsha Walia and other activists, and the Solidarity Across Borders group, established in Montreal/Mooniyaang/Tiohtià:ke in 2003, were prime examples of this phenomenon.[28] These groups called for broad-based immigration reforms. They also drew attention to instances of individualized and generalized injustice, often using intersectional categories of analysis to highlight the connections between the treatment of disparate communities. Solidarity Across Borders explained its core principles as follows:

> Our main demands are an end to deportations, detentions and double punishment, and support for a full, comprehensive and ongoing regularization program (ie. Status for All!). We also actively campaign to build a Solidarity City, the creation of a community that rejects a system that engenders poverty and anguish, not solely for immigrants and refugees, but also for other Montrealers confronting these same realities. We support open borders and the free movement of people seeking justice and dignity, meaning freedom to move, freedom to return, and the freedom to stay.[29]

Historians have underscored how "as a social movement, sanctuary is born in and responds to emergency"; however, part of what Solidarity Across Borders and other organizations were arguing against were the increasingly complex and bewildering immigration regimes that increased the likelihood of people falling through the cracks and violating their terms of entry in the first place.[30] They were taking issue with the structure of it all.

Modern sanctuary requires that lawyers, refugee advocates, and sanctuary supporters become experts in the merits of individual cases. During the 1980s Sanctuary Movement, church congregations and refugee-support organizations in the United States and Canada scrutinized international affairs issues and asylum rules; they studied law and foreign policy in order to assist Central American refugees fleeing civil war in their homelands.[31] The same occurred again in the early 2000s when refugee acceptance rates tumbled in the United States and Canada. Activists and supporters informed themselves about events abroad and at home, and they acted. National church organizations, as well as individual churches, made increasingly frequent public declarations about the systemic failures they were witnessing.

In offering sanctuary and speaking about injustice, church congregations and activists weren't just taking the law into their own hands; they were making judgments and pronouncements about the operation of the law as it existed and about the merits of the individual cases they encountered. In the United States, sanctuary was interwoven with concerns about the securitization (even militarization) of immigration and the fate of undocumented migrants. There were also many concerns about the state of immigration and refugee determination cases in Canada in the post 9/11 period. In Montreal/Mooniyaang/Tiohtià:ke, expert reports identified chronic problems with the operation of the Immigration and Refugee Board in the city, which had a disproportionately high refusal rate.[32]

This was no small matter.

As historian Peter Gatrell has observed, refugee determination processes "are supposed to be fair but also fast." They require "that the individual refugee produce a clear narrative of the circumstances that led to them seeking asylum." As a result, the "individual applicant plays for high stakes. He or she might be tripped up through interrogation of some kind or accused of misleading an official by omitting some crucial detail or offering an inconsistent account, with potentially far-reaching consequences for their claims to asylum."[33] The documented excesses in refusals by the Immigration and Refugee Board in Montreal/Mooniyaang/Tiohtià:ke, and the difficulties people had in accessing refuge generally, meant that many found themselves in rotten situations in the very societies where they had moved to seek refuge.[34] When the system appeared to fail, some people chose to pursue sanctuary in willing churches in an effort to buy time and convince the public and various levels of government of the merits of their cases.

In the early 2000s, there were several sanctuary cases involving church congregations in the Montreal/Mooniyaang/Tiohtià:ke area. Some of the congregations that participated had extensive histories of community engagement; for others, the offer of sanctuary was rather novel. The Union United Church, located on rue Delisle just adjacent to the Lionel-Groulx Metro station, had long been involved in social justice issues. The church sits in the shadow of a massive Catholic Church, St-Irenaeus, but its own exterior is adorned by murals and plaques that speak to the church's unique history. These include an image and quote from Nelson Mandela, whom the church actively supported during his time in prison in apartheid South Africa, as well as a memorial to twelve children who perished on a church outing to the Lac des Deux Montagnes in 1954. Nestled between Little Burgundy, the city's historic Black neighbourhood, and St-Henri, a historic working-class, though rapidly gentrifying, neighbourhood, the Union United Church literally and figuratively sits at the intersection of multiple histories of struggle and self-reliance.

Established in 1907 as the Union Congregational Church, the Union United Church is described as the city's "oldest Black congregation," forged out of community and in the face of racism that denied Black parishioners a place of worship among white churches.[35] The church's history was regularly repeated in sanctuary coverage in the early 2000s, giving moral weight to its contemporary activities. Indeed, akin to historic Black churches across North America, over the years, the Union United Church has been home and sanctuary for generations of congregants who have confronted racism, exploitation, oppression, and hostility in their own lives.

Over the years, the Black community in Montreal/Mooniyaang/Tiohtià:ke has often turned inwards for self-reliance and support. Racism encountered by railway porters led to considerable union organizing and the creation of the St Antoine District Coloured Women's Club of Montreal (CWCM) in 1902.[36] The CWCM collected and distributed clothing and assisted people looking for homes. It also organized "social activities to foster a sense of cohesion in a city where opportunities for Blacks to integrate into mainstream organizations were extremely limited as a result of the overt racism that existed."[37] As noted in "The Hostile City" chapter, the Union United Church was instrumental in supporting congregation members with soup kitchens and other relief efforts during the economic turmoil of the Great Depression. Even on a quotidian basis, the Union United Church was a kind of centrifugal source. According to historian Dorothy Williams, it was (and remains) "truly a community church because it brought together the different religious denominations of the black community."[38]

In the aftermath of 9/11, the Union United Church, under the leadership of Reverend Darryl Gray, became one of the most prominent sanctuary providers in the city. Gray's energy and convictions are almost legendary and he proved a dynamic, charismatic figure throughout his time in Montreal/Mooniyaang/Tiohtià:ke.[39] One refugee lawyer described him as a kind of Martin Luther King, with "very strong moral principles."[40] Originally from the United States, where he had been involved in the civil rights movement and worked with Reverend Jesse Jackson, Gray preached in the Maritimes before becoming the pastor at the Union United Church in 1998. During his time at the head of the church, Gray became an outspoken critic of Quebec sovereignty and head of Alliance Quebec (a rights-advocacy group established in 1982 to advocate for English-language rights in the province). He later ran for federal office as an independent candidate. The congregation of the Union United Church grew under his watch, and when he left in 2005, the church struggled to find a permanent replacement.[41] The Union United Church has not been involved in any sanctuary offers since Gray's departure. The cases that the congregation accepted during Gray's tenure, therefore, reveal a great deal about the church leadership as well as the contingencies that underpinned sanctuary efforts in the early twenty-first century. By way of illustrating what was at stake, I outline one of the cases that the Union United Church was engaged with here. It was the shortest one and presumably (and hopefully) less traumatic and difficult than some of the others.

Family Protection

In the early 2000s, an Algerian Canadian family took sanctuary in the Union United Church. The man had been born in Algiers, and it is unclear whether he later called a different part of Algeria home. He came to Canada from the United States in the mid-1990s as civil war raged in his homeland and filed an asylum claim. It was rejected by Aimable Ndjeuru and Corianne Côté-Lévesque of the Immigration and Refugee Board. The man's lawyer appealed on the basis that these same two members of the Immigration and Refugee Board had also heard and rejected his brother's claim, which meant that there was a "reasonable apprehension of bias on their part."[42] Meanwhile, the man went about his days, first finding work as a taxi driver, a profession with a storied history of activism and community solidarity in Montreal/Mooniyaang/Tiohtià:ke.[43] Soon after, the conservative Federal Court judge Marc Nadon (who had ruled against another family in sanctuary) denied the man's appeal, supporting the Immigration and Refugee Board's negative decision based on the man's "lack of credibility, the fact that he did not claim refugee status during the three months he spent in the United States and the fact that he did not seem to have a sincere fear of persecution since he had left Algeria one year after obtaining his passport."[44] By this time however, the federal government had introduced a moratorium on deportations to Algeria as a result of the turmoil caused by the civil war in that country. The man was stuck.

The moratorium recognized the dangerous conditions in Algeria. At the time, the civil war had left an estimated 150,000 people dead. Twelve thousand people had disappeared, and a million people, out of a population of almost thirty million, had been displaced. Reports described "a civilian population harassed by regular kidnappings, summary executions and violent repression."[45] The moratorium kept people safe from the raw conditions in Algeria, but it did not guarantee they could stay in Canada permanently. As a result, people operated in a kind of in-between space, an extreme example of the liminality so often associated with refugee experiences. Mirroring the sans-papiers movement in France, activists organized the Action Committee of Non-Status Algerians in Quebec/Comité d'Action des Sans-Statut (CASS) to address the plight of failed refugee claimants in Canada who were caught as a result of the moratorium on deportations. They had been denied protection in Canada, but there was no immediate return for them to Algeria.

The man's wife, whom he had met after arriving in Canada, had also filed an asylum claim, but she, too, was refused by the Immigration and Refugee Board even though she insisted that she had been subject to persecution as a result of her role as a polling clerk in the 1997 elections.[46] These elections had been marred by "rampant political violence" according to reports by Human Rights Watch.[47] Nevertheless, Michel Jobin and Madeleine Dupont-Lévesque ruled against her claim and she was ordered deported. The moratorium on deportations to Algeria remained in place, however, and the woman was also stuck. She and her husband, therefore, continued with their lives as best they could.

When the federal government eventually lifted the moratorium, it acted swiftly.[48] Within months, thirty-two people had been deported to Algeria even though Amnesty International affirmed that human rights violations in the country had become "institutionalized." The deportation of the man and woman was scheduled to follow suit.[49] The fact that they had a Canadian-born son and the woman was experiencing a difficult pregnancy did nothing to dissuade Canadian immigration officials.

For community members and activists who had been organizing around the situation of Algerians in Quebec during the moratorium years, the family represented an important test case of the humanitarian capacity of both the provincial and federal governments. Mohamed Cherfi, who led the CASS, worked with organizations such as No One Is Illegal to raise public awareness about the family's situation and that of others caught up in the shifting refugee determination and deportation practices in this period. CASS and No One Is Illegal held sit-ins in immigration offices, forcing federal officials to confront the tangible realities of the people bound up with evolving circumstances that were beyond their control and yet who were affected by them so profoundly. CASS and No One Is Illegal specifically demanded that the government halt all deportations, reinstate the moratorium, and regularize the status of all non-status Algerian residents in Canada.[50] These efforts echoed the earlier attempts by Chilean refugees in Canada to effect broad-based change (see "The Occupied City" chapter), as did the emotional and deliberate decision to use sanctuary to try and sway public opinion and stop the deportations.

In drawing attention to the merits of the family's case, advocates highlighted two things: the ongoing danger in Algeria and the length of time they had spent in Canada. Numerous press conferences featured the family, with prominent images of their smiling two-year-old son, along with stories of what they had been doing in Montreal/Mooniyaang/Tiohtià:ke and what they hoped to accomplish if they were permitted to stay. The woman explained that she wanted to work in a daycare, while the man expressed his desire to return to his taxi business. The emphasis on gainful employment and the amount of time they had spent in Canada was used to portray the parents as contributing members of society, something that was meant to foster sympathy for their situation.

When the family went into sanctuary, they went into hiding on one level, but on another, they moved to the forefront of public scrutiny. Newspaper coverage featured bewildered-looking agents at Dorval Airport, wondering where the family was when they failed to appear for their scheduled deportation. No One Is Illegal was also at the airport (and may have invited the journalists to document the event), distributing information flyers to waiting passengers and immigration agents. Advocates organized several press conferences in which the family presented themselves for consideration to the public, and supporters railed against the federal government's deportation policies. In addition to presenting the image of a wholesome family, the parents benefited from the fact that they were French speakers, a key factor in a province that regularly defined itself along linguistic and cultural lines.[51] The fact that the woman was Muslim and wore a veil did not seem to faze the public, though this issue would become a focal point of the debate about the place of religion in public life in Quebec society a decade and a half later.[52] Indeed, the combination of family wholesomeness and the shared French language preempted any concerns about accepting Muslim refugees, or refugees from the Middle East, at a time when Islamophobia was quite peaked. It also reflects the established nature of the Algerian community in Quebec in this period, which had roots in the province dating to the 1950s and 1960s because of the migration that occurred as a result of decolonization processes in North Africa.[53]

In contrast to the extended stays for Chilean refugees in the 1990s, the family spent a total of eleven days in the church before being permitted to stay in Canada and apply for residency on humanitarian and compassionate grounds. In the process, the federal and Quebec governments agreed to a regularization program for Algerian nationals. It permitted people who were facing deportation and who had no criminal record to apply for permanent residence (for a fee of $550 per adult, $150 per child) without first leaving the country, as was the standard legal requirement.[54] They had three months from the date of announcement to do so or three months from a negative refugee status decision. It was an offer of help, but it was not unequivocal. While the government introduced new moratoriums on deportation, the federal minister of immigration, Denis Coderre (who as mayor would be a key proponent of the 2017 sanctuary declaration in Montreal/Mooniyaang/Tiohtià:ke), presented new citizenship legislation that made it easier for the federal government to strip people of their citizenship and deport them.[55]

The family left sanctuary shortly after the announcement of the regularization program. Meanwhile, campaigns continued on behalf of those who didn't have the money to pay the application fees required for processing applications under the lifted moratorium. The family's presumed relief stood in stark contrast to the sentiments of other Algerians who did not have people to sponsor them and could not afford to apply. CASS leader Mohammed Cherfi ultimately went into sanctuary himself when he failed to meet the criteria established by the government. On his entry into sanctuary, Cherfi criticized the limited reprieve: "The selection process was based on criteria linked to an evaluation of our ability to 'integrate' into Quebec society, a very ambiguous and arbitrary process, in particular for war refugees who have lived for years without status and with the continual anxiety of being eventually deported. … I have found myself, at the end of the day, among the people refused within the framework of the selection procedure, with the explanation that I lack 'integration' into Quebec society."[56] In turn, Cherfi decided that his only recourse was to seek sanctuary and while the outcome was much more circuitous in his case, he did eventually obtain legal status in Canada.[57]

The experience of offering sanctuary to the Algerian Canadian family was seen as a positive by all those involved. Indeed, people began to celebrate the event as a very cosmopolitan moment, something unique to the city. The relative speed and the community-wide reprieve may have contributed to this sense of triumph and solidarity. It is certainly worth remarking upon and celebrating. Yet, this case might also have been one of the peaks in terms of collaborations. Subsequent situations would prove more challenging, in part because they involved longer sanctuary stays and deeper divisions among advocates and supporters about possible and desirable outcomes.

As noted previously, Darryl Gray left the Union United Church in 2005. His departure came on the heels of an acrimonious fight with the hierarchy of the United Church of Canada, which some speculated had to do with his political activism, including his determined efforts around sanctuary.[58] Although the Union United Church did not provide sanctuary to anyone else following Gray's departure, it did advocate on behalf of a number of other people in sanctuary in other churches in the city in the early 2000s. This included a woman who fled the Ivory Coast when threatened with forced genital mutilation and other cases involving a Colombian family and a Palestinian family. On these occasions, people were again supported by a variety of church congregations as well as groups such as the Coalition Against the Deportation of Palestinian Refugees, the Interfaith Sanctuary Coalition, No One Is Illegal, and Solidarity Across Borders. Indeed, Solidarity Across Borders would play a principal role in sanctuary events throughout the next decade, including the case of an elderly and ailing Pakistani woman. This particular situation distilled in stark ways the uneasy alliances that shaped the possibility of sanctuary in this period.

Protracted Sanctuary

In 2013, Solidarity Across Borders took the lead in a case that lawyers considered to have been badly mismanaged from the outset. The situation involved an older woman from Pakistan who was ordered deported following a complex series of twists and turns in her efforts to stay in Canada. Her daughter and grandson had received refugee status in Canada in 2000. In 2011, the woman and her husband travelled to Canada on a tourist visa and eventually filed refugee claims. In Lahore, with its famed walled city and busy, congested roadways, the couple had been active community leaders. The man was a prominent member of the Shia minority community in the city and claimed to have been targeted by the extremist anti-Shia group Ahle Sunnat Wal Jamaat. Nevertheless, the couple's claims were refused on the basis that they lacked credibility, and in 2013, the woman and her husband were ordered deported. The husband was sent back relatively swiftly and forced to go into hiding in Pakistan; however, the woman's deportation was delayed because she suffered from a chronic heart condition and was too sick to travel at the time.[59] Stories of her husband's renewed persecution soon surfaced, exacerbating concerns about the Immigration and Refugee Board's decision to return the couple to Pakistan.

The evolving situation and the narrowing window of opportunity to resolve the case prompted Solidarity Across Borders to reach out to potential churches to provide sanctuary. In August 2013, working through an intermediary, they contacted Reverend Chris Barrigar.[60] Barrigar is a warm, curious, and thoughtful conversationalist who describes his work as one of leading "a community of faithful disciples of Christ."[61] Born in New Brunswick and raised in Ontario, Reverend Barrigar can trace genealogical connections to Huguenot refugees and United Empire Loyalists who made their way to British North America at the time of the US Civil War. Barrigar pursued studies in Toronto/Tkaronto, doctoral studies at McGill University, and then graduate teaching in India. He had been ministering for more than a decade when the request came to provide sanctuary.

Barrigar's response was to organize an emergency board meeting, and a rather intense discussion followed about whether to provide support. The participants at the meeting weighed many factors as well as concerns about what they were being asked to undertake. There were critical questions about the expected duration of the sanctuary offer and the nature and depth of the assistance being requested.[62] People only had a small sense of what offering sanctuary entailed though they quickly grasped that what they were being asked to do was rather exceptional.[63] As Reverend Barrigar recalls, the conversations as they unfolded during a series of meetings over the next few days were "difficult."[64] There were concerns about whether the woman was a "genuine sanctuary case," and there were related anxieties about the implications of doing something illegal.[65] The board members were aware that other churches had offered sanctuary in Canada (Solidarity Across Borders had provided them with examples) without any legal action being taken against providers but they were nevertheless concerned. They worried about being raided and about the woman's health. They also had very pragmatic concerns about hygiene and how the woman would be fed, with some members wondering if the church would "smell of spices." As Reverend Barrigar puts it, there was simply "a lot of doubt."[66]

Ironically, one of the people who most opposed the decision to offer sanctuary had worked at Romero House in Toronto, a welcome centre founded by Mary-Jo Leddy of the Southern Ontario Sanctuary Coalition. Of all the congregation members, he was probably the most well-versed in the politics of sanctuary. He opposed the idea because he didn't think the case met the requirements as outlined by the leadership in other churches, including the Evangelical Lutheran Church of Canada, which had prepared a guide on the subject.[67] The pamphlet advised that there be a very clear sense of the parameters of the undertaking, especially in terms of the potential length of time in sanctuary. The board member in question did not think these issues had been addressed and was especially worried about the implications of "unbounded time."[68]

Ultimately, however, the board was inclined to accept. Many members were sympathetic, and Reverend Barrigar was convincing. The congregation had a history of involvement with refugee protection issues, including with refugees from Vietnam, Cambodia, and Laos in the 1970s and Rwandan refugees in the 2000s. Reverend Barrigar viewed the potential offer of sanctuary in this light.[69] For Reverend Barrigar, the opportunity to become involved in offering sanctuary was also "an answer to (his) prayers." He had been worrying about the spiritual health of the congregation, and the request to help was a chance for people to think deliberately about the question: What does the commitment of faith mean? Barrigar explained that one of the strengths of religion can be its capacity to provide security and that one of the downsides is that it "it can lead people to a comfort zone" where their focus is almost entirely inward, on the self, with little engagement with broader issues.[70] On some levels, Barrigar and the congregation wrestled with the decision to offer sanctuary, but, in other ways, it seemed the obvious thing to do. Many of the congregation members later spoke of their desire to help "an elderly lady." They underscored the specific merits of the case, as well as the need to do something since she was "far away" from home.[71]

The woman entered sanctuary on a fall day and spent fifty weeks in the church. It was longer than anyone expected, and it had everything to do with the uncomfortable alliance and divergent objectives that various supporters imagined with the act of sanctuary. Stewart Istvanffy, a lawyer involved with the case, recalled that at the time, he "was pleased when she went into sanctuary" because he "didn't want her to be deported."[72] However, the confidence in the decision to pursue sanctuary would fray with time as debates and divisions about how best to organize politically around the case, and to what ends, became more pronounced. For Istvanffy, the case was a human rights one. His focus was on the woman's well-being in terms of her immediate legal situation, which meant that people shouldn't "organize the political struggle around the day of deportation."[73] For Solidarity Across Borders, the issue was immigration reform more broadly. Their goals were similar but not entirely aligned, and this led to considerable tension.

Some of this strain may have originated with the very location of the church in an affluent neighbourhood, as well as the structure of the church itself. Built in 1940 in an Early English Gothic style, the church was quite large, and much of the space was consumed by the physical sanctuary. It was not designed with housing in mind. To accommodate the woman in sanctuary, the congregation arranged for a room in the basement to be repurposed and ensured there were hotplates for cooking. Bathing and showering facilities were also installed. The church provided the physical space, but all the additional assistance came from the woman's family, Solidarity Across Borders, and other supporters who organized food and medical care. The woman's daughter often visited or stayed with her. Additionally, her grandson regularly visited after school. According to congregation members I interviewed, the woman spent much of her time knitting or watching Bollywood videos.

Congregation members sought to make the woman's time in sanctuary as comfortable as possible, and Reverend Barrigar emphasized that there were regular discussions about the importance of "dignity" for anyone in sanctuary.[74] Nevertheless, it is clear that being in sanctuary was not easy for an ailing woman.[75] When no one else was in the church, she would have been living in a large, cold, dark building all on her own. The lights beyond her living quarters would have been turned off. Faced with language and cultural barriers, the woman proved "shy" and was reluctant to be presented to the congregation, though she did join them for coffee on one occasion following Sunday services.[76] In other rare instances, the woman was joined by supporters, including prominent political figures for mid-day lunches but she was a ghost-like presence for many of the congregation members, with one person describing her as the "Phantom of the Opera" in their recollection of events.[77]

Despite the woman's reticence within the church, over the course of her time in sanctuary, her case became quite mediatized as supporters sought to garner public backing and sway the federal government in its approach. To protect the anonymity of the congregation, Bishop Barry Clarke of the Anglican Diocese, whom Reverend Barrigar described as a "person of compassion," became the media spokesperson.[78] Several press conferences were held in which prominent individuals and organizations made their solidarity readily apparent. Supporters included Amir Khadr (one of the founders of Québec Solidaire), the South Asian Women's Community Centre, the Canadian Council of Muslim Women, La Féderation des Femmes, the South Asian Legal Clinic of Ontario, the South Asian Women's Centre, the Action Committee Against the Racial Profiling of Pakistanis, Shaine Hiadery Islamic Association, Babul Hawej Imamburgah, the South Asian Women's Rights Organization, and Le Regroupement des Maisons Pour Femmes Victimes de Violence Conjugale.

Meanwhile, lawyer Stewart Istvanffy worked through legal channels, including a judicial review with the Federal Court of Canada, the preparation and consideration of a Pre-Removal Risk Assessment, and an application on humanitarian and compassionate grounds to the federal government. Some of these efforts operated at cross-purposes with attempts to publicize the woman's case and raise public awareness, and vice versa. Solidarity Across Borders considered the woman's case as part of a larger systemic problem. Describing an "attack" on refugees, Solidarity Across Borders demanded a repeal of the conservative government's 2012 "Refugee Exclusion Act," officially known as the Protecting Canada's Immigration System Act.[79] This legislation made it more difficult for people who applied for refugee protection to later become permanent residents and was part of the Harper government's efforts to deter people from seeking refuge in Canada at all.[80] The government was resistant to any of these broad-based demands and the possibility of resolution in this specific case often seemed doubtful.

The woman's time in sanctuary was, therefore, much more extended and more difficult than anyone had initially expected. She eventually came out of sanctuary after being there for almost a year. She returned to her family, but her poor health never improved. She died in May 2019, and people involved in the case worry that her extended time in sanctuary may have contributed to her further decline.[81] Reverend Barrigar and the board of the church lost touch with the woman and her family, as well as members of Solidarity Across Borders, after she left sanctuary. Activists and congregation members crossed paths only briefly during the 2018 protests against religious accommodation laws in Quebec, a provincial initiative that banned the wearing of religious symbols in public, which many critics condemned as anti-Islamic in character.[82] Other than that, their connections ended with the woman's departure. Nevertheless, in reflecting on this specific sanctuary case, Reverend Barrigar evinces an enduring belief in having done something right and good.[83]

Conclusions

Sanctuary in the early twenty-first century has generally been understood as a last, desperate option. Lawyer Rick Goldman, who first heard about church sanctuary in the US context, described it as a form of "house arrest." In conversation, Goldman underscored that given the stress and anxiety involved, sanctuary was a last resort for people in desperate circumstances, a sentiment echoed by others, including people involved with the United Church of Canada.[84] Nobody considered sanctuary to be desirable in and of itself. People were often housed in makeshift and uncomfortable conditions.[85] It was often a lonely and isolating experience, and of course, it was woven through with uncertainty because there was no guarantee that people would ultimately be permitted to stay.

Significantly, it is in some ways with the public forms of sanctuary that the carceral dimensions of taking refuge in the physical space of a church were most obvious. Physically, people were limited in terms of their movements. Adults and children alike had to stay within the confines of the physical sanctuary. People were also constrained in how they presented themselves and their cases to the public, reflecting concerns among critical refugee studies scholars about the inadvertent harm that even well-intentioned humanitarian efforts can invite.[86] In cases where there were larger political reforms at stake, the particular needs of migrants and refugees are often repurposed to suit a broader activist campaign. As a result, in modern sanctuary cases, refugees have been at once hyper-visible as subjects of sanctuary and almost entirely invisible as fully-fledged subjects and historical actors.[87] Ironically, I have perpetuated that invisibility here in some respects, seeking to restore some measure of privacy and some ca-pacity for living away from the public's gaze even as I can envision the mass of digital information that remains accessible (making this task the equivalent of a Sisyphean stone in some respects).

Of all the churches discussed in *Sanctuary in Pieces*, only the Union United Church and the church in Kalamazoo (traditional territory of the Ojibwe, the Odawa, and the Potawatomi) remain as consecrated spaces with a permanent congregation. The Oratory of the Holy Cross in Liverpool, where John Harrison Surratt sought sanctuary, was sold and torn down in 2001. Similar to the Church of St-Jean-de-la Croix, discussed in "The Occupied City," the sanctuary church described in the latter part of this chapter was closed and put up for sale in the spring of 2019. With the sale of the church, the congregation that had offered sanctuary was displaced and forced to relocate. As this move got underway, there were a series of sharing moments when people reflected on the life of the church. A number of participants mentioned the woman's time in sanctuary as an important moment in the life of the community.[88] When I asked people to consider their offer of sanctuary six years after the fact, some expressed regret that they hadn't gotten to know the woman better or at all.[89]

Instead of building deeper personal relationships, much of the energy in this sanctuary case went into the advocacy work that was intended to find a resolution. The alliances that formed around the provision of sanctuary to a stranger existed only because of the woman involved. As Reverend Barrigar observed, the act of the woman "coming into sanctuary" was not achieved in isolation. It required a community of supporters.[90] That her community included her family, lawyers, members and supporters of Solidarity Across Borders, and the congregation of the church and the Anglican Diocese is, at once, surprising and entirely understandable given the political, social, and philosophical influences that have inspired the work around sanctuary and solidarity in recent years.

Although Reverend Barrigar never asked the members of Solidarity Across Borders about their experiences with organized religion, he appreciated the "neat set of relationships" that emerged, given that "church folk" and "SAB folk" didn't necessarily move in the same circles.[91] As part of this bridge building, members of Solidarity Across Borders came and spoke to the congregation, which Reverend Barrigar hoped would lead to deeper connections. Yet congregation members ultimately described a sense of Solidarity Across Borders activists projecting a "fish out of water feeling" whenever they were in the church.[92]

In the end, the connection between these various groups was fleeting. Efforts to protect an older and infirm Pakistani woman from deportation had the makings of a cross-cultural alliance, in the way that people celebrated efforts to come together and help an Algerian Canadian family at the Union United Church in 2002, but they did not manifest on this occasion. The federal government proved reticent to resolve the case, and there were more opinions and divisions about how best to help this particular family, and refugees in search of protection more generally. It was an uneasy time as actors on all sides flexed their intellectual and political (and in some cases spiritual) commitments, and migrants and their families navigated openings and closings with whatever knowledge, insights, and acumen was available to them.

For many sanctuary seekers in more recent times, their involvement in broader social justice issues was in some ways accidental. In seeking refuge, they had initially sought legal protection, nothing more. This didn't mean they were passive or apolitical, but their goal in seeking refuge was not to necessarily transform the political order, it was first and foremost about obtaining protection for themselves and their loved ones under the law. When people failed to obtain refugee status and the implicit protection this legal recognition provides, they pursued whatever options beyond deportation that were available to them. In this way, they became bound up with broader campaigns around immigration reform, regularization, and refugee determination processes. They and their supporters often needed to simultaneously prove the merits of their individual cases and speak to the plight of others. It was a heavy load.

Part of this heaviness stemmed from the fact that sanctuary seekers in the early twenty-first century needed to be exemplary. This is a recurring theme in the work of critical refugee studies scholars, and it is worth underscoring that it is a relatively recent phenomenon. As noted previously, one of the key differences between historic forms of sanctuary and those that have been pursued over the past half-century is that sanctuary now is only for those who are perceived to be innocent and deserving (in contrast to similar practices in ancient and medieval times, which were bound up with systems of criminal justice).

In the cases discussed here, people had to prove they were innocent, deserving, and vulnerable. It wasn't enough to underscore the dangerous conditions that people might face if they were returned to their homelands. Sanctuary seekers also needed to show that they were deserving. This could be done in a number of ways, such as by pointing to corrupt lawyers or a biased Immigration and Refugee Board panel. People could also outline the merits of their specific cases in terms of the persecution they had endured or the length of time they had already spent in Canada. In making appeals to supporters, the general public, and the federal and provincial governments, there was little room for sanctuary seekers to express any unease about sanctuary itself.

I feel the lack of fullness keenly. I hope that someday we might hear about people's lives and about sanctuary on their own terms. While there is an important story to be told about the particular and uneasy contingencies that led to the New Sanctuary Movement of the early twenty-first century, this was not necessarily the main story for those involved. Those in sanctuary might have a very different take on what was important to them. If the people at the heart of these stories were to document their lives, their time in sanctuary might appear as a passing reference, a footnote, or not at all. Or it might take up many hours and many pages.

Conclusion

Beyond the City

AS I WROTE AND REVISED this work over the course of 2023, discussions about the US-Canada border intensified, especially following the announcement of an Additional Protocol that extended the 2004 Safe Third Country Agreement. This agreement limits the capacity for people to make asylum claims in a second country if their application has been refused in the first. It rests on the generous assumption that the law and justice are infallible. As of 25 March 2023, the agreement applied to the entirety of the border, with no exceptions for unofficial crossings. However, exemptions in the original agreement, including for those with relatives in Canada or the United States, remained.

A week later, there was terrible news out of Ahkwesáhsne about a community member who had gone missing and eight migrants, including an infant and a three-year-old, who perished trying to cross the St Lawrence River/Kaniatarowanenneh on a cold, rough March night. Feminist scholar Robyn Maynard's assertion that the US-Canada border was "a grave" and the desperation with which people venture cross-border movements in our current moment came back to haunt even as people's various attempts at crossings also signified a determined sense of opportunity and possibility.[1] Crossing a contemporary international border is both a distressed and hopeful act for many.

In the days that followed, questions of responsibility loomed large: Were the changes to the Safe Third Country Agreement to be blamed? Were the Canadian and US governments responsible for this tragedy? What about the man who was suspected of transporting the families? And what of the responsibilities of the families themselves?

The question of responsibility was layered and sharp, like shards of cold, brilliant glass.

There was no single or simple answer to these questions, but the debate in and of itself was revealing for it pointed to an ongoing contest over how responsibilities towards any kind of migrant or stranger are understood. In addition to the physical "architecture of exclusion," there is now a rhetorical one. It is now all too easy for people to be dismissed with a single phrase or even term, "illegal," "refugee," or "border crosser." As political scientist Rebecca Hamlin has shown in her work on migration categorizations, the US public (and presumably the general public in other settler societies) is more likely to want to assist people if they are presented as "vulnerable refugees" rather than "vulnerable immigrants," even though it is often difficult to contain experiences within tidy definitional containers.[2]

As Hamlin's analysis underscores, the term *refugee* has conventionally evoked a sense of responsibility to assist, if not necessarily a sense of responsibility to address root causes. This is no longer the case. And much of what is substantive about the term *refugee*, in terms of meaningful understanding about the experiences involved, has similarly been lost or deliberately obscured with the passage of time. Crucially, if we want to recover its meaning and its significance, we need to make sure that we recognize broader life experiences alongside moments of tragedy and persecution. We don't need to absorb every personal detail, but we do need to understand what it takes to seek refuge, the wild contingencies required for sanctuary to be offered, taken, or received, and the ease with which any one of us could become sanctuary seekers or sanctuary providers of some sort.

The desire to elaborate the complexities and shifting contingencies in the search for sanctuary and the making of refuge is at the heart of *Sanctuary in Pieces*.

The case studies in this book were deliberately chosen to explore the ways in which people have historically sought to locate and forge refuge in all kinds of ways, in all kinds of places, and with all kinds of communities. This need has not gone away. If anything, it has become more urgent given the pervasive economic exploitation, racism, sexism, and oppression in our world, and the renewed intensity of attacks on Black, Indigenous, Asian, Muslim, and LGBTQIA+ people to pull but a few examples from recent headlines. Building on the power of "queering space," of changing political and public expectations by refusing to be invisible, those targeted have become more vocal about their needs and rights while simultaneously confronting considerable societal pushback, including harassment and pointed legal persecution.[3] The confusion and isolation (some of which stems from the messiness of going public) are palpable; people have, in many instances, chosen to seek community among peers and supporters rather than the state. At the same time, communities have shown that they can be a source of considerable conflict and pain, as we saw in the case of Chilean refugees and migrants seeking refuge (discussed in the chapter "The Occupied City"). People must sometimes flee communities that they don't consider safe, making the need for refuge all the more urgent, and the possibility of sanctuary all the more difficult to grasp, in the present.

Sanctuary in Pieces foregrounds refuge among non-state actors as a reminder that neither protection nor hospitality has ever been uniquely the purview of the state. There was a need for refuge in the context of imperial state formation, and this need endures beyond the context of the nation-state in our current moment. Yet, even though the state is not the central character in the cases explored here, and even though this book seeks to demonstrate why the state doesn't have to be the main actor in the provision of refuge, the state is nevertheless always there. Sometimes, it is there simply in terms of creating and safeguarding legal frameworks around mobility and protection, and sometimes, it is actively involved in determining fates. In some ways, the state apparatus has become increasingly prominent in terms of sanctuary as the legal frameworks around migration and asylum have become more complex. Sanctuary and refuge now operate in dialogue with shifting laws, regulations, and policies. As detailed in the case studies here, in some instances, the state's influence on sanctuary was very pronounced in terms of official sanction, as was the case for war resisters opposed to the United States' wars in Vietnam, Cambodia, and Laos. In later instances, the state figured prominently in terms of the laws and policies that were being evoked, and which, in some instances, contributed to the need for sanctuary such as with the number of deportation cases explored in the last chapter.

In outlining the substance of sanctuary, beyond the law and beyond the discursive significance of these practices, the goal is to see the interplay between state and non-state actors, including sanctuary seekers, rather than seeing the state as the end-all and be-all of sanctuary. In 2002, when an Algerian Canadian family was in sanctuary, then federal immigration minister Denis Coderre insisted that he would not "conduct negotiations in a church." He urged the family to leave, assuring them that they would be safe. He told reporters, "There will be no arrest warrant, and there isn't even any deportation process organized at this time." He then said, "I'm asking them to show some confidence in me."[4] On another occasion, he said simply, "Trust me."[5] These were extraordinary, deeply personalized moments in which Coderre seemed to fully embody the federal state, complicating the idea of trust, especially for those in sanctuary who had fled oppression by state authorities in their homeland. How could one simply trust?

In some ways, the 2017 sanctuary city declaration of which Coderre was a keen proponent in his capacity as mayor was another invitation to trust – to trust that municipal authorities would be able to make the city safe for undocumented migrants, that the Montreal Police Service would not share information with other law enforcement authorities, and that citizens would buy into the idea of Montreal/Mooniyaang/Tiohtià:ke as a sanctuary city. None of this happened.[6] As in the case of other jurisdictions where sanctuary has been publicly declared, the city gained plaudits in some quarters but did a great disservice to the very people it intended to assist by raising expectations and then proving incapable or unwilling to meet them.

In the months that followed, the idea of Montreal/Mooniyaang/Tiohtià:ke as a sanctuary city was put on display and to the test as thousands of migrants sought refuge from the shifting political situation in the United States. These included many people targeted by the Muslim Ban and Haitians whose temporary status in the United States had been terminated by the Trump administration in the fall of 2017.[7] In response, many people crossed into Quebec from New York/Manahàhtaan, using unofficial border crossings such as the one at Roxham Road, which is due south of Kahnawà:ke (about forty-seven kilometres or twenty-nine miles as the crow flies). In response, the city opened the Big O stadium (a legacy of the 1976 Summer Olympic games) to house new arrivals in a gesture eerily reminiscent of the way the Louisiana Superdome in New Orleans was used following the devastation of Hurricane Katrina in 2005. The scale of the building alone spoke to the gravity of the situation, as did the public pronouncements. Mayor Denis Coderre took to Twitter to welcome the refugees and blame Donald Trump for the situation. He also explained that because Montreal/Mooniyaang/Tiohtià:ke had become a sanctuary city in February, new arrivals would have access to city services.[8] Yet, disappointment stemming from the gulf between the city's sanctuary declaration and the lived experience of being in Montreal/Mooniyaang/Tiohtià:ke quickly became evident. People regularly pointed to official claims of being a sanctuary city to highlight shortcomings in the services and protection being offered and to demand better access to health care and social housing.[9]

The lack of substance or effective sanctuary policies to support the city council's declaration and the related Access to Municipal Services Without Fear policy ultimately led to a repeal of the initiative in December 2018 by the newly elected mayor and former opposition leader, Valérie Plante. In introducing the city's plan for immigration and integration, and acknowledging the limitations of the previous declaration, Plante insisted on "setting the record straight" and indicated that Montreal/Mooniyaang/Tiohtià:ke would no longer be a sanctuary city but rather would be "responsable et engagée" (a "responsible and engaged" city).[10] In an implicit condemnation of this shift, the *Montreal Gazette* ran a two-part story about a twenty-three-year-old man who had grown up in Montreal/Mooniyaang/Tiohtià:ke over the course of the previous decade and was arrested after a bar fight. According to news accounts, this man was deported to Guinea two weeks after city council abandoned the idea of being a sanctuary city. However, the police action against him predated the December decision, confirming fears among advocates that information-sharing between the Montreal Police Service and federal immigration enforcement authorities with the Canadian Border Services Agency had been ongoing.[11] Solidarity Across Borders, which had consistently advocated for more substantial policy changes both in the lead up to and in the wake of the sanctuary city declaration, stressed that "a true sanctuary city is supposed to be safe and people living undocumented in the city shouldn't live in fear of any sort of encounter with police."[12]

Detailing the history of sanctuary in a single place is an important way of understanding the changing values, moral compasses, practices, and politics in the making and unmaking of community. In the case of Montreal/Mooniyaang/Tiohtià:ke, we can trace the shifting currents around the provision of sanctuary in three main ways. The first is the shift from private to public, from sanctuary that had to be concealed underground, in the dark of the night, and away from the gaze of scrutinizing eyes to one that was not only visible but broadcast loudly. In the era of the "Underground Railroad" of the late eighteenth and early nineteenth centuries, the greatest form of safety came from not being seen and not being found. By the turn of the twenty-first century, the situation was radically different. Those facing deportation or expulsion sought shelter in physical spaces where they felt they were protected from law enforcement and turned to the public for support. Engaging the public in their plights was a way of garnering additional layers of protection. The results, as we have seen, were mixed. This was sometimes an effective strategy, especially if there was an extended community beyond the immediate sanctuary of the church to provide support. In other cases, however, even determined media and legal campaigns failed to effect sufficient change. In such instances, sanctuary disappointed. Indeed, given the difficulty I had finding people who had once been in sanctuary to speak with, I wonder if these experiences didn't ultimately discourage some people from making long-term commitments to the city, the province, or the country.

The other major shift has to do with the role of organized religion in offering sanctuary over the years. This was certainly the received custom, but as the case studies in *Sanctuary in Pieces* have shown, sanctuary was never uniquely about physical protection in sacred spaces, which according to customary law, could not be transgressed by secular authorities such as law enforcement or immigration control. Among Indigenous Peoples, there were and remain distinct adoption and kinship practices. And historically, people also forged refuge among other communities, most notably political ones as in the case of Emma Goldman during her time in exile and the war resisters who made their way to Montreal/Mooniyaang/Tiohtià:ke in the late 1960s.

While organized religion was only ever part of the story, it was an important one, especially in Montreal/Mooniyaang/Tiohtià:ke. The city was, from its very origins, a largely religious space dominated initially by various Catholic orders. This dominance changed over the course of the period under study, most notably with the arrival and official sanction of Protestant influences in the eighteenth century and later with Jewish, Muslim, and others. In the 1960s, there was a marked rupture in the close relationship between church and state even though religion continues to play an important, if complicated, role in Quebec society. The secularist outlook in Quebec treats religion largely as culture. Yet for sanctuary seekers, churches represented more than a cultural practice, in theory, they also offered physical safety. In entering religious sanctuary, people were giving weight to the historic authority of the Christian church, even if they were often not of the same faith as their hosts. In seeking help, those in sanctuary raised the profile of the church in much-needed ways.

By the early twenty-first century, churches across Montreal/Mooniyaang/Tiohtià:ke were hurting financially and socially. They had seen their influence wane in the preceding decades. While the 2021 national census revealed that 64.8 per cent of people in Quebec still identified with a Christian religion, this figure did not speak to the active participation of people in religious communities, which is significantly less. Meanwhile, 27.3 per cent of respondents reported having "no religious affiliation or a secular perspective."[13] Offering sanctuary was one way for churches to reinvigorate themselves, though as this study has shown, this approach was not without its difficulties. Participating in sanctuary acts encouraged congregations and church leaders to become more vocal and explicit about moral obligations and ethical responsibilities. This sometimes worked in favour of those in sanctuary, and in other cases, it did not.

The final notable evolution is in terms of the politics and practices of sanctuary from the nineteenth to the twenty-first century is the fact that the idea of sanctuary as protest is a rather recent phenomenon, one that dates only to the 1970s. In the earliest case explored here, sanctuary was about safety, it was about hiding, having legal refuge, having some kind of community, and having some kind of shelter. Abolitionists wanted to help people, and they wanted an end to slavery. They were willing to help people escape bondage to make that happen, but the people seeking refuge were doing so first and foremost for safety. The same is true today. Since the

1980s, however, acts of sanctuary have been imbued with additional layers of meaning and symbolism. People in sanctuary have had to take on the added responsibility of speaking to their own situations but also to larger structural inequalities and injustices. Some have been willing and able to do so. But not all.

And some have moved very far away from this time in their lives in the intervening years. Seeing the distance that some people have sought to create for themselves with regards to their time in sanctuary hints at the toll that seeking refuge can take, even if the outcome is ultimately understood as a positive or successful one.

Throughout the research and writing of this work, I kept returning to the idea of leaving history, and if and how it is possible, for whom, and under what terms. I suppose part of this line of questioning is shaped by the dominance of social media in our current moment and its oppressive pervasiveness. Scholars have identified the particularly harmful impacts of social media on the politics of mourning, especially of Black bodies. Scholar Tonia Sutherland, for instance, has shown how social media results in the commodification of memorializations, making it impossible to forget, a right that she insists is paradoxically denied to those who have lost the most.[14]

The notion that one might want to forget or that one might want to leave history is a profoundly disconcerting idea for some. Since the 1990s, and the publication of Michel Rolph-Trouillot's monumental *Silencing the Past: Power and the Production of History* (a work that I absolutely treasure and which has meant so much to me) and a rich body of literature around archival silences, especially in the colonial archive, the discipline of history has fixated on the idea of silences and addressing exclusions and absences. Such interventions have worked well when they have led to a fundamental reconceptualization of what was happening in the past based on new evidence, especially from different language sources, oral histories, and previously unexplored materials that invite us to interrogate dominant narratives. It has worked less well when it has been simply about writing people in. In such cases, people have become historical subjects, not historical actors, and are made to carry the weight of representation beyond their own personal experiences.

Such is the challenge in the fields of refugee history and refugee studies where the burden of representation is practically all-consuming. Critical refugee studies scholar Y-Dang Troeung, for instance, wrote of being photographed as a baby upon her arrival in Canada and the ways in which the production of "refugee poster child" was used to "sanitize and deflect from" the country's "systemic structure of ongoing settler colonial violence."[15] When Troeung requested that this image be removed when it was repurposed for commemorative coverage, the journalist in question refused.[16] This was an egregious response. The flight from genocide was already horrendous, and here was the settler state and its agents making it worse.[17]

Beyond questions of justice in the past, present, and future, the experience of sanctuary is distinguished by a critical temporal dimension. The impact of migrating, being displaced, or being violently apprehended, living in camps, and many other possible facets of what we have come to understand as a refugee experience can stay with people forever. So, too, can the desire to be described and to describe oneself as a refugee. In other ways, however, the experience of being a refugee is temporally bounded. The time spent in physical sanctuary in our contemporary context is meant to be limited, even if the ultimate length is unknown at the outset. It is precisely because the bounded nature of these experiences is so paramount to our understanding of what is at stake in anyone needing or seeking refuge in the present that we should ask about when and how people can carve out a space, choose silence, or leave history. As oral historian Anna Sheftel has compellingly insisted, we should also recognize the power in silence, the power in being able to turn away from a probing researcher and to leave the past in the past, or to keep it contained within oneself or a chosen circle.[18]

One of the things that I wrestled with in writing *Sanctuary in Pieces* was the disciplinary imperative to detail the process of seeking refuge in order to better understand what this experience felt like and signified, while at the same time recognizing that this history was only ever one part of people's lives, and that for some people, it was a very painful period that they did not wish to revisit. Torn between the imperatives of the historical discipline and the ethical dimensions of writing about painful histories, I began to see that the requests by some actors to have their stories left untold was a way of speaking to the temporality of what they experienced, of reframing sanctuary so that it was only ever one part of their lived experience, while at the same time being a critical part of the social and political landscape that

I sought to elaborate. My understanding of the significance of sanctuary at different historical junctures evolved as a result.

Throughout the research and writing processes, I was rightfully pressed about what this book was ultimately about. There was always a lot of interest in the idea of sanctuary (especially when it involved some of the more sensational aspects of the project such as John Harrison Surratt's escapades or Emma Goldman's provocations), but inevitably, people wanted to know more about what was at stake, and what it all meant.

I often found it hard to provide a simple, straightforward answer.

As I noted in the introduction, this is ultimately because I didn't like the conclusions that I was drawing. Long a critic of state practices around refugee protection and humanitarian assistance, I put my faith in the activists and the sanctuary seekers themselves. And while there were beautiful, inspiring moments, I realized that seeking or offering sanctuary does not in and of itself amount to radical change. Even with the Sanctuary Movement of the 1980s, the New Sanctuary Movement of the early 2000s, and now the Solidarity City movement, the state's power to include and exclude, to exploit, cast away, marginalize, and disregard remains. The changes described over the course of these case studies, from refuge in the shadows to public refuge, represent a shift in tactic. However, many of the exclusionary structures that people were up against historically endure in the present and, in some ways, have been reinforced, especially when it comes to differences in gender, race, and class.

At the same time, the sanctuary cases described here point to moments when people have sought to do things differently; when they have imagined alternative futures for themselves, their families, and others; and when they have acted (again for themselves, their families, their communities, or on behalf of others). Sometimes these actions resulted in important changes, and sometimes they did not. But people acted regardless.

This is the crucial point.

In acting, people created precedent, and this is the key to effecting change in the realm of migrant justice and refugee protection. Once something has happened or been tried, then there is precedent for others to do the same and to go beyond. We see this among both state and non-state actors. Civil servants in Canada were famously told to read the *None Is Too*

Many manuscript by Harold Troper and Irving Abella during the refugee crisis in Southeast Asia in the 1970s so that the recognized racism and mistakes of the Second World War period vis-à-vis Jewish refugees would not be repeated. When the Canadian federal government finally acted on behalf of Syrian refugees in 2015, officials looked to the precedent of the large-scale movement of refugees out of Southeast Asia in the 1970s and 1980s to think about all that might be possible. And when the federal government introduced a novel temporary visa for Ukrainians fleeing the attacks by Russia in 2022, observers paid attention in part because a precedent had seemingly been set.[19] Although many pointed to the discrepancies between the treatment of Syrian and Ukrainian refugees, the more significant dimension was the fact that the federal government had established a new precedent in terms of the scale of temporary assistance, one that might be very difficult to walk away from in the future given the broad appreciation for this initiative nationally and internationally, as well as among members of the affected diasporic community. In the case of non-state actors, the importance of precedence is perhaps all the more critical because stories of what was done previously can serve as inspiration (albeit sometimes in problematic ways).

It is ultimately for possible futures that I wrote *Sanctuary in Pieces*. The emphasis on individual and collective action, the significance of networks, the reflections, the critiques, and the praise were all teased out from the historical record with the idea that if people know more about what was possible in the past, then we might dream of even bigger, brighter, and more creative ways to transform the structures and contingencies that continue to create the need for refuge in the present. In an age of rampant capitalism and climate catastrophe, this work is all the more urgent as I suspect the ragged condition of our planet means that the need for refuge and the capacity for providing sanctuary are going to be severely tested in the coming years.

I worry about how people will find refuge in the present and the future given the accumulated weight of history and the long-standing practice of denying sanctuary. As economic and political oppression mounts and the planet burns and drowns, the capacity for sanctuary seems all the more necessary and illusory. Given our current moment, it seemed that the past might have a lot to say about sanctuary in the present. I also felt compelled to write this book to address fundamental issues in the fields of refugee history and migration history. The starting point for this project was, therefore, a keen intellectual commitment to exploring what was at stake in questions of mobility, protection, and hospitality. I was determined to ask certain questions at the outset, but these were quickly transformed through my interactions with the archival record and, more importantly, with the people who helped me do this work. Some people moved this project in new directions by refusing to participate, either explicitly or implicitly, and this made me consider what I was doing and how. Others helped by disagreeing with my existing approaches, pointing to new avenues of inquiry, or offering insights and evidence that led to shifts in how I was doing this work. Still others helped by affirming the project, in big and small ways.

What this means is that the research evolved from a very particular intellectual space to one that engaged with all kinds of different ideas, histories, and lived experiences. In this way, it represents a bit of a middle ground or transition work between conventional approaches in the western academy and the new emphasis on not just community-based research but also community-led research. This shift has been unfolding for some time, especially because scholars are increasingly interested in nurturing their community bonds as opposed to severing them. It is an important change and one that this book captures in terms of its methodological approach. In leaving deliberate silences and gaps, this book is also expressing the wish that community-based researchers and communities themselves will lead in documenting histories of sanctuary in the future, beyond the politics and practices described here.

After all, there is still so much to learn about sanctuary within, and beyond, any given city.

Notes

Introduction

1 Elie Wiesel, "The Refugee," *Cross Currents* (Winter 1984–5): 390.
2 Translation by author. Minutes, Assemblée Ordinaire du Conseil Municipal, Version 2, 20 February 2017.
3 Translation by author: "This is a historic moment. I've been through a lot in politics, but to see a council, unanimously, make Montreal a sanctuary city, given the context on a global scale and even on our continent, I think it sends a very, very strong message." Jeanne Corriveau, "Vote unanime pour faire de Montréal une 'ville sanctuaire,'" *Le Devoir*, 21 February 2017, https://www.ledevoir.com/politique/montreal/523554/montreal-n-est-pas-une-ville-sanctuaire-reconnait-valerie-plante.
4 Idil Atak and Graham Hudson, "Montreal's Sanctuary Policy for Non-Status Migrants: Opportunity and Obstacles," *Refuge: Canada's Journal on Refugees* (September 2022), DOI: 10.25071/1920-7336.40787.
5 Ibid.
6 Harald Bauder, *From Sovereignty to Solidarity, Rethinking Human Migration* (London, New York: Routledge, 2022), 284.
7 Translation by author: "A lot of words have been said, especially in tweets, but at the end of the day, we're not a 'sanctuary city' per se." Marion Scott, "Montreal not a sanctuary city, but a responsible one, Plante says," *Montreal Gazette*, 6 December 2018, A4.
8 Although scholars have pointed to how cities such as Nairobi are, in fact, sanctuary cities given the number of refugees they host, the declaration of sanctuary city status is a North American and European phenomenon. See Derese G. Kassa, *Refugee Spaces and Urban Citizenship in Nairobi: Africa's Sanctuary City* (Lanham, MD: Lexington Books, 2019); Philip Marfleet, "Understanding 'Sanctuary': Faith and Traditions of Asylum," *Journal of Refugee Studies* 24, no. 3 (2011): 452.
9 William Chester Jordan, *From England to France: Felony and Exile in the High Middle Ages* (Princeton, NJ: Princeton University Press, 2017), 31–2. For an example, see brief references to ancient sanctuary practices in Lauren Collingwood and Benjamin Gonzalez O'Brien, *Sanctuary Cities: The Politics of Refuge* (New York: Oxford University Press, 2019), 4.
10 John Peter Sexton, "In the Saint's Embrace: The Sanctuary Privilege in Medieval Religious Writing" (PhD diss., University of Connecticut, 2007), 54–5; Karl

Shoemaker, "Sanctuary for Crime in the Early Common Law" in *Sanctuary Practices in International Perspectives: Migration, Citizenship, and Social Movements*, eds. Sean Rehaag and Randy Lippert, (New York: Routledge, 2021), 19.

11 Victor M. Uribe-Uran, "Iglesia Me Llamo1": Church Asylum and the Law in Spain and Colonial Spanish America," *Comparative Studies in Society and History* 49, no. 2 (2007): 448.

12 Shannon McSheffrey, *Seeking Sanctuary: Crime, Mercy, and Politics in English Courts, 1400–1550* (Oxford: Oxford University Press, 2017), 193.

13 William C. Ryan, "The Historical Case for the Right of Sanctuary," *Journal of Church and State* 29, no. 2 (1987): 212. The heavily prescribed "rituals" around sanctuary in ancient times were preserved in modified forms in the medieval era in England, including practices around abjuration. See Krista Kesselring, "Abjuration and its Demise: The Changing Face of Royal Justice in the Tudor period," *Canadian Journal of History* 34, no. 3 (1999): 349; Elizabeth Allen, "'As Mote in at a Munster dor': Sanctuary and Love of This World," *Philological Quarterly* 87, no. 1–2 (2008): 107.

14 McSheffrey, *Seeking Sanctuary*, 9.

15 Ibid., 10.

16 Fatiha Cherfouh, "La Déchéance de l'Asile Religieux Sous l'Ancien Régime," *Revue Historique de Droit Français et Étranger*, 8 no. 3 (2009): 396.

17 *Jesuit Relations and Allied Documents: Travels and Explorations of the Jesuit Missionaries in New France* 34 (Cleveland, OH: Borrows, 1901), 195.

18 By contrast, ecclesiastic immunity, which was "enacted in some Iberian kingdoms as early as 610 AD" was guaranteed among Spanish colonial holdings. Uribe–Uran, "Iglesia Me Llamo," 448. As historian Michelle McKinley has shown, the *Nueva Recopilación* issued in 1567 "contained several references to ecclesiastical immunity," as did the *Recopilación de Leyes de los Reinos de las Indias*, issued in 1680. So, too, did the *Curia Philipica* (1615), which detailed King Philip II's insistence on the use of ecclesiastical immunity in the colonies, one that lasted until the 1820s. Michelle McKinley, "Standing on Shaky Ground: Criminal Jurisdiction and Ecclesiastical Immunity in Seventeenth-Century Lima, 1600–1700," *U.C. Irvine Law Review* 141 (2014): 145.

19 Kesselring, "Abjuration and its Demise," 353; Marfleet, "Understanding 'Sanctuary,'" 448.

20 McSheffrey, *Seeking Sanctuary*, 192.

21 Ibid.

22 According to McSheffrey, Manchester was, therefore, replaced by Chester, which protested in turn, and was subsequently replaced by Stafford, 195; A. Naomi Paik, "Abolitionist Futures and the US Sanctuary Movement," *Race and Class* 59, no 2. (2017): 3–25.

23 Jacques Derrida, *On Cosmopolitanism and Forgiveness* (London: Routledge, 2001), 4, https://doi.org/10.4324/9780203165713. Relatedly, the European idea of free

cities (such as Basel, Augsburg, Cologne, or Strasbourg) reflected a secular solution for entities seeking to operate independently from other levels of authority. They weren't strictly about sanctuary but reflect a historic negotiation of power amongst various state levels.

24 Julie Anne Sweet, "A Very Extraordinary Kind of a Creature: Conflicting Contemporary Perspectives on Christian Priber," *The South Carolina Historical Magazine* 118, no. 1 (2017): 74.

25 Ibid., 64; Christina Snyder, *Slavery in Indian Country* (Cambridge, MA: Harvard University Press, 2010), 110. Some of these aspirations are also evident in the history of mixed communities such as Great Crossings, Kentucky, which Christina Snyder evokes with such grace in terms of the "diverse dreams" and, later, the promise of education in overcoming the violence of US imperialism. *Great Crossings* (Oxford: Oxford University Press, 2017), 298.

26 Philip Marfleet, "Understanding 'Sanctuary,'" 452; Vicki Squire has coined the term "mobile solidarities" to reflect the fluid and shifting nature of support networks. See "From Community Cohesion to Mobile Solidarities: The City of Sanctuary Network and the Strangers into Citizens Campaign," *Political Studies* 59 (2011): 292. On the solidarity as a moral imperative, see Rose Cuison-Villazor, "What is a Sanctuary?" 61 *S.M.U. L. Rev.* 133 (2008): 145; Jennifer Bagelman, *Sanctuary City: A Suspended State* (New York: Palgrave Macmillan, 2016), 8.

27 Allen, "'As Mote in at a Munster Dor'," 106; Villazor, "What is a Sanctuary?"135; Jennifer Bagelman, "A Politics of Ease?" *Alternatives: Global, Local, Political* 38, no. 1 (2013): 50.

28 Rachel Ida Buff, "Sanctuary Everywhere: Some Key Words, 1945–Present," *Radical History Review*, no. 135, (2019), https://doi.org/10.1215/01636545-7607809, 17.

29 Stephanie Pettigrew, "The Hidden Narratives of Clandestine Communities: Digital History and the Religious Minorities of New France," https://earlycanadianhistory.ca/2018/12/03/the-hidden-narratives-of-clandestine-communities-digital-history-and-the-religious-minorities-of-new-france%EF%BB%BF/, accessed 18 February 2023; Tiya Miles, *All That She Carried: The Journey of Ashley's Sack, a Black Family Keepsake* (New York: Penguin Random House, 2022), 56.

30 See John Peter Sexton, "In the Saint's Embrace"; Karl Shoemaker, "Sanctuary for Crime in the Early Common Law," in *Sanctuary Practices in International Perspectives: Migration, Citizenship, and Social Movements*, ed. Sean Rehaag and Randy Lippert (New York: Routledge, 2021), 19; Uribe-Uran, "Iglesia Me Llamo," 448. The idea of history in keys is inspired by Paul A. Cohen's approach in *History in Three Keys: The Boxers as Event, Experience, and Myth* (New York: Columbia University Press, 1998).

31 A. Naomi Paik uses this phrase in the context of sanctuary policies, but I see it as equally relevant in the context of sanctuary practices by non-state actors. See *Bans, Walls, Raids, Sanctuary: Understanding US Immigration for the Twenty-First Century* (Oakland, CA: University of California Press, 2020), 110.

32 Ananya Roy, "The City in the Age of Trumpism: From Sanctuary to Abolition," EPD: *Society and Space* 37, no.5 (2019): 762. As Roy notes, this has been most marked in terms of police violence that has played out at the local level, and which has galvanized the Black Lives Matter movement.

33 Patti Lenard and Laura Madokoro, "Introduction: The Stakes of Sanctuary," *Migration and Society: Advances in Research* 4, no. 1 (2021): 1–15; Melvin Delgado, *Sanctuary Cities, Communities, and Organizations: A Nation at a Crossroads* (New York: Oxford University Press, 2018, x.

34 Collingwood and O'Brien, *Sanctuary Cities*, 36, 39, 96.

35 Mireille Paquet, "Sanctuary Cities," *Routledge Handbook of Immigration and Refugee Studies* (Oxfordshire, UK: Routledge, 2022), 436, 437.

36 As I revised this introduction in the summer of 2023, I did so in the wake of human tragedy caused by the failure to respond to distress signals from a ship, the Messenia fishing trawler, in the Mediterranean. Over five hundred people perished. As families and loved ones grieved (a national day of mourning was declared in Pakistan), the Global North's attention turned to the fate of five people aboard a Titan vessel, which had gone down to explore Titanic and failed to resurface. The contrast between the rich and poor, and the levels of caring and uncaring (manifest in the dedicated Coast Guard and military resources that went to recovering the Titan and its victims) could not have been more obvious. On sanctuary in the Mediterranean, see Jonathan Darling and Harald Bauder, *Sanctuary Cities and Urban Struggles: Rescaling Migration, Citizenship, and Rights* (Manchester: Manchester University Press, 2019), 1. See also Harald Bauder, *From Sovereignty to Solidarity: Rethinking Human Migration* (London, New York: Routledge, 2022), 3.

37 See the organisation pledge in https://cityofsanctuary.org, accessed 4 October 2020.

38 Graham Hudson, "City of Hope, City of Fear: Sanctuary and Security in Toronto, Canada," in *Sanctuary Cities and Urban Struggles: Rescaling Migration, Citizenship, and Rights*, ed. Jonathan Darling and Harald Bauder (Manchester: Manchester University Press, 2019), 79.

39 Christopher Curtis, "'If You Deport Me, You Might as Well Just Kill Me': Asylum-seeker," *Montreal Gazette*, 18 December 2018, A1.

40 Idil Atak, "Toronto's Sanctuary City Policy — Rationale and Barriers," in *Sanctuary Cities*, ed. Darling and Bauder, 120.

41 David Harvey, "The Right to the City," https://davidharvey.org/media/righttothecity.pdf, accessed 14 January 2024.

42 Henri Lefebvre, "Industrialization and Urbanisation" in *Writings on Cities*, trans. Eleonore Kofman and Elizabeth Lebas (London: Blackwell, 1996), 71.

43 Dimitros Roussopoulos, *The Rise of Cities: Montreal, Toronto, Vancouver and Other Cities* (Montreal: Black Rose Books, 2017), 19–20.

44 Miriam Davidson, *Convictions of the Heart: Jim Corbett and the Sanctuary Movement* (Tucson, AZ: University of Arizona Press, 1988).

45 Jennifer Ridgely, "Refuge, Refusal, and Acts of Holy Contagion: The City as a Sanctuary for Soldiers Resisting the Vietnam War," ACME: *An International Journal for Critical Geographies*, 10, no. 2 (2015): 200.
46 Cited in Robert Tomsho, *The American Sanctuary Movement* (Austin, TX: Texas Month Press Inc., 1987), 31.
47 There was also considerable sanctuary work in Texas, but this was undertaken quite quietly compared to the public-facing work in other parts of the country.
48 "Research–-Borders + Crossings 1" MS 502, File 11, Box 2, Jim Corbett Collection, University of Arizona, Special Collections.
49 Barbara Sostaita, "Escape-Bound: Juana Luz Tobar Ortega's Fugitive Poetics," *Southern Cultures* 26, no. 4 (Winter 2020): 42–59, https://doi.org/10.1353/scu.2020.0054.
50 A. Naomi Paik, "Deportations in the 21st Century and the New Sanctuary Movement," National Museum of American History, https://americanhistory.si.edu/explore/stories/new-sanctuary-movement, accessed 17 July 2023.
51 Annie Correal, "Trump Can Withhold Millions From 'Sanctuary' States, Court Rules," *New York Times*, 26 February 2020, https://www.nytimes.com/2020/02/26/nyregion/sanctuary-cities-funding.html.
52 See Audrey Macklin, "Working Against and with the State: From Sanctuary to Resettlement," *Migration and Society: Advances in Research* 4, no. 1 (2021): 31–46, https://doi.org/10.3167/arms.2021.040105.
53 Damien M. Sojoyner, "Another Life is Possible: Black Fugitivity and Enclosed Places," *Cultural Anthropology* 32, no. 4 (2017): 514–36.
54 Paik, *Bans, Walls, Raids, Sanctuary*, 105.
55 Jeremy Hainsworth, "Border Service Visits Alarm Singh Supporters," *Globe and Mail*, 14 July 2008, https://www.theglobeandmail.com/news/national/border-service-visits-alarm-singh-supporters/article954566/; "Montreal Imam Faces Deportation Over Refugee Status," *CBC News*, 15 October 2007, https://www.cbc.ca/news/canada/montreal/montreal-imam-faces-deportation-over-refugee-status-1.662156.
56 Beatrix Hoffman, "Immigrant Sanctuary or Danger: Health Care and Hospitals in the United States," *Migration and Society: Advances in Research* 4, no. 1 (2021): 62–75, https://doi.org/10.3167/arms.2021.040107.
57 Benjamin Hoy, *A Line of Blood and Dirt: Creating the Canada-United States Border across Indigenous Lands* (New York: Oxford University Press, 2021), 8.
58 Ibid., 109, 165; Bruce Trigger, *Children of Aataentsic: A History of the Huron People to 1660* (Montreal-Kingston: McGill-Queen's University Press, 1976), 802.
59 Daniel Rück, "Kahnawá:ke Timeline: Some Key Events Related to Land and Resources to 1957," 2012, http://kahnawakeclaims.com/wp-content/uploads/2014/11/KahnawakeTimeline2012.pdf.
60 For instance, contemporary statistics show that "urban Indigenous people are eight times more likely to experience houselessness than those who are

non-Indigenous." Stéphane Guimont Marceau, Jennifer Buckell, Marie-Ève Drouin Gagné, Naomie Léonard, Raphaëlle Ainsley Vincent, "Settler Urbanization and Indigenous Resistance: Uncovering an Ongoing Palimpsest in Montreal's Cabot Square,"*Urban History Review* 51 no. 2 (2023): 313.

61 See Max Hamon, *The Audacity of His Enterprise: Louis Riel and the Métis Nation That Canada Never Wass, 1840–1875* (Montreal-Kingston: McGill-Queen's University Press, 2019); Max Hamon, "Contesting Civilization: Louis Riel's Defence of Culture at the Collège de Montréal," *The Canadian Historical Review* 102, no.1 (2021): s285–s308.

62 Hamon, "Contesting Civilization," 67.

63 Snyder, *Slavery in Indian Country*, 109.

64 Lorenzo Veracini, "Imagining the Settler-Colonial City: Introducing Urban Indigeneities and the Settler-Colonial City," *Urban History Review* 51, no. 2 (2023): 182.

65 Marceau et al. "Settler Urbanization and Indigenous Resistance," 313.

66 I did not receive permission to name the person with whom I spoke and so I am describing the conversation in only broad terms. The person I spoke with continued by emphasizing harm done in Indian Residential Schools in particular. Telephone conversation 26 November 2018. As this discussion shows, I was immediately sympathetic to their point even as I understand that the relationship between Western and Eastern religions and Indigeneity has been complicated. See Tolly Bradford and Chelsea Horton, eds, *Mixed Blessings: Indigenous Encounters with Christianity in Canada* (Vancouver: UBC Press, 2016).

67 Aimee Villarreal, "Sanctuaryscapes in the North American Southwest," *Radical History Review*, no. 13 (2019), 43–70, https://doi.org/10.1215/01636545-7607821.

68 Lenard Monkman, "'No ban on stolen land,' say Indigenous activists in U.S.," 6 February 2017, https://www.cbc.ca/news/indigenous/indigenous-activists-immigration-ban-1.3960814.

69 Elizabeth Ellis, "The Border(s) Crossed Us Too: The Intersections of Native American and Immigrant Fights for Justice," *Emesférica* 14, no. 1 (2018): https://hemisphericinstitute.org/en/emisferica-14-1-expulsion/14-1-essays/the-border-s-crossed-us-too-the-intersections-of-native-american-and-immigrant-fights-for-justice-2.html.

70 See discussion in Peter Nyers, *Irregular Citizenship, Immigraiton, and Deportation* (London, New York: Routledge, 2019).

71 As in on other instances in this book, I consider the cases described here to be private matters, shaped by adoption and kinship practices that do not necessitate the naming of individuals to be understood as significant.

72 Kimberly Tallbear, *Native American DNA: Tribal Belonging and the False Promise of Genetic Science* (Minneapolis: University of Minnesota Press, 2013). Writing about the history of the Algonquian nation, historian Richard White notes that in the eighteenth century "each group of refugees sought ties with strangers precisely because they feared outsiders." He explains, "the whole logic" of such actions "was

that dangerous strangers had to be turned into either actual or symbolic kinspeople if the refugees were to survive hunger, disease and Iroquois attack." Richard White, *The Middle Ground: Indians, Empires, and Republics in the Great Lakes Region, 1650–1815* (Cambridge: Cambridge University Press 2012), 15.

73 Guimont Marceau et al., "Settler Urbanization and Indigenous Resistance," 319.

74 Randy Lippert, "Rethinking Sanctuary: The Canadian Context, 1983–2003," *International Migration Review* 39, no. 2 (2005): 381–406, https://doi.org/10.1111/j.1747-7379.2005.tb00271; Sean Rehaag, "Bordering on Legality: Canadian Church Sanctuary and the Rule of Law," *Refuge*, 26, no. 1 (2009): 43–56.

75 McSheffrey, *Seeking Sanctuary*, 6.

76 The treatment of the term "Underground Railroad" by putting it in quotation marks is deliberate. The "Underground Railroad" did not exist as an institution, per se, and the term is often used in a manner that marginalizes the significant actions of those in flight. Nevertheless, it remains an important concept. The term is, therefore, capitalized to recognize its symbolic importance but is placed in quotation marks as an acknowledgment of its limited capacity to convey the centrality of the very people who moved in search of safety and freedom and the fluidity of flight in this era.

77 Saidiya Hartman, *Scenes of Subjection: Terror, Slavery, and Self-Making in Nineteenth-Century America* (New York: W.W. Norton and Company, 2022), 16. Hartman's focus is largely on what happened to people post-emancipation in the United States while I am interested in understanding emancipation as it involved the movement across juridical and international borders.

78 Sojoyner, "Another Life is Possible," 516.

79 Tina Campt, "Black Feminist Futures and the Practice of Fugitivity." Helen Pond McIntyre '48 Lecture, Barnard College, 7 October 2014, http://bcrw.barnard.edu/blog/black-feminist-futures-and-the-practice-of-fugitivity. Campt calls fugitivity "the quotidian practice of refusal," citing Judith Butler's ideas about "refusing to stay in one's proper place."

80 Ananya Roy, "The City in the Age of Trumpism: From Sanctuary to Abolition," *Society and Space* 37, no.5 (2019): 775, https://doi.10.1177/0263775819830969.

81 Allison Mountz, "Seeking Status, Forging Refuge: U.S. War Resister Migrations to Canada," *Refuge: Canada's Journal on Refugees* 36, no. 1 (2020): 97–107, https://doi.org/10.25071/1920-7336.40648. Mountz is also a co-producer of the film *Safe Haven* on this topic, made with Lisa Molomot.

82 Begoña Aretxaga, *Shattering Silence: Women, Nationalism, and Political Subjectivity in Northern Ireland* (Princeton, NJ: Princeton University Press, 1997), 21.

83 Tonia Sutherland, "Making a Killing: On Race, Ritual, and (Re)Membering in Digital Culture," *Preservation, Digital Technology & Culture* 46, no. 1 (2017), https://doi.org/10.1515/pdtc-2017-0025.

84 Elie Wiesel, "The Refugee," *Cross Currents* (Winter 1984–85), 390.

85 Harald Bauder, "Migrant Solidarities and the Politics of Place," *Progress in Human Geography* 44, no. 6 (2020): 1066.

Before the City

1 Brett Rushforth, *Bonds of Alliance: Indigenous and Atlantic Slaveries in New France* (Chapel Hill, NC: University of North Carolina Press, 2012), 304.
2 Jacques Cartier, *The Voyages of Jacques Cartier*, ed. Ramsay Cook (Toronto: University of Toronto Press, 2017), 64–5.
3 Translation by author. [François Dollier de Casson], *Histoire de Montréal, 1640–1672* (Montreal, 1871), 18.
4 Brett Rushforth, *Bonds of Alliance: Indigenous and Atlantic Slaveries in New France* (Chapel Hill, NC: University of North Carolina Press, 2012), 305.
5 Ibid., 304.
6 Vimont Barthelemy, Andre Richard, and Isaac Jogues, eds, vol.24, *Jesuit Relations and Allied Documents* (Cleveland, OH: Burrows Brothers, 1901), 263.
7 Jean-François Lozier, *Flesh Reborn: The Saint Lawrence Valley Mission Settlements through the Seventeenth Century* (Montreal-Kingston: McGill -Queen's University Press, 2018), 75. Other scholars emphasize geographic isolation as a prominent feature in the city's development. Dany Fougères and Roderick Macleod, eds, vol.1, *Montreal: History of a North American City* (Montreal-Kingston: McGill-Queen's University Press, 2018), xxv.
8 Lozier, *Flesh Reborn*, 76.
9 Paul-André Linteau, "Montreal, 1850–1914," *Urban History Review* 1, no.75 (1975): 50. Over the years, the use of the walls evolved from a palisade to repel attacks to a means of controlling movement in and out of the city. According to Brett Rushforth, "soldiers posted at each of the city's gates inspected goods, checked papers, and questioned anyone who seemed not to belong." *Bonds of Alliance*, 310.
10 Fougères and Macleod, eds, vol. 1, *Montreal*, 117.
11 Rushforth, *Bonds of Alliance*, 307.
12 Ibid., 304.
13 Ibid.
14 Ibid.
15 Max Hamon, *The Audacity of His Enterprise: Louis Riel and the Métis Nation That Canada Never Wass, 1840–1875* (Montreal-Kingston: McGill-Queen's University Press, 2019), 212.
16 Desmond Morton, "How Lower Canada Won the War of 1812," *American Review of Canadian Studies* 42, no. 3 (2012): 321–8, https://doi.org/10.1080/02722011.2012.707050; Sean Mills, "French Canadians and the Beginning of the War of 1812: Revisiting the Lachine Riot," *Histoire Sociale/Social History* 38, no. 75 (2005): 40.
17 Jean-Pierre Sawaya, *Des braves et des guerriers. Les Amérindiens du Québec et la guerre de 1812* (Québec: Les Presses de l'Université Laval, 2015), 41.
18 During the war, Indigenous allies including the Haudenosaunee in Ahkwesáhsne and Kahnawà:ke were often loyal to the British, but they generally sought to remain neutral, even with their participation in battle at Chateauguay. Others, such

as Joseph Brant of the Grand River First Nation fought for the British, only to be betrayed when promises were not fulfilled in the 1814 Treaty of Ghent. Elizabeth Elbourne, *Empire, Kinship and Violence: Family Histories, Indigenous Rights and the Making of Settler Colonialism, 1770–1842* (Cambridge: Cambridge University Press, 2022), 154, 164, 173; Elizabeth Dickson-Gilmore, "Resurrecting the Peace: Separate Justice and the Invention of Legal Tradition in the Kahnawake Mohawk Nation" (PhD diss., University of London, 1995), 350.

19 Vincent Geloso and Vadim Kufenko, "Can markets foster rebellion? The case of the 1837–38 rebellions in Lower Canada," *Journal of Economic Behavior & Organization* 166 (2019): 266, https://doi.org/10.1016/j.jebo.2019.06.005; Allan Greer, "1837–38: Rebellion Reconsidered," *The Canadian Historical Review* 76, no. 1 (1995): 11.

20 Allan Greer, "From Folklore to Revolution: Charivaris and the Lower Canadian Rebellion of 1837," *Social History* 15, no. 1 (1990): 34.

21 Allan Greer, *The Patriots and the People: The Rebellion of 1837 in Lower Canada* (Toronto: University of Toronto Press, 1993), 335.

22 Ibid., 49.

23 Greer, "Rebellion Reconsidered," 15; John Duffy and H. Nicholas Muller, "The Great Wolf Hunt: The Popular Response in Vermont to the 'Patriote' Uprising of 1837," *Journal of American Studies* 8, no. 2 (1974): 156.

24 Duffy and Muller, "The Great Wolf Hunt," 162.

25 Greer, *The Patriots and the People*, 333.

26 Sherry Olson and Patricia Thornton, *Peopling the North American City: Montreal, 1840–1900* (Montreal-Kingston: McGill-Queen's University Press, 2011), 21.

Notes from the Field (The Lonely City)

1 Saidiya Hartman, *Scenes of Subjection: Terror, Slavery, and Self-Making in Nineteenth-Century America* (New York: W.W. Norton and Company, 2022), xxxvii.

The Lonely City

1 Charles Smallwood, *On Ozone and on the Meteorology of the Vicinity of Montreal* (Montreal: John Lovell at the Canadian Directory Office, 1857), 16.

2 Gary Collison, *Shadrach Minkins: From Fugitive Slave to Citizen* (Cambridge, MA: Harvard University Press, 1997), 174.

3 Residents of Kahnawà:ke recall massive ice build ups in the earlier years. As one Elder remembered, "The ice was so thick to the river it would pile up during the night close to our house. The ice was so thick that it took until May to melt." Joe Cross Interview. Angela Morris, *Old Kahnwà:ke*, (Kanien'kehá:ka Onkwawén:na Raotitióhkwa Language and Cultural Center), 26.

4 Indeed, a map produced by the National Parks Service in the United States shows Minkins crossing the vast waters of the St Lawrence at La Prairie, https://www.nps.gov/articles/-rescued-from-the-fangs-of-the-slave-hunter-the-case-of-shadrach-minkins.htm, accessed 20 February 2023.
5 Collison, *Shadrach Minkins*, 171.
6 Sherry Olson and Patricia Thornton, *Peopling the North American City: Montreal, 1840–1900* (Montreal-Kingston: McGill-Queen's University Press, 2011), 5.
7 Dorothy Williams, *The Road to Now: A History of Blacks in Montreal* (Montreal: Véhicule Press, 1997), 14.
8 Ibid., 27.
9 Hartman, *Scenes of Subjection*, xxviv, xxxv, 11.
10 Elsbeth Heaman, *Civilization: From Enlightenment Philosophy to Canadian History* (Montreal-Kingston: McGill-Queen's University Press, 2022), 4.
11 Tyler Stovall, *White Freedom: The Racial History of an Idea* (Princeton: Princeton University Press, 2022, 5). A similar story can be told about the exclusive nature of formal, legal citizenship. See Christina Snyder, *Great Crossings* (Oxford: Oxford University Press, 2017), 315.
12 On refugeehood, freedom, and the cold war see, Daniel Cohen, *In War's Wake: Europe's Displaced Persons in the Postwar Order* (Oxford: Oxford University Press, 2011).
13 I am relying on the Oxford English Dictionary here.
14 Charmaine Nelson, "The Canadian Fugitive Slave Archive and the Concept of Refuge," ESC 45, no. 3 (2019): 96.
15 Benjamin Drew, *The Refugee, or The Narratives of Fugitive Slaves in Canada* (Boston: J.P. Jewett, 1856), 85.
16 Ibid., 25.
17 Ibid., 42, 39.
18 Tiya Miles, *All That She Carried: The Journey of Ashley's Sack, a Black Family Keepsake* (New York: Penguin Random House, 2022), 124.
19 Ibid. Jonathan Goldberg-Hiller argues that Black mobility at night has been consistently "identified as dangerous to white interests." *Law by Night* (Durham, NC: Duke University Press, 2023), 25.
20 Hartman, *Scenes of Subjection*, 7, 226, 266.
21 See Sunil Amrith's *Crossing the Bay of Bengal: The Furies of Nature and the Fortunes of Migrants* (Cambridge, Massachusetts: Harvard University Press, 2013) in which he deftly marries a study of environmental history and migration history in the shaping of communities around the Bay of Bengal. In this work, "furies" refers largely to environmental conditions.
22 Carla Marano, "'For the Freedom of the Black People': Case Studies on the Universal Negro Improvement Association in Canada, 1900–1950" (PhD diss., University of Waterloo, 2018), 50.

23 Dorothy Williams, *Blacks in Montreal, 1628–1986: An Urban Demography* (Montreal: Éditions Yvon Blais, 1989), 8.
24 Ibid., 23.
25 James Walker, *Black Loyalists, The Search for a Promised Land in Nova Scotia and Sierra Leone, 1783–1870* (Toronto: University of Toronto Press, 2019), 7, https://doi.org/10.3138/9781442671447. See also Jason Silverman, *Unwanted Guests: Canada West's Response to American Fugitive Slaves, 1800–1865* (Associated Faculty Press, 1985), 3; Frank Mackey, *Done With Slavery: The Black Fact in Montreal, 1760–1840* (Montreal-Kingston: McGill-Queen's University Press, 2010), 382, 402; Raymond Paul Zirblis, "The Vermont Underground Railroad Survey Report," for the State of Vermont, Vermont Department of State Buildings, Vermont Division for Historic Preservation (1996), 19.
26 Williams, *Blacks in Montreal*, 12.
27 Robin Winks, *The Blacks in Canada: A History* (Montreal-Kingston: McGill-Queen's University Press, 2021) 29–30, 33. Johnson apparently had fourteen people with him upon arrival. Johnson's signature appears on an undated document titled "Return of Negroes brought in by Scouts and sold at Montreal," preserved at Library and Archives Canada. Of the over fifty enslaved people named on this list, about half were sold in Montreal/Mooniyang/Tiohtià:ke. One person was sold to Rev. David C. DeLisle, an Episcopal rector in the city, for twenty pounds, http://www.sfredheritage.on.ca/Early%20Slavery.htm.
28 See discussion in Charmaine Nelson, *Slavery, Geography, and Empire in Nineteenth-Century Marine Landscapes of Montreal and Jamaica* (London, New York: Routledge, 2019).
29 Charmaine A. Nelson, "'Tone of Voice Peculiar to New-England' Fugitive Slave Advertisements and the Heterogeneity of Enslaved People of African Descent in Eighteenth-Century Quebec," *Current Anthropology* 61, no. 22 (2020): S303.
30 Ken Alexander and Avis Glaze, *Towards Freedom: The African-Canadian Experience* (Toronto: Umbrella Press, 1996), 29.
31 Afua Cooper, *The Hanging of Angélique: The Untold Story of Canadian Slavery and the Burning of Old Montreal* (Toronto: Harper, 2006), 86.
32 William Renwick Riddell, "Lower Canada," *The Journal of Negro History* 5, no. 3 (1920): 305–15.
33 Silverman, *Unwanted Guests*, 11; Robin Winks, "Negroes in the Maritimes: An Introductory Survey," *Dalhousie Review* 48 (1968), 459.
34 Wilfrid Emmerson Israel, "The Montreal Negro Community," (MA thesis, McGill University, 1928), 65.
35 Harvey Amani Whitfield, *The Problem of Slavery in Early Vermont, 1777–1810* (Burlington, VT: Vermont Historical Society, 2020), 119.
36 Silverman, *Unwanted Guests*, 12.
37 In a study of the history of the Underground Railroad in Vermont, for instance, Michelle Arnosky Sherburne cites a figure of forty thousand fugitive slaves being

assisted. See *Abolition and The Underground Railroad in Vermont* (Charleston, SC: The History Press, 2013), 1.

38 Damian Alan Pargas, *Fugitive Slaves and Spaces of Freedom in North America* (Gainesville, FL: University Press of Florida, 2018), 11.

39 Robert Keith Collins, "How African Americans Met Native Americans During Slavery" *Contexts* 19, no. 3 (2020): 16–21; Eric Foner, *Gateway to Freedom: The Hidden History of the Underground Railroad* (New York, London: W.W. Norton & Company, 2015), 16, 30.

40 Miles, *All That She Carried*, 229.

41 Zirblis, "The Vermont Underground Railroad Survey Report," 2.

42 William Still, *The Underground Railroad: A Record of Facts, Authentic Narratives, Letters, and c., Narrating the Hardships, Hair-Breadth Escapes, and Death Struggles of the Slaves in their Efforts for Freedom, as Related By Themselves or Witnessed by the Author, Together With Sketches of Some of the Largest Stockholders, and Most Liberal Aiders and Advisors, of the Road* (Philadelphia, PA: Porter & Coates, 1872), 4–5.

43 Frederick Douglass, *Narrative of the Life of Frederick Douglass, An American Slave, Written by Himself* (Boston: Anti-Slavery Office, 1845), 101.

44 *Afro-Can* publications (1984), Negro Community Centre Fonds, Concordia University.

45 Williams, *Blacks in Montreal*, 17.

46 Katherine McKittrick, "Freedom is a Secret" in *Black Geographies and, the Politics of the Place*, ed. Katherine McKittrick and Clyde Woods (Toronto: Between the Lines Press, 2007), 101.

47 Ibid., 101, 102.

48 Mimi Nguyen, *The Gift of Freedom: War, Debt, And Other Refugee Passages* (Durham, NC: Duke University Press, 2012).

49 In this regard, I am thinking of Audrey Macklin's fascinating analysis of the different dynamics around refugee sponsorship and sanctuary. See "Working Against and With the State," *Migration and Society: Advances in Research* 4 (2021): 31–46, https://doi.org/10.3167/arms.2021.040105.

50 Wendell Nii Laryea Adjetey, *Cross-Border Cosmopolitans: The Making of a Pan-African North America* (Chapel Hill, NC: University of North Carolina Press, 2022), 183.

51 See, for example, Renny Golden and Michael McConnell, *Sanctuary: The New Underground Railroad* (Ossining, NY: Orbis Books, 1986).

52 J.A. Shantz, "No One Is Illegal: Organizing Beyond Left Nationalism in Fortress North America," *Socialism and Democracy* 19, no. 2 (2005), 184; Maurice Stierl, "How Migrants and their Supporters are Reviving the Ethos of the 19th-century Underground Railroad," https://theconversation.com/how-migrants-and-their-supporters-are-reviving-the-ethos-of-the-19th-century-underground-railroad-128445, 19 December 2019; Jake Halpern, "The Underground Railroad for

Refugees," 5 March 2017, https://www.newyorker.com/magazine/2017/03/13/the-underground-railroad-for-refugees.

53 *Detention Empire: Reagan's War on Immigrants and the Seeds of Resistance* (Chapel Hill, NC: The University of North Carolina Press, 2022), 172.

54 Robert H. Churchill, *The Underground Railroad and the Geography of Violence in Antebellum America* (Cambridge: Cambridge University Press, 2020), 12. Even in ancient times, enslaved people could not "seek freedom through accessing consecrated ground." Michelle McKinley, "Standing on Shaky Ground: Criminal Jurisdiction and Ecclesiastical Immunity in Seventeenth- Century Lima, 1600–1700," *U.C. Irvine Law Review* 141 (2014): 149.

55 William M. Mitchell, *The Underground Railroad: From Slavery to Freedom* (London: W. Tweedie, 1860), 39.

56 Foner, *Gateway to Freedom*, 124–5.

57 Ibid., 128.

58 Ibid., 65.

59 Wilbur Siebert, *The Underground Railroad from Slavery to Freedom: A Comprehensive History* (New York: MacMillan Company, 1898), 191. See also "J. Theodore Holly to Henry Bibb, Voice of the Fugitive, 2 July 1851," cited in Afua Cooper, "Doing Battle in Freedom's Cause: Henry Bibb, Abolitionism, Race Uplift, and Black Manhood, 1842–1854" (PhD diss., University of Toronto, 2000), 173; Collison, *Shadrach Minkins*, 199. On refuge in Mexico and the Texas-Mexico borderlands see Alice Baumgartner, *South to Freedom: Runaway Slaves to Mexico and the Road to the Civil War* (New York: Basic Books, 2020); Mekala Audain, "'Design his Course to Mexico': The Fugitive Slave Experience in the Texas-Mexico Borderlands, 1850–1853"; and James David Nichols, "Freedom Interrupted: Runaway Slaves and Insecure Borders in the Mexican Northeast," in *Fugitive Slaves and Spaces of Freedom in North America*, ed. Pargas.

60 Douglass, *Narrative of the Life of Frederick Douglass*, 101.

61 Ibid.

62 Foner, *Gateway to Freedom*, 164.

63 Douglass, *Narrative of the Life of Frederick Douglass*, 107.

64 This silence is another example of the limitations of the "Underground Railroad" as a conceptual framework. The Seminoles were themselves refugees from the Creek and were later resettled on Creek territory and in Mexico following settler encroachment and conflict in present-day Florida in the mid-1800s. See William Loren Katz, *Black Indians* (New York: Macmillan, 1986), 50, 69. See also Claudio Saunt, "'The English Has Now a Mind to Make Slaves of Them All': Creeks, Seminoles, and the Problem of Slavery," in *Confounding the Color Line: The Indian-Black Experience in North America*, ed. James F. Brooks (Lincoln, NE: University of Nebraska Press, 2002), 47–75; Evan Taparata "No Asylum for Mankind: The Creation of Refugee Law and Policy in the United States, 1776–1951" (PhD diss, University of Minnesota, 2018), 139. The Creek signed a treaty in 1721 in which

they promised the return of fugitive slaves though it is unclear about the extent to which this was enforced. Pargas, *Fugitive Slaves and Spaces of Freedom in North America,* 10. On Black refuge with other Indigenous communities, see discussion of Joseph Brant in Katz, *Black Indians,* 111. Fugitive slaves also found refuge in Shawnee villages and used their established trails in their bid for safety. See also Roy E. Finkenbine, "The Underground Railroad in 'Indian Country': Northwest Ohio, 1795–1843," in Pargas, *Fugitive Slaves and Spaces of Freedom in North America,* 76–7. The situation changed significantly in the years following the 1830 Indian Removal Act, which forced the displacement of Indigenous Peoples west of the Mississippi. Alaiana Roberts' astonishing work, *I've Been Here All the While: Black Freedom on Native Land* (Philadelphia: University of Pennsylvania Press, 2021) sheds further light on the complex implications of this forced removal, documenting how Indigenous Peoples who were being forcibly removed brought with them enslaved people and also contributed to the further dispossession of Indigenous Peoples on the lands in present-day Oklahoma where they resettled. See also Elizabeth Ellis, *The Great Power of Small Nations: Indigenous Diplomacy in the Gulf South* (Princeton, NJ: Princeton University Press, 2022).

65 McKittrick, "Freedom is a Secret," 101. Scholars now identify key flaws in Wilbur Siebert's ground-breaking work on the Underground Railway, most notably in terms of his focus on particular sites of refuge and an over-emphasis on abolitionist efforts. See Churchill, *The Underground Railroad,* 13.

66 Douglass, *Narrative of the Life of Frederick Douglass,* 106–7.

67 Ibid.

68 Miles, *All That She Carried,* 96.

69 Hartman, "Scenes of Subjection," 11.

70 Miles, *All That She Carried,* 106.

71 Siebert, *The Underground Railroad from Slavery to Freedom,* 195.

72 Foner, *Gateway to Freedom,* 82.

73 Little information survives about Isaacson's law practice in this period, though records show that he assumed Power of Attorney responsibilities for one Robert Naxon and, later, one Sarah Gill, in 1856. See Archives des notaires, Québec, Canada, 1637 à 1935, Bibliothèque et Archives Nationale du Québec (BANQ).

74 "Record of Fugitives," Sydney Howard Gay, Columbia University Archives. There are several references of people being sent to Albany and Syracuse, and it is unclear whether they continued from there. "Dolly's Chop House" by S.M.B., Etat Civil - Robert Philips Isaacson, C002/A, 94, M68846, McCord Museum.

75 Benjamin Hoy, *A Land of Blood and Dirt: Creating the Canada-United States Border Across Indigenous* Land (New York: Oxford University Press, 2021), 28. Surveyors in the west referred to mosquitoes as "our tormenters."

76 This area is long rumoured to have been a site on the "Underground Railroad" as well as the site of an old Black cemetery. Alfie (Alphie) Roberts wrote about the

search for this history in the July 1984 of *Afro-Can* on behalf of "The Emancipation 150 Cttee," Negro Community Centre Fonds, Concordia University.

77 Roland Viau, "The Times and Trials of a Distinctive Colony: 1702–1760," in Dany Fougères and Roderick McLeod, vol. 1 *Montreal: History of a North American City* (Montreal-Kingston: McGill-Queen's University Press, 2018), 165.

78 See also "A new map of the province of lower Canada, describing all the seigneuries, townships, grants of land, &c." http://digitalarchive.mcmaster.ca/islandora/object/macrepo%3A81318, accessed 28 January 2024; "To his most excellent majesty King William IVth this map of the provinces of Lower & Upper Canada, Nova Scotia, New Brunswick, Newfoundland & Prince Edwards Island, with a large section of the United States," https://mdlcollections.library.utoronto.ca/islandora/object/fishermaps%3AG3410_1831_B6-2, accessed 28 January 2024.

79 Siebert, *The Underground Railroad from Slavery to Freedom*, 52; Frank Mackey, *Steamboat Connections: Montreal to Upper Canada, 1816–1843* (Montreal-Kingston: McGill-Queen's University Press, 2000), 3.

80 Rück, *The Laws of the Land*, 61.

81 John Scott, 1 September 1859, cited in Still, *The Underground Railroad*, 105.

82 See discussion in Siebert, *The Underground Railroad from Slavery to Freedom*.

83 1893 letter from Reverend Joshua Young of Burlington to Wilbur Siebert, the Underground Railroad historian, suggesting railroads were the principal means of flight. Cited in Collison, *Shadrach Minkins*, 164; Ellen R. Smith's letter to Wilbur Siebert, 4 May 1935, https://ohiomemory.org/digital/collection/siebert/id/24617.

84 Allan Downey, "Indigenous Brooklyn: Ironworking, Little Caughnawaga, and Kanien'kehá:ka Nationhood in the Twentieth Century," *American Quarterly* 75, no. 1 (2023): 29. The geographic locations and extended relations of the communities in both Kahnawà:ke and Ahkwesáhsne make it possible that fugitives from slavery may have stayed there for a time or been adopted into community, but neither the archival record nor available oral histories are forthcoming in this regard. This is, in some ways, not surprising given the limitations of the documentary record for highly mobile populations. See Jean Teillet, "Understanding the Historic and Contemporary Métis of the Northwest," *Canadian Issues* (2008): 36–49. There is no evidence of any permanent presence of fugitives from slavery in nineteenth-century census records for Kahnawà:ke, which was recorded by census takers only as the Sault Saint-Louis seigneury. In 1852, there were 1259 "Indians" in Sault Saint-Louis and no recorded "coloured persons," though there were seven people whose country of origin was the United States. Nine years later, there were 1352 "Indians" in Sault Saint Louis, in addition to one Swiss, eight French, four English, five Scottish, and one Irish person as well as five whose origins were unknown. In 1872, there were 1,351 Indigenous Peoples in the count, along with two Scotch, three English, 223 French, and one German. These records do not reveal the presence of fugitive slaves. Their rigid construction nevertheless raises questions about who might have come and gone in the intervening years. Census,

Government of Canada, Sault-St Louis, 1871. In the case of Kahnawà:ke, historian Daniel Rück describes a "long and proud history of successful adoption and naturalization of outsiders," of both Indigenous Peoples and non-Indigenous people, including a number of Black people. Rück, *The Laws of the Land*, 90.

85 Rück, *The Laws of the Land*, 105.

86 Daniel Rück, "When Bridges Become Barriers," in *Metropolitan Natures: Environmental Histories of Montreal*, ed. Stéphane Castonguay and Michèle Dagenais (Pittsburgh, PA: University of Pittsburgh Presss, 2011), 233.

87 Ibid., 234.

88 Siebert, *The Underground Railroad from Slavery to Freedom*, 133. St John, New Brunswick is located on the traditional territory of the Wəlastəkwiyik (Maliseet).

89 Elizabeth Montour, "Treasures Revealed: Episode 8," Discover Library and Archives Canada Podcast. Decades later, Josie Day offered her own recollections of crossing the bridge to work on the island because there was "no work" on the reserve: "We had to cross the bridge on food, this is why we're all thin and had small waists … We worked all day picking raspberries at twenty-five cents an hour. It was nice, we joked while were picking and sometimes women got mad at each other. I remember one time just as we were finishing for the day, the sky became dark and looked like rain. We asked one another if we should attempt the bridge. We did and about halfway across the bridge, it started to pour, thunder, and lightning. We were scared because we knew that we were walking on steel, but we got home safe." Morris, *Old Kahnawà:ke*, 20.

90 Samuel Ringgold Ward to Henry Bibb, 16 October 1851, *Voice of the Fugitive*, https://proxy.library.mcgill.ca/login?url=https://www.proquest.com/newspapers/letter-samuel-ringgold-ward-henry-bibb/docview/2522665606/se-2.

91 By way of illustration, hospital records after 1857, when steam power changed the nature of industrial activity in the city, show significant worker solidarity as people passed "the hat in the shop or yard of a foundry" or covered the cost of an ambulance, recorded by drivers as "Paid by friends." See Sherry Olson, "Setting the census household into its urban context: Visualizations from 19th-century Montreal," *Demographic Research* 36 (2017): 1416.

92 Harriet Beecher Stowe, *Uncle Tom's Cabin* (New York: Quarto Publishing Group USA, 2016).

93 Miles, *All That She Carried*, 299; Stowe, *Uncle Tom's Cabin*, 438.

94 President Abraham Lincoln purportedly claimed that the book helped pave the way for the US Civil War. *The Maple Leaf*, a monthly periodical, serialized the book from July 1852 to June 1853. Meanwhile, the original publisher promoted the book with "merchandise, such as mementos, card games and puzzles, porcelain figures, needlework and items of clothing." Cheryl Thompson, *Uncle: Race, Nostalgia, and the Politics of Loyalty* (Toronto: Coach House Books, 2021), 8. The book and the buzz captured the "public's imagination," and, as Thompson has observed, in some ways it has never left; although historical details, such as the limited nature of refuge in Montreal/Mooniyaang/Tiohtià:ke, have become blurry. Thompson, *Uncle*, 14.

95 Thompson, *Uncle*, 7, 18.
96 Siebert, *The Underground Railroad from Slavery to Freedom*, 134, 141, 149, 218.
97 Williams, *Blacks in Montreal*, 18. Gary Collison points out that there were very few Blacks in New England, comparatively speaking and this might have also made Montreal a "weak magnet" for fugitives. See Gary Collison, "Loyal and Dutiful Subjects of her Gracious Majesty, Queen Victoria": Fugitive Slaves in Montreal, 1850–1866," *Quebec Studies* 19 (1995): 60.
98 Foner, *Gateway to Freedom*, 19; Harvey Amani Whitfield, *Black Slavery in the Maritimes* (Peterborough, ON: Broadview Press, 2018), 4.
99 Community histories emphasize the significance of local organizing and consolidation only as the size of the population grew with the advent of new migration and settlement due to railway work in the late nineteenth and early twentieth centuries. Stanley Clyke, "A Community Within a Community?" A Paper Presented to the Church-Welfare Institute, April 26, 1961," Negro Community Centre Fonds, Concordia University.
100 Collison, "Loyal and Dutiful Subjects," 60.
101 Williams, *The Road to Now*, 27.
102 Collison, "Loyal and Dutiful Subjects," 60; Still, *The Underground Railroad*, 105.
103 Collison, *Shadrach Minkins*, 189.
104 John Scott, 1 September 1859. This letter, one of the few from the city, has been widely cited. See Still, *The Underground Railroad*, 105. The 1861–2 city directory shows a William Taylor, milkman, at 31 Durham Street. Edmund Turner is named as a barber in the 1861 and 1863 Mackay's Montreal Directory.
105 Charmaine Nelson, *Slavery, Geography and Empire*, 162.
106 The 1851 census does not record any Black or Indigenous Peoples in the city; however, Gary Collison notes that the 1852 city census shows fifty-one Black people living in three different wards. Collison, *Shadrach Minkins*, 196.
107 Ward to Bibb, October 16, 1851.
108 "Once enslaved in Virginia, Montrealer Shadrach Minkins commemorated at cemetery," 28 October 2023, https://www.cbc.ca/news/canada/montreal/shadrach-minkins-plaque-cemetery-montreal-1.7011679.
109 Collison, "Loyal and Dutiful Subjects," 61, 65.
110 A Report from Israel Lewis, Founder of the Wilberforce Colony, National Anti-Slavery Standard, 3 June 1841; Silverman, *Unwanted Guests*, 32.
111 Collison, *Shadrach Minkins*, 177.
112 Samuel Ringgold Ward to Henry Bibb, 16 October 1851, *Voice of the Fugitive*, https://proxy.library.mcgill.ca/login?url=https://www.proquest.com/newspapers/letter-samuel-ringgold-ward-henry-bibb/docview/2522665606/se-2.
113 Zirblis, "The Vermont Underground Railroad Survey Report," 35.
114 Landon, "The Negro Migration," 36. Pape's letter is widely cited. See also Samuel May, *The Fugitive Slave Law and Its Victims* (New York, 1861).
115 The fact that some of these establishments were Confederate hangouts has been a subject of interest for latter-day Montrealers. Barry Sheehy, "Opinion:

A Haven for Escaped Slaves — and Confederate Operatives," 27 February 2018, https://montrealgazette.com/opinion/opinion-a-haven-for-escaped-slaves-and-confederate-operatives.

116 Collison, *Shadrack Minkins*, 209. Collison suggests that those newcomers who gave their place of birth as a Southern state, were "probably fugitive slaves." He adds, "Many had a skill or trade, including Matthew Bell, a carpenter; John Wilson, a brickmaker; Thomas Cook, listed variously as a whitewasher, a cook, and a coffee house operator beginning in 1856; and seven barbers, William Briscoe, David Johnson, William Francis Jones, Edwin Moore, Isaac Newton, William Medley, and Clarence F. Selden." Collison, "Loyal and Dutiful Subjects," 60.

117 Nicole St-Onge, "'He Was Neither a Soldier nor a Slave: He Was under the Control of No Man': Kahnawake Mohawks in the Northwest Fur Trade, 1790–1850," *Canadian Journal of History* 51, no. 1 (2016): 1–32.; Simpson, *Mohawk Interruptus: Political Life Across the Borders of Settler States* (Durham, NC: Duke University Press, 2014), 50, 51; David Blanchard, "Entertainment, Dance, and Northern Mohawk Showmanship," *American Indian Quarterly* 7, no. 1 (1983): 2, 22.

118 Collison, "Loyal and Dutiful Subjects," 63.

119 Ibid., 64.

120 Ibid.

121 Clyke, "A Community Within a Community?"

122 Rück, *The Laws of the Land*, 46.

123 Charon was a former trader who had been afflicted by serious illness and sought to ensure assistance for others. The Sulpicians helped the Charon brothers receive royal approval for their initiative. John Alexander Dickinson and Ollivier Hubert, eds, *Les Sulpiciens de Montréal: Une Histoire de Pouvoir et de Discrétion* (Montreal: Les Éditions Fides, 2007), 244.

124 Olivier Maurault, "1742" *Les Cahiers des Dix* 7 (1942): 172.

125 To help with this work, for which demand grew steadily, the Grey Nuns purchased the Seigneury of Chateauguay from the French Crown in 1765. In doing so, they came into conflict with the Kanien'kehá:ka, who accused them of encroaching on their lands. Rück, *The Laws of the Land*, 46.

126 It is also important to note that during her lifetime, Marguerite d'Youville received several enslaved people as gifts. Upon her death in 1771, she willed five Indigenous slaves in her personal possession and another four at the Hôpital Général. See Alanna Loucks, "The Governor, the Merchant, the Soldier, the Nun, and Their Slaves: Household Formation and Kinship in Seventeenth and Eighteenth-century Montréal" (MA thesis, Queen's University, 2019), 105. Historian Marcel Trudel provides details for three enslaved people at the hospital; a "panis" given by the widow Saint-Blin in 1763, Marie-Marguerite, identified as "pains" given by Grasset de Saint-Sauver at the age of nineteen in 1764; and Henry-Thérèse, "Sioux," aged twenty-one, born in Châteauguay in 1774. Marcel Trudel, *Dictionnaire des esclaves et de leurs propriétaires au Canada français* (Montreal: Hurtubise HMH, 1990), 347.

127 Williams, *Blacks in Montreal*, 15.

128 Douglass, *Narrative of the Life of Frederick Douglass*, 107–8.

129 See "Spirit World: Director's Cut," *Ahkwesáhsne* TV, https://www.youtube.com/watch?v=kocX8COeQIw, accessed 8 April 2023.

130 North Country Underground Railroad Historical Association, https://northcountryundergroundrailroad.com/franklin-county.php, accessed 28 January 2024. The other tangential connection to the Underground Railroad involves Matilda Joslyn Gage, who was adopted into the Wolf Clan in 1893 and given the name, Karonienhawi ("she who holds the sky"). Gage grew up in Cicero, New York where her family's home was "the intellectual centre" of the community. She was an advocate for women's rights and native rights, and lived for part of her life in Fayetteville, Onondaga County, New York. There she sheltered fugitives in her handsome colonial revival home (now adorned with a historical plaque), with its proud Greek ionic columns and peaked pediment. Gage described "helping black slaves on to freedom" as "one of the proudest acts of my life." Gage undertook her work on behalf of fugitive slaves before she was adopted by the Wolf Clan and it seems that her adoption was largely as a result of the community relations that stemmed from her advocacy for women's rights, rather than her abolitionist engagements. See Sally Roesch Wagner, *Matilda Joslyn Gage: She Who Holds the Sky* (Aberdeen, SD: Sky Carrier Press, 1998), 34; Leila Brammer, *Excluded from Suffrage History: Matilda Joslyn Gage, Nineteenth-Century American Feminist* (Westport, CT: Greenwood Press, 2000), 1; Matilda Joslyn Gage, "Old Times and New," *National Citizen and Ballot Box*, May 1880, column 5, 3.

131 See references in *Akwesasne Notes*, American Indian Digital History Project, https://www.aidhp.com, accessed 23 January 2024.

132 Transcribed in Mackey, *Done With Slavery*, 331.

133 Ibid., 109.

134 Ibid.

135 Steward, *Twenty-Two Years A Slave*, 283. There is no record of Israel Lewis in the registers of the Hôpital Général nor at the Hôtel Dieu. A search of the Montreal General Hospital records also came up empty. However, his presence in the city is confirmed by historian Frank Mackey who also reports that Lewis was buried in "'the Poor Ground' off the Protestant cemetery on Papineau street." *Black Then*, 126.

Notes from the Field (The Fugitive City)

1 Assessment of James O. Hall analysis in Frederick Hatch, *John Surratt: Rebel, Lincoln Conspirator, Fugitive* (Jefferson, NC: McFarland & Company, Inc., Publishers, 2016), 168.

2 Entry dated 5 September 1965, John H. Surratt, *The Private Journal and Diary of John H. Surratt, the Conspirator* (New York: Frederic A. Brady, 1866).

The Fugitive City

1 William Edwards and Edward Steers, *The Lincoln Assassination: The Evidence* (Champaign, IL: University of Illinois Press, 2009), 1227.

2 Max Hamon, *The Audacity of his Enterprise: Louis Riel and the Métis Nation That Canada Never Was, 1840–1875* (Montreal-Kingston: McGill-Queen's University Press), 223.

3 Damien M. Sojoyner, "Another Life is Possible: Black Fugitivity and Enclosed Places," *Cultural Anthropology* 32, no. 4 (2017), 516.

4 Ibid. Sojoyner recognizes the influential work of Audra Simpson on the politics of refusal. See *Mohawk Interruptus: Political Life Across the Borders of Settler States* (Durham, NC: Duke University Press, 2014). See also Leanne Betasamosake Simpson, *As We Have Always Done: Indigenous Freedom through Radical Resistance* (Minneapolis, MN: University of Minnesota Press, 2017).

5 Tina Campt, "Black Feminist Futures and the Practice of Fugitivity," Helen Pond McIntyre '48 Lecture, Barnard College, 7 October 2014, https://bcrw.barnard.edu/event/black-feminist-futures-and-the-practice-of-fugitivity. Campt calls fugitivity "the quotidian practice of refusal," citing Judith Butler's ideas about "refusing to stay in one's proper place." In this framework, the law and other social structures are called into question rather than the qualities of the individuals involved.

6 Kenneth J. Zanca, *The Catholics and Mrs. Mary Surratt* (Lanham, MD: University Press of America, 2008), 21.

7 See Matthew McCullough, *The Cross of War: Christian Nationalism and U.S. Expansion in the Spanish-American War* (Madison, WI: University of Wisconsin Press, 2014).

8 Jessica Harland-Jacobs argues that even though anti-Catholicism was obvious, the significant influence of the Roman Catholic Church meant that it had to be accommodated and couldn't simply be marginalized. See "Incorporating the King's New Subjects: Accommodation and Anti-Catholicism in the British Empire, 1763–1815," *Journal of Religious History* 39, no. 2 (2015): 203–23. On the changing place of the Catholic Church in the United States and the Province of Canada, as well as the social lives of Irish Catholics, see Willie Jenkins, *Between Raid and Rebellion: The Irish in Buffalo and Toronto, 1867–1916* (Montreal-Kingston: McGill-Queen's University Press, 2013), 9.

9 Stephen Kenny, "A Prejudice that Rarely Utters Its Name: A Historiographical and Historical Reflection upon North American Anti-Catholicism," *American Review of Canadian Studies* 32, no. 4 (2002), 649. Historian William Kurtz argues that anti-Catholic sentiment dates "back to the earliest foundations of the original colonies by Great Britain." *Excommunicated From the Union: How the Civil War Created a Separate Catholic America* (New York: Fordham University Press, 2015), 2.

10 Hamon, *The Audacity of His Enterprise*, 93.

11 Shawn McCutcheon, "Honnêtes Hommes et Gentilshommes: L'éducation Classique des Garçons et la Formation du Soi Masculin au Bas-Canada à L'âge Des Révolutions (1791–1840)" (PhD diss., McGill University, 2021), 36. Somewhat ironically, historian Max Hamon sees the education offered by the Sulpicians as a form of sanctuary in and of itself. As he writes, "The strength of the seminaries and colleges in North America was in reaction to the French revolution … Some felt that this 'exile' jeopardized their calling as philosophers. Others, however, saw an opportunity, and they abandoned Europe to revolutionary liberalism and moral corruption, while they embraced the sanctuary of the New World and its opportunities." See "Contesting Civilization: Louis Riel's Defence of Culture at the Collège de Montréal" *Canadian Historical Review* 97, no. 1 (2016): 78, https://doi.org/10.3138/chr.3337.

12 Tiya Miles, *The Journey of Ashley's Sack, a Black Family Keepsake* (New York: Random House, 2022), 224.

13 Kurtz, *Excommunicated from the Union*, 4.

14 Ibid. See also, Willie Jenkins, *Between Raid and Rebellion*, 5.

15 Riel ultimately helped the government of Manitoba ward off a Fenian attack in 1871. See J.M. Bumsted, "Louis Riel and the United States," *The American Review of Canadian Studies* 29, no. 1 (1999): 22.

16 Alfred Isaacson, *The Travels, Arrest and Trial of John H. Surratt* (Middletown, NY: Vestigium Press, 2003), 4.

17 Kurtz, *Excommunicated from the Union*, 108, 109; Stephen Kenny, "A Prejudice that Rarely Utters Its Name: A Historiographical and Historical Reflection upon North American Anti-Catholicism," *American Review of Canadian Studies* 32, no. 4 (2002): 665.

18 Kurtz, *Excommunicated from the Union*, 6. On the search for equality of treatment, see Dean Duncan, *Citizens or Papists? The Politics of Anti-Catholicism in New York, 1685–1821* (New York: Fordham University Press), 2005.

19 As Michael Gauvreau and Olivier Hubert underscore, the historiography on religion and social beliefs has long been divided along linguistic lines in Canada. See *Churches and Social Order in Nineteenth and Twentieth Century Quebec* (Montreal-Kingston: McGill-Queen's University Press, 2006), 5. The notion of blind followers needs to be heavily critiqued, particularly in the context of sanctuary offers in which individual inclination is critical. Nevertheless, is still necessary to recognize the extensive social regulation and the close relationship between religion and identity in the mid-nineteenth century. As Gauvreau and Hubert suggest, "Over time, bishops controlled their clergy with growing efficiency, developed more precise ways of knowing and managing their personnel, and calibrated instruments by which to measure faith." Gauvreau and Hubert, *Churches and Social Order in Nineteenth and Twentieth Century Quebec*, 2. See also Michael Gauvreau and Nancy Christie, *Christian Churches and Their Peoples, 1840–1965: A Social History of Religion in Canada* (Toronto: University of Toronto Press, 2010), 6.

20 Preston Jones, "Civil War, Culture War: French Quebec and the American War between the States," *The Catholic Historical Review* 87, no. 1 (2001): 57. Louis Riel would spend time in many of their settlements during his time in exile.
21 Ibid., 61.
22 Ibid.
23 Ibid., 53–4.
24 Ibid, 63–4.
25 Ibid.
26 According to Zanca, slave-owning was consonant with Catholic teaching in "that buying, selling, and owning slaves were not immoral activities. Catholic teaching insisted on the humane treatment of slaves because they were rational human beings possessing souls, but slavery itself was a consequence of fallen human nature, and not condemned." Zanca, *The Catholics and Mrs. Mary Surratt*, 18, 19.
27 Zanca, *The Catholics and Mrs. Mary Surratt*, 19. See also 'Sisters of Charity," https://www.emmitsburg.net/archive_list/articles/history/stories/sisters_of_charity.htm, accessed 14 June 2023.
28 Zanca, *The Catholics and Mrs. Mary Surratt*, 19.
29 "L. J. Wiechmann Examined by Col. Foster Old Capitol Prison, May 2, 1865," in Steers, *The Lincoln Assassination: The Evidence*, 1324.
30 Miles, *All That She Carried*, 53, 56.
31 "Letter of Archbishop Eccleston, 1838," cited in Bernard Christian Steiner, *History of Education in Maryland* (Washington, DC: United States Bureau of Education, 1894), 167.
32 Ibid., 169.
33 Ibid., 168.
34 Ibid., 167.
35 Edward Steers, *Blood on the Moon: The Assassination of Abraham* Lincoln (Lexington, KY: University of Kentucky Press, 2001), 80.
36 John Surratt, "A Remarkable Lecture: John H. Surratt Tells His Story," *Lincoln Herald* 51, no. 4 (1949): 22, https://rogerjnorton.com/Lincoln55.html.
37 Jill Lepore, *These Truths: A History of the United States* (New York: W.W. Norton & Company, 2018), 290, 296. The Davis family first sent their children to safety at Bishop's College School in Lennoxville, Quebec (traditional N'dakina and Wabanaki territory), about an hour from the Vermont border, and then later moved there themselves. Later in life, Varina Davis (the wife of Jefferson Davis) emphasized Catholic support in helping her and her family. See Barry Sheehy, *Montreal: City of Secrets, Confederate Operations in Montreal during the American Civil War* (Montreal: Baraka Books, 2017), 187.
38 Lepore, *These Truths*, 293.
39 Hamon, *The Audacity of His Enterprise*, 212.
40 Bettina Bradbury, *Working Families: Age, Gender, and Daily Survival in Industrializing Montreal* (Toronto: University of Toronto Press, 2003), 23, 24.

41 Thomas W. Raphael, *Annual Review of the Trade and Commerce of Montreal: With a Glance at The Resources of Canada, 1866* (Montreal: Herald Steam Press, 1867), 1, 4.

42 Andrew D. Smith and Laurence B. Mussio, "Canadian Entrepreneurs and the Preservation of the Capitalist Peace in the North Atlantic Triangle in the Civil War Era, 1861–1871," *Enterprise & Society* 17, no. 3 (2016): 545; John W. Headley, *Confederate Operations in Canada and New York* (New York; Washington, DC: Neale Pub. Co.), 221.

43 Gerald J. J. Tulchinsky, "Augstin Cantin, *Dictionary of Canadian Biography*, http://www.biographi.ca/en/bio/cantin_augustin_12F.html, accessed 29 January 2024.

44 Cited in Wilfrid Bovey, "Confederate Agents in Canada During the American Civil War," *The Canadian Historical Review* 21, no. 1 (1921): 46.

45 Ibid., 51.

46 Michelle Arnosky Sherburne, *The St. Albans Raid: Confederate Attack on Vermont* (Charleston, SC: History Press, 2014), 23.

47 Mayers, *Dixie & the Dominion*, 158.

48 Sherburne, *The St. Albans Raid*, 23.

49 Sheehy, *Montreal*, 30.

50 Ibid. 23. On the cotton trade in the Civil War, see Ludwell H. Johnson, "Contraband Trade During the Last Year of the Civil War," *The Mississippi Valley Historical Review* 49, no. 4 (1963): 635–52; Ludwell H. Johnson, "Northern Profit and Profiteers: The Cotton Rings of 1864–1865," *Civil War History* 12, no. 2 (June 1966): 101–15. By 1864, there was certainly a lot of cotton trade for meat. For details, see "W.H. Carroll to S.P. Walker, 20 March 1865," in Speers, *The Lincoln Assassination: The Evidence*, 327.

51 Sheehy, *Montreal*, 127.

52 Josh Ellerbock, "Abolitionist Exhibit created by the Saint Albans Museum opens up in St. Albans City Hall," *St Albans Messenger*, 19 October 2021, https://www.samessenger.com/news/abolitionist-exhibit-created-by-the-saint-albans-museum-opens-up-in-st-albans-city-hall/article_bcd46f58-3132-11ec-8689-e33018b61c2d.html.

53 Headley, *Confederate Operations in Canada and New York*, 262. A former soldier from Tennessee, Headley makes his pro-Confederate sympathies very clear throughout his account of the war.

54 Adam Mayers, *Dixie & the Dominion: Canada, the Confederacy, and the War for the Union* (Toronto: the Dundurn Group, 2003), 25.

55 Ibid., 176.

56 American Consul Potter to Secretary of State Seward, May 2, 1865, Despatches from United States consuls in Montreal, 1850–1906, National Archives and Records Administration (NARA).

57 Ibid. See newspaper clippings included in the same series.

58 Sherburne, *The St. Albans Raid*, 128; Bovey, 55.

59 Cited in Michelle Arnosky Sherburne, *The St. Albans Raid*, 133. "Outrage at St. Alban's," *Montreal Gazette*, 20 October 1864, 2.

60 Ibid.

61 Mayers, *Dixie & the Dominion*, 191.

62 "Our Relations With Canada," *New York Times*, 3 February 1865, 2, https://timesmachine.nytimes.com/timesmachine/1865/02/03/issue.html.

63 Ibid.

64 Bradley Miller, *Borderline Crime: Fugitive Criminals and the Challenge of the Border, 1819–1914* (Toronto: University of Toronto Press, 2018), 29.

65 Although this is the generally accepted chronology and timeline of Surratt's whereabouts, there are differing accounts. One of the members of the Military Commission that investigated Lincoln's assassination maintained that Surratt was in the capital on the day of the assassination. Thomas Harris declared "Surratt himself told his old acquaintance, St. Marie, with whom he renewed his acquaintanceship in the ranks of the Papal Zouaves at Velletri, in Italy, that he left Washington early on the morning of the 15th of April, disguised as an English tourist; and that he had a very hard time to make his escape." Thomas Mealey Harris, "Chapter VIII," *Assassination of Lincoln: A History of the Great Conspiracy Trial of the Conspirators by a Military Commission, and a Review of the Trial of John H. Surratt*, 1892. Project Gutenberg, 2013.

66 Testimony by Stephen F. Cameron, *Trial of John H. Surratt in the Criminal Court for the District of Columbia: Hon. George P. Fisher Presiding* (Govt. Print. Off., 1867), Volume 2, 794.

67 Surratt, "Lecture," 31; Lewis J.A. McMillan, *Trial of John H. Surratt in the Criminal court for the District of Columbia, Hon. George P. Fisher Presiding* (Washington, Govt. Print. Off., 1867), 472, https://babel.hathitrust.org/.

68 Julian Sher, *The North Star: Canada and the Civil War Plots Against Lincoln* (Toronto: Penguin Random House Canada, 2023), 278. This style of coat referred to a "new Garibaldi pleated jacket with four buttons down the front and a belt." Sher, *The North Star*, 239.

69 Cited in Mayers, *Dixie & the Dominion*, 208.

70 Winks, *The Civil War Years*, 367. For details on Booth's meetings with Confederate agents while in Canada in October 1864, see "Confederate S.A. Documents No. 1, H.R. 361," "John Deveney to Secretary of War, 22 April, 1865," and "G.B. Scrummond to Consul Potter, 20 April 1865" in Speers, *The Lincoln Assassination: The Evidence*, 317, 432, 1134. See also American Consul Potter to Secretary of State Seward, 25 April 1865, despatches from United States consuls in Montreal, 1850–1906 (NARA), for American Consul correspondence on possible support for Surratt from St Alban's raiders.

71 "The Booth Conspiracy: Various Statements Respecting It," *The Globe*, 6 May 1865, 2. There was also an initial search for John Wilkes Booth, who had spent ten days in Montreal in October 1864, until he was apprehended and killed in

Virginia (though rumours that he was actually alive and well in Canada circulated for years after). Two of Booth's trunks mysteriously appeared in Rimouski, furthering the speculation. See American Consul Potter to Secretary of State Seward, 30 May 1865, Despatches from United States consuls in Montreal, 1850–1906 (NARA).

72 "Assssinat du President Lincoln, et de MM. Seward, Père et fils." *Courrier de St. Hyacinthe*, 18 April 1865, 2.

73 Ibid.

74 Winks, *The Civil War Years*, 367.

75 Harris, "Chapter VIII," *Assassination of Lincoln*.

76 "Memorandum of facts connected with the case of J. H. Surratt, alias John Harrison; Montreal," in *The Lincoln Assassination: The Evidence*, 1222; Alexandra Lee Levin, "Who Hid John H. Surratt, The Lincoln Conspiracy Case Figure?" *Maryland Historical Review* 60, no. 2 (1965): 175.

77 Surratt, "Lecture," 32; McMillan testimony in *Trial of John H. Surratt in Criminal Court*, 472.

78 Frederick Hatch, *John Surratt: Rebel, Lincoln Conspirator, Fugitive* (Jefferson, MD: McFarland & Company, 2016), 92.

79 Headley, *Confederate Operations in Canada and New York*, 292–3; Andrew C.A. Jampoler, *The Last Lincoln Conspirator: John Surratt's Flight From the Gallows*, (Annapolis, MD: Naval Institute Press, 2008), 46; *Le Courier du Canada*, 55, 12 June 1865, 1, https://numerique.banq.qc.ca/patrimoine/details/52327/2534110; Sher, *The North Star*, 279.

80 McMillan testimony in *Trial of John H. Surratt in Criminal Court*, 472–3; Harris, "Chapter VIII," *Assassination of Lincoln*.

81 Sher, *North Star*, 307. Lapierre would later become priest for the new parish of St Henri des Tanneries on 12 August 1868 after Canon Bourget received permission from Rome to subdivide the parishes in Montreal where there were an estimated 80,000 Catholics at the time. Pierre Georges Roy, "Recherches Historique," 41 (1935), 43, https://numerique.banq.qc.ca/patrimoine/details/52327/2657413ER.

82 Kenneth J. Zanca, *The Catholics and Mrs. Mary Surratt: How They Responded to the Trial and Execution of the Lincoln Conspirator* (New York: University of America Press, 2008), 84n18.

83 Translation by author: Surratt arrived in Canada bearing a letter of introduction given by General Lee to a Catholic priest who welcomed him purely from charitable motives, in a spirit independent of any political preoccupation, as he would have given shelter to a fugitive slave coming to claim the hospitality that a Christian priest never refuses to the afflicted and proscribed. *Le Courrier do Canada*, 14 August 1867, 1. A general reference to this editorial appears in Sher, *The North Star*, 310.

84 "David R.P. Bigley and James A. Mcdevitt, 20 April 1865," *The Lincoln Assassination: The Evidence*, 134; Harris, "Chapter VIII," *Assassination of Lincoln*. Julian Sher

suggests that Surratt may have in fact stayed with tailor John Reeves for two days before going to St Liboire, but no other account confirms this. See Sher, *The North Star*, 280.

85 Father Charles Boucher testimony, vol. 2, *Trial of John H. Surratt in the Criminal Court for the District of Columbia : Hon. George P. Fisher Presiding* (Washington, DC: Govt. Print. Off., 1867), 896.

86 C.H.A. Bulkley, Canandaigua, N.Y, to Hon. E.M. Stanton, Secretary of War, 16 May 1865, *The Lincoln Assassination: The Evidence*, 218.

87 McMillan testimony in *The Trial of John H. Surratt in Criminal Court*, 474.

88 "Nouvelles Américaines," *Journal de Québec*, 12 May 1865, 2.

89 Surratt, "Lecture," 32.

90 Isaacson, *The Travels, Arrest and Trial of John H. Surratt*, 3.

91 McMillan testimony in *The Trial of John H. Surratt in Criminal Court*, 473.

92 Jampoler, *The Last Lincoln Conspirator*, 69. There are some historical discrepancies here. The biographical entry for Lapierre in the *Dictionnaire biographique du clergé canadien-français (Les Anciens)* (1910) indicates that he was only at La Prairie in 1866 and it is likely that he was newly appointed to La Prairie when he began to visit with, and assist, Surratt. https://numerique.banq.qc.ca/patrimoine/details/52327/2022769.

93 Lewis J.A. McMillan, *The Trial of John H. Surratt in Criminal Court*, 473.

94 Jampoler, *The Last Lincoln Conspirator*, 49.

95 Consul Potter to William Hunter, Acting Secretary of State, 25 May 1865, Despatches from United States consuls in Montreal, 1850–1906, NARA.

96 This same ship would carry hundreds of settlers between Europe and Canada from 1875 until she was broken up in 1905, https://www.mharchives.ca/a-picture-from-our-history/s-s-peruvian/.

97 McMillan testimony in *Trial of John H. Surratt in the Criminal Court*, 464.

98 Ibid. 474.

99 Ibid., 463.

100 Ibid., 464.

101 Ibid., 472.

102 Ibid., 474.

103 David Richardson, Suzanne Schwarz and Anthony Tibbles, eds, *Liverpool and Transatlantic Slavery* (Liverpool: University of Liverpool Press, 2017); 4; Jampoler, *The Last Lincoln Conspirator*, 81.

104 Isaacson, *The Travels, Arrest and Trial of John H. Surratt*, 6.

105 Jampoler, *The Last Lincoln Conspirator*, 87.

106 G.A.: oblation formula, 18 personal documents and 435 letters to about ten Oblates. Missions OMI, 1864–1908, passim. Cited in https://www.omiworld.org/lemma/jolivet-charles/.

107 Isaacson, 8. The idea of being "secreted" is drawn from a letter that Surratt sent years later to Father Jolivet in which he mentioned his continued gratitude, writ-

ing "I have never forgotten your kindness to me at a time when I was without friends and penniless ... It seems impossible that only a wall separated us."

108 Cameron testimony in *Trial of John H. Surratt in the Criminal Court for the District of Columbia*, 808.

109 Harris, "Chapter VIII," *Assassination of Lincoln*.

110 Isaacson, *The Travels, Arrest and Trial of John H. Surratt*. 8.

111 Ibid., 9.

112 Sher, *The North Star*, 324.

113 Jampoler, *The Last Lincoln Conspirator*, 101.

114 Indeed, there are some suggestions that the "organizational capacity" evident in the "nationalist and ultramontane networks established during the Zouave campaign" were later repurposed in the campaign to secure Louis Riel's amnesty. Certainly, one correspondent was "willing to send Zouaves to fight for the Métis cause." Hamon, *The Audacity of his Enterprise*, 210, 249, 262.

115 Isaacson, *The Travels, Arrest and Trial of John H. Surratt*, 24.

116 Jampoler, *The Last Lincoln Conspirator*, 131.

117 Harris, "Chapter VIII," *Assassination of Lincoln*.

118 Cameron testimony in *Trial of John H. Surratt in the Criminal Court for the District of Columbia*, 794, 808; Sher, *The North Star*, 309.

119 Campt, "Black Feminist Futures and the Practice of Fugitivity."

The Hostile City

1 Yvonne Maisonneuve, unpublished autobiography, Archives Le Chaînon, courtesy of Annick Desmarais, 8.

2 Andrée Lévesque, *Résistance et Transgression : Études en Histoire des Femmes au Québec* (Montreal : Éditions du Remue-ménage, 1995), 135.

3 1936 Letters Patent. See Gazette officielle du Québec. Québec official gazette., 1936–03–14, Collections de Bibliothèque et Archives nationale du Québec (BAnQ).

4 "L'Accueil aux Fillettes, Avant la Protection de la Jeunesse," https://ville.montreal.qc.ca/memoiresdesmontrealais/laccueil-aux-fillettes-avant-la-protection-de-la-jeunesse, accessed 30 December 2023.

5 Anne MacLennan, "Charity and Change: Montreal English Protestant Charity Faces the Crisis of Depression," *Urban History Review / Revue d'histoire urbaine* 16, no. 1 (1987): 1–2. https://doi.org/10.7202/1017942ar.

6 Emma Goldman, *A Woman Without a Country* (New York: Oriole Press, 1934), 2, https://archive.org/details/AWomanWithoutACountryByEmmaGoldman/page/n1/mode/2up, accessed 29 January 2024.

7 Joseph Ishill to Emma Goldman, April 22, 1934, C – Feb 1934 – April 1934, The Emma Goldman Papers Project, International Institute for Social History, Microfilm Edition.

8 In 1934, one writer complained to the federal Minister of Justice about her presence, referring to her as a "Jewess" and suggesting that "Jews in this country" were making "important preparations … for future disturbed occasions." Acrian Rand, *Le Patriote,* to Min. HH Stevens, 15 January 1934, RCMP Fonds, RG18-F-3, Vol 3317, File "Emma Goldman, Mrs. James Colton," Library and Archives Canada (LAC).

9 Albalate de Cinca (A Collectivized Village) by Emma Goldman, draft, 1937, W-1935–1940, The Emma Goldman Papers Project, International Institute for Social History, Microfilm Edition.

10 Report of the Investigation Committee re Unemployment, June 23, 1937, 14, CA M001 XCD00-P6212, Boîte: 105-04-01-02, Ancien côte: V.1510.1-5, Archives de Montréal. Population figures are pulled from correspondence on the "chiffre official de la population," 28 January 1946. See Sante – Demographie, 8II.2-1, VM166-1-1-D2453 D811-2-1 : Santé - Démographie - Population - Montréal et sa banlieue : Tableaux. - [18-]-[19-], Archives de Montréal.

11 Report of the Investigation Committee re Unemployment, June 12, 1937, 14, Archives de Montréal.

12 Unemployment Relief Commission, 12 April 1935, Département du chômage. – 1936–1938, CA M001 VM002-07-8-D006 and CA M001 VM002-07-8-D008, Boîte: 047-02-04-03, Archives de Montréal. These schemes included the federal Auger-Rogers plan and were largely directed at those who had moved from rural areas. See Jean-Philippe Bernard, "'Emparons-nous u sol!' Chômage, retour à la terre et colonialisme durant la Grande Dépression au Québec" (PhD diss., Université de Québec à Montréal, 2022). They echoed previous settlement efforts undertaken by state and private authorities alike (most notably Jewish colonization efforts in Manitoba in the late nineteenth century undertaken at the behest of the Baron de Hirsch Institute in Montreal). See John C. Lehr ,"Doomed to Failure: The Jewish Farm Colony of Hirsch, Saskatchewan," Manitoba Historical Society 89 (2019), http://www.mhs.mb.ca/docs/mb_history/89/jewishfarmcolony.shtml.

13 Todd Miller, *Storming the Wall: Climate Change, Migration, and Homeland Security* (San Francisco, CA: City Lights, 2017), 32; Sonya Roy, "Une Catégorie de Chômeurs à Part: Les Cols Blancs de Montréal, 1930–1935." *Labour* 84, no. 1 (2019): 107–40.

14 Angela Morris, *Old Kahnwà:ke* (Kanien'kehá:ka Onkwawén:na Raotitióhkwa Language and Cultural Center), 12.

15 Roy, "Une catégorie de chômeurs à part," 112.

16 See Brian McKenna, "Camillien Houde," https://www.thecanadianencyclopedia.ca/en/article/camillien-houde.

17 Report of the Investigation Committee re Unemployment, 23 June 1937, Archives de Montréal.

18 Gabrielle Roy, *The Tin Flute* (New York: Reynal & Hitchcock, 1947), 348.

19 I was alerted to this phenomenon by Sonya Roy who has done important, compelling research in this area. For example, the city's Executive Committee deter-

mined in December 1934 that only those who had resided "regularly" in the city since 1 May 1934 were eligible for relief. See report by the Unemployment Relief Commission, 12 April 1935, Archives de Montréal.

20 Report of the Investigation Committee Regarding Unemployment, 23 June 1937, 28-9, Archives de Montréal.

21 David Este, Christa Sato, and Darcy McKenna, "The Coloured Women's Club of Montreal, 1902–1940: African-Canadian Women Confronting Anti-Black Racism," *Canadian Social Work Review* 34, no. 1 (2017), 93–4, https://doi.org/10.7202/1040996ar.

22 Ibid., 93.

23 Oral History Transcript, Pauline Paris, V.5, pt.2, FC 2947.9 B6B53 1988, Negro Community Centre Fonds, Special Collections, Concordia University; Este et al., "The Coloured Women's Club of Montreal," 93.

24 John English, *Citizen of the World: The Life of Pierre Elliott Trudeau* (Toronto: A.A. Knopf Canada, 2006), 40; Michael Brown, *Jew or Juif? Jews, French Canadians, and Anglo-Canadians, 1759–1914* (New York: Jewish Publication Society, 1986), 254. See also Baron de Hirsch Annual Report, 1940, Montreal Jewish Public Library.

25 "For 75 Years, The Coloured Women's Club Has Served the Community," F013-006-F46, Negro Community Centre Fonds, Special Collections, Concordia University.

26 "Carte du Réseau d'Institutions de Régulation Sociale de Montréal Entre 1841 et 1921," https://chrs.uqam.ca/index.php/carte-du-reseau-dinstitutions-de-regulation-sociale-de-montreal-entre-1841-et-1921.

27 This organizing would continue in later years, most notably with the establishment of the Chez Doris shelter and Assistance aux Femmes (discussed in chapter five) in 1977, and the Native Women's Centre of Montreal in 1987.

28 Translation by author: "her only reward was that of serving others." Annick Desmarais, "Yvonne Maisonneuve : Mère du Chaînon," Encyclopédie du MEM, https://ville.montreal.qc.ca/memoiresdesmontrealais/yvonne-maisonneuve-mere-du-chainon

29 Maisonneuve, unpublished autobiography, 8.

30 Ibid., 1.

31 Yvonne Maisonneuve, Première Conférence "Comment Ai-Je Été Amenée à fonder notre œuvre?," Archives Le Chaînon, courtesy of Annick Desmarais, 2.

32 Translation by author: "taken rooms in the wrong places." Maisonneuve, unpublished autobiography, 8.

33 Ibid.

34 Maisonneuve, Première Conférence, 2; Lévesque, *Résistance et Transgression*, 52.

35 Maisonneuve, unpublished autobiography, 58.

36 Translation by author: "there were all kinds: ruined, abandoned, discouraged by life ..." Maisonneuve, unpublished autobiography, 26.

37 Lévesque, *Résistance et Transgression*, 11.

38 Translation by author: "I loved them: I saw them return to God ever so slowly, and when I saw a poor girl with a smile on her face, do you think that the burdens I carried or the snide comments I received bothered me at all?" Maisonneuve, unpublished autobiography, 26.
39 Maisonneuve, unpublished autobiography, 11.
40 Ibid.
41 Maisonneuve, Première Conférence, 3.
42 Maisonneuve, unpublished autobiography, 8.
43 Ibid., 23.
44 Ibid., 32. It would move again in 1940 to 101 De La Gauchetière West, and in 1975 to 4373 l'Esplanade Avenue, once again close to the heights of Mont-Royal.
45 Maisonneuve, Première Conférence, 5.
46 Translation by author: "We looked in different parts of the city for accommodation; we were not stable; we were poor; we had faith in Providence, blown here and there on her wings; could we really worry about anything, guided as always by the Lord? In this way, everything worked!" Maisonneuve, unpublished, 32.
47 Translation by author: "We were out of step the neighbourhood. We were doing poor people's work, which was more or less appreciated." Maisonneuve, unpublished autobiography, 31–2.
48 Translation by author: Downtown was "more in keeping with our work; the working class, the good pious people, as well as the Oblate Fathers who cultivated devotion in their parish." Maisonneuve, unpublished autobiography, 31–2.
49 Interview with Annick Desmarais, 12 December 2023.
50 Hélène-Andrée Bizier, *Une Histoire des Québécoises en Photos* (Montreal: Fides, 2007), 233.
51 "Partie de cartes au profit de Notre-Dame-de-la-Protection," *Le Devoir*, 21 November 1938.
52 Interview, Annick Desmarais, 12 December 2023; Maisonneuve, unpublished autobiography, 14.
53 Maisonneuve, Première Conférence, 3.
54 Maisonneuve, unpublished autobiography, 25–6, 58.
55 Sylvie Taschereau, "The Years of the Great Depression," in *Montreal: The History of a North American City* vol. 2, ed. Dany Fougères and Roderick MacLeod (Montreal-Kingston: McGill-Queen's University Press, 2018), 29.
56 Alice Wexler, *Emma Goldman: An Intimate Life* (New York: Pantheon Books, 1984), 37.
57 Martha Solomon, *Emma Goldman* (Boston: Twayne Publishers, 1987), 155; Candace Falk also uses the term "unmoored" to describe Goldman's state of mind in 1931. See *Love, Anarchy, and Emma Goldman* (New York: Holt, Rinehart, and Winston, 1984), 322. Kathy Ferguson, *Emma Goldman: Thinking in the Streets* (Lanham, MD: Rowman & Littlefield Publishers, 2011), 268.
58 Edward Said, *Out of Place: A Memoir* (New York: Vintage Books, 2000), 217.

59 Edward Said, *Reflections on Exile and Other Essays* (Cambridge, MA: Harvard University Press, 2002), 273.
60 Walter Benjamin, "Theses on the Philosophy of History," in *Illuminations: Essays and Reflections by Walter Benjamin*, ed. Hannah Arendt (New York: Mariner Books, 2019), 259–360.
61 Wexler, *Emma Goldman in Exile*, 5.
62 This essay is discussed in detail in Marian Morton, *Emma Goldman and the American Left "Nowhere at Home"* (Woodbridge, CT: Twayne Publishers, 1992), 139.
63 Emma Goldman, "The Tragedy of Political Exiles," *The Nation*, 10 October 1934; Hannah Arendt, *The Origins of Totalitarianism* (New York: Harcourt Brace Jovanovich, 1979). Arendt does not explicitly engage with Goldman's ideas in her own work, though I see a number of parallels and overlaps in their discussions of political refugees.
64 Goldman, "The Tragedy of Political Exiles."
65 Ibid.
66 Emma Goldman to Frank Heiner, 22 May 1934, The Emma Goldman Papers Project, International Institute for Social History, Microfilm Edition.
67 Emma Goldman to H. Fromkin, 6 December 1934, C Nov 34 to Feb 1935, The Emma Goldman Papers Project, International Institute for Social History, Microfilm Edition.
68 See references in letter to Emily Holmes Colman, February 24, 1939, C-Dec 1938–March 1939; 7 February 1939 letter to William and Lillian Medelsohn, C-Dec 1938–March 1939; and 2 March 1939 letter to Ethel Mannin, C-Dec 1938–March 1939, The Emma Goldman Papers Project, International Institute for Social History, Microfilm Edition.
69 Rebecca Margolis, *Jewish Roots, Canadian Soil: Yiddish Cultural Life in Montreal, 1905–1945* (Montreal-Kingston: McGill-Queen's University Press, 2011), 19.
70 Israel Medres, *Montreal of Yesterday: Jewish Life in Montreal 1900–1920* (Montreal: Véhicule Press, 1998), 30.
71 Rebecca E. Margolis, "A Tempest in Three Teapots: Yom Kippur Balls in London, New York and Montreal," *Canadian Jewish Studies* 9 (2001), 52–3. Groups such as the Arbiter Freund in Montreal joined the Anarchist Federation in New York. See reference in *Mother Earth* 2, no. 12 (1908). Montreal donors also contributed to the publication of *Mother Earth*, including O. Kritzer and F. Yelast. *Mother Earth* 4 (1909–10).
72 David Rome, *On Our Forerunners — at Work (Epilogue: Notes on the Twentieth Century)* (Montreal: Canadian Jewish Congress, 1978), 110; Margolis, "A Tempest in Three Teapots," 39–40, 54, 55. Hershman does not figure prominently in Emma Goldman's correspondence though he established the Jewish People's Kitchen in 1933, which also operated as a site for anarchist lectures including some by Emma Goldman. See also Mathieu Houle-Courcelles, *Sur les Traces de L'anarchisme au Québec (1860–1960)*, (Montreal: Lux, 2008) 47.

73 Medres, *Montreal of Yesterday*, 13; Margolis, *Jewish Roots*, 19.

74 Brown, *Jew or Juif?*, 5.

75 Marilyn Reizbaum, "Yiddish Modernisms: Red Emma Goldman," *Modern Fiction Studies* 51, no. 2 (2005): 460; Wexler, *Emma Goldman in Exile*, 40; Paul Avrich, *Anarchist Voices: An Oral History of Anarchism in America* (Princeton, NJ: Princeton University Press, 1995), 51. Their daughter Vera Shlakman, a famed economist, was fired from her teaching position at Queens College in New York in 1952 for refusing to reveal whether she was card-carrying member of the Communist Party; Emma Goldman to Tom Keell, November 25, 1926, Emma Goldman Papers, Sallie Bingham Center for Women's History & Culture, Duke University Library.

76 See correspondence in Harry Joshua Stern Fonds, Volume 1, File 19, MG31-F12, R4243-5-2-E, Library and Archives Canada.

77 Emma Goldman, vol. 2, *Living my Life* (New York: Alfred A. Knopf, 1934), 992.

78 Emma Goldman, vol. 1, *Living My Life* (New York: Alfred A. Knopf, 1931), 246, 522. Goldman also lectured in German on occasion. See "Our Propaganda," *Mother Earth* 2, no. 12 (Feb 1908), 581.

79 Paul and Karen Avrich, *Sasha and Emma: The Anarchist Odyssey of Alexander Berkman and Emma Goldman* (Cambridge, MA: Harvard University Press, 2012), 336.

80 Emma Goldman, "Joys of Touring," *Mother Earth* 3, no. 11 (1909): 36.

81 Emma Goldman, "Patience and Postage," *Mother Earth* 3, no. 6 (1927): 6–7.

82 Ibid.

83 Taschereau, "The Years of the Great Depression," 9. Emma Goldman to Frank Heiner, December 19, 1934, Frank Heiner and Montreal Newspaper Clippings, International Institute of Social History. See Theresa Moritz and Albert Moritz, *The World's Most Dangerous Woman: A New Biography of Emma Goldman* (Toronto: University of Toronto Press, 2010), 141.

84 Brown, *Jew or Juif?*, 134–5.

85 English, *Citizen of the World*, 145; Acrian Rand, *Le Patriote*, Library and Archives Canada.

86 English, *Citizen of the World*, 28.

87 Ibid. There were an estimated seven hundred to one thousand party supporters in Quebec when the party was founded in 1934. See Taschereau, "The Years of the Great Depression," 9. Emma Goldman to Frank Heiner, 19 December 1934, Frank Heiner and Montreal Newspaper Clippings, The Emma Goldman Papers Project, International Institute for Social History, Microfilm Edition. See also Moritz and Moritz, *The World's Most Dangerous Woman*, 24.

88 Alti Rodal "Nazi War Criminals in Canada: The Historical and Policy Setting from the 1940s to the Present," 109. MG31-F6, Volume 250, Gunther Plaut Fonds, Library and Archives Canada.

89 Ibid. On debates over religious education in Quebec in this period, see Roderick MacLeod and Mary Anne Poutanen. "Little Fists for Social Justice: Anti-Semitism, Community, and Montreal's Aberdeen School Strike, 1913," *Labour/Le Travail* 70, no. 1 (2012): 61–99, http://www.lltjournal.ca/index.php/llt/article/view/5657/6520; Jacques Langlais and David Rome, *Jews and French Quebecers Two Hundred Years of Shared History* (Waterloo, ON: Wilfrid Laurier University Press, 1991), 122.

90 See Irving Abella and Harold Troper, *None is Too Many: Canada and the Jews of Europe, 1933–1948* (Toronto: University of Toronto Press, 2013). Many Jewish German refugees would nevertheless be interned in Canada as a result of a wartime agreement with the British government.

91 Franca Iacovetta, *Gatekeepers: Reshaping Immigrant Lives in Cold War Canada* (Toronto: Between the Lines, 2006), 49. The Bernonville case led to a tense situation between federal and provincial authorities over whether he should be permitted to remain. The federal government certainly pursued the deportation of other Vichy war criminals, most notably Georges Benoît-Montel, but the Bernonville case was complicated by the vocal support that emerged on his behalf including the organization of the "Comité de défense des réfugiés politiques français" (in Montel's case the support was quieter and manifested largely in plans to have him go into sanctuary at the Séminaire du Québec). Historian Robert Rumilly and leading church figures in Quebec befriended de Bernonville and his family (who also received support from Camille Houde, the mayor of Montreal). Friends received regular updates and seasonal Christmas cards filled with affectionate greetings. Supporters insisted on the man's innocence and charged that he was being persecuted by communists (Bernonville had also been sheltered by the Catholic Church in France, seeking initial refuge in a monastery before leaving the continent). Nevertheless, after a series of court cases and investigations, de Bernonville was deported in 1951 (something that the Jewish community in Canada had lobbied for). See Robert Rumilly Fonds, P303, S6, SS9, D1, BANQ (Montreal); Yves Lavertu, *L'Affaire Bernonville: Un Criminel de Guerre en Cavale au Québec* (Édition Yves Lavertu, 2013), 28, 57, 60. See also Katelyn Arac, "'War Criminals, Multiculturalism, and Post-war Liberalism in Canada" (PhD diss., Queen's University, 2022).

92 "Emma Goldman to Alexander Berkman, February 12, 1935," in *Feminist Interpretations of Emma Goldman*, Penny Weiss and Lorretta Kensinger (University Park: Pennsylvania State University Press, 2007), 263.

93 Emma Goldman to Max Nettlau, 8 February 1935, C-Nov 1934–Feb 1935, The Emma Goldman Papers Project, International Institute for Social History, Microfilm Edition.

94 See discussion in Todd Miller, *Storming the Wall: Climate Change, Migration, and Homeland Security* (San Francisco, CA: City Lights, 2017).

95 See discussion in Barbara Roberts, *Whence They Came: Deportation from Canada, 1900–1935* (Ottawa: University of Ottawa Press, 1988).
96 Goldman, vol.1, *Living My Life*, 122–3.
97 Goldman, vol. 2, *Living My Life*, 523.
98 Ibid., 524.
99 Wexler, *Emma Goldman in Exile*, 158.
100 Emma Goldman letter (multiple copies), 11 May 1934, Emma Goldman Papers, Sallie Bingham Center for Women's History and Culture, Duke University Library.
101 The latter was particularly interested in her views on the situation in France and noted that "Il lui parait que le Canadien français est bien plus Français que Canadien. Ses traditions françaises remontent à bien plus loin que ses traditions canadiennes." See "Anarchie dit paix, pour Emma Goldman," *La Presse*, 4 May 1934, 3.
102 "Red Emma" Denounces Hitler and Hindenburg," *Montreal Daily Herald*, 15 May 1934.
103 Wexler, *Emma Goldman in Exile*, 237.
104 "Emma Goldman on Hitlerism," *Toronto Star*, 17 January 1934.
105 Wexler, *Emma Goldman in Exile*, 237.
106 Emma Goldman to Emmy Eckstein (undated), C Nov 34 to Feb 1935, The Emma Goldman Papers Project, International Institute for Social History, Microfilm Edition.
107 Moritz and Moritz, *The World's Most Dangerous Woman*, 141.
108 Emma Goldman to Alexander Berkman, 20 January 1935, C Nov 34 to Feb 1935, The Emma Goldman Papers Project, International Institute for Social History, Microfilm Edition.
109 Emma Goldman to Jeanne Levey, 10 December 1934, Emma Goldman Papers, Sallie Bingham Center for Women's History and Culture, Duke University Library.
110 Taschereau, "The Years of the Great Depression," 9.
111 Ibid.
112 Ibid.
113 Ibid.
114 Moritz and Moritz, *The World's Most Dangerous Woman*, 140.
115 Emma Goldman to "Joe, Sophie, Becky and my dearest secretary," 6 November 1934, C Nov 34 to Feb 1935, The Emma Goldman Papers Project, International Institute for Social History, Microfilm Edition.
116 Emma Goldman to Tom Keell, 19 December 1934, Emma Goldman Papers, Sallie Bingham Center for Women's History and Culture, Duke University Library.
117 Emma Goldman to J. H. Holmes, 8 February 1935, C Nov 34 to Feb 1935, The Emma Goldman Papers Project, International Institute for Social History, Microfilm Edition.

118 Emma Goldman to Alexander Berkman, 27 December 1934, C Nov 34 to Feb 1935, The Emma Goldman Papers Project, International Institute for Social History, Microfilm Edition.

119 Emma Goldman to Tom Keell, 27 November 1934, Emma Goldman Papers, Sallie Bingham Center for Women's History and Culture, Duke University Library.

120 Emma Goldman to Jeanne Levey, 10 December 1934, Emma Goldman Papers, Sallie Bingham Center for Women's History and Culture, Duke University Library.

121 Ibid.

122 Theodor Adorno's *Minima Moralia: Reflections from Damaged Life* (London: Verso Books, 2020) often falls into this category, as does Edward Said's work, discussed previously in this chapter.

123 Emma Goldman to Alexander Berkman, 20 January 1935, C Nov 34 to Feb 1935, The Emma Goldman Papers Project, International Institute for Social History, Microfilm Edition.

124 Emma Goldman to Jeanne Levey, 10 December 1934, Emma Goldman Papers, Sallie Bingham Center for Women's History & Culture, Duke University Library.

125 Emma Goldman to H. Fromkin, 6 December 1934, C Nov 34 to Feb 1935, The Emma Goldman Papers Project, International Institute for Social History, Microfilm Edition.

126 Emma Goldman to J. H. Holmes, 8 February 1935, C Nov 34 to Feb 1935, The Emma Goldman Papers Project, International Institute for Social History, Microfilm Edition.

127 Emma Goldman to Rabbi Stern, 15 October 1935, Harry Joshua Stern Fonds, MG31-F12, Vol 1, File 19, Library and Archives Canada.

128 Emma Goldman to Alexander Berkman, 9 December 1934, C Nov 34 to Feb 1935, The Emma Goldman Papers Project, International Institute for Social History, Microfilm Edition.

129 Emma Goldman to Alexander Berkman, 23 February 1935 Montreal, cited in Richard and Anna Maria Drinnon, eds, *Nowhere at Home: Letters from Exile of Emma Goldman and Alexander Berkman* (New York: Shocken Books, 1975), 242–423.

130 Emma Goldman to Alexander Berkman, 7 February 1935, C Nov 34 to Feb 1935, The Emma Goldman Papers Project, International Institute for Social History, Microfilm Edition.

131 Emma Goldman to Alexander Berkman, 14 November 1934, C Nov 34 to Feb 1935, The Emma Goldman Papers Project, International Institute for Social History, Microfilm Edition.

132 Emma Goldman to Alexander Berkman, 24 January 1935, C Nov 34 to Feb 1935, The Emma Goldman Papers Project, International Institute for Social History, Microfilm Edition.

133 Emma Goldman to Alexander Berkman, 12 February 1935, in *Nowhere at Home*, ed. Drinnon and Drinnon, 114–15.

134 Emma Goldman to Alexander Berkman, 16 June 1934, in Drinnon and Drinnon, eds, *Nowhere at Home*, 108.
135 Emma Goldman to Alexander Berkman, 5 January 1935, C Nov 34 to Feb 1935, The Emma Goldman Papers Project, International Institute for Social History, Microfilm Edition.
136 Emma Goldman to Roger Baldwin, 19 June 1935, Harry Joshua Stern Fonds, MG31-F12, Vol 1, File 19, Library and Archives Canada.
137 Emma Goldman to Rudolf Rocker, 21 March 1935, C Feb 1935–June 1935, The Emma Goldman Papers Project, International Institute for Social History, Microfilm Edition.
138 Ibid.
139 Emma Goldman to Jeanne Levey, 10 December 1934, Emma Goldman Papers, Sallie Bingham Center for Women's History & Culture, Duke University Library.
140 Emma Goldman to Leon Malmed, 20 April 1935, C Feb 1935–June 1935, The Emma Goldman Papers Project, International Institute for Social History, Microfilm Edition.
141 Emma Goldman to Rose Pesotta, 13 December 1938, C-Jan 1938–Mar 1939, The Emma Goldman Papers Project, International Institute for Social History, Microfilm Edition.
142 Taschereau, "The Years of the Great Depression," 24.
143 Goldman, *Living My Life*, vol. 1, 226.
144 Ibid., 456.
145 Samuel Abramson to H.M. Caiserman, 29 October 1938, H.M. Caiserman Fonds, Alex Dworkin Canadian Jewish Archives.
146 Emma Goldman to Marjorie Goldstein, 13 December 1938, The Emma Goldman Papers Project, International Institute for Social History, Microfilm Edition.
147 Elaine Leeder, *The Gentle General: Rose Pesotta, Anarchist and Labor Organizer* (Albany, NY: State University of New York Press, 1993), 114–15; Hugues Théorêt, *La Peur Rouge: Histoire de l'Anticommunisme au Québec* (Québec: Les Éditions du Septentrion, 2020), 89.
148 Gornick, 135.
149 Translation by author. "As long as I am alive and breathing, I will spare nothing, and I will do everything in my power to eradicate communism from the province of Quebec." Maurice Duplessis, "Propagande Communiste," *Débats de l'Assemblée Nationale*, 3 March 1937, 216; English, *Citizen of the World*, 28.
150 Recent scholarship emphasizes the breadth of anti-communist sentiment in Quebec and Canada in this period, despite the relatively small number of people formally registered with the Communist Party of Canada. Théorêt, *La Peur Rouge*, 9.
151 Ibid. Rose Bernstein, one of Emma Goldman's most faithful correspondents, confirmed Pesotta's assessment of the situation. Rose Bernstein to Emma Goldman,

9 February 1939, C-Dec 1938 to March 1939, Emma Goldman Papers, International Institute for Social History, Microfilm Edition.

152 Marjorie Goldstein to Emma Goldman, 1 April 1939, Emma Goldman Papers, International Institute for Social History, Microfilm Edition.

153 Paul-Etienne Rainville, "Au Nom de l'Ordre ou de la Liberté? Le Congrès Juif Canadien Face à la Répression des Libertés Civiles et des Droits des Minorités Religieuses au Québec (1945–1954)," *The Canadian Historical Review* 99, no. 2 (2018): 196–224.

154 Jack Fitzgerald, "Is Canada Going Fascist?," *The Vanguard*, April 1938, 9–10, https://libcom.org/article/vanguard-vol-4-no-3-april-1938.

155 Indeed, the term Montreal appears regularly in keyword searches of Emma Goldman's digitized correspondence largely because of her travel plans.

156 Emma Goldman to Max Zahler, 29 July 1938, Emma Goldman Papers, International Institute for Social History.

157 Wexler, *Emma Goldman in Exile*, 236–7; Moritz and Moritz, *The World's Most Dangerous Woman*, 158.

158 Emma Goldman to Leon Malmed, 8 August 1938, C-Jan 38 to Mar 39, The Emma Goldman Papers Project, International Institute for Social History, Microfilm Edition.

159 Théorêt, *La Peur Rouge*, 117.

160 English, *Citizen of the World*, 47. English suggests that Trudeau's views were the largely the product of French Canadian nationalist thinking that objected to war based on the country's previous imperial engagements.

161 Michael Petrou, *Renegades: Canadians in the Spanish Civil War* (UBC Press, 2008), 22. In contrast to the rootlessness I have emphasized here, Petrou includes Goldman in the list of Canadian volunteers. See Appendices.

162 Falk, *Love, Anarchy, and Emma Goldman*, 390.

163 Translation by author. Original: "Yvonne Maisonneuve a voué sa vie entière à la cause des femmes marginalisées et à l'amélioration de leurs conditions de vie. Alors que la société change, que les œuvres charitables et sociales s'adaptent et se modernisent, l'essence de son accueil unique et familial traverse le temps. Son œuvre demeure, à ce jour, incomparable et inestimable." https://ville.montreal.qc.ca/memoiresdesmontrealais/yvonne-maisonneuve-mere-du-chainon, accessed 9 December 2023.

164 For example, in conversation with Moishe-Volf Dolman, who translated news articles from the *Keneder Odler* for this project, he mentioned hearing stories of Emma Goldman organizing workers while in Montreal/Mooniyang/Tiohtià:ke, 24 January 2022.

165 Emma Goldman, August Strindberg, 1935 (draft), W-1935–1940, The Emma Goldman Papers Project, International Institute for Social History, Microfilm Edition.

166 "Emma Goldman to Harry Kelly," 13 August 1934, Toronto, C-Aug1934–Oct1934, The Emma Goldman Papers Project, International Institute for Social History, Microfilm Edition.

167 Albalate de Cinca (A Collectivized Village) by Emma Goldman, draft, 1937, W-1935–1940, The Emma Goldman Papers Project, International Institute for Social History, Microfilm Edition.

Notes from the Field (The Wartime City)

1 Email correspondence with Bonnie Klein, 19 October 2021.

2 David Rapaport *No Justice, No Peace: The 1996 OPSEU Strike against the Harris Government in Ontario* (Montreal-Kingston: McGill-Queen's University Press, 1999), 3.

The Wartime City

1 Jennifer Ridgley, "Refuge, Refusal, and Acts of Holy Contagion: The City as a Sanctuary for Soldiers Resisting the Vietnam War," *ACME: An International Journal for Critical Geographies* 10, no. 2 (2011): 203.

2 Michael Klein puts the estimate at closer to 200,000. *Dissident Doctor: Catching Babies and Challenging the Medical Status Quo* (Toronto: Douglas & McIntyre, 2018), 98. Sweden was also another major destination. On the deserter experience in Sweden, see Paul Benedikt Glatz, *Vietnam's Prodigal Heroes: American Deserters, International Protest, European Exile, and Amnesty* (Lanham, Maryland: Lexington Books, 2021); Terry Whitemore, *Memphis, Nam, Sweden: The Autobiography of a Black American Exile* (New York: Doubleday, 1971); Thomas Lee Hayes, *American Deserters in Sweden: The Men and Their Challenge* (New York: Association Press, 1971).

3 At this point, Prime Minister Pierre Trudeau and Minister of Manpower and Immigration Alan McEachen clarified that draft status would not be a factor in determining admissions or landed immigrant status. This decision provoked considerable correspondence, both for and against the decision. See the seven files of correspondence in RG 76, Volume 726, File 5560-2, Parts 7–14, Library and Archives Canada (LAC). In the same year, the government clarified that those deserters already in Canada legally could apply for landed immigrant status and that desertion would be a consideration, but not a determining factor, in their eligibility. The whole question of draft evasion or desertion provoked debates about loyalty and citizenship in government quarters and officers on the border had considerable power in interpreting the regulations, which emphasized "legal, moral and contractual obligations." "Allan McEachen to R.B. Muclure, 30 April 1969," RG 76, Volume 893, File 5560-1 "Draft Dodgers - General," Part 6, LAC.

4 Bruce Garside, Zoom Interview, 11 July 2021; Jurgen Dangwort, email exchange with author, 15 April 2023.

5 Steven High, *Deindustrializing Montreal: Entangled Histories of Race, Residence, and Class* (Montreal-Kingston: McGill-Queen's University Press, 2022), 15.

6 David Rapaport, Zoom interview, 17 June 2021.

7 Comments from Dorothy Day, social activist, upon her visit to Montreal/ Mooniyaang/Tiohtià:ke. Interview with Bruce Garside, 4 September 2021.

8 High, *Deindustrializing Montreal*, 15.

9 Audra Simpson, *Mohawk Interruptus: Political Life Across the Borders of Settler States* (Durham, NC: Duke University Press, 2014), 21.

10 Simpson, *Mohawk Interruptus*, 51–2.

11 Sean Mills, *The Empire Within: Postcolonial Thought and Political Activism in Sixties Montreal* (Montreal-Kingston: McGill-Queen's University Press, 2010), 4. Other work emphasizes the 1960s as a "phenomenon," underscoring the importance of the New Left and social movements in forging "an historical moment that fomented a revolution in education, racial divisions, anxieties about national security, consumerism, Aboriginal mobilization, anti-Americanism, the search for national identity, clashes between capital and labour, innovations in public policy, and debates surrounding the family, health, and the environment." Lara Campbell and Dominique Clement, "Introduction" in *Debating Dissent: Canada and the Sixties*, eds., Lara Campbell and Dominique Clément (Toronto: University of Toronto Press, 2012), 6, 10.

12 Labour unrest continued beyond the 1960s. In 1972, there was a major Common Front strike involving all the major unions such as the Confederation of National Trade Unions (CSN), Quebec Federation of Labour (FTQ); and the Quebec Teachers Corporation (CEQ). An estimated 210,000 people participated in the general strike, which lasted ten days. José Iguarta, "The Sixties in Quebec," in Campbell and Clément, eds. *Debating Dissent*, 261, 266.

13 Ibid., 257.

14 Pierre Vallières, *White N*** of America*, translated by Joan Pinkham (Toronto: McLelland and Stewart, 1971), 211.

15 Will Langford, *The Global Politics of Poverty: Development Programs and Democracy, 1964–1979* (Montreal and Kingston: McGill-Queen's University Press, 2021), 89–90.

16 Iguarta, "The Sixties in Quebec," 249.

17 Ibid., 250.

18 Jean Lesage victory speech on 14 November 1962. Cited in Ibid.

19 Mario Polèse, "Montreal's Economy Since 1930," in *Montreal: The History of a North American City* vol. 2., ed. Dany Fougères and Roderick Macleod, 181.

20 Darel E. Paul, "World Cities as Hegemonic Projects: The Politics of Global Imagineering in Montreal," *Political Geography* 23, no. 5 (2004): 573; Bryan Palmer,

Canada's 1960s: The Ironies of Identity in a Rebellious Era (Toronto: University of Toronto Press, 2008), 319.

21 Paul, "World Cities as Hegemonic Projects," 582. Paul notes further, "The remarkably anti-democratic nature of the city's electoral system through the 1960s, which reserved the franchise for property owners and rate payers alone, also contributed to Drapeau's longevity and his insulation from popular will."

22 Paul, "World Cities as Hegemonic Projects," 583; Polèse, "Montreal's Economy Since 1930," 181.

23 Gilles Sénéchal and Nathalie Vachon, "Metropolitan Expansion: The Challenge of Polycentricity," in *Montreal: The History of a North American City*, vol. 2, ed. Dany Fougères and Roderick Macleod, 75. See also Anne-Marie Séguin, Paula Negro and Philipe Apparicio, "Poverty and Wealth in the Post-War Montreal Area," in *Montreal: The History of a North American City*, vol. 2, ed. Dany Fougères and Roderick Macleod, 367, 371.

24 Sean Mills, "Democracy, Dissent and the City," in *The Sixties in Canada: A Turbulent and Creative Decade*, ed. M Athena Palaeologu (Montreal: Black Rose Books, 2009), 155.

25 Langford, *The Global Politics of Poverty*, 105. See also Steven High, "Little Burgundy: The Interwoven Histories of Race, Residence, and Work in Twentieth-Century Montreal," *Urban History Review/Revue d'histoire urbaine* 46, no. 1 (2017): 23–44, https://doi.org/10.7202/1059112ar.

26 High, *Deindustrializing Montreal*, 13; "1962 Report of the Economic Research Corporation of Montreal," cited in Palmer, *Canada's 1960s*, 319.

27 Palmer, *Canada's 1960s*, 319.

28 Mills, *The Empire Within*, op.cit, 21, 26.

29 Vallières, *White N*** of America*, 91–2. Of the "ills afflicting Montreal," including traffic congestion and overcrowding and overpopulation, housing was considered of paramount importance. See "Urban Ills" in André Lortie, ed., *The 60s: Montreal Thinks Big* (Montreal: Canadian Centre for Architecture, 2004), 116.

30 Vallières, *White N*** of America*, 99.

31 Bruno Cornellier, "The Struggle of Others: Pierre Vallières, Quebecois Settler Nationalism, and the N-Word Today," *Discourse* 39, no. 1 (2017): 35.

32 Wendell Nii Laryea Adjetey, *Cross-Border Cosmopolitans: The Making of a Pan-African North America* (Chapel Hill, NC: The University of North Carolina Press, 2022), 167. Vallières, *White N*** of America*, 275.

33 Vallières, *White N*** of America*, 275.

34 David Austin, *Fear of a Black Nation: Race, Sex, and Security in Sixties Montreal* (Toronto: Between the Lines Press, 2013), 38.

35 LOGOS reprinted Carmichael's telegram in full, alongside an article titled "Vallières & Gagnon: Prisonniers Politiques," and an article called "What is the FLQ?" by Claude Savoie 1, no. 6, 12. The telegram read: "Courage nos frères: SNCC experiences government chicanery and deception daily. We refuse to be divided from our

FLQ brethren by malicious lies. We support you in your trial. Your experiences are no different from those of true patriots everywhere and anytime who revolt against tyranny. We are confident of your complete vindication. Washington SNCC. Stokely Carmichael." See https://archive.org/details/logosvo1no6/page/8/mode/2up, accessed 10 October 2021. Some FLQ supporters and members became more tangibly involved in the Black Power movement, including Michelle Duclos who famously conspired to blow up the Statue of Liberty.

36 Stokely Carmichael's speech was transcribed and reprinted in David Austin, ed., *Moving Against the System* (London: Pluto Press, 2018), 214.

37 Vallières, *White N*** of America*, 21.

38 Cited in Mills, *Empire Within*, 103.

39 Cited in Mills, *The Empire Within*, 6. See also Richard Gordon Kicksee, "Scaled Down to Size: Contested Liberal Commonsense and the Negotiation of Indian Participation in the Canadian Centennial Celebrations and Expo '67, 1963–1967," (MA thesis, Queen's University, 1995), 56.

40 David Austin, "Narratives of Power: Historical Mythologies in Contemporary Québec and Canada," *Race & class* 52, no. 1 (2010): 24. Pierre Vallières, *The Impossible Quebec*, trans. Jeffrey S. Moore (Montreal: Black Rose Books, 1980), 125–6. Vallières concluded this essay, titled "The Emergence of Anti-Statists and the Inuit Question," by suggesting, "For those Québécois who have chosen to structure their existence outside the State and established institutions, the Inuit movement *has* to succeed, even if it means compromising the James Bay project and other 'northern developments.' After all, the dignity of man and communities is well worth the loss of a little electricity."

41 Cornellier, "The Struggle of Others," 32.

42 René Levesque, *Option Québec*, cited in D'Arcy Jenish, *The Making of the October Crisis* (Toronto: Doubleday, 2018), 121.

43 For more on this topic, see Scott Rutherford, *Canada's Other Red Scare Indigenous Protest and Colonial Encounters during the Global Sixties* (Montreal-Kingston: McGill-Queen's University Press, 2020); Scott Rutherford, "'We Have Bigotry All Right—but No Alabamas': Racism and Aboriginal Protest in Canada during the 1960s," *The American Indian Quarterly* 41, no. 2 (Spring 2017): 158–79. See also Gerard Taiake Alfred, *Heeding the Voices of our Ancestors: Kahnawake Mohawk Politics and the Rise of Native Nationalism* (Toronto: Oxford University Press), 1995.

44 A fact noted in the seminal two-volume Hawthorn Report on the health and welfare of Indigenous Peoples in Canada, which appeared in 1966. See J.B. Hawthorn, vol. 1, *A Survey of the Contemporary Indians of Canada: A Report on Economic, Political, Educational Needs and Policies in Two Volumes* (Ottawa: Indian Affairs Branch, 1966), 132. This debate has carried over more recently, see for example, "Pourquoi encore parler de colonialisme et donc de décolonisation au Canada et au Québec?" https://ici.radio-canada.ca/espaces-autochtones/1382859/pourquoi-encore-parler-de-colonialisme-et-donc-de-de-

colonisation-au-canada-et-au-quebec, accessed 5 October 2021. As I worked on this chapter, the Mohawk Council was making representations to hearings on Bill 96 about language rights in Quebec: https://montreal.ctvnews.ca/quebec-indigenous-communities-wonder-how-french-charter-amendments-will-affect-their-languages-growth-1.5430113, accessed 10 October 2021.

45 David Rapaport, Interview, 26 October 2021. This subject would become more familiar in later years and Rapaport recalls going to Kanesatake with other members of the Ontario labour movement to lend support to the community during the 1990 Oka Crisis.

46 Jürgen Dankwort, Zoom interview, 8 August 2021.

47 Mary Harman, Interview, 4 September 2021.

48 Adjetey, *Cross-Border Cosmopolitans*, 184. In investigating the experience of Black war resisters in Toronto, Adjetey notes that some appear to have sheltered with Black residents in the city. See *Cross-Border Cosmopolitans*, 185.

49 "Michael Klein," short film, Canadian Museum of Human Rights.

50 "Interview with Bill," Box 3, Folder 11, Renée Kasinsky Fonds, Rare Books and Special Collections, University of British Columbia.

51 Ibid.

52 Mary Harman, Interview, 4 September 2021.

53 Ibid.

54 Email exchange with author, 14 June 2021; Klein, *Dissident Doctor*, 97.

55 Jürgen Dankwort, Zoom interview, 8 August 2021.

56 Klein, *Dissident Doctor*, 96; Bonnie Sherr Klein, Zoom interview, 4 August 2021.

57 Inderbir Riar, "Expo 67, or the Architecture of Late Modernity" (PhD diss., Columbia University, 2014), 20.

58 Myra Rutherdale and Jim Miller, "'It's Our Country': First Nations' Participation in the Indian Pavilion at Expo 67," *Journal of the Canadian Historical Association/Revue de la Société historique du Canada* 17, no. 2 (2006): 148–73.

59 Dorothy Todd-Hénaut, "The 60s – imagining a better world," November 2010.

60 Keith Bolender, "When Cuban-American Terrorism Came to Canada," in *Other Diplomacies, Other ties: Cuba and Canada in the Shadow of the United States*, ed. Cynthia Wright, Lana Wylie, Tabio Fernández and Luis René (Toronto: University of Toronto Press, 2017), 118. On the Cuban presence at Expo 67, see also Asa McKercher, "Lifting the Sugarcane Curtain: Security, Solidarity, and Cuba's Pavilion at Expo 67," in Cynthia Wright et al., *Other Diplomacies*.

61 For a fuller discussion, see David Meren, *With Friends Like These: Entangled Nationalisms and the Canada-Quebec-France Triangle, 1944–1970* (Vancouver: UBC Press, 2012).

62 Ken Hyman and Jackie Hyman, Interview, 22 June 2021. In advance of Expo 67, city council had embarked on "rapid modernization projects" but these did not benefit the more impoverished communities, which often suffered deleterious effects as a result. See Steven High, "Little Burgundy," 39.

63 Analyses of the historical experiences of French Canadians and intellectual influences on discourses of decolonization in Quebec suggest as much. See Papa Dramé et Magali Deleuze, "Les Idées Phares du Processus de Décolonisation et le Québec," *Bulletin d'histoire politique* 15, no. 1 (2006): 118.
64 Vallières, *White N*** of America*, 235.
65 Ibid., 233.
66 Jürgen Dankwort, Zoom interview, 8 August 2021.
67 Bruce Garside mentioned language as a key factor in shaping his sense of isolation. Zoom interview with Bruce Garside, 11 July 2021. Dorothy Todd-Hénaut shared similar sentiments even though she arrived in Quebec over a decade prior. She highlights the stifling of Quebec writers under the Duplessis regime, oppression that led many to leave, "Significant Voices: The Lessons of Quebec Culture and Nationalism," *Canadian Forum* (June 1995), 24.
68 Vallières, *White N*** of America*, 275.
69 Sheila McLeod Arnopoulos, *English Fact in Quebec* (Montreal-Kingston: McGill-Queen's University Press, 1984), 234. Only very recently did the French-speaking population start to decline relative to others. For example, in the 2021 National Census only 58.4% of respondents identified as French speakers for the district of Montreal Island. This was relatively low compared to the rest of the province, with only the district of Nord-du-Québec reporting lower figures (31.1%), https://www150.statcan.gc.ca/n1/daily-quotidien/220817/dq220817a-eng.htm#, accessed 19 July 2023.
70 E-mail exchange with author, 11 June 2021.
71 In Michèle Lalonde's famous 1970 poem of the same name, she links the French Canadian experience to a broader anti-colonial struggle, "We know that liberty is a black word/Just as poverty is black/ And just as blood mixes with dust in the streets of Algiers And Little Rock."
72 Dorothy Todd-Hénaut, Interview, 9 September 2021.
73 Bonnie Sherr Klein, e-mail exchange, 19 October 2021.
74 Dorothy Todd-Hénaut, Interview, 9 September 2021.
75 Zoom interview with Bonnie Sherr Klein, 4 August 2021. Michael Klein also emphasized the importance of political solidarity. Klein was hired by the Montreal Children's Hospital and recalls that "the staff could not have been more welcoming. They were generally opposed to the war, so they felt good about supporting their 'draft dodger.'" Klein, *Dissident Doctor*, 97.
76 Bruce Garside, Interview, September 4, 2021.
77 "Immigration to Canada and its relation to the Draft, Broadsheet of instructions (March 1968, Montreal Revised No.1" Courtesy of Bruce Garside, personal papers.
78 "Memorial march erupts in violence," *Montreal Star*, 6 May 1970.
79 Klein, *Dissident Doctor*, 95.
80 David Rapaport, Interview, 17 June 2021.

81 Barbara Sostaita, "Escape-Bound: Juana Luz Tobar Ortega's Fugitive Poetics," *Southern Cultures* 26, no. 4 (Winter 2020): 42–59.

82 Andy Doherty, "Montreal Means Never Having to Say You're Sorry: Amnesty for Jesse Winchester?" *ZooWorld* (November 1974).

83 Renée G. Kasinsky, *Refugees from Militarism: Draft-Age Americans in Canada* (New Brunswick, NJ: Transaction Books, 1976), 128, 134.

84 Cited in Roger Neville Williams, *The New Exiles: American War Resisters in Canada* (N.Y., Liveright Publishers, 1971), 10.

85 Williams, *The New Exiles*, 58. For more on Ed Miller, "Ed Miller: Lifelong War Resister" in Rita Deverell, *American Refugees: Turning to Canada for Freedom* (Regina, SK: University of Regina Press, 2019), 169. My thanks to Dr. Joanne Tompkins and Marion Miller for taking the time to speak with me.

86 Interview with Dorothy Todd-Hénaut, 9 September 2021.

87 James Endicott (Canadian Peace Congress) to Tommy Douglas, 29 May 1970, Tommy Douglas Fonds, MG32-C28, Volume 35, File 17-3, Manpower and Immigration, Draft Dodgers, LAC.

88 "MCAWR Circulár," preserved in RG 76, Volume 983, File 5660-1, "Military Personnel - Draft Dodgers – General, 1966 – 1973 Part 1, LAC.

89 The house appears to have been made available to non-Americans as well. https://www.montrealundergroundorigins.ca/logos-and-montreal-counter-culture/, accessed 19 August 2021.

90 Bruce Garside, MCAWR, to Professor Gilles Langevin (cc Canon Wilkinson, Claude de Mestral), 6 March 1970, and "Immigration to Canada and its relation to the Draft, Broadsheet of instructions (March 1968, Montreal Revised No.1" Bruce Garside, personal papers.

91 Doherty, *ZooWorld*.

92 Bruce Garside mentions the influence of John Southin in the School of Medicine at McGill (who had been involved in supporting the communist revolution in Cuba) in establishing MCAWR. Zoom interview with Bruce Garside, 11 July 2021.

93 Bruce Garside, MCAWR to Rev. Roger Balk, Student Christian Movement, McGill, 25 September 1969, Bruce Garside, personal papers.

94 Letter from Ed Miller, MCAWR Secretary to Organizations listed by the Central Committee of Correspondence, and other organizations, individual draft counsellors, and others, Bruce Garside, personal papers.

95 Bruce Garside remembers Bill Mullen as remembered as "quiet" and also "skilled and dedicated." Email exchange with author, 6 October 2021. See also Williams, *The New Exiles*, 59.

96 Email exchange with author, 13 February 2021.

97 On occasion, however, MCAWR would adopt a more overtly political tone. For instance, MCAWR members were some of the signatories on an "Open Letter to the McGill University Community" in which signatories noted the following: "It is with considerable regret that we note that both the Student's Council and the

University Placement Committee have requested that any legal corporation be permitted to utilize the McGill Placement Service ... we pledge ourselves to use every peaceful means to protest, though not to attempt to prevent, the occurrence of job interviews with corporations proven to be involved in selling war material to the United States." Bruce Garside, personal papers.

98 Zoom interview with Bruce Garside, 11 July 2021.

99 Bruce Garside, MCAWR, to Professor Gilles Langevin (cc Canon Wilkinson, Claude de Mestral), 6 March 1970, and "Immigration to Canada and its relation to the Draft, Broadsheet of instructions (March 1968, Montreal Revised No.1" Bruce Garside, personal papers.

100 Interview with Bruce Garside, 4 September 2021.

101 Doherty, *ZooWorld*. There is little information about the American Refugee Service, though it is briefly mentioned in Jessica Squires, "A Very Major Wheel That Helped Grind the War Down": The Canadian Anti-Draft Movement, 1966–1973," in *Worth Fighting For: Canada's Tradition of War Resistance from 1812 to the War on Terror*, eds. Lara Campbell, Michael Dawson and Catherine Gidney (Toronto: Between the Lines, 2015), 273, FN46.

102 Email correspondence with Michael Hendricks, 22 October 2021.

103 Ibid.

104 Interview with Bruce Garside, 4 September 2021. For more on this dynamic, see Doherty, *ZooWorld*.

105 Jessica Squires, *Building Sanctuary: The Movement to Support Vietnam War Resisters in Canada, 1965–73* (Vancouver, BC: UBC Press, 2014), 154.

106 See correspondence in "Draft Dodgers – General," RG76, Volume 121, File number: 5660-1, Part 4, LAC.

107 The government labelled entire files related to war resisters as complaints and criticisms, see "Military Personnel - Draft Dodgers - Complaints and Criticisms – General, 1969–1973," File 5660-2, Volume 726, LAC.

108 "FLQ Backers from 'Schools' Hold Parade," *Montreal Gazette*, 10 September 1963, 45.

109 I am tremendously grateful to Wendell Nii Laryea Adjetey for this insight and for the reference to Vincent Brown's ideas of a "war within a war" in *Tacky's Revolt: The Story of an Atlantic Slave War* (Cambridge, MA: Harvard University Press, 2020).

110 Angela Morris, *Old Kahnwà*:ke (Kanien'kehá:ka Onkwawén:na Raotitióhkwa Language and Cultural Center), 14.

111 Jürgen Dankwort, Zoom interview, 8 August 2021.

112 Langford, *The Global Politics of Poverty*, 127, 136.

113 Velma Rounding (Secretary to Canon Wilkinson, Canadian Council of Churches to Bruce Garside, MCAWR, 26 October, 1970, Bruce Garside, personal papers.

114 David Rapaport, Zoom interview, 5 October 2021.

115 E-mail exchange with author, 11 June 2021.

116 E-mail exchange with author, 9 June 2021. Feminist groups were becoming increasingly organized in this period, which included the establishment of the Montreal Women's Liberation Movement in 1969.
117 Email exchange with author, 11 June 2021.
118 Ibid.
119 Mary Harman, Interview, 4 September 2021; Williams, *The New Exiles*, 391.
120 Roger Williams, "Strong-Arm Rule in Canada; the War Measures Act and its Aftermath," *New Republic*, 30 January 1971, 16, 17. Few were in actual danger, though people like Karl and Dwight Armstrong, who were wanted by US authorities for their role in the bombing of the Army Research Center (Sterling Hall) in Madison on 24 August 1970, were certainly more vulnerable to arrest. Tom Bates, *Rads: The 1970 Bombing of the Army Math Research Center at the University of Wisconsin and Its Aftermath* (Toronto: HarperCollins, 1992), 339; Christopher Powell, "'Vietnam: It's Our War Too:' The Antiwar Movement in Canada: 1963–1975," (PhD diss., University of New Brunswick, 2010), 422.
121 David Rapaport, Zoom interview, 17 June 2021.
122 Ibid. Rapaport's reference to the Underground Railroad is significant (mentioned in "The Lonely City" chapter as well). Wendell Nii Laryea Adjetey underscores that during the 1960s, radical newspapers referred to the Underground Railroad as a way of connecting, and convincing, Canadian and American readers about the deservedness of the resisters' cause. *Cross-Border Cosmopolitans*, 170.
123 David Rapaport, Zoom Interview, 17 June 2021.
124 Ibid.
125 Email exchange with author, 24 August 1970; Langford, *The Global Politics of Poverty*, 136.
126 Email exchange with author, 15 April 2023.
127 Jürgen Dankwort, Zoom interview, 8 August 2021.
128 Interview with Dorothy Todd-Hénaut, 9 September 2021. Police surveillance of anti-poverty activists in a number of Canadian cities has also been well-documented. Langford, *The Global Politics of Poverty*, 10.
129 Adjetey, *Cross-Border Cosmopolitans*, 170.
130 Ken Hyman and Jackie Hyman, Interview, 22 June 2021.
131 Ibid.
132 Ibid.
133 Years later, Garside would learn that the RCMP had also visited the secretary in the department to request that she provide them with information about any travels he might undertake to the United States. Zoom interview with Bruce Garside, 11 July 2021.
134 Statement of Principles for the Greater Montreal Anti-Poverty Coordinating Committee, Adopted by the GMAPCC Annual General Assembly, 27–29 October 1972, Pointe Ste Charles Fonds, File 2008-024.01.4.3, McGill University Archives. Jürgen Dankwort also insisted on the significance of the fight against poverty

undertaken by the GMAPCC coalition, suggesting that it is impossible to consider the history of the civil rights movement in Canada without considering the anti-poverty work that took place in this period. Email exchange with author, 15 April 2023.

135 "Editorial Statement," *Up to the Neck* 1, no. 1 May 1974, McGill University Rare Books and Special Collections.

136 Bruce Garside, Zoom interview, 11 July 2021.

137 Dorothy Todd-Hénaut, Interview, 9 September 2021.

138 Email exchange with author, 13 February 2021.

139 Ibid.

140 Email exchange with author, 13 February 2021. On a related note, Jürgen Dankwort recalls his active efforts to offer sanctuary to members of the Black Power movement. As he explained, his activism brought him "back to Boston briefly. I had decided in 1969 when the Black Panthers were being pursued and murdered, it was time to offer them sanctuary. I contacted the *Boston Mole* underground paper, and they facilitated a meet up with the Panthers in Roxbury, a section of greater Boston familiar to me where I used to drive a cab before 1967. The meeting with the Panthers was brief and a sanctuary offer never materialized from that, but the RCMP soon after raided an apartment in Ottawa that had harboured Black Panthers as I recall in working with the *Octopus* newspaper. The RCMP never got them as they had already left the premises before they made the raid, but the communal house I lived in we called Nobis on Daily Avenue, was raided at least monthly by the RCMP primarily in search of drugs (and there were many users amongst us). It was obviously unnerving for the several US deserters also living there." Email exchange with author 15 April 2023.

141 David Rapaport, Zoom interview, 5 October 2021.

142 Email exchange with author, 6 October 2021.

143 David Rapaport, Zoom interview, 5 October 2021.

144 Email exchange with author, 13 February 2021.

145 Langford, *The Global Politics of Poverty*, 10. Jürgen Dankwort, email exchange with author, 15 April 2023.

146 Briefing notes and pamphlets prepared by GMAPCC on a wide variety of issues are now preserved in the Pointe Ste Charles Fonds, File 2008-024.01.4.3, McGill University Archives.

147 "Committee to Aid Refugees from Militarism, ExNet Bulletin, Number 22, March 18, 1971," AMEX / Canada Records, Wisconsin State Archives.

148 MCAWR Circular, May 1971, Bruce Garside, private papers.

149 Jürgen Dankwort explains that the "Carter amnesty pleased most Americans in exile." As he says, "Many Americans were prepared to go home" while "others preferred to stay in Canada." While Jürgen opted to stay in Canada, as did the other people I interviewed for this project, the amnesty was important because it

enabled people to return freely, and without repercussion. Email exchange with author, 5 October 2021.

150 Some of these themes are explored in the novel *Ru*, first published in French in 2009, by author Kim Thúy. The story is based in part in Granby, Quebec (traditional territory of the Wabanaki and N'dakina) about eighty kilometres (fifty miles) from the downtown of Montreal/Mooniyaang/ Tiohtià:ke.

151 Kwok B. Chan and Doreen Marie Indra, *Uprooting, Loss and Adaptation: The Resettlement of Indochinese Refugees in Canada* (Ottawa: Canadian Public Health Association, 1987).

The Occupied City

1 Yến Lê Espiritu, *Body Counts: The Vietnam War and Militarized Refugees* (Berkeley, CA: University of California Press, 2014), 203, https://doi.org/10.1525/9780520959002.

2 David Fitzgerald, *Refuge Beyond Reach: How Rich Democracies Repel Asylum* (Oxford: Oxford University Press, 2019), 13, 6.

3 Translation by author. Noël St-Pierre, Interview, 10 March 2022. I only had the chance to meet with Noël St-Pierre once in person and it was a truly inspiring and enlightening afternoon. I was saddened to learn that he passed away in January 2024.

4 Francis Peddle, *Young, Well-Educated, and Adaptable: Chilean Exiles in Ontario and Quebec, 1973–2010* (Winnipeg, MB: University of Manitoba Press, 2014), 10.

5 Geoffrey Pearson, "Pearson Report Situation in Chile – Refugees, Immigrants, Asylees, November 28, 1973," RG 25, Volume 8634, File number: 20-1-2-CHILE, Part 7, Library and Archives Canada (LAC).

6 José Del Pozo, *Les Chiliens au Québec* (Montréal : Les Éditions du Boréal, 2009), 37.

7 Thomas C. Wright and Rody Oñate Zúñiga. "Chilean Political Exile," *Latin American Perspectives* 34, no. 4 (2007): 33, http://www.jstor.org/stable/27648032.

8 Manuel Bastías Saavedra, "The Unintended Legacy of September 11, 1973: Transnational Activism and the Human Rights Movement in Latin America," *Iberoamericana*, 13, no. 51 (2013): 102; Wright and Zúñiga. "Chilean Political Exile," 34.

9 "Memo Concerning the Work Done by the Embassy in Santiago de Chile in Giving Protection to Refugees," Political Affairs – Political Asylum – Chile, 1973 to 1974, RG 35, Volume 9337, File 20-15-CHILE, LAC.

10 "Santiago to Ottawa, October 24, 1973," Refugees - Chilean Movement - Situation Report to the Minister, 1973 RG76, Volume 986, File number: 5781-3-8, LAC.

11 On relief efforts see "Aid, Development and Export Finance – Relief – Canadian to Foreign Countries – Chile," RG25, Volume 20992, File 38-11-1-CHILE, all parts, LAC. It is important to note that some of the material donations, including by the

United States and the Communist Bloc during the 1960s, were especially generous in part because they were part of the Cold War battle for "hearts and minds." Relief was another way of expressing solidarity and Chilean Canadian communities were notably active in this regard. On foreign debt financing, see correspondence in Aid, Export, Finance, RG 25, Volume 12080, File 38-10-3-CHILE, Part I – 1964 – 1965, LAC.

12 Del Pozo, *Les Chiliens au Québec*, 26.

13 Saavedra, "The Unintended Legacy of September 11, 1973"; Mark Overyer-Velazquez and Enrique Sepulveda III, eds, *Global Latin(o) Americanos: Transoceanic Diasporas and Regional Migrations* (New York: Oxford University Press, 2018), 235.

14 "Ambassador Ross A.F. Hart, Director, Security & Intelligence, Liaison Divison, Department of External Affairs, 3 January 1972," RG 25, Volume 8940, File number: 20-CHILE-1-4, Part 2, LAC. On Allende, see "Political Affairs – Chile – Policy and Background – Internal Policy Affairs, 1970 – 1971," RG 25, Volume 8940, File number: 20-CHILE-1-4, Part 6, LAC.

15 "Meet the Canadian envoy who hid hundreds of Chileans," https://www.utoronto.ca/news/meet-canadian-envoy-who-hid-hundreds-chileans, accessed 19 February 2022.

16 Del Pozo, *Les Chiliens au Québec*, 55; Peddle, *Young, Well-Educated, and Adaptable*, 60.

17 "Memorandum, Task Force on Chile," 25 November 1973, RG 25, Volume 13766, File 83-10-CHILE, Part 2, LAC; "Pierre Charpentier, Latin American Division, to GW Division," December 4, 1973," Political Affairs – Political Asylum – Chile, 1973 to 1974," RG25, Volume 9337, File 20-15-CHILE, LAC.

18 "Diplomatic Asylum – Chile," Political Affairs – Political Asylum – Chile, 1973 to 1974, RG25, Volume 9337, File 20-15-CHILE, Part 2, LAC.

19 Maurice Demers, *Connected Struggles: Catholics, Nationalists, and Transnational Relations between Mexico and Quebec, 1917–1945* (Montreal-Kingston: McGill-Queen's University Press, 2014), 46.

20 Del Pozo, *Les Chiliens au Québec*, 39.

21 Clément Trudel, "Un Panorama Qui Fait Penser au Brésil de l'Escadron de la Mort," *Le Devoir*, 29 September 1973, 3.

22 The conference was held at St James United Church attended by a number of delegates from Latin America, as well as leaders of the Black Panthers in the United States and celebrities such as pediatrician Dr Benjamin Spock. Paul Lacnarce, "Une violente diatribe contre l'impérialisme Américain," *Le Soleil*, November 30, 1968, 52; "Bomb Halt Won't Stop Viet Conference," *Montreal Gazette*, 2 November 1968, 26.

23 Sean Mills, *Empire Within: Postcolonial Thought and Activism in 1960s Montreal* (Montreal-Kingston: McGill-Queen's University Press, 2010), 214, 258, 273;

Daniel Gay, *Les élites québécoises et l'Amérique latine* (Montréal: Nouvelle optique, 1983), 8.

24 Peddle, *Young, Well-Educated, and Adaptable*, 51, 52; Nikolas Barry-Shaw, "Rêve/Cauchemar: Allende's Chile and the Polarization of the Québec left, 1968–1974," (Master's thesis, Queen's University), 2014.

25 "Telex, Santiago to Ottawa, September 21, 1973," RG25, Volume 13766, File 83-10-CHILE, Part 2, LAC.

26 Suzanne Chartrand, Michel's daughter, was also actively involved from 1979 to 1980. My thanks to Geneviève Dorais for these insights.

27 "Bilan - Comité Québec - Chili, 1973–1978," https://40ans.cdhal.org/revues/quebec-chili-informations/, accessed 18 April 2022.

28 Memo to the Minister, "Demonstrations by Members of the Chilean Solidary Committees at Immigration Offices on November 19, 1973," RG 76, Volume 986, File 5781-5-5, LAC; "Embassy of Chile, Memorandum, October 16, 1973," RG25, Volume 8941, File 20-CHILE-1-4, Part 8, LAC. The activism in Quebec and Canada also drew critiques from the Ministry of Foreign Affairs in Chile. "Telex, Santiago to Ottawa, October 30, 1973," RG76, Volume 987, File 5781-9-2, LAC; Memo to the Minister, "Demonstrations by Members of the Chilean Solidary Committees at Immigration Offices on November 19, 1973," RG 76, Volume 986, File 5781-5-5, LAC; "Allan Gotlieb to Minister, November 20, 1973," Representations – Chilean Solidarity Committee, RG 76, Volume 986, File 5781-5-5, LAC.

29 Ibid.

30 "Gotlieb to Minister, Forthcoming visit of Mrs. Allende to Canada, November 22, 1973," RG76, Volume 715, File HQ3-94624, LAC.

31 Cabinet Conclusions, "Asylum for Chilean Citizens," 29 November 1973; "Robert Andras to Prime Minister, November 30, 1973," and "Prime Minister's reply, December 6, 1973," Political Affairs – Political Asylum – Chile, 1973 to 1974, RG 25, Volume 9337, File 20-15-CHILE, LAC. For more on the government's response, see Suha Diab, "Fear and (In) Security: The Canadian Government's Response to the Chilean Refugees," *Refuge: Canada's Journal on Refugees* 31, no. 2 (2015): 51–62.

32 "Situation Report on People Seeking Admission to Canada from Chile," RG76, Volume 986, File 5781-3-8, LAC.

33 Del Pozo, *Les Chiliens au Québec*, 65. Raphael Girard explained "acceptable" as within the limits of acceptable dissent in a liberal democratic society. Zoom interview, 29 March 2022. According to Girard, "the outreach to political prisoners focussed on those who had been convicted of offences that do not appear in the Criminal Cole or for activities that would be considered legitimate dissent in a democracy." Email exchange, 29 March 2023.

34 Flora Fernandez, interview with Maurice Demers, https://www.youtube.com/watch?v=mJIpI4-rdo4, posted 8 July 2021.

35 "Flora Fernandez et son expérience d'incarcération au Chili," https://www.youtube.com/watch?v=mJIpI4-rdo4, accessed 22 February 2022.

36 These efforts eventually fed into the Political Prisoners and Oppressed Persons (PPOP) designated class, developed in 1980 to address the situation in El Salvador but which the federal government used in Chile and other parts of Latin America as well. It was a class that made migration possible for people in refugee-like situations, who had not been able to cross an international border as required by one of the conditions for protection enshrined in the 1951 Convention Relating to the Status of Refugees. By 1982, the PPOP had facilitated the arrival of an additional 349 former political prisoners from Chile, as well as their dependents. 13.2% of all Chileans arriving in Canada moved to the province of Quebec by the early 1980s, bringing first-hand knowledge and perspectives with them "Current Situation," RG25, Volume 12620, File 20-22-2-CHILE, 1978 to 1979, LAC; interview with Raphael Girard, Zoom Interview, March 29, 2022. See statistics in RG 25, Volume 18508, File 20-CHILE-1-4, LAC.

37 See "Current Situation," RG25, Volume 12620, File 20-CHILE-1-4, LAC.

38 Premier Rene Lévesque took up the issue of the disappeared in Chile as well, with correspondence that was later reprinted in the press. "Rene Levesque to Pierre Trudeau, June 5, 1978," Political Affairs – Internal Security – Political Prisoners – Chile, RG25, Volume 9388, File 20-22-2-CHILE, Part 2, LAC. This correspondence, and Trudeau's reply, were published in *La Presse*. See "Correspondance Trudeau – Levésque," *La Presse*, 21 July 1978, A4. When relatives of the victims began a hunger strike in Chile in 1978, this led to a "coordinated world-wide strike." Across Canada, many young people participated in the strike, which received considerable media coverage – so much so that officials worried whether the Assistant Deputy Minister for External Affairs Allan Gotlieb should attend a black-tie dinner at the home of the Chilean ambassador in honour of Canadian justice Bora Laskin (who himself was not attending). Gotlieb attended regardless. See "Roger Gilbert, Director, Latin American Division to JGG, 8 June 1978," RG 25, Volume 9388, File 20-22-2-CHILE, Part 2, LAC.

39 Geneviève, "'Un Impérialisme Bien de Chez Nous' : La Campagne du Comité de Solidarité Québec-Chili Contre les Activités de la Minière Noranda, 1975-1980," *Bulletin d'histoire politique* 31, nos 1–2 (2023): 200–22.

40 See correspondence in RG25, Volume 9389, 20-22-2-CHILE, LAC.

41 As Patrick Barrett has argued, the military regime was all about capital accumulation and this seemed to be a successful strategy until it collapsed in 1982, "triggering the most severe economic crisis experienced by any of Latin America's authoritarian regimes." See "Patrick S. Barrett, "The Limits of Democracy: Socio-Political Compromise and Regime Change in Post-Pinochet Chile," in *Studies in Comparative International Development* 34, no. 3 (1999): 8. The influence of economists from the Chicago School has been well documented in this regard. See Gilberto Aranda Bustamante, "Human Rights, Economic Liberalism and Social Affairs in Post-Pinochet Chile," *Contexto Internacional*, 31, no. 1 (Jan/Apr 2016): 146; Michael J. Lazarra, *Civil Disobedience : Complicity and Complacency in Chile*

Since Pinochet (Madison, WI: University of Wisconsin Press, 2018), xiv.; Peddle, *Young, Well-Educated, and Adaptable*, 129.

42 As historian Francis Peddle observes, the exile period as well as the politics of the 1970s in Canada and the rise of second-wave feminisms resulted in "changing relationships between parents and children, and the rethinking of accepted gender roles and responsibilities within couples." Peddle, *Young, Well-Educated, and Adaptable*, 116.

43 McWhirter, "La Violencia Privada," 38.

44 In 1988, for instance, a delegation led by Louise Harel (Quebec MNA for Hochelaga Maisonneuve) went to Chile to assist women political prisoners in detention. See "Ottawa to Santiago, June 13, 1988," RG76, Volume 1835, File 8680-1, Part 6, LAC. Lawyer Noël St-Pierre was also involved in these efforts. Interview, 10 March 2022.

45 Del Pozo, *Les Chiliens au Québec*, 77; James Hathaway, "Selective Concern," 694; Frelick, Bill, Ian M Kysel, and Jennifer Podkul, The "Impact of Externalization of Migration Controls on the Rights of Asylum Seekers and Other Migrants," *Journal on Migration and Human Security* 4, no. 4 (2016): 195.

46 Coverage in *La Presse*.

47 See correspondence in Refugees and Displaced Persons — Special Movement — Chile and South America (SMC) – General, 197 – 1989, RG 76, Volume 1835, File 8680-1, Part 6, LAC.

48 Jaime Escandon describes the cases of two men who both came to Canada on tourist visas in the early 1980s and sought to make a refugee claim after the fact. See "Le Vécu Des Réfugiés En Attente De Statut À Montréal Et Les Mouvements De Défense De Leurs Droit," (PhD diss., Université de Montréal, 1987), 25, 28. See also RG76, Volume 1835, File 8680-1, Part 6, LAC.

49 "Case Summary Update," RG 76, Volume 1834, File 8680-1, Part 5, LAC.

50 Importantly, the initial visa already indicated that the Canadian government considered migration from a particular country suspect. Statistics show 753 asylum claims from Chile in 1986 (out of a total of 13,540) and 1,114 in 1987 (out of a total of 13,973). No claims were listed for the years 1988–90. See Yolande Frenette, *Les Revendicateurs du Statut de Réfugié au Québec* (Annex A) (Conseil des communautés culturelles et de l'immigration. April 1991).

51 Coverage in *La Presse*.

52 Coverage in the *Montreal Gazette*.

53 Ibid. In addition to the hunger strike, seventeen protesters traveled to Ottawa (traditional territory of the Algonquin Anishnabek) to make a direct appeal to parliamentarians. They received considerable media attention. Journalists from *La Presse* took a heightened interest in some of the protest's supporters, including one member from the Plains Cree Nation (in present-day Saskatchewan). At the time, this support was considered noteworthy because of how it exemplified

a sense of "Indigenous solidarity in the Americas." See press clippings in RG 76, Volume 1834, File 8680-1, LAC.

54 Press Coverage in the *Montreal Gazette.*

55 Ibid.

56 Ibid.

57 Ibid.

58 Crucially, as Mireille Paquet has shown, this dynamic was not limited to the province of Quebec after 1990. See discussion in *Province Building and the Federalization of Immigration in Canada* (Toronto: University of Toronto Press, 2019).

59 Peddle, *Young, Well-Educated, and Adaptable,* 130, 134.

60 Part of the shift may also have had to do with the nature of the prisoners themselves, at least as assessed by Canadian immigration officials. Joe Bissett, the director general of immigration, observed: "Those imprisoned today in Chile for activities with political overtones are for the most part hard-core activists and appear to be quite different from the high proportion of political slogan painters and pamphleteers languishing in Chilean jails in 1975 and 1976." RG25, Volume 25035, File 20-22-CHILE, LAC.

61 Julia Paley, *Marketing Democracy: Power and Social Movements in Post-Dictatorship Chile* (Berkeley, CA: University of California Press, 2001), 1. See also Lois Hecht Oppenheim, *Politics in Chile: Socialism, Authoritarianism, and Market Democracy* (Boulder, CO: Westview Press, 2007), 170; Patrick S. Barrett, "The Limits of Democracy: Socio-Political Compromise and Regime Change in Post-Pinochet Chile," 4. Zoom interview with Flora Fernandez, 23 February 2022. "The Report of the Chilean National Commission on Truth and Reconciliation" also makes note of the continuity in economic approach, see 86, https://www.usip.org/sites/default/files/resources/collections/truth_commissions/Chile90-Report/Chile90-Report.pdf.

62 Cath Collins, "The Moral Economy of Memory: Public and Private Commemorative Space in Post-Pinochet Chile" in *Accounting for Violence: Marketing Memory in Latin America,* ed. Bilbija and Payne, (Durham, NC: Duke University Press, 2011), 235; Zuleta and Gajardo, "The task of the museum in shaping the aesthetic-political field of memory in post-Pinochet chile," 95. See also Michael J. Lazarra, *Civil Disobedience : Complicity and Complacency in Chile Since Pinochet* (University of Wisconsin Press, 2018), xiii.

63 Translation by author. Flora Fernandez, Zoom interview, 23 February 2022.

64 Gonzalo Bacigalupe, "Family Violence in Chile: Political and Legal Dimensions in a Period of Democratic Transition." *Violence Against Women* 6, no. 4 (2000): 430.

65 McWhirter, "La Violencia Privada," 39.

66 Rachel Ida Buff, "Sanctuary Everywhere: Some Key Words, 1945–Present," *Radical History Review* 2019, no. 135 (2019): 24.

67 The administration was deporting between 500 and 1,000 people to El Salvador *a month* in 1980. Ibid, 27.

68 Kristina Shull, *Detention Empire: Reagan's War on Immigrants and the Seeds of Resistance* (Chapel Hill, NC: University of North Carolina Press, 2022), 160, 166.
69 Brian McDonough, Zoom Interview, 16 December 2021.
70 Coverage in *La Presse*.
71 Caroline Patsias and Nastassia Williams, "Religious Sanctuary in France and Canada," in *Sanctuary Practices in International Perspectives: Migration, Citizenship and Social Movements*, ed. Randy K. Lippert and Sean Rehaag (London, New York: Routledge, 2013): 175–88. Brian McDonough recalls that André Boisclair, angered by the presence of people in sanctuary, did contact the church. This suggests that the tactic was an effective one. Zoom interview, 16 December 2021.
72 Brian McDonough, Zoom interview, 16 December 2021.
73 Brian McDonough served in that capacity for twenty-four years. Ibid.
74 Ibid.
75 Ibid.
76 The year before, in France, thousands of people had protested over the country's punitive deportation laws, some of which punished citizens for having non-citizens in their homes. Hundreds of "sans-papiers" had entered the St-Bernard Church in Paris in 1996, only to be forcibly evicted, arrested, and deported by law enforcement. These actions drew the ire of many French citizens and created an enduring legacy. Crucially, none of the sanctuary seekers themselves acknowledged any inspiration or insights from events in France. In fact, Flora Fernandez reminded me that Chileans had a long history of activism through hunger strikes and didn't need to rely on the French precedent for their campaign. Flora Fernandez, Zoom interview, 23 February 2022. On the sans-papiers movement, Danielle Mitterrand, *Sans Papiers?: Pour Lutter Contre les Idées Reçues* (Paris: Utopia, 2018); Miriam Ticktin, *Casualties of Care: Immigration and the Politics of Humanitarianism in France* (Berkeley, CA : University of California Press, 2011); Sarah Waters, *Social Movements in France: Towards a New Citizenship* (London : Palgrave MacMillan, 2003).
77 Brian McDonough, Zoom interview, 16 December 2021. Laura Lopez recalls Cardinal Turcotte in fond terms, explaining that he visited and sought to comfort the children. When he sought to reassure Lopez as well, she remembers saying "you are closer to God than I am," and acknowledged during out interview that she was not a particularly religious person. Laura Lopez, phone interview, 23 March 2022.
78 Brian McDonough, Zoom interview, 16 December 2021; Father Denis Prescott, email exchange with author, 1 February 2022.
79 Brian McDonough, Zoom interview, 16 December 2021.
80 "Santiago to Ottawa, September 24, 1973," in RG 25, Volume 13766, File 83-10-CHILE, Part 2, LAC.

81 Interview with Laura Lopez, phone interview, 23 March 2022. This work was literally underground, two floors beneath an underground parking lot. The working conditions were terrible.
82 Laura Lopez, telephone interview, 23 March 2022.
83 Ibid.
84 Ibid.
85 Ibid.
86 These guidelines addressed situations where countries were unwilling or unable to protect or assist women in situations of domestic violence. These were reinforced by the 1996 Supreme Court decision in Canada v. Ward in which judges ruled that "gender" constituted a "social group" in interpreting the definition of the 1951 Convention Relating to the Status of Refugees. The effects of this changes continue to be felt. See "Chairperson's Guideline 4: Gender Considerations in Proceedings Before the Immigration and Refugee Board," https://irb.gc.ca/en/legal-policy/policies/Pages/GuideDir04.aspx#:~:text=3.2%20The%201993%20Guideline%20was,Court%20of%20Canada%20in%20Ward%20.&text=Among%20other%20things%2C%20the%20Ward,in%20a%20particular%20social%20group.
87 Ibid.
88 Flora Fernandez was able to provide me with some context and background about the participants named in the media. Email correspondence with author, 5 April 2022. Coverage in *Le Devoir.*
89 See examples in Shull, *Detention Empire.*
90 Nayan Shah, *Refusal to Eat: A Century of Prison Hunger Strikes* (Oakland, CA: University of California Press, 2022), 1–2.
91 See discussion throughout Shull, *Detention Empire.*
92 Del Pozo, *Les Chiliens au Québec*, 73.
93 "House of Commons Book – Briefing Note," RG25, Volume 25040, File 20-22-2-CHILE, LAC.
94 Ibid.
95 Coverage in *La Presse.*
96 Flora Fernandez, Zoom Interview, 23 February 2022.
97 Brian McDonough, e-mail exchange, 24 July 2023.
98 Ibid.
99 Ibid.
100 Ibid.
101 Del Pozo, *Les Chiliens au Québec*, 107.
102 Laura Lopez eventually despaired of the process and presented herself to immigration authorities to be deported only to be granted entry as an immigrant by a sympathetic officer. Email exchange with author, 18 April 2022.
103 Del Pozo, *Les Chiliens au Québec*, 108.
104 Translation by author: "Supporters highlighted cases involving cases of risk of return, particularly for hunger strikers, cases of domestic violence, sexual orien-

tation cases and cases involving the care of minors." "1998 Declaration, August 25, 1998," provided by Flora Fernandez via email, 28 January 2022.

105 Translation by author: "(the families) are excluded from the healthcare system, their children cannot attend school, they do not have work permits, and they take on work for $3 or $4 an hour without benefits or job security." "1998 Declaration, August 25, 1998," provided by Flora Fernandez via email, 28 January 2022.

106 Translation by author: "We had to do it, because Canada had started deporting people: they went looking for people everywhere, entering schools to take children, and people were forced to surrender … So the occupation was a way of completing what we'd started with the hunger strike, to stop the arrests." Cited in Del Pozo, *Les Chiliens au Québec*, 107.

107 Coverage in *Le Devoir*. Fernandez was a member of the executive committee of the Table de concertation d'organismes latino-américains du Québec.

108 Translation by author: resulted in "tensions, including threats of violence from certain individuals in the neighbourhood." Email exchange with Father Prescott, 1 February 2022.

109 Coverage in *La Presse*. Prescott was more sympathetic than his parishioners in this regard, noting that children needed to expend their energy and that they couldn't do so outside for fear of being apprehended by the immigration agents.

110 Julia Paley, *Marketing Democracy: Power and Social Movements in Post-Dictatorship Chile* (Berkeley, CA: University of California Press, 2001), 1. The changing situation also affected people's sense of the merits or importance of being in exile. See Peddle, *Young, Well-Educated, and Adaptable*, 7.

111 Reverend Warren, E-mail correspondence with author, 17 November 2021.

112 Michel Gagnon, Zoom interview, 18 November 2021.

113 Ibid.

114 Reverend Robert Warren, email exchange with author, 17 November 2021.

115 Ibid.

116 Ibid.

117 Ibid.

118 Janice Simpkins, telephone interview, 13 November 2021.

119 Ibid.

120 Michel Gagnon, Zoom interview, 18 November 2021.

121 Janice Simpkins, telephone interview, 13 November 2021. This longer connection was repeated in news coverage in the *Montreal Gazette*.

122 Janice Simpkins, telephone interview, 13 November 2021.

123 Ibid.

124 Ibid.

125 Ibid.

126 Ibid.

127 Ibid.

128 Ibid.

129 Michel Gagnon, Zoom interview, 18 November 2021.
130 Janice Simpkins, telephone interview, 13 November 2021; Rivka Augenfeld interview with author, Montreal, 15 November 2021.
131 Rivka Augenfeld, interview with author, Montreal, 15 November 2021.
132 Reverend Robert Warren, email exchange with author, 17 November 2021.
133 Janice Simpkins, telephone interview, 13 November 1991.
134 Ibid.
135 Reverend Robert Warren, email exchange with author, 17 November 2021. Emphasis in original.
136 News coverage in the *Montreal Gazette*.
137 Fitzgerald, *Refuge Beyond Reach*, 265.

Notes from the Field (The Uneasy City)

1 Azar Masoumi, *Refugees Are (Not) Welcome Here: The Paradox of Protection in Canada* (Vancouver: UBC Press, 2023), 4.

The Uneasy City

1 This was part of a huge spike in interest in sanctuary, something Reverend Alison Harrington witnessed, and helped facilitate, from Southside Presbyterian Church in Tucson, Arizona (located on the site of a former Tohono O'odham village), which continues to work on behalf of migrant justice issues. Zoom interview, 25 October 2022.
2 Reported in the *New York Times* in 2021.
3 Domenic Vitiello, *The Sanctuary City: Immigrant, Refugee, and Receiving Communities in Postindustrial Philadelphia* (Ithaca, NY: Cornell University Press, 2022), 15.
4 A. Naomi Paik, "Abolitionist Futures and the US Sanctuary Movement," *Race & Class* 59, no. 2 (2017): 8.
5 Randy Lippert, "Rethinking Sanctuary: The Canadian Context, 1983–2003," *International Migration Review* 39, no. 2 (2005): 382, https://doi.org/10.1111/j.1747-7379.2005.tb00271.x.
6 See press release by the Canadian Council of Refugees, "Pourquoi Sanctuaire," https://ccrweb.ca/sites/ccrweb.ca/files/static-files/pourquoisanctuaire.htm, accessed 8 November 2022.
7 See Jennifer Bagelman, *Sanctuary City: A Suspended State* (London: Palgrave Macmillan, 2015), 94–104.
8 Note that religious attendance was still significant and, in some cases, growing amongst newly arrived communities.
9 Jennifer Bagelman, "Sanctuary: A Politics of Ease?" *Alternatives: Global, Local, Political* 38, no. 1 (2013): 55.

10 Didier Bigo, "Security and Immigration: Toward a Critique of the Govemmentality of Unease," *Alternatives* 27, no. 1 (2002): 82.

11 Barbara Sostaita, "Escape-Bound: Juana Luz Tobar Ortega's Fugitive Poetics," *Southern Cultures* 25, no. 4 (2020): 42–59. The emphasis on carcerality stands in stark contrast to suggestions of church sanctuary as the "flip side" to "spaces of state detention." See Katharyne Mitchell and Key Macfarlane, "Sanctuary Space, Racialized Violence, and Memories of Resistance," *Annals of the American Association of Geographers* 112, no. 8 (2022): 2364.

12 Interview with congregation numbers, 3 November 2019. Certainly, when sanctuary first appeared as a phenomenon in Canada in the 1980s and 1990s the federal government considered possible legal actions. An undated government memorandum titled, "'Sanctuary Movements' — Government Recourse Under the Act," (meaning the Immigration Act) spelled out the ways in which a church congregation might be charged under the Immigration Act for offering sanctuary. Staff noted that Canadian church groups could be prosecuted "under 95(m) of the IA if they knowingly induce, aid, or abet any person to contravene any provision of the Act or the Regulations (likely eluding examination), or if they knowingly attempt to do so." They noted further that "charges under the Canadian Criminal Code could also be applicable; for example, conspiracy to violate the Immigration Act." Although the government never pursued this route, it is interesting to observe that the early conversations around a potential sanctuary movement in Canada were grounded in discussions about prosecution. The memorandum explained that civil servants had "received reports that certain church groups are considering offering 'sanctuary' (note the air quotes) to illegal entrants in response to the recent control initiatives." See "'Sanctuary Movements' — Government Recourse Under the Act," Refugees and Displaced Persons — Special Movement — Chile and South America (SMC) — General, 1979–1989, RG76, Volume 1834, File 8680-1 (LAC).

13 Reverend Barrigar, Interview, 27 August 2019.

14 Rick Goldman, Interview, 26 November 2021.

15 Shannon McSheffrey, for instance, investigated the surviving legal records of the King's Bench for the period from 1400–1550 and uncovered 1,800 sanctuary seekers as a result. See Chapter Two, in *Seeking Sanctuary: Crime, Mercy, and Politics in English Courts, 1400–1550* (Oxford: Oxford University Press, 2017).

16 Yến Lê Espiritu, Lan Duong, Ma Vang, Victor Bascara, Khatharya Um, Lila Sharif, and Nigel Hatton, eds, *Departures: An Introduction to Critical Refugee Studies* (Oakland, CA: University of California Press, 2022), 120.

17 Ibid.

18 Maria Cristina Garcia, *The Refugee Challenge in Post-Cold War America* (New York: Oxford, 2017), 114.

19 Ibid., 128, 129.

20 Howard Adelman, "Canadian Borders and Immigration Post 9/11," *The International Migration Review* 36, no. 1 (2002): 15–28.
21 Canadian Council for Refugees, *Closing the Front Door on Refugees: Report on the First Year of the Safe Third Country Agreement* (December 2005), ii.
22 Constance MacIntosh, "Insecure Refugees: The Narrowing of Asylum-Seeker Rights to Freedom of Movement and Claims Determination Post 9/11 in Canada," *Review of Constitutional Studies* 16, no. 2 (2011): 181–210.
23 Robyn Maynard, "Black Life and Death across the U.S.-Canada Border: Border Violence, Black Fugitive Belonging, and a Turtle Island View of Black Liberation," *Critical Ethnic Studies* 5, no. 1–2 (2019): 134.
24 "Pakistan," Human Rights Watch, https://www.hrw.org/world-report/2011/country-chapters/pakistan.html, accessed 18 March 2023.
25 Stewart Istvanffy, Zoom interview, 25 March 2021.
26 Cited in Myriam Hachimi Alaoui, "L'exil des Algériens au Québec," *Revue Européenne des Migrations Internationales* 13, no. 2 (1997): 200, https://doi.org/10.3406/remi.1997.1558.
27 Obiora Chinedu Okafor, *Refugee Law after 9/11: Sanctuary and Security in Canada and the US* (Vancouver: UBC Press, 2020), 9.
28 Randy Lippert identified key differences in the US and Canadian contexts in terms of the more diffuse, and localized, nature of sanctuary in Canada. Lippert, "Rethinking Sanctuary," 383.
29 "Our Principles," Solidarity across Borders, https://www.solidarityacrossborders.org/en/a-propos/our-principles, posted 4 December 2018.
30 Rachel Ida Buff, "Sanctuary Everywhere: Some Key Words, 1945–Present," *Radical History Review* 2019, no. 135 (2019): 33.
31 See Robert Tomsho, *The American Sanctuary Movement* (Austin, TX: Texas Monthly Press, 1987).
32 Cécile Rousseau, François Crepeau, Patricia Foxen, France Houle, "Determining Refugeehood: A Multidisciplinary Analysis of the Decision-Making Process of the Canadian Immigration and Refugee Board," *Journal of Refugee Studies* 15, no. 1 (2002): 43–70.
33 Peter Gatrell, "Raw Material: UNHCR's Individual Case Files as a Historical Source, 1951–75," *History Workshop Journal* 92, no. 1 (2021): 239.
34 See discussion on the violence of immigration and refugee determination systems and an emphasis on "livability" instead of fear in Yến Lê Espiritu et al, eds, *Departures*, 54.
35 Leo Bertley, *Montreal's Oldest Black Congregation: Union Church* (Pierrefonds, QC: Bilongo Publishers, 1976).
36 As historian Melissa Shaw has shown of women's involvement in the District 21 Branch of the United Negroes Improvement Association in Toronto/Tkaronto, women were critical to ensuring the well-being and welfare of members in their various communities. Melissa N Shaw, "'Who Used to Run the UNIA Hall': Black

Canadian Women's Leadership of Toronto Division #21, 1919–1939," *Journal of African American History* 109, no. 2 (Spring 2024): 200–30.

37 Este et al., 91.

38 Dorothy Williams, *The Road to Now: A History of Blacks in Montreal* (Montreal: Véhicule Press, 1997), 52, 55.

39 Noël St-Pierre, Interview, 10 March 2022.

40 Rick Goldman, Interview, 26 November 2021.

41 "The measured return of Montreal's 'renegade' pastor, the Reverend Darryl Gray," *Montreal Gazette*, 6 March 2012, https://montrealgazette.com/entertainment/the-measured-return-of-montreals-renegade-pastor-the-reverend-darryl-gray. Reverend Darryl Gray left Montreal in 2014 and returned to the United States. Following the murder of Michael Brown, he became involved in federal politics and the Black Lives Matter movement and undertook considerable community organizing in his hometown of St Louis, Missouri.

42 IMM-1808-96, Federal Court of Canada.

43 See Sean Mills, "Quebec, Haiti, and the Deportation Crisis of 1974," *The Canadian Historical Review* 94, no. 3 (2013): 405–35.

44 CanLII 5076 (FC), https://www.canlii.org/en/ca/fct/doc/1997/1997canlii5076/1997canlii5076.html?resultIndex=1, accessed 18 March 2023.

45 Nyers, "Abject Cosmopolitanism," 1082.

46 IMM-841-00, Federal Court of Canada.

47 "Algeria — Elections in the Shadow of Violence and Repression," Human Rights Watch, 29 May 1997, https://www.hrw.org/news/1997/05/29/algeria-elections-shadow-violence-and-repression.

48 Jean McDonald, "Migrant Illegality, Nation-Building, and the Politics of Regularization in Canada," *Refuge* 2, no. 26 (2009): 67.

49 Nyers, "Abject Cosmopolitanism," 1085.

50 Ibid.," 1083, 1084.

51 Noël St-Pierre, Interview, 10 March 2022.

52 Scholars have pointed to language ties as a key reason for the general affinity resident Quebecers feel towards North African migrants. See Marie McAndrew and Mahsa Bakhshaei, "The Difficult Integration of Muslims into Québec Since 9/11: International or Local Dynamics?" *International Journal* 67, no. 4 (2012): 938. Still, others emphasize that linguistic affinity has not always been sufficient to overcome or ease cultural differences. Alaoui, *Les Chemins de L'Exile*, 91, 165.

53 Marion Camarasa-Bellaube et Aurélien Yannic, *La Méditerranée sur les Rives du Saint-Laurent: Une Histoire des Algériens au Canada* (Paris: Éditions PubliBook, 2010), 95.

54 Nyers, "Abject Cosmopolitanism," 1086. The significant fees meant that 174 Algerians simply went "underground" and continued to avoid deportation in Canada, but they also remained without status.

55 Bruce Cheadle, "L'Expulsion Sera Plus Facile: Projet de Loi Sur la Cityonneté," *La Presse*, 31 October 2002, A3.
56 No One Is Illegal used Cherfi's entry into sanctuary to make broader demands, namely: (1) the regularization of all non-status Algerians; (2) an end to deportations; and (3) a return of the moratorium on removals to Algeria. See "Statement by Mohamed Cherfi on Taking Sanctuary," https://noii-van.resist.ca/page/410/?p=l-lyxmrcwiktz, accessed 13 January 2024.
57 Cherfi's case was one of the few instances where police raided a church sanctuary to effect an arrest and proceed with a deportation.
58 Stewart Istvanffy, Zoom Interview, 22 July 2021.
59 This decision is interesting given long standing laws and regulations that make it difficult for people to stay in Canada permanently if there is a sense that someone might be a burden on the medical system.
60 Nicholas Keung, "Border Officials Slammed for Arresting Woman in Hospital Emergency Room," *The Toronto Star*, 16 July 2013, https://www.thestar.com/news/canada/border-officials-slammed-for-arresting-woman-in-hospital-emergency-room/article_ecb21fac-bc75-5ca9-a161-90ce9d9d9fe9.html.
61 Reverend Barrigar, Interview, 27 August 2019.
62 Group interview with congregation members, 19 November 2019.
63 Ibid.
64 Reverend Barrigar, Interview, 15 March 2018.
65 Ibid; Reverend Barrigar, Interview, 27 August 2019.
66 Reverend Barrigar, Interview, 15 March 2018.
67 "Evangelical Lutheran Church in Canada: Guidelines for Congregations Considering Offering Sanctuary," https://elcic.ca/wp-content/uploads/2021/12/ELCICSanctuaryandGuidelines.pdf, accessed 18 March 2023.
68 Group interview with congregation members, 19 November 2019.
69 The history of the Rwandan diaspora in Montreal has been powerfully documented and explored in the "Life Stories of Montrealers Displaced by War, Genocide, and Other Human Rights Violations" project at Concordia University. See https://storytelling.concordia.ca.
70 Email correspondence with Reverend Barrigar, 25 September 2019.
71 Group interview with congregation members, 19 November 2019.
72 Stewart Istvanffy, Zoom Interview, 22 July 2021.
73 Ibid.
74 Reverend Barrigar, Interview, 15 March 2018.
75 The difficulties associated with being in sanctuary have been documented elsewhere. Jennifer Bagelman, *Sanctuary City: A Suspended State* (London: Palgrave Macmillan, 2016) xiv, 5.
76 Reverend Barrigar, Interview, 15 March 2018.
77 Email correspondence with Reverend Barrigar, 25 September 2019; Group interview with congregation members, 3 November 2019.

78 Interview, Reverend Barrigar office, 15 March 2018.
79 See https://www.solidarityacrossborders.org/en/, accessed 18 March 2023.
80 Jennifer Ditchburn and Graham Fox, *The Harper Factor* (Montreal-Kingston: McGill-Queen's University Press, 2016), 192.
81 Stewart Istvanffy, Zoom interview, 22 July 2022.
82 Reverend Barrigar, Interview, 15 March 2018.
83 Ibid.
84 Rick Goldman, Zoom interview, 26 November 2021.
85 Bagelman, "Sanctuary: A Politics of Ease?" 50, 58.
86 Yến Lê Espiritu et al., eds, *Departures*, 78.
87 Vicki Squire and Jennifer Bagelman, "Taking not Waiting: Space, Temporality and Politics in the City of Sanctuary Movement" in. *Citizenship, Migrant Activism and the Politics of Movement*, ed. Peter Nyers and Kim Rygiel (London: Routledge, 2012), 152.
88 Reverend Barrigar, Interview, 27 August 2019.
89 Group interview with congregation members, 3 November 2019.
90 Reverend Barrigar, Interview, 15 March 2018.
91 Ibid.
92 Group interview with congregation members, 3 November 2019.

Conclusion: Beyond the City

1 Robyn Maynard, "Black Life and Death across the U.S.-Canada Border: Border Violence, Black Fugitive Belonging, and a Turtle Island View of Black Liberation," *Critical Ethnic Studies* 5, no. 1–2 (2019): 124.
2 Rebecca Hamlin, *Crossing: How We Label and React to People on the Move* (Stanford, CA: Stanford University Press, 2021), 8. See also Erin Goheen Glanville, "About," https://www.eringoheenglanville.com/bio, accessed 18 April 2023.
3 Yến Lê Espiritu et al., *Departures: An Introduction to Critical Refugee Studies* (Oakland, CA: University of California Press, 2022), 61–2.
4 As reported in the *Sudbury Star* and *La Presse*.
5 As reported in the *Montreal Gazette*. Somewhat ironically, Mayor Coderre cited the precedent of church sanctuary as part of his public justifications of the need for a sanctuary city declaration. "Entrevue avec Denis Coderre: Montreal, Ville Sanctuaire," Radio Canada, 17 August 2017, https://ici.radio-canada.ca/info/videos/1-7768388/entrevue-avec-denis-coderre-nbsp-montreal-ville-sanctuaire.
6 For policy analyses on Montreal as a sanctuary city, see Mireille Paquet and Meghan Joy, "Canadian Sanctuary Policies in Context," *Canadian Public Administration* 65, no. 4 (2022): 629–46; Idil Atak and Graham Hudson, "Montreal's Sanctuary Policy for Non-Status Migrants: Opportunity and Obstacles," *Refuge: Canada's Journal on Refugees* 38, no. 2 (2022): 1–13.

7 Sarah R. Champagne, "Les Demandeurs d'Asile Haïtiens Mal Informés et Bientôt Désillusionnés," *Le Devoir*, 11 August 2017.
8 Jesse Fitch and René Bruemmer, "Big O Among Shelters Housing Influx of Haitians," *Montreal Gazette*, 3 August 2017, A3.
9 "City must do more to combat social and racial profiling, committee hears," *Montreal Gazette*, 22 June 2017, A2; Nazila Bettache et Samir Shaheen-Hussain, "Lorsque les Politiques de Santé Tuent," *Le Devoir*, 7 August 2017; Sophie Mangado et Michel Huneault, "Privés de Services Médicaux et Sociaux," *Le Devoir*, 24 March 2018.
10 Marion Scott, "Montreal not a sanctuary city, but a responsible one, Plante says," *Montreal Gazette*, 6 December 2018, A4; Pierre Saint-Arnaud, "L'annonce de la Réduction du Nombre d'Immigrants Inquiète Valérie Plante," *Le Devoir*, 5 December 2018, and "Immigration: Montréal se Veut «Responsable et Engagée," *Le Devoir*, 6 December 2018.
11 See coverage in the *Montreal Gazette*. Reports of information sharing between police and CBSA were flagged in March 2018 by Huffington Post Quebec, "Montreal Police Calls to CBSA Suggest It Is Far From A Real Sanctuary City," 29 March 2018, https://www.huffingtonpost.ca/2018/03/29/montreal-sanctuary-city-police-cbsa-migrants_a_23399044/.
12 "No Fear in 'True Sanctuary City,'" *Montreal Gazette*, 18 December 2018, A2.
13 "Ethnocultural and religious diversity – 2021 Census promotional material," https://www.statcan.gc.ca/en/census/census-engagement/community-supporter/ethnocultural-and-religious-diversity#, accessed 19 July 2023.
14 Tonia Sutherland, "Making a Killing: On Race, Ritual, and (Re). Membering in Digital Culture," *Preservation, Digital Technology & Culture* 46, no. 1 (2017): DOI 10.1515/pdtc-2017-0025.
15 Y-Dang Troeung, *Refugee Lifeworlds: The Afterlife of the Cold War in Cambodia* (Philadelphia, PA: Temple University Press, 2021), 7–9.
16 Ibid.
17 Novelist Jeanne Truong evokes some of these horrors in her work, *Ceux qui sont restés là-bas* (Paris: Gallimard, 2021).
18 Anna Sheftel, "'I don't fancy history very much': Reflections on Interviewee Recruitment and Refusal in Bosnia-Herzegovina," in *Oral History off the Record: Toward an Ethnography of Practice*, ed. Stacey Zembrzycki and Anna Sheftel (New York: Palgrave Macmillan, 2013), 255–72. See also Melanie Ng's important discussion of community and silence in "Open Secrets: Methods and Archives in Asian Canadian Histories," *Journal of the Canadian Historical Association* 34, no. 1 (2024): 183–207.
19 In fact, as Krenare Recaj has argued, the temporary resettlement of Kosovar refugees in 1999 is an equally important precedent in this vein.

Index